Plato's First Interpreters

Plato's First Interpreters

Harold Tarrant

Cornell University Press

Ithaca, New York

First published 2000 by Cornell University Press

ISBN 0-8014-3792-X

Librarians: Library of Congress
Cataloging-in-Publication Data are available.

Printed in Great Britain

Contents

In Memoriam

George and Nellie Topley

Harold Alfred Tarrant

Preface

I have long wanted to give an account of ancient Platonism that concentrated on the interpretation of Plato rather than on the collecting of doctrines. It is widely acknowledged that a Platonist's doctrine and his interpretation of Plato went hand in hand. If this is the case, then there is a case for occasionally trying to focus on interpretation. This is particularly so with those Platonic texts that were read, but not read for the sake of doctrine. The priority that has been traditionally given to doctrine has meant that Platonic interpretation seldom attracts attention except where texts were mined for doctrine. This seldom happened with some of the dialogues, and it was certainly not the only use to which Plato's writings were put in antiquity.

Platonic interpretation is today at a crossroads. The corpus is being read in a variety of ways, and an authoritative approach to the whole seems elusive. I want to explore ancient attempts to wrestle with this corpus, and to see how the problems were approached before us by philosophers whose philosophical armoury was less sophisticated, but who had the advantage of speaking a Greek not greatly removed from that of fourth-century Athens. I have had to concentrate on the Middle Platonist period, which I believe is the most interesting as long as enough evidence is available. Neoplatonists and others have been drawn upon for supplementary material. I have tried to avoid an excessively historical approach, as I believe that it is the options that were available that is interesting, not who introduced each new reading and when. The ultimate object is not to understand little known Platonic figures, but to encourage a fresh, almost primitive reading of Plato himself.

It is difficult to know who to thank. I have benefited particularly from discussion with Matthias Baltes, John Dillon, Franco Ferrari, Christopher Gill, Jan Opsomer, David Runia, David Sedley, and Carlos Steel, as well as from colleagues in the Australasian Association for Ancient Philosophy and the International Plato Society. I owe a considerable debt to the generous reader who acted on behalf of Cornell University Press, and am sure that I should have produced an even better book if I had been able to spend longer pondering this person's comments. Work was carried out chiefly in Cambridge UK, thanks to the hospitality of the Faculty of Classics, with important visits to the Center for Hellenic Studies at

Washington, and the Universities of Aarhus, Exeter, Leiden, Leuven, London, Lund, and Münster. I should make special mention of Gerry Press, who sought from me the article that first made me realise that such a book as this was possible.

Concentrated work of this kind is only possible in the right background circumstances, and I should perhaps reserve the last word for my excellent group of colleagues at the University of Newcastle, NSW, and for a very patient wife and son.

February 2000   Harold Tarrant
Newcastle, NSW

PART ONE

1

What kind of text is this?

i. Encountering Plato

Plato is a notoriously difficult author to interpret. Sometimes deeply philosophic, sometimes almost sophistic; sometimes open, sometimes obscure; sometimes great literature, sometimes tortuous. Insofar as he penned the earliest significant Greek philosophic works to survive for us, he is the Homer of philosophy. Just as Homer stands at the head of the Western literary tradition so that his poems attract constant attention from a variety of quarters, so Plato stands at the head of the Western philosophic tradition. He is therefore a figure of widespread and permanent interest. Just as Homer had great influence over the formation and development of a variety of genres, so Plato has played a role in the growth of a variety of branches of learning, from ethics and politics to mathematics and the sciences. We still want to know him, to appreciate how he felt, to find truth in his words, to have him on our side. But the task is difficult, for the gulf that separates the written texts from the author's mind can seem extraordinarily wide.

The art-form that Plato employed is one that is largely alien to us, and perhaps has more to do with the way in which Plato himself had experienced intellectual inquiry. He wrote 'dialogues', cast mostly in an elegant prose that mirrored the speech of the Athens which he knew, most of them employing an astute main speaker in conversation with one or more other speakers – the interlocutors as they are known. Nevertheless the genre itself was still in its infancy, and permitted many differences of form, of content, of purpose, and of length. The rules of the genre were limited by little other than the inventiveness of those who wrote within it, and the purposes that they could find for it. In other words, it had practically no limitations at all.

One convention, however, was of far-reaching importance: the writer did not employ himself as a speaker, and rarely made any reference to himself. He manipulated his 'speakers' in much the same way as the tragic poet manipulated his actors, but in general he was distanced from the discussions that the dialogue presented by a variety of literary techniques, from placing those conversations in a world of Socratic mythology (as in the *Symposium*) to actually denying that the author was present (as in the *Phaedo*). In this way Plato denies us a secure authorial voice, though he is usually thought to be communicating with us in some way through the words of 'Socrates' or another principal speaker.

Socrates himself remains almost as much an object of our search as Plato. Widely viewed as the first moral philosopher, he had a depth and decisiveness that most of us would like to emulate, an originality that the majority of his fellow Athenians viewed with intense suspicion, and a commitment to his adopted principles that was strong enough to see him martyred. He was apparently the inspiration behind the development of the philosophic dialogue by Plato's contemporaries, and most if not all of its earliest examples must have involved Socrates as a central character. His philosophising was apparently so dependent on frank and cooperative question-and-answer inquiry that it could only be conducted through conversation. Hence works that depicted philosophy had to resemble conversations rather than lectures. Socrates was also one of the major reasons why intellectuals wanted to write at all. His conduct and manner was that of somebody who had found the personal goal that he was pursuing, pervaded by an inner calm that was never more apparent than at conversations after his conviction on capital charges. So he was the model both for the manner in which inquiry was to be pursued, and for its desired result: unshakable inner prosperity. Written works of philosophy were needed so that Socrates should not be lost: to preserve, promote, and develop the Socratic legacy. His inspiration was such that very few philosophers in the Greek, Hellenistic, and Roman worlds (at least until the rise of Christianity and of Neoplatonism) did not consider him a predecessor in some significant manner. So we want to know Socrates as well as Plato, even though for many of us Socrates scarcely exists outside the latter's writings, since we do not trust Xenophon or Aristophanes to tell his story.

So Plato writes dialogues, initially ones centred on his 'Socrates', but later giving prominence to other speakers. That he should have written dialogues remains a key problem: we must inevitably ask what basis his characters have in history, and what non-historical use Plato is making of them. In particular, is the chief speaker manipulated so as to speak for Plato, or can his authorial message emerge only through a careful study of the *interaction* between speakers? That he should have written dialogues of many different types and many different sizes makes the problem worse. Are the solutions the same for all dialogues, or do they differ from one dialogue to another? Should we be looking for doctrines in them, and if so where? Was Plato perhaps some kind of sceptic? Or was he determined to keep his most important doctrines out of his dialogues, as certain *Epistles* would suggest? Is it right to be looking at Plato as somebody trying to bring enlightenment to readers, whether within his school or outside it? Or are the dialogues just as much his personal method of following problems through – are they motivated by considerations of research rather than of teaching? Indeed, did Plato believe that his own progress in philosophy somehow depended on his interaction with others, through the written word as well as through oral discussion, so that research documents and 'teaching' documents were one and the same thing?

The daunting task of supplying definitive answers to these problems will remain in the background throughout this study, though the way in which the very questions have been framed must inevitably give clues as to the present writer's leanings. Rather we shall attempt to understand better the choices before us today by examining the choices open to earlier interpreters. For all these problems were confronted by ancient interpreters just as by modern ones. Some of them really wanted to know what Plato meant, others just wanted him to be saying things that they could agree with: but looking to him as a source of inspiration nevertheless. Often comparing their problems with ours can be the source of useful insights into both Plato and his ancient interpreters. One issue that was much discussed in relation to the dialogues was the basic subject: the fundamental thing that Plato wanted our reading of the work to teach us about. Even such a simple question as this can generate considerable debate. The problems were often worse in the case of works that were not unanimously thought to offer positive teaching on a subject: those trying, in whole or part, to undermine the activities of Plato's intellectual rivals, or gently prompting self-examination and deeper thinking among their generally youthful readers and listeners. These works were generally called 'inquisitive' in antiquity.

Today we come to Plato under the guidance of others: those who work at university departments of philosophy or classics, or other teachers, or the authors who write the basic books on him or the introductions to the dialogues which we read. On many issues we meet several different perspectives at an early stage, and there is no obstacle to our consulting the rival volumes of hundreds of modern interpreters, or listening to appropriate radio or television programmes, or even visiting informative sites on the internet. Communications have multiplied the number of 'Platos' available to us, even though most of us will remember with special reverence the approach of those who first made us enthusiastic about him. One must therefore ask the reader to imagine a time when a complete set of the works of Plato might have been difficult to acquire, when some of the most important cities of the Graeco-Roman world might have no teacher of Platonic philosophy, and when only the most intellectually prestigious of them, perhaps only Athens itself, could offer a recognised Platonist with an authoritative approach to Plato's writings.

Let us imagine the young intellectual of prosperous background in an ordinary city, either in the dying days of the Roman Republic or under the early empire. He is likely to accept that he must travel for higher studies such as those involving philosophy, and he will travel to a centre that boasts one or more eminent teachers. In their circles, whether they are sophists, philosophers, or teachers of rhetoric and expression, he will encounter a variety of writings, not just those of a single school, and become aware that the reputation of some classical authors was particularly high. He will want to be able to derive the same pleasure from their study that he sees others enjoying, and in particular he is likely to want to make an educated attempt to understand what Plato had to say. He may have already encountered writings that purport to be by Plato, perhaps through owning them himself, but perhaps only through having heard others reading them at small gatherings. Now, at his chosen centre of philosophic studies, he will probably encounter other works with the same claim to be by Plato, in some of which he will find a connection with what he knew before, while in others he sees quite a different message and quite a different approach. He may wonder how Plato can be the author of them all and where the voice of the true Plato is to be found. He may feel in one case that he stands at the threshold of the truth, and in another that he can make no progress. His questions may lead him to search in particular for an expert on Plato, something that may lead him to travel elsewhere if the present city cannot satisfy him.

Until early in the first century BC those desiring to find the true Plato would naturally wish to go to Athens, where the Academy still traced its heritage back to Plato its founder. There was, even there, some dispute as to what this Plato had really been like, and the rival Stoa would by now have been claiming that in significant ways Plato had had more in common with their own discipline. Whatever was the case at Athens, Posidonius' influential Stoic school on Rhodes was interested in promoting its own view of Plato, and in employing ideas from Plato's dialogues when discussing the nature of the soul in particular. From now on there would indeed be competition for Athens from other centres, such as Alexandria, Smyrna, and eventually Rome, where the student could hope to receive an authoritative view of Platonic philosophy, but once there the student would usually only hear the one view of Plato, a view which would be firmly stamped upon his mind. His teacher was likely to be treated with considerable respect – at least by his more serious followers – and his manner of understanding Plato would have been questioned only rarely.

Greek notions of the authority of the teacher meant that ideas tended to change slowly now. The very interest in authors of Greek antiquity was connected with a deep respect for the past and for ancient tradition, and it was very rarely that somebody calling himself a teacher of philosophy could attract much respect and attention without attaching himself to a school that had its origins in the fourth or very early third centuries BC. Potamo of Alexandria did so in the age of Augustus, when he founded an 'eclectic' philosophy, but he was not rejecting the authority of the past as much as announcing his intention to draw on all parts of it selectively. Normally teachers thrived by demonstrating above all their intimacy with and faithfulness to a respected philosophy from ancient Greece:[1] Platonism, Aristotelianism, Cynicism, Scepticism, Epicureanism, or Stoicism. Their opponents delighted above all in pointing out ways in which they did not follow the founders of their school.[2] Successors were frequently faithful to those whom they succeeded, at least in matters of principle. Ideas about philosophy proper tended to develop in parallel with ideas about the interpretation of philosophical authorities, so that, in all probability, Platonic interpretation would only change slowly within the confines of a particular school unless there were pressing reasons for it to develop.

Yet changes did assuredly take place, and attitudes towards interpretation became constantly more sophisticated as time went on. Some would say that they became too sophisticated, as allegory and symbolism came to be detected in seemingly quite innocent passages. The confident application of established strategies of exegesis was liable to produce what are for us most implausible interpretations, a fact which should warn us that we cannot expect to be able to take our own interpretative strategies to extremes without seeming somewhat ridiculous in the eyes of future generations. Nothing is of less help in the sensible interpretation of an author than the failure to be aware of the ways in which our basic interpretative assumptions – our metainterpretation, in fact – is not itself beyond challenge, however satisfying the results that it has yielded may seem to us and to those who think like us. Hence this book will concentrate on the principles of interpretation which we find being employed, rather than the details, though naturally the details need often to be recorded in order to establish principles in the first place.

ii. Dramatic literature or philosophy?

Nobody would deny that there is philosophy in Plato's dialogues. Few would deny that Plato was himself a 'philosopher', even in the modern sense. But some works in the corpus, of largely undisputed authenticity, seem to have quite a small proportion of their total length dedicated to what we should see as philosophic debate. The *Critias*, consisting largely of the narration by 'Critias' of a portion of the Atlantis story, may be unfinished, but what we have of it is not given over to the discussion of any philosophic issues. There may be some elusive moral message, but the same could be said of a great deal of ancient literature. The *Menexenus* consists of an introduction followed by a funeral oration, a rather mechanical production that employs standard materials of epideictic oratory for some obscure purpose: possibly satirical. The well-known *Apology* sets out what purport to be the words of Socrates at his infamous trial of 399 BC, and its content is mostly quite serious even when it hides beneath a comic veneer. But the fact that it is serious, and the fact that it is spoken by a philosopher obsessed with his own mission, does not necessarily make it uniformly philosophic. And even if there is philosophy within it, that philosophy might belong to Socrates' own words in court rather than to his follower's portrayal of him. The *Symposium* has a variety of important speakers, the seemingly light-hearted topic of Love (appropriate for post-prandial discussions), and only one interlude of any great depth – at least to the inexperienced reader.

Other works of course contain a much higher proportion of neat philo-sophy, but the *Laws* has a large proportion of legislation, and the *Republic* much description of the ideal state and its generation, many stories, some mathematics, and some allegory. Their philosophic content is considerable, but then many an Athenian tragedy was rich in serious thought about human beings, their cities, their world, and their gods. There is consider-able overlap between the issues raised in Sophocles' *Antigone* concerning the relationship of state to individual and those raised in Plato's *Crito*. In both cases the dramatic setting gives these issues a great sense of urgency, and in both cases one cannot fail to admire the calm resolve of the heroic figure who is destined to die. To a lesser degree drama and philosophy might be said to have become merged in episodes of Homer's epics, and poetry and philosophy had coalesced in the writings of Hesiod, Xeno-phanes, Parmenides, and Empedocles. Philosophy is not foreign to the prose writings of non-philosophers either. The Pericles Funeral Oration and the Melian Dialogue are two highlights of Thucydides' histories that raise fundamental questions of human existence in fresh and interesting ways. Philosophy within literature, particularly dramatised philosophy, was nothing new. So what makes a work philosophy rather than litera-ture? What, if anything, sets Plato apart as one who wrote philosophy? Why should we approach him in the expectation of enjoying his theories rather than the works in which those theories are embedded?

These problems were not foreign to the ancient world. The earliest arrangement of Plato's works of which we are aware, that of the hellenistic scholar Aristophanes of Byzantium,[3] grouped fifteen of them into trilogies in the same way as tragedies had been grouped for their original perform-ances. The groupings were based on dramatic considerations, such as shared characters or related dramatic dates as well internal cross-refer-encing, so that the *Sophist* and *Politicus*, or *Timaeus* and *Critias*, or *Laws* and *Epinomis*, are kept together because the same faces are present at both conversations, while *Theaetetus*, *Euthyphro*, and *Apology* belong together (Socrates before prison) as do *Crito* and *Phaedo* (Socrates in prison).

An introduction to Plato known to us from a papyrus, *Oxyrhynchus Papyrus* no. 3219, adopts (at least in the portion which we possess) a similar dramatic approach to the corpus. It apparently distinguishes 'narrated' from 'dramatic' dialogues, and investigates origins of the 'purely dramatic' dialogue in fr. 1, accepting that Sophron the mimographer was a literary model but denying that Alexamenos was.[4] It examines Plato's use of characters in fr. 2, mentioning variations in the identity of his principal speaker (2 ii, 5-8); Dionysus and acting are mentioned in fr. 3.2-3, the name of Sophocles apparently occurs in fr. 4.4, and tragedy and drama are found again in frs 5.4 and 6.

A modest move away from this approach is made in the introduction to Plato followed by Diogenes Laertius in his discussion of Plato's works at 3.48ff., though even here some dramatic material overlaps with the papyrus. The literary predecessors of Plato's dialogues are discussed at 3.48.[5] Material relevant to tragedy and tragic festivals is prominent at 3.56, with emphasis given to Thrasyllus' notion that the dialogues were promulgated like tragedies in *tetralogies*; for the three principal plays used to be followed by a satyr-drama. Thrasyllus it seems had been trying to improve upon Aristophanes of Byzantium, whose trilogies are mentioned rather dismissively at 3.61. Again there is an attempt to correct the papyrus' claim (fr. 2 i) that the Athenian Stranger is simply Plato, and the Eleatic Stranger simply Parmenides, given different names so as not to detract from the dramatic illusion; in Diogenes this simple identity is denied (3.52). Dissent is again registered in the case of the proper classification of Plato's dialogues, with Diogenes' source shunning the literary division, known to the author of the papyrus, into 'dramatic', 'narrative', and 'mixed' works in favour of an elaborate classification of dialogue 'character' according to philosophical approach. 1 have therefore argued[6] that Diogenes' source is arguing with some consistency *for* a broadly Thrasyllan and more philosophic position *against* details of Aristophanes' more literary treatment, which the papyrus appears to adopt.

By the time of the Platonist Albinus in the second century AD Thrasyllus' treatment from the first century AD was itself seen as too non-philosophic. In chapter 4 of his brief *Prologue*, another introduction to reading Plato, Thrasyllus and the undatable Dercyllides are criticised for proposing tetralogical reading orders that are based upon the cast-list and setting rather than the requirements of philosophy. It was not that literary considerations had become irrelevant, for Albinus opens with a definition of 'dialogue' which makes question-and-answer and characterisation fundamental,[7] and has its counterpart in Diogenes too, but Albinus belonged to the era when Platonic texts were documents regularly used in the teaching of Platonic philosophy, and he was probably writing less for the general reader than Diogenes' source had been.

So we see in the ancient world a mirror-image of the twentieth-century move away from an exclusively philosophical approach to Plato. At that time there was a strong tendency to take the dialogues out of the hands of the literary scholar and place them in the philosophic schoolroom. No such trends are ever uniform or unbroken, but it is worth noting that by the middle of the second century even a figure such as Apuleius, who had wide-ranging literary skills, built creatively on Platonic themes, and recognised Plato's enormous literary merits,[8] could produce a handbook on Plato which largely reduced the Platonic heritage to a collection of doctrines. The dialogue form, which was still being experimented with as a means for the communication of Platonising philosophy by Plutarch, perhaps two generations earlier, did not attract Apuleius' pen. While Plutarch discussed the divine sign of Socrates in a rather successful dialogue set in fourth-century Boeotia, Apuleius treated the same subject in a linguistically polished oration designed, it seems, for oral delivery in the theatre.[9] What he appreciated in Plato was his diction, not his literary form; he followed Plato the supreme orator rather than Plato the dramatist. And meanwhile the use of dialogue-form in the tradition of Plato was appropriated by another performer, Lucian, for purposes that were largely associated with parody and polemic at philosophy's expense.[10]

iii. History or fiction?

Neither Plato's philosophic purposes nor his dramatic purposes are fully compatible with another response to Plato that one may adopt with at least *some* plausibility in the case of *some* of the dialogues. This is the 'transcript' response, which views many dialogues as little more than a record of actual historical conversations. That response is in fact encouraged by a straightforward reading of the opening of the *Theaetetus*, where Euclides gives his account of a meeting between Socrates, Theodorus, and Theaetetus; he has remembered the whole conversation, written it down shortly afterwards, and gone back to check with Socrates that he has the details right. He even says that the book was without the embellishment of a narrative structure, *just as he had originally written it down*. It seems that the production of a Platonic book might involve little more than the faithful record of a conversation that Plato thought worth recording. No thoughtful person in antiquity seems to have held such a view, and this may in part be due to the preservation of the writings of Socratics such as Aeschines and Antisthenes, which led to a greater appreciation of the conventions of Socratic literature than is available to us, and a greater awareness of how individual Plato's picture of Socrates was.[11] Anecdotes may occasionally be based upon Plato's dialogues, showing that individual episodes had been retold as historical fact, but this does not imply anything like a transcript theory. And one anecdote from antiquity has Socrates complaining to Plato that the latter's portrait of him in the *Lysis* was quite fictitious (DL 3.35). Even the *Apology* was not likely to be treated as a record of what Socrates said at his trial, simply because of the existence of a good deal of other literature about the trial, as one may see from the extant *Apology of Socrates* by Xenophon – particularly the first chapter which speaks of Socratic trial-literature as if he had many rivals.

More interesting is what one might call the hypothetical transcript theory. In this case the dialogue is not supposed to be historical, but accurately to depict the way in which historical characters might have conversed had they met in a given set of circumstances. Socrates would ask questions according to his usual methods and converse in a manner consistent with his normal set of beliefs; interlocutors would answer in character. We should only consider such a transcript theory in relation to a selection of dialogues in the corpus, and so too would the ancients. Even so, Plato's depiction of Socrates and others was regularly taken to illustrate the actual historical characters and their opinions, and the same would often be true today. But the real question here was not whether the dialogues could be used as evidence for Socrates, the sophists, and their prominent contemporaries, but whether Plato was writing for the purpose of illustrating what these people were actually like and how they actually conversed. Did historical motives outweigh literary and philosophical motives? Here there is a problem of how we are to classify those works in which we suspect that Plato is striving to defend Socrates or to attack rival interlocutors. If apologetic and polemical motivation is coupled with the conviction that individuals really were to be applauded or to be avoided, then a historical picture might well have been an aim. If the author is less sure that the picture which he wants to paint conforms with historical truth, then the characters who are defended or blackened may well become paradigms and caricatures, and transcript theory would have to be rejected.

Where might the ancients have stood on this matter? Certainly the ancient introductions to Plato were liable to see certain works as offering, with the help of Socrates, a kind of paradigm of the philosophic life. In the Thrasyllan arrangement of the corpus the first tetralogy, consisting of *Euthyphro*, *Apology*, *Crito*, and *Phaedo*, was supposed to have had this purpose, and Albinus certainly agreed in respect of the *Phaedo*.[12] Yet one may be fairly confident that either would have seen such a purpose as intrinsically philosophical, and a useful lesson for the new philosophy student. From non-Platonists one occasionally does get the criticism that historical truth has been ignored, as perhaps when Panaetius objects to the *Phaedo* because it depicts 'Socrates' committed to the immortality of the soul, which he regards as only a possibility in the *Apology*;[13] or when Aristides complains of unfairness in Plato's treatment of Gorgias and others. For Platonists, however, the dialogues regularly appear to have a philosophical purpose that takes precedence, and dialogues were regularly held to be *about* some matter that is a regular topic of philosophy. Nearly all were given by Thrasyllus a second title, i.e. a subtitle, of the form 'about S' where S is an appropriate subject, though there were a few exceptions, including *Apology*, *Critias*, and *Menexenus*.[14] None of this should be taken to imply that Platonists did not detect a considerable degree of historical fidelity within dialogues, and one can see from Olympiodorus' treatment of the historical setting of the *Gorgias* and deduce from the remains of column 1 of the anonymous *Theaetetus*-Commentator that the actual historical background was widely considered important. In all probability, however, both would have acknowledged that Plato chose the historical setting for fictional conversations to suit his philosophic purposes.

Are there doctrines here?

i. Scepticism and dogmatism: the sceptic reading

After Plato most works of philosophy, though by no means all, took the form of treatises designed to be instructive. This is because most schools of philosophy saw their role as being inextricably linked with determining which propositions are true and which false. It is far from clear that Platonism had worked like this; the dialogues might be held rather to *suggest* ways in which a problem might be approached or a question answered. When a person new to Plato tried to read a dialogue he may have expected the author to be visibly arguing for some thesis or against some other. He probably expected to learn something, and to have part of the work done for him. He expected the work to be treating some single announced topic, and to be trying to make some advance in our understanding of it. His first taste of Plato was therefore likely to be a bewildering one. Plato's characters may seem to be intent on changing the subject, or digressing without obvious purpose. Subjects are rarely announced at the outset, if at all. There may be two or more subjects that vie in importance. Conclusions may be limited in scope, provisional, paradoxical, or simply absent. Where they do occur, it may not be clear that the author is serious, or they may depend on argumentation that seems either humorous or trivial. Theses apparently approved by one dialogue, or rather by the chief character within it, may be denied in another; and opposite theses might seem to be approved within the same dialogue. We have learnt to associate these characteristics primarily with those works which are referred to as 'early' or 'Socratic', but our concepts of the earliness or socraticity of certain dialogues are far from uncontroversial, and have in any case only come about through the careful study of the whole corpus.

Bewilderment at Plato's failure to give his audience a clear lead had been evident in his own lifetime. We do not know who wrote the *Clitophon* or exactly when,[1] but it seems to indicate the impatience of some who were well-disposed to Plato that his version of Socrates was very good at encouraging young people to philosophy, but incapable of giving them any serious help when they took these studies up. Clitophon wanted to discover what justice was, not simply to hear Socrates praise it, but came to the conclusion that Socrates either did not know or would not tell (410c); in fact he seemed to be just an obstacle to those already committed to learning (410e). Details show that the Clitophon relates in some way to the discussion of justice in *Republic* 1, though not to the version that has come down to us. In fact the same passionate dissatisfaction with Socrates' lack of obvious direction is expressed by Thrasymachus there (336b-d); he too sees Socrates as unwilling to teach (338b); and Socrates' tendency to underestimate his own cognitive abilities is charged with being obstructive (337a).

That Plato differs from those philosophers who straightforwardly set out their doctrines was obvious. The nature of this difference was not easy to determine, and consequently it was liable to be seen in terms belonging rather to an interpreter's own time. The Hellenistic age saw philosophy sharply divided between those who claimed to have the answers to important questions of philosophy, and those who did not profess to do so. For whatever reason, the Academy, Plato's own educational foundation, taught only the issues and the arguments, and made no pronouncements about the correct conclusions. They were especially tough in their criticism of theories of knowledge or truth, and, without giving any strong indications that they deeply doubted matters which humans in general would accept, they became viewed as willfully embracing ignorance and obstructing the progress of philosophy. We call them Sceptics. We cannot be sure that they did so themselves, but we do have many arguments which are designed to support what may be called a sceptic view of Plato, though I prefer to refer to it as a non-dogmatic view. The main requirement of these arguments is that Plato should not have fixed doctrines in the way the Epicureans and Stoics had done: doctrines capable of being reduced to fill handbooks to philosophy, the kind of 'short cuts to philosophic glory' which were favoured at least from the first century BC onwards,[2] or doctrines that could credibly be utilised in doxographical summaries of the views of various philosophers on a range of set philosophical topics, another product of the same age.[3]

How did these anti-dogmatists argue for a non-dogmatic view of Plato? We may suspend judgment ourselves for the moment concerning which arguments were used when, and whether certain of them were used by Academic or Pyrrhonist sceptics or both. We shall concentrate rather on the view of Plato that they imply. It is usual to treat them as primarily 'Academic', as for instance do Annas and Shields in their contributions to a recent volume,[4] and at least the arguments encountered in Cicero's *Academica* must go back to Academic sources. Following a representation of (Plato's) Socrates as a (marginally less rigorous)[5] predecessor of Arcesilaus, the first Academic sceptic, it is observed that:

1. Nothing is affirmed in Plato's books;
2. They contain many examinations of both sides of an issue;

3. All things are under investigation;
4. Nothing is represented as certain.[6]

These four claims about Plato's dialogues seem not to be restricted to any specially 'Socratic' group of works. The non-affirmation argument is best illustrated by the way in which the much respected physics and theology of the *Timaeus* is constantly represented as a likely story. The reader is clearly discouraged from taking what is said on trust. Yet if the clear exposition of Plato's ideas by a figure widely taken to be Plato's spokesman does not amount to telling us what we should believe, how much less is the reader expected to believe ideas that only emerge in the course of conversations? The argument is really trying to show us that Plato does not speak to us like a Stoic or Epicurean might, nor does he expect us to make up our minds in favour of what he says without further reflection.

Argument 2 picks out a feature of various dialogues where the conversation is led by Socrates; another source mentions *Lysis*, *Euthydemus*, and *Charmides*,[7] but the *Meno* for instance might also have been mentioned since it seems to argue for, then against, the very important thesis that virtue is knowledge, and so might the *Theaetetus*, which at 152a begins to *build up* a theory of sensation based upon Protagorean theory, only to start *undermining it* at 157e.[8] Even in the *Philebus* the same 'Socrates' who begins arguing that intellectual activity is the highest good for intelligent creatures (11), goes on to show that the mixed life of intellectual activity and pleasure is to be preferred (21-2), and ends by hinting that something like measure might in fact be the highest good: with intellectual activity being split into two kinds which come only third and fourth (66). So even in what we see as the late dialogues we find a 'Socrates' who can change sides in the argument. Nor is Socrates the only protagonist to change direction, for the Eleatic Stranger does so several times to arrive at a variety of seemingly incompatible definitions of the sophist,[9] or to find himself arguing against the validity of a previous definition of the statesman.[10] Nor must argument for contrary or contradictory positions be within a single dialogue in order to be relevant to the sceptic thesis. It is just as relevant that Plato should appear to be arguing for the equation of virtue with moral knowledge in the *Protagoras* and against it the *Meno*, or for hedonism in the *Protagoras* and against it in the *Gorgias* and *Phaedo*. These were among the most important issues of moral philosophy, and Plato's writings surely appeared to the Hellenistic age to be far less consistent in their treatment of them than the writings of Epicurus, Zeno, or Chrysippus. As for hedonism, there is a passage in the *Attic Nights* of the North African writer Gellius, derived no doubt from his studies at Athens in the second quarter of the second century AD, which claims that Plato's treatment of it had been so multi-faceted that he seemed to be the origin of all other positions on pleasure that had been discussed: that it had been (i) good, (ii) bad, (iii) indifferent, (iv) inferior to freedom from pain, and (v) dangerous. Whether or not this is a sceptic view of Plato,[11] it is a splendid illustration of the perplexity which can follow from the different positions that Plato appears to be adopting in different dialogues, leaving some readers with the feeling that the writer had refused to make up his mind on one the critical issues of moral philosophy.

Argument (3) follows from this. If Plato kept treating the same topic in different ways, it showed not only that he did not make up his mind, but also that he *continued thinking* about the subjects that he discussed. This is one of the key ideals of the ancient Sceptics, and one which gave rise to two of their four names;[12] they kept *examining* the issues (and so were *sceptics*), and they kept *searching* (and so were *zetetic*). Hence it relates closely to the Academic ideal of *inquiry* which prevails in Cicero.[13]

The final argument also seems important to me, and relates more closely to the epistemology lurking behind Plato's works. If nothing is represented as certain, then one plausible explanation for it is that Plato does not hold that certainty is possible. Here one could point to passages where Plato's 'Socrates' begins to adopt a remarkably confident tone, compatible with didacticism of Hellenistic philosophy, only to remind us of his doubts about his own knowledge. The best example would be *Gorgias* 508e-509a, where he had even spoken about the argument being bound by bonds of iron and adamant. If such statements are not supposed to be unequivocal, what could be? Another example would be *Meno* 98b, where 'Socrates', after a variety of bold epistemological statements, reminds us of his ignorance and says that if he were to claim that he knew anything (and there were few things of which he could make this claim) he would claim that he knew knowledge differed from correct opinion. This proposition is not an exception of great moment, since it virtually follows from his well-known claim that he *knows* that he knows nothing. If the champions of the Sceptic Plato were honest, they would find a rather different conviction in Socrates at the end of his days. At *Crito* 54d one set of arguments reverberates through his brain so that he cannot hear the opposite side of the question; and at *Phaedo* 107b he urges Simmias to carry on investigating what he believes unless everything finally becomes clear, when he need search no longer – as seems to have been the case with Socrates. These two passages seem to run counter to the sceptic ideal of perpetual inquiry, but in a sense they still support it. For Socrates, the time for thinking how he is to live his life is past; he has not made premature decisions; he does not expect his followers to be wholly persuaded, and he expects *them* to continue the search. That is, indeed, what Plato has done. In his apotheosis Socrates transcends the shackles of mortality and the ignorance to which mortals are doomed; has he not also transcended Plato?

The overall picture of these arguments is of a Plato who does not finally make up his mind, does not expect us to do so, and so continues to investigate the arguments from every side. It is not an extreme picture,

and would have considerable plausibility for those struggling to understand Plato after previous encounters with the more forceful systems of
Zeno, Epicurus, or even Aristotle. Others, however, went beyond, seeing
Plato as cautious and uncommitted, arguing that he was *systematic* in his
non-commitment, or even that he took a stance that was *hostile to commitment*.

A later collection of five arguments for showing that Plato was a sceptic
seems more of this kind. The anonymous author of the *Prolegomena to
Plato's Philosophy* belongs to the Alexandrian school of Olympiodorus in
the sixth century BC, but the arguments themselves have an earlier origin.
They purport to show that Plato was an Academic sceptic in so far as he (i)
suspends judgment, and (ii) shows signs of maintaining that things cannot
be cognitively grasped in such a way as to exclude the possibility of error.
One argument, that Plato argues for both sides of many questions, parallels the second in Cicero, and will not be further discussed. The other four
are as follows:[14]

5. Plato uses frequent expressions of uncertainty, such as 'perhaps';
6. He refutes all accounts of knowledge in the *Theaetetus*;
7. He thinks knowledge has two foundations, sensation and thought;
   The senses are very unreliable, while –
   Thought is badly hindered by the senses, so –
   Neither foundation of knowledge is secure, so –
   There is no securely founded knowledge.
8. His 'Socrates' denies that he has views of his own in *Theaetetus*.

Argument (5) is known from a number of authors of the Alexandrian
school, and needs little explanation. Certainly these little words of caution
are used often in Plato as compared with Hellenistic and later authors;
many occurrences are in the responses of interlocutors, but that still seems
to be an indication of the level of Plato's commitment. Take the responses
of Protarchus to Socrates' enumeration of the five principal goods at the
very climax of the *Philebus*. The issues have profound implications for
human life, and one might justly hope for some authoritative pronouncements after the taxing travails of this work. Instead we get:

(i) 'It's certainly (*goun*) what emerges from *the present discussion*.'
(ii) 'It's certainly (*goun*) likely.'
(iii) 'Perhaps.' (*isôs*)
(iv) 'Maybe.' (*tach' an*)
(v) 'Perhaps.' (*isôs*)

The irony is that the first answer, the most positive of them all, is given to
the least clear of Socrates' claims, while the second, the next most positive,
is still given to a claim that could warrant considerable clarification.[15] I

have chosen this example because it comes from a dialogue that shows
little debt to the Socratic spirit and employs a largely cooperative interlocutor, so that it does seem to reflect Plato's own doubts. If Plato was
always as hesitant in assenting to his conclusions then one could indeed
see him as non-dogmatic: as fundamentally different from the confident
system-builders of a later age.

Argument (6) and argument (8), both relying on the *Theaetetus*, belong
together. Socrates there attributes his own failure to set forth his views to
his having no wisdom of his own (150c); Plato himself pictures a fruitless
search for an explanation of knowledge. If the former is being honest, and
the latter is not hiding what he knows, then both have no epistemology
such as could legitimately provide a basis for confident utterances on
matters of dispute. Furthermore, that Plato should have wanted to write
a work in which his barren questioner demolishes all accounts of knowledge seems to show a positive desire to set forth the sceptic position and
to *communicate* his doubts systematically. Argument (7) makes clever if
unconvincing use of the *Phaedo*. It does, however, illustrate how Plato can
bewilder the less experienced reader. He does indeed have serious criticisms of the senses in many works, but the words of *Phaedo* 83a are
particularly strong:

> ... investigation through the eyes is full of deception, and so too is that which
> takes place through the ears and the other sensations ...

Strictly speaking it is sensations involving pleasure and pain which the
sequel regards as a hindrance to our thought, and we have to turn rather
to 66b-67b to fill out the picture as the Sceptic requires. The body there is
responsible for hindering us by arousing loves, desires, fears, a variety of
images, and empty nonsense, so that it becomes impossible for us ever to
fix our minds on anything (66c); we can't see the truth because of it (66d).
Plato wants to stress the difficulties of intellectual endeavour until such
time as we have shed the body, in order that he may demonstrate the logic
of Socrates' willingness to die. But in so doing he presents a rather
desperate situation for those of us who are less attracted to his ultimate
solution:

> For if it is impossible, in the body's company, to get a clean grasp of anything,
> then one of two things: either it is impossible to achieve cognition anywhere,
> or it is only possible for the dead.

Plato is denying that the living can have the kind of knowledge for which
Socrates sought, and this is the position of one who sees no path to
certainty for human beings qua human beings. It is right for anybody
reading such passages to be asking how Plato's words here left any room
for sure cognition, and though the sentiments are extreme we do not have

to suppose that Plato ever regretted them. To transcend scepticism the reader needs to transcend the superficial reading of the text, and realise perhaps that Plato only associates human beings with such knowledge to the extent that they can transcend their mortality.

However, the champions of this interpretation did not want to transcend scepticism. Whereas arguments 1-4 were fully in accord with the representation of Academic scepticism at *Academica* 2.7-9, painting Plato as a fallibilist keen to avoid rash assent and to examine issues from all perspectives, arguments 6-7 are representing Plato as one who based a more systematic scepticism upon the rejection of all accounts of how cognition might be achieved. The dilemmatic structure of argument 7 is reminiscent of the sharpest Academic and Pyrrhonist arguments against cognition. Whereas for Cicero's Academics Plato embraced a fallibilism whose ultimate objective could still be represented as the truth or a close approximation to it, our second picture sees him arguing, with some determination, that truth will never be reached. Furthermore there is no suggestion that it might even be approached. In conformity with this the Platonic Socrates in argument 8 turns into a mere critic, an educator without a positive idea to his name. The whole thrust of this view is to claim Plato's unequivocal embrace of suspension of judgment.

This enables one to see how there did not have to be one 'sceptic' view of Plato. Even if there was no outright attempt by Pyrrhonists to paint him as an archetypal *Pyrrhonist* sceptic (and hence to run the risk of creating a rival for the founder of their own school), there were at least three kinds of non-dogmatic Academics to whom he could be assimilated: those painted by Sextus in his *Outlines of Pyrrhonism* (1.221-34) as Second, Third, and Fourth Academies. Even here, different interpretations could be offered of the positions of both Arcesilaus and Carneades, key questions involving whether one claimed to *know* that one knew nothing, whether one permitted oneself private doctrine on either philosophical or everyday issues, and whether one adopted scepticism as a way of life or merely as a dialectical strategy. The sceptical view of Plato could be modified to conform with most kinds of ancient scepticism, and it was easy for those who doubted their ability to recover the truths of history to argue for any interpretation that happened to suit their own position.

ii. Scepticism and dogmatism: reading
Plato as doctrine

We have seen how the reader's perplexity and frustration can lead to the view that Plato has no fixed views of the kind that would support confident philosophical instruction. But as the reader of much of Plato knows, perplexity can be the beginning rather than the end of philosophy. In fact the three dialogues with the most obvious epistemological content both signify this. In the *Meno* Socrates demonstrates to a perplexed and frustrated Meno that his similarly perplexed slave boy has benefited from becoming perplexed:

> We have done something that contributes, apparently, to his finding out the real position; for now in his ignorance he'd be happy to search, but then he lazily believed that he could speak well ... about the doubling of an area ....

Besides including a passage which speaks directly of amazement as the beginning of philosophy (155d), the *Theaetetus* promises that recognition of the inadequacies of early ideas may lead to one's later ideas being better (210b-c); and this message is reinforced at *Sophist* 230c-d:

> [the soul] will not have the benefit of the lessons that are administered until such time as some interrogator reduces the one being tested to a sense of shame, removing the opinions that are a hindrance to the lessons, ...

For those who have experienced ignorance with Plato, the opportunity exists to go on to find treasures.

Not all of those who found deeper messages in Plato can have come through such a route. Like many of us today, the Stoics and Cynics of the Hellenistic age were deeply interested in Socrates, whose philosophical activities had been presented to the Greeks from a number of perspectives and by a variety of authors. The elusive 'Socrates' of Plato's shorter works in particular, who prefers questions to answers and manages the progress of a conversation round to a state of final indecision, was not the only 'Socrates' available. Xenophon's 'Socrates' we know to be far readier to reveal his views and to teach his pupils positive moral lessons; other writers might easily have been closer to Xenophon than to Plato in this regard. But the key point is that Xenophon and others would have provided a clear framework within which to understand Socrates' philosophy, a framework which could then be applied to Plato's dialogues, and give additional help in revealing the moral assumptions which underlie the Platonic protagonist's treatment of the argument. They could give clues as to when 'Socrates' is arguing more seriously against a position which he holds to be wrong, and when he is more frivolous; they could suggest times when he is being ironic, and others when he is being earnest. Thus the reader can begin to feel more at ease with the Platonic 'Socrates', and more confident of messages that Plato might have intended.

The Stoics in particular would have been able to find in Socrates many themes of relevance to their own moral philosophy, including the priority of virtue and its relation to knowledge. As they read many of the dialogues they would feel they were reading literature inspired by similar moral beliefs to their own. Some emphases may have been different, some key planks of the system may have been missing, but there was enough which they could warm to and feel they understood to make them convinced that Plato did indeed speak – albeit in a very different manner from that of their own school. Over the centuries several interpreters and groups of interpreters have found different – often conflicting – messages in Plato, messages which they could respond to. When they have done so, it has been hard to deny that their own message had been intended by the author, and that the author had once anticipated their own beliefs. A variety of philosophic visions has been read into Plato's text, with varying levels of justification. Plato is the fellow-traveller on many a philosophic journey.

Once meaning has been found in the works of Plato it is difficult to treat him as a sceptic. Perhaps he was less than sure of many things, and lacked the epistemology that could justify certainty; but messages abounded. These messages could be expressed in new philosophic language, and clarified with the help of new distinctions. They could even be improved on. But that Plato had doctrines, that he was prepared to communicate them to readers with their eyes open, and that they constituted a major contribution to the progress of philosophy, was for many impossible to doubt.

Agreement that Plato held and communicated doctrine of some kind did not imply any unanimity as to what the doctrine was or what processes one could adopt for identifying it. The same issues that were directly fought out between philosophers could be fought out a second time within the corpus of Plato, where both sides found agreement with their own position. In a sense even the Sceptics were involved in this. Once their own themes and tactics were found in Plato, it was hard to accept they were present by accident. Even the Pyrrhonist Sceptics, according to Diogenes Laertius 9.72, numbered Plato among their less developed predecessors, and the arguments for the Sceptic Plato can themselves be seen to rely on the notion that Plato was conveying his own messages in parts of the dialogues.

iii. Scepticism and dogmatism:
the combined reading

Controversy between those who saw Plato as a straightforward teacher and those who saw him as something of a sceptic took various forms, sometimes no doubt closely related to strong beliefs about the Platonic corpus, at other times turning into a mere dialectical battle about an ancient text. Hence it seems that some took the sceptics' most important text, the *Theaetetus*, and turned it into a positive contribution to theory concerning the criterion of truth,[16] while their opponents took the most important text for the didactic Plato, the *Timaeus*, and argued on the basis of 40b that Plato 'leaves the truth to gods and the children of gods' while seeking only the likely story himself (DL 9.72).

More circumspect interpreters were prepared to take each text on its merits. They were prepared to accept that Plato was far from teaching in many works, while realising that in others he communicates views seemingly his own. This view was probably widespread, though we know it explicitly thanks to Sextus Empiricus (*PH* 1.221): some believed that Plato is *aporetic* in *gymnastic* works where he contends with rival intellectuals or when sporting with others, but *dogmatic* when expounding his own views through his 'Socrates' or 'Timaeus' etc. The terminology suggests that Plato was seen as engaging in a kind of mental wrestling with others, or having his 'Socrates' do so, and that the mental wrestling could either be an earnest struggle, as when he challenges views needing refutation, or playful when he is merely exercising with friends. Such works would pose problems rather than suggesting answers. The result of a distinction in these terms is inevitably the downgrading of the *aporetic* works, just as one would not value mere exercise as highly as the activities which one wanted to remain fit for. There is a strong tendency in Platonist sources of Sextus' era to refer to works likely to be labelled *dogmatic* much more frequently than to those of polemic or less serious exercise.

Clearly Plato himself is not thought to be both a sceptic and a dogmatist, as this would attribute to him incompatible psychological states. Rather Platonists were distinguishing between two sets of works with fundamentally different purposes. Similar distinctions are made using slightly different terminology in various documents of that age, particularly in an elaborate classification of dialogue-character present in both Diogenes Laertius and Albinus, where the contrast is between fifteen dialogues of an *inquisitive* character, and twenty that are *expository*.[17] Here too Plato is seen as a thinker with both convictions and the ability to offer straightforward answers.[18] However, he refuses to do so in a certain group of his works, which are there to challenge the young or to refute rivals: or perhaps he *cannot* do so if he is to achieve his purpose, as is suggested by our *Theaetetus*-commentator (59). His distinction is not, it seems, between groups of dialogues, but between types of activity, and it is Platonic (or Socratic) *inquiries* that he chooses to separate from *declarations*.[19] The *Theaetetus* is principally an inquiry into knowledge, but the passage on Socratic midwifery (150-1) and no doubt the ethical digression too (172-7) offer teaching on topics outside the main inquiry. This type of distinction between activities within the dialogue has the merit of avoiding the simple division of the corpus into more helpful and less helpful works, and so preserves an important place for dialogues like the *Meno* and *Theaetetus*, both of which are clearly held to contain important doctrine even if they are supposed to conceal it on the central issue: for the *Meno* too, after appearing to reach positive conclusions, undercuts them in the closing speech of 'Socrates'.[20]

iv. Does Plato withhold doctrines?

So we see that the ancients had broadly three positions open when trying to assess whether Plato expounded doctrines through his dialogues. The position that sees Plato as doctrine-free has few further interpretative problems, but it is overall the least plausible position, and the least use to most of those who wanted to offer themselves as philosophic teachers during the centuries of Roman domination – for the Roman mind was often rather practical, and had little time for mere intellectual exercises that could be written off as sophistic quibbles. Therefore the other two positions dominated, and both raise many further questions concerning these doctrines. The first is the *extent* of Plato's willingness to commit his doctrines to writing.

This question begins with the *Phaedrus*, and the fascinating question of why he seems there, in a work that is itself written, to diminish the authority of the written word (274-8). A considerable amount has been written about this passage, but what interests us is the likely reactions of readers in antiquity on and beyond the boundaries of philosophy (of whom there were a considerable number).[21] What would be their reaction, when reading Plato for either literary enjoyment, or rhetorical examplars, or philosophic edification, to find this admired author criticising the very manner in which he was communicating with them so successfully? The messages which the passage would convey to him are that writings are only able to have the correct effect on those they are intended for, and can't make provision for others, or give supplementary details that may be needed. They are therefore inferior to oral communication, and a wise man will not attach much importance to what he has written. They are written for amusement, and as a reminder, for himself and others like him, of what they already know.

The immediate question that this raises is how the dialogues could have been intended as vehicles for teaching, if all they are able to do is remind oneself and those who tread the same path of what they already know (276d3-4, 278a1). Perhaps Plato's theory that learning is a process of recollection might be implied here, yet, if it is, how is it that written 'teaching' can be contrasted with oral/aural teaching? It does seem that if the *Phaedrus* gives a reasonable account of Plato's views then Plato does not believe his works are *sufficient to teach*. In a later age they need somebody other than Plato to help explain them, to assist the student to follow the Platonic path, and to answer questions that may arise. This is all useful for the Platonist teacher, whose role is fully justified if Plato's works rely on him to sow the right seeds in the student's mind first.

The *Phaedrus* is quite perplexing enough on its own, but when one adds to it material in the *Seventh Epistle* which denies that there ever has been or will be a book by Plato on certain matters pertaining to metaphysics (341c-d), and another from the *Second Letter*, which goes on to arrange for its own burning ostensibly to prevent the esoteric content falling into the wrong hands (314c), one realises that there is no shortage of material in the corpus to suggest that Plato was committed to keeping his most deep and fundamental doctrines off the written page: except, apparently, the written pages of the *Epistles* which were not themselves intended to survive. Precisely when these letters made their mark on the world of

Platonic interpretation is uncertain; the bulk of the *Seventh Epistle* was known to Cicero, but it is unclear whether the particular passage in question, clearly marked as a digression, was noticed before the second century AD.[22] It is, however, improbable that anything in our surviving collection of letters was absent from the materials arranged by Thrasyllus in the early first century AD, and some evidence that esoteric theological material in the *Sixth Epistle* (323d) was in fact alluded to by Thrasyllus.[23] What seems certain is that nobody who knew these passages from the *Epistles* and accepted them at face value could ignore them. We do not know of attempts in antiquity to deny their authenticity, even though all are regularly challenged today. Without the evidence of the *Epistles* the evidence of the *Phaedrus* might seem to indicate only passing doubts of the validity of writing, or perhaps that these doubts were only those of the non-writer Socrates; with them it seems to confirm that the content of the dialogues represents only the tip of the dogmatic iceberg, the real foundations of which lie hidden forever from Plato's readers. Again, without the *Epistles* the *Phaedrus* would not be thought to have in mind some special category of doctrine that may not be written; with them it would be suggesting that the central tenets of metaphysics are not safely communicable in writing, and Plato would be an esotericist, teaching important doctrines only behind closed doors.

The next piece in the rather untrustworthy jigsaw puzzle is Aristotle's evidence that the Academy had known *agrapha dogmata* under Plato: unwritten, or unwritable, doctrines. The phrase is used by Aristotle at *Physics* 209b15 in the context of Plato's unwritten views on matter and place, which are supposed to be in conflict with those in the *Timaeus*. But other passages in Aristotle also introduce us to a Plato whom we certainly do not instantly recognise from the dialogues, and concern the principal doctrines of metaphysics, concerning the One, the Indefinite Dyad, Ideal Numbers, Mathematicals, and the Ideas themselves.[24] Some scholars do feel that the *agrapha dogmata* actually explain how mysterious passages in the allegedly later dialogues, in particular the second half of the *Parmenides* and the *Philebus*, should be understood,[25] though they can only offer an *additional* level of explanation, for these dialogues are intelligible without them. Aristotle's evidence is not to be ignored, though it may well constitute a considerable simplification, and it may relate only to the later years of Plato's life, when much of his time was presumably taken up with his great political project – the *Laws*. For our present purposes, however, it is important that Aristotle is not evidence that the dialogues did not teach doctrine; it is not evidence that some doctrines were actually incommunicable; it is only evidence for a body of doctrine beyond the dialogues.

The position is further complicated by Plato's successors within the Academy, his nephew Speusippus and also Xenocrates, who succeeded Speusippus as Head of the school. They apparently left later readers the impression that they were trying to say something about Platonic doctrine from time to time, though the status of what they were claiming remains obscure. It seems that straightforward exegesis was not yet an important task; rather they were trying to develop or adapt certain aspects of Plato's theory, such as his views on the identity of the Gods[26] or on Soul,[27] and to make other aspects more approachable. Hence Proclus seems to believe that Speusippus had something meaningful to offer on the subject of the Pythagorean background to Plato's *Parmenides*,[28] and Plutarch deals with Xenocrates' approach to the Platonic World-Soul in *On the Procreation of the Soul*.[29]

The principal tenet of interpretation which the Old Academy has left us is the belief that the creation of Plato's *Timaeus* should not be understood as a *temporal* creation-process; the creation-story is seen as a mere expository device helping to explain *how the universe works*.[30] This is of great importance, because, like Aristotle's dismissal of the Atlantis-story as fiction,[31] it shows Plato's immediate descendants declining to recommend that the dialogues should be taken as a literal reflection of his beliefs, and legitimises the non-literal approach to various Platonic issues adopted by many subsequent Platonists. But their internal disagreements, over the doctrines to which they themselves subscribed if not over matters of interpretation, also made it legitimate for later Platonists to doubt whether these earlier successors had inherited any deeper insights into Plato than were available to much later generations. Certainly it did not become usual to appeal to Speusippus or Xenocrates as authoritative interpreters.

Two other successors who may be briefly mentioned are Hermodorus, who is little known, but is thought to have preserved, via the similarly shadowy figure of Dercyllides, a very important doctrine of Platonic 'categories' for late antiquity;[32] and Philip of Opus, who was often supposed to be the author of the *Epinomis*, but who was nevertheless usually assumed to be true to the spirit of Plato's final doctrines. At any rate we are often told of what *Plato* says in the *Epinomis*.

Both Aristotle and Plato's successors in the Academy present a challenge to interpreters of Plato, irrespective of their knowledge of or confidence in the *Epistles*, for it is clear evidence of a side of Plato that one does not know from literal interpretation of the dialogues. It makes the task of interpretation complex by introducing the possibility that dialogues may be alluding to ideas not fully developed within them. They could not be fully interpreted internally, yet how could the necessary extra material be understood from Aristotle – a largely unsympathetic witness?

The possibility that Plato withholds some significant beliefs actually becomes quite plausible in the light of modern scholarship on certain supposedly earlier dialogues, such as the *Euthydemus*, *Euthyphro*, and *Lysis*. It is difficult to read these works without feeling that we have a kind of forward reference to works such as the *Republic* and *Symposium* (supposing these to be 'middle'), and if we follow this feeling we need to develop a 'proleptic' reading such as has recently been advocated by Kahn.[33] If this feeling is justified at all, it probably means that Plato is already experimenting with certain themes well before they are clearly articulated. It is likely that when the *Euthydemus* was written it was alluding to 'unwritten doctrines' that subsequently were entrusted to writing; adherence to the same practice would mean that Plato's later works are likely to be alluding to other themes not yet clearly enunciated in writing. The interpreter's task now involves discussion of background Platonic doctrine of which no satisfactory account is available; he is dependent to some extent on correct Platonist intuitions; and he has no controls beyond an interpretation's ability to make sense to other readers of Plato. This is dangerous territory!

Let us take as our example the earliest part-extant Platonic commentary from antiquity, the anonymous *Theaetetus*-commentary. The author believes that Socratic inquiries employ a methodology which keeps Plato's own views on the principal topic of investigation *theoretically* hidden – though accessible to those readers who can read between the lines (59.12-21). The experienced reader is supposed to absorb the message *imperceptibly*. This constitutes a legitimisation of reading between the lines, or at least of reading between the lines after one has first read the lines very carefully. Our commentator makes much of tiny details in Plato's text, and overall he is guided towards his answers by a combination of noting these details and attempting to harmonise them with what occurs in other relevant dialogues. He does not wander far from what is written *somewhere* in the corpus, and indeed interprets the epistemological inquiries of the *Theaetetus* largely in the light of themes openly revealed in the *Meno*. But then he is not committed to the view that Plato conceals any of his doctrines *consistently*, but only when they would pre-empt the results of some Socratic *investigation* and stand in the way of the interlocutor revealing his own ideas – and ultimately his own ignorance. It is a view that would no doubt assist him to interpret all those shorter dialogues which search inconclusively for definitions of virtues and similar qualities that Plato is quite happy to define elsewhere: the *aporia*, or final impasse, is something contrived to suit the requirements of an investigation into the ideas of others. Plato can easily supply definitions of the various virtues in Book 4 of the *Republic*, and of the beautiful at *Gorgias* 474d; but, if he is to remain true to the paradigm of Socratic inquiry, he does not have the option of doing so in *Laches*, *Euthyphro*, *Charmides*, and *Hippias Major*, or indeed in *Republic* 1.

Others of this period were much more inclined to assume that Plato was making an effort to hide his innermost thoughts, and revealing them *nowhere* clearly. Hence in the introduction to Plato followed by Diogenes Laertius there had been material which showed how Plato kept his doctrines obscure by (i) using many terms for the same thing, the Platonic Ideas for example, and (ii) using the same terms for a variety of things.[34]

No doubt this esotericism was thought to be connected with the notion of philosophy as a kind of initiation, in which nobody would come to see the inner rites without the appropriate preparation.[35] Another text which attributes an esotericism to Plato, at least on theology, is Apuleius' *De Platone* (1.5.191), which is interesting in view of the straightforward didacticism about all aspects of Platonic doctrine that one encounters in this work. Apuleius has no intention of going beyond underlining Plato's own statement concerning the impossibility of revealing the Father to all persons (*Tim.* 28c), though the number of negative attributes that Apuleius here applies to the divinity does contribute to an effect of esotericism. For stronger proof of Apuleius' tendency to see Platonism's inner doctrine as something denied to the profane majority one might turn to the *Apology*, where the accusers are conveniently put into this group while Apuleius and the presiding judge are given privileged insights.[36] Apuleius' tantalising account of his *alter ego*'s initiation into Isaic mysteries at *Metamorphoses* 11.23 also suggests that he warms to the idea of privileged doctrines. Since Apuleius places himself in the same tradition as Plutarch, it might be wise to quote the following revealing passage of the treatise *On Isis and Osiris* (370f), discussing two opposing cosmic forces, one good and one bad:

> But Plato, though in many locations he muddies the waters and hides behind a veil, calling one of the opposite principles The Same and the other The Different, speaks in the *Laws*, when he is older, not through riddles or symbols but in explicit language, saying that the universe is moved not by one soul but perhaps by many, and at very least not less than two, ...

Plutarch accepts that Plato normally shrouds his theology in obscure terminology, presumably so that it shall not be perceived by the profane, but believes that old age has somehow led him to be more open. Plutarch himself, though sometimes more coy, is certainly anxious to impart his message by any means possible in the *De Iside*, and perhaps welcomes the example that the mature Plato offers him.

It is far from obvious why such straightforward teachers are keen to see Plato as one who conceals. The answer in some cases might be a link with the Pythagorean tradition. Often, as at *De Platone* 1.3, Plato is supposed to have been deeply indebted to Pythagoras. But the reticence is then linked rather with the early influence of Socrates, who was seen by the Pythagorean Numenius as being an unhelpful influence in this regard.[37] Numenius, operating probably at about the same time as Apuleius, could thus openly expound Plato's alleged doctrines, on the grounds that they are Pythagoras' too, and Pythagoras, whom he claimed to follow, was not reluctant to express his views! In general the alleged esotericism of Plato was not the cause of any similar reticence on the part of later Platonists, who were only too happy to say what they meant.[38] It merely gave them more scope to develop their own individual strains of Platonism without seeming to go too far beyond anything that Plato would privately have assented to. This is not a criticism; the liberties taken by interpreters today in the belief that Plato left many things unsaid, or was unable to say them clearly, are often worse.

v. Socratic irony

Whether or not Plato is sometimes responsible for the withholding of doctrine, there is a serious additional question of the same nature about Socrates. Plato's Socrates professes ignorance of a wide range of things in a number of dialogues, admitting his expertise only in matters relating to love and the delivery of intellectually 'pregnant' young men.[39] It is difficult for the reader to understand his diffidence, since he always seems better able to grasp the essentials of a topic than his interlocutors. An opponent of the Platonic 'Socrates' such as Thrasymachus (*Rep.* 337a) is quite ready to view his adversary as an habitual ironist, implying some pretence of being unable to grasp what he in fact grasps perfectly well. Whatever the exact meaning of the term, Alcibiades in the *Symposium* accuses Socrates of spending his whole life 'playing the ironist'.[40] If this means that Socrates makes a practice of concealing his views, then Plato too might be supposed to be under an obligation to present Socrates concealing his views. It might be hard to accuse 'Socrates' of being an ironist in *Symposium*, *Phaedrus*, *Phaedo*, and the later books of the *Republic*, but all these works show 'Socrates' talking in private with his friends, far from his normal public haunts of the gymnasium or wrestling-school, or even from such less familiar surroundings as the houses of those who entertained sophists. In those cases he could be more open. That he conceals his views in other works with more public settings is easier to believe, and often interlocutors are unable to judge whether or not they should take his professions of ignorance at face value;[41] on other occasions they find it difficult to believe that 'Socrates' is serious about other views that he espouses;[42] and in the *Hippias Major* 'Socrates' conceals his own reactions to the simplistic answers of 'Hippias' by explaining this as the reaction that a friend would have: a friend who emerges as the double of 'Socrates' himself, sharing the same house and father! Here there is little doubt that the principal speaker is concealing his own grasp of the topic by inventing an *alter ego* with greater expertise. Is Plato's 'Socrates' an ironist?

Those who believed in a dogmatic Plato, a dogmatist who immortalised in his writings a Socrates whose views were also strong, could easily claim as much. They could resort to the notion that the more unconvinced 'Socrates' of certain works, who leads the argument around in circles, and engineers paradoxical or inconclusive endings, is in actual fact merely indicative of the irony of Socrates: not of the ignorance of either Socrates or Plato. To many commentators it would have been far more damning that Socrates should have been ignorant, than that he should have concealed

his knowledge. Olympiodorus, for example, resists strongly the implication that Socrates is ignorant,[43] even though he only very occasionally
allows that he may be being ironic.[44] In general it would seem to have been
an attractive tactic for those convinced of Plato's and Socrates' knowledge
of the subject investigated to appeal to Socrates' irony in order to avoid the
charge that he is indecisive.

Such tactics had clearly been employed in Platonic interpretation before
the time of Plutarch and the anonymous *Theaetetus*-commentator, both of
whom launch an attack on those who have advocated reading 'Socrates' as
an ironist.[45] Both want to view the aporetic dialogues as an important part
of the Platonic corpus, with a positive purpose of its own independent of
any ironic tendencies that the historical Socrates may have had. They can
appeal to two important aspects of the 'midwife'-image of Socrates in the
Theaetetus: the first that the god himself has forbidden him to conceal the
truth, and the second that he actually compares himself with that god – in
one case suggesting that the procedure of concealment would be illegiti-
mate, and in the other case showing that any concealment could not
possibly be attributed to any kind of modesty!

The debate between those who saw 'Socrates' as an ironist and those
who did not can be traced back before Cicero's *Academica*, though we do
not have the same details about which individual passages were being
argued over. A number of Ciceronian passages seem to advance the idea
that Socrates, perhaps even in the works of Xenophon and Aeschines,[46]
was an ironist who concealed the level of his expertise.[47] This irony may
sometimes appear as a stylistic device quite as much as any kind of
dishonesty.[48] It is of course usually Cicero's more pro-stoic characters who
are inclined to explain away Socratic ignorance by appealing to irony,
while he himself, *in propria persona*, may resist;[49] yet even his 'Varro', a
spokesman for the dogmatist cause and for the dogmatist view of Plato,
seems to be taking the Socratic confession of ignorance quite seriously at
Academica 1.15-17.[50] One does not have to appeal to irony in order to see
Socrates as having made a positive contribution to philosophy.

Appeals to Socrates' irony may have the effect of relieving Plato himself
of the responsibility for failed investigations; he can remain committed.
The claim that Plato writes inconclusively *only* in order to be faithful to
Socratic irony is another case of the modified transcript theory, and takes
much of the responsibility for the inconclusiveness of some dialogues away
from Plato. If one goes one step further and argues that Plato himself is
being ironic, having inherited this trend from his mentor, then one is left
with the view that he himself often conceals what he knows, and this leads
into other interpretative issues.

3

Where do I look for Plato's doctrines?

i. Plato's spokesmen

The problem of Socratic irony is at its trickiest for those interpreters who wish to see 'Socrates' as little more than a spokesman for Plato himself. If 'Socrates' consistently says things which Plato would say, and takes on a character much like the author himself, then we would expect to have a reliable guide to what Plato believed and how he would himself have conversed. However, at one moment 'Socrates' is firm and outspoken, at another he is in doubt on the same issues; at one moment he will appear a hedonist, at another an anti-hedonist; at one moment an implacable opponent of rhetoric, at another a champion of scientific rhetoric. At one moment he will attack the sophists, at another he will act like them. Above all perhaps, he will frequently undermine his own credibility as a spokesman, by questioning his own intellectual capacity for sorting out the issues before him. Clearly it will be difficult to claim that he is a spokesperson in all dialogues, and those who saw Plato as part dogmatic, part aporetic, can claim that he acts as a spokesperson in the works which convey doctrine, but not otherwise. They can associate Socratic irony, with some credibility, with the aporetic works rather than the doctrinal ones. Then they can give 'Socrates' the job of expounding doctrine in works such as the *Phaedo*, *Republic*, and *Phaedrus*.

It is not only 'Socrates' who was seen as a spokesman for Plato. In Diogenes Laertius (3.52) we are told that Plato reveals 'that which seems so to him' through four characters: 'Socrates', 'Timaeus', and the Athenian and Eleatic Strangers. On the other hand he uses the characters of 'Thrasymachus', 'Gorgias', 'Protagoras', 'Euthydemus', 'Hippias' *and others like them* for the victims of his refutation-processes. In effect we have a list of 'good' and 'bad' characters, a list which leaves out many others, most of whom could be regarded as Socrates' acquaintances. The Athenian Stranger is an obvious choice, since that figure is clearly meant as a spokesman for Athens as opposed to Sparta or Crete, and not for democratic Athens. That 'Timaeus' should usually have been considered a spokesman was inevitable, since he expounded theories directly, and those theories relate closely to views expressed by the protagonists of other dialogues. The Eleatic Stranger's inclusion follows naturally from the view, expressed by Diogenes, that the *Sophist* and *Politicus* are works expounding positive doctrine (3.50); this leaves the Platonic 'Socrates' as the remaining spokesman. The list is hardly a complete list of 'main speakers', since it excludes Parmenides, Critias, Clitophon, and Menexenus in the dialogues named after them. This has interesting implications for the *Parmenides*, which was regarded as a work of instruction at 3.50. Who can it be who is doing the instructing?

The Athenian Stranger, though regarded as a vehicle for Platonic doctrine, is not seen simply as a mask for Plato; nor is the Eleatic Stranger identified with Parmenides or any other Eleatic. Diogenes' source sees both Strangers as nameless Platonic inventions, distinct from Plato himself (like 'Socrates' and 'Timaeus') as well as from Parmenides; he sees them as vehicles of Plato's approved doctrine *without* their *standing for* Plato. How can it be that the Athenian is a mouthpiece for Platonic doctrine without his actually representing Plato? I argue elsewhere[1] that Diogenes' source has uncritically adopted earlier mouthpiece-theory and then had qualms about applying it rigidly. A more thorough-going application of the 'mouthpiece' idea, making the Athenian Stranger the thinnest of disguises for Plato, and his Eleatic counterpart the thinnest of disguises for Parmenides, is found in the Introduction to Plato partially preserved in *Oxyrhynchus Papyrus* no. 3219.

Fragment 1 of this work discusses the alleged precedents for Plato's 'direct' or 'dramatic' dialogues, accepting that Sophron was a model but denying that Alexamenos was.[2] The first column of fragment two then reads something like this:

> ... Protagoras [is among] those being refuted in his works. But he reveals what seems to him to be the case through [4] characters, Socrates, Timaeus, the Athenian Stranger, the Eleatic Stranger; the Eleatic Stranger and the Athenian Stranger are Plato and Parmenides, but because he constructs his dialogues to be dramatic right through [...][3] and creates an imaginary unnamed Athenian ...

The same four characters are singled out as the vehicles through which Plato expresses his view, and the wording is very close to that of Diogenes, signifying at very least a common source. But in the case of the papyrus-work the unknown author applies his mouthpiece-theory uncritically. Perhaps he sees the need to achieve a plausible drama as the only reason why Plato had thinly disguised the Strangers' identities. Here the absence of Parmenides from the list of spokesmen is even more striking, bearing in mind that the Eleatic does have spokesman-status and is here identical with Parmenides! I have argued[4] that Diogenes' source is arguing with some consistency *for* a broadly Thrasyllan position and *against* details of Aristophanes' treatment, which is reflected in the papyrus. If so, then the list of four spokesmen in both the papyrus and Diogenes is ultimately

Aristophanes of Byzantium's list, and includes all those who might be reasonably regarded as spokesmen *from the fifteen works which Aristophanes arranged* into trilogies;[5] since no candidates from outside the works of the arrangement are present, 'Parmenides' is not included.

In both cases in which we have discovered reference to Plato's spokesmen the material seems to derive from introductions to the reading of Plato,[6] and consequently one might suspect that very many who encountered Plato had come to him with the expectation that they should be learning from the words of a single respected character in each dialogue. It is likely that introductions to the reading of Plato would have incorporated this spokesman theory from the period of Aristophanes of Byzantium in the early second century, at least until the flurry of Plato-scholarship in the second century AD. What then would have been the case in works of more advanced exegesis?

A substantial portion of the third book of Galen's *Commentary on the Medical Claims in the Timaeus* survives, and in it we find the author constantly referring to what Plato says or does without any regard to the fact that his character 'Timaeus' is speaking.[7] Excerpts from other works referring to this commentary also speak of what 'Plato says'.[8] Galen's practice differs at first in his compendium of the *Timaeus*, where he begins by carefully distinguishing speakers; as time goes on, however, this approach is dropped, and Galen seems to believe once again that he is dealing simply with 'Plato'.[9] One might add that the kind of author who is content to write summaries of Platonic dialogues is also likely to be committed to the view that doctrine can easily be extracted with little consideration for the literary form; this in turn strongly suggests that there must be characters whose words regularly express what Plato thought. However, we may receive an unnecessarily one-sided view by confining our discussion to the *Timaeus*, where there seems little reason for Plato to have chosen Timaeus to expound a view of the world's operations unless he was disposed to agree with that view. For a balanced approach we must consider a range of dialogues, as may be seen from an examination of the complex position of Plutarch.

In Plutarch's *Quaestiones Platonicae* and *De Animae Procreatione in Timaeo*, we find a strong tendency to talk as if Plato employed spokesmen for his views. In the *Quaestiones* Plutarch generally writes as if Plato speaks through 'Timaeus' in the *Timaeus*;[10] through the Eleatic Stranger in the *Sophist* (1009b); and through 'Socrates' in *Republic* 6 (1001c, e, 1006e),[11] *Symposium* (1002e), and *Phaedrus* (1008c). However, in the first *Quaestio* he is much more cautious, and begins by speaking of the words which Plato attributes to 'Socrates' in the *Theaetetus*, and concludes by denying that *Socrates* taught anything (999d, 1000e). It seems logical to suppose that Plutarch himself recognised certain works in which 'Socrates' operated in a more authentically Socratic manner, had no 'teaching' (in the straightforward sense of the term), and consequently had an identity of his own. Probably these would have included most of the so-called early works, along with the *Theaetetus* itself. Certainly *De Animae Procreatione* treats most of the so-called middle- and late-period works as if the chief speaker cannot meaningfully be distinguished from Plato. Plutarch speaks of *what Plato says* in the *Phaedo, Republic, Phaedrus, Sophist, Politicus, Philebus, Laws*, and of course *Timaeus*.[12] The one exception, at 1017c, is noteworthy, since he here supports his view that the creation-process in the *Timaeus* must be taken literally by referring to what 'Timaeus' says in *Critias*, what the 'Parmenidean Stranger' says in *Politicus*, and what 'Socrates' says in *Republic* 8. I argue that he is showing how a plurality of Plato's alleged spokespersons agrees with the *Timaeus* in postulating a creation in time.[13] Galen likewise seeks to strengthen one's confidence that 'Timaeus' is putting forward Plato's own point of view, by showing that the same doctrines are to be found expounded elsewhere by Plato's 'Socrates', especially in the *Republic*.[14]

Strictly speaking, if Plato has a 'spokesman', then that person ought to be in agreement with everything which Plato thinks right, and any of the spokesman's opponents, *qua* opponents, would only be able to make such contrary points as Plato thought to be mistaken. This seems not far from the position of Diogenes Laertius, for whom the opponents are there to be refuted. Wherever such figures as 'Gorgias', 'Callicles', 'Hippias', and 'Protagoras' make good points, and appear to be correcting 'Socrates', then it diminishes Socrates' claim to be a spokesperson in the full sense. Even where less sophisticated characters who are not direct opponents seem to be helping the argument to progress, it is natural to believe that the lessons which emerge from the work as a whole amount to far more than the propositions being voiced by the official 'philosopher' of the drama. If there is really some point in writing philosophy as drama, then it is surely because drama can somehow transcend a treatise or handbook, and the leading character is less than self-sufficient.

This kind of problem about the status of certain 'voices' within a written work is not one that normally surfaces explicitly within surviving Platonist literature. However, it is not altogether different from a similar problem affecting early Christians in their dealing with the Old Testament. Take for example the voice of some prophet in a book written down by another: a voice, which is taken to be an authoritative voice. There can be real debate as to one's obligation to understand the exact words of the text as ideally conveying the real meaning. Was the real author of these words simply a historian? Do we really have the voice of the prophet? And does the voice of God itself speak these words through the prophet? As can be seen in Justin Martyr (I *Apol*. 36.2), this kind of problem was already being compared in the middle of the second century with similar issues confronting pagans committed to interpreting texts. We are not told *which* texts, but there is a high probability that Justin had in mind the texts of Plato, whose interpretation was already a sophisticated task. Are the words of

'Socrates' at the end of the *Phaedo* when he describes what awaits us after death (i) the voice of Plato (who according to the text at 59b never even heard him speak), (ii) the true voice of the man 'Socrates', or even the voice of Apollo heard through the words of his human spokesman?[15] Contemporary literature also seems acutely conscious of issues involving the status of voices heard speaking within, and nowhere is this more in evidence than in the *Golden Ass* – the novel written by the Platonist Apuleius.[16] Furthermore these problems are also the problems of the Platonist's schoolroom: the voice of Socrates, as interpreted by Plato, is reinterpreted once again by the Platonist teacher as he communicates the meaning to the pupil. This was an age when the status of the voice which one hears was particularly at issue, for the reworking of old messages constituted a huge proportion of serious literature. Indeed Seneca had recently been saying of the intellectuals of the Roman Empire 'numquam auctores, semper interpretes': 'never authors, always interpreters'. The public was used to trying to distinguish between old message and new elaboration.

The question of the relationship between the protagonist of Platonic dialogues and Plato himself touches on another question of importance to the attentive reader. What is the status of those voices in Plato's dialogues that are themselves neither authorial nor authoritative, but that still speak sense? A number of passages demonstrate that the ancients were aware of less desirable characters making useful contributions to the discussion, for even a statement which errs in certain details can nevertheless be founded on important intuitions. Important testimony is found in Aulus Gellius' *Noctes Atticae* (10.22), where Plato's 'Callicles', the most important interlocutor from the *Gorgias*, is supposed to be correct in condemning certain kinds of aimless intellectual pursuits when undertaken by those of mature years. Gellius finds deeper meaning, with profound implications for how a dialogue is read, in a character who is not a spokesman, discouraging the simplistic division between characters who put Plato's views and the inferior minds of the their opponents.

Olympiodorus' commentary on the *Gorgias* (26.2) also attributes a worthwhile lesson on reasoning to Callicles, even though he is regarded as anything but an insightful character on matters of ethics. The same author can find useful lessons in the words of 'Gorgias' too (8.7; 8.12). Plutarch can also find truth in the words of 'Gorgias' at 458b; his remarks about the need to consider how the spectators are feeling is alluded to twice in the *Quaestiones Conviviales*.[17] Deeper meaning is found in the words of Pausanias in the *Symposium* by a variety of Middle Platonist authors, who regularly take the theory of two Aphrodites and two Erotes seriously. Plutarch and Apuleius could both be mentioned here,[18] but most important is probably Calvenus Taurus, as reported by Gellius (*Noctes Atticae* 17.20.4-6); here Taurus finds much to commend in the speech of Pausanias at *Symposium* 180e, and calls upon his pupil to appreciate a deep inner meaning.

Enough has been said to show that the issues concerning Platonic spokesmen, and their supposed differences from other characters in the dialogues, are quite complex and relate closely to other issues of interpretation. But one further point should be made: Plato's spokesmen, at least in the eyes of his devoted supporters, must be saying things that can be reconciled. If the messages seem to conflict, then the interpreter's task is to explain away the differences, and show that the deeper meaning of any two passages is the same. The task was awesome, and a starting-point was required.

ii. Which dialogues does one follow?

There is scarcely any reader of Plato who does not attach more importance per page to one dialogue than to another. Those who seek Socrates' philosophy pay much more attention to some supposedly early works than to others, and those who seek Plato's mature philosophy do likewise. All who search for Platonic doctrine require some kind of canon of works, or some single authoritative work on which to build their reconstruction. Issues of authenticity are here of some importance, and the need to exclude some dialogues was felt quite early on. Panaetius, in his search for Socrates, seems to have denied that the *Phaedo* was 'genuine', in all probability denying that it was Socratic rather than Platonic.[19] Those searching for Plato were likewise compelled to reject material, though not always because of the philosophic content. A list of *spuria* is found in the introduction to Plato used by Diogenes Laertius (3.62), and it contains some but not all of the material conventionally listed among Plato's *spuria* today. The thirty-six works arranged in tetralogies by Thrasyllus (DL 3.58-60) would normally have been accepted as 'genuine' in some sense, though it was obvious that not all the *Epistles* were genuine;[20] furthermore the tradition that Philip of Opus had composed the *Epinomis* was strong,[21] and there seem to have been doubts concerning *Alcibiades II*, *Hipparchus*, and *Erastae*.[22] Whether these four dialogues have been included because of the belief that Plato wrote them, the acceptance of their usefulness, or some other reason is not clear. What is obvious, however, is that none assumed great importance for Platonism late antiquity. It is worth noting, perhaps, that the two dialogues that generate most controversy today, *Alcibiades I* and *Hippias Major*, seem not to have been questioned in antiquity. Of these the former was seen to have great importance,[23] partly because of the controversial nature of the interlocutor and of Socrates' relationship with him, but also because of the manner in which it depicts the education of Alcibiades and the way in which both he and the reader are encouraged to reflect upon what their true selves really are (129-33). But the latter remained in comparative obscurity, because much of what it hints at concerning the nature of the 'fine' or 'beautiful' (*to kalon*) emerged more clearly in other works, such as the *Symposium* and *Phae-*

drus. The latter were attractive works of literature with the additional
benefit of making Socrates speak as if inspired, and the more pedestrian,
if amusing, *Hippias* was no match for them.

This imparity between the influence of the dialogues should remind us
that even the subtlest interpreters needed to establish some kind of
priority within the undisputed works if they were ever to produce a
coherent picture of Plato. Iamblichus appears to have narrowed the corpus
down to twelve important dialogues, plus *Republic* and *Laws* which had
some unspecified status ensuring continued detailed treatment.[24] The
Iamblichan canon was aimed at positive instruction, so the only work
included in it that ends inconclusively was the *Theaetetus*, widely thought
to offer authoritative instruction in certain parts. Within the canon the
Timaeus and *Parmenides* were afforded special status, but were not studied until late. One started with dialogues permitting a more literal or less
controversial interpretation. But the later Neoplatonists were already
privileged insofar as the key passages for interpretation had already been
inherited from Plotinus, and perhaps from even earlier. They did not have
to struggle to find a starting-point for their views, for that had been done
for them earlier.

A simple approach to trying to determine the foundations upon which
one can build one's interpretation of Plato was to look for those works
which seemed to be saying things most openly: those where the dialectical
situation could not be suspected of determining the views to which Plato's
protagonist was drawn. There was little point in selecting a passage as
being particularly important, if it could easily be argued that Plato is
indulging in *ad hominem* argument, or that he is only committed to such
a point of view when the wider issue is seen as it is in a particular work.

It may have been partly for this reason that the most consistently
important dialogue throughout antiquity was the *Timaeus*. In this work
the character Timaeus, viewed normally both as Plato's spokesman and as
a Pythagorean, expounds his view of the physical world, the soul that
moves it, and the divinity which creates it, *in continuous didactic speech*.
It feels as if the reader is being *told* something, for nothing that Timaeus
says is tailored to suit the particular requirements of his audience: Socrates, Critias, and Hermocrates, who are all seemingly addressed, even
though the discourse is being told for Socrates in particular. While repeated reference was made by Timaeus to the fact that his account (or part
of it) was no more than 'likely' owing to its dealing largely with the mutable
world of the senses, the work became an important battleground for any
ancient Platonist teacher seeking to establish his credentials. Right up to
the time of Proclus in the fifth century AD, one could almost rely on a
serious Platonic commentator having commented on some part of this
crucial but atypical dialogue. Hence Proclus' own commentary on this
work was far richer in material about the views of his predecessors than
were his other commentaries. The work had been mined for its views on

physics, metaphysics, theology, epistemology, medicine, and even the moral goal. Consequently the appendix on Plato's doctrines in Diogenes Laertius (3.67-80) is heavily dependent on this one work, and Alcinous' *Didascalicus*, of which the physical chapters – 12 to 23, approximately one quarter of the entire handbook – draw on little else, utilises the *Timaeus* for a wide variety of subjects.

The *Timaeus* was not only studied for the light which it could throw on Plato's views, but also as a source for Pythagoreanism with which Plato was assumed to agree. Hence Cicero dedicates his translation of part of the work to the Pythagorean P. Nigidius Figulus, and an extant Pseudo-Pythagorean work, 'Timaeus Locrus' *On the Universe and the World-Soul*, appeared. Pythagoreans such as Numenius and Nicomachus made considerable use of the *Timaeus*. Philo of Alexandria, associated rather problematically with Pythagoreanism by Clement of Alexandria,[25] uses it extensively in his treatment of the creation story in *Genesis*. It was occasionally used as a justification of the sceptic or part-sceptic views of Plato,[26] but is the dominant source for a dogmatic epistemology attributed to Plato by Sextus Empiricus in *Adversus Mathematicos* 7.141-4, and a significant source of Alcinous in his *Handbook of Platonism*, ch. 4. It had also attracted the attention of Stoics such as Panaetius and Posidonius.[27] Thus it was a text of some importance for philosophy in general, not for Platonism alone.

In general, passages involving continuous exposition of a philosophic topic were likely to be given comparatively more attention than those involving rapid changes of speaker, and it can be seen from the dialogues of Cicero or Plutarch that the presence of longer speeches was thought to improve a dialogue, at least from the point of view of communicating ideas. Socrates' account of Diotima's instructions in Love in the *Symposium* or his long explanation of the mechanics of Love in the *Phaedrus* were both well-known and influential. Myths were seen as containing important doctrine, however veiled it might be. Though politics was not a discipline that greatly attracted philosophers of the Roman Empire, the *Republic* was well known, as was the *Laws*, and it is in some ways surprising how much their non-political content was taken into account by interpreters.

What more can one say about the choice of authoritative texts? Clearly for those who were more interested in support for their own philosophic positions any dialogue could be authoritative if it seemed to be leading in the required direction. Hence we have good evidence that the *Theaetetus* was of special interest to the Sceptics because it failed to arrive at any explanation of knowledge after what seemed to be a thorough investigation, and because it also seemed to take Socrates' disavowal of knowledge to an extreme. In general, however, there seems to have been relatively little weight attached to works (or parts of works) with an obvious polemical purpose, and not a great deal more to those where 'Socrates' examines young men: for in either case the setting out of doctrine seemed not to be a matter of priority. This is particularly so for those who would claim that the inconclusive endings of many of these dialogues are contrived, and do not reflect any ignorance on the part of Plato. On the whole they seem not to have been interested in trying to show that Plato's handling of the discussion points the sensitive reader firmly in the direction of a solution, which is one (well justified) modern way of explaining these aporetic dialogues; rather they took comparatively little notice of anything in them. They were read and alluded to by serious Platonists, but only the *Gorgias*, *Meno*, *Alcibiades I* and *Theaetetus* were prominent: the first three (and possibly all four) because of the considerable element of positive teaching on offer. By contrast, dialogues in which Socrates is *explaining* things to *less youthful* friends tend to be seen as important, as do those parts of the *Sophist* and *Politicus* in which the Eleatic Stranger explains things. It is of interest, perhaps, that Plato's debt to Pythagoras was also sought in these works, and that Plato's 'Eleatic' is described by Clement as the 'Pythagorean'.[28]

These considerations may be behind the elaborate classification of dialogue *character* found in Diogenes Laertius and (for the most part) in Albinus, and partially reflected elsewhere. All Plato's works were divided into *hyphegetic* (instructional) and *zetetic* (inquisitive), with the former being ultimately divided into physical, ethical, political, and logical,[29] and the latter being divided firstly into combative and gymnastic works. This subdivision seems important, and distinguishes works intended to *refute* from those aimed merely at mental exercise for the young. Clearly one does not accept as important for doctrine anything intended as an exercise document, while one may well take note of what Plato tries to refute, but the dialogues where Plato wishes to teach positively will clearly be the most important *for doctrine*. Others may be more important for certain kinds of educational activity and for public debate, and there is no suggestion that any of these dialogues should be *ignored* simply because they do not point the way forward to positive conclusions. Indeed, when Albinus relates dialogue character to five educational stages, we find that the works of positive educational instruction are *all* confined to the central stage. Before this one has the works primarily concerned with the encouragement and testing of young men, and with helping them to express their own ideas; after doctrine come the logical dialogues, which are seen as giving students the strength of reasoning that will allow them to realise when demonstration has been achieved, and the anti-sophistic works that will enable them to argue against the onslaughts of the opponents of philosophy. All parts of the corpus had their uses, but only some had any direct bearing in revealing to the student what a Platonist's doctrines should be. Platonism is not just doctrine; it is an educational process *involving* doctrines, but neither begins with them nor ends with them.

iii. Which dialogues must be read in conjunction?

Many would now emphasise that each dialogue is a self-contained unit, in which argument and doctrine are tailored to a particular dramatic setting, and are therefore not always directly comparable with the philosophic doctrine of other dialogues. Even so, it is difficult to allow that there are not some benefits to be gained for the interpreter by experience of the wider corpus, whether the connections between works are doctrinal or dramaturgical. Ancient interpreters tended to the other extreme, expecting some kind of unity of philosophic thought right across the corpus, regardless of the differences in dramatic settings. For the most part they were unitarians, convinced that there was a single philosophic approach, or stance, or doctrine, which could be discovered through a sensitive reading of almost any work in the corpus. They sought for Plato, not for early Plato, or late Plato, or esoteric Plato, or political Plato.

An obvious tactic when trying to build one's interpretation of Plato on a secure foundation was to find groups of dialogues that could easily be read in conjunction, in such a way as to yield a coherent picture on the central issues. Well before the Neoplatonist canon was established in the fourth century AD, Platonists were quite used to interpreting certain texts in conjunction with certain others. Plutarch chooses to view the metaphysics of the *Timaeus* in terms of a selection of other texts in his essay *On the Generation of the Soul in the Timaeus*. These texts in rough order of importance are the myth of the *Politicus* (1015a-d, 1017c), the *Phaedrus* (1016a, 1026d, cf. 1013c), *Laws* 10 (1013e-f, 1015e), *Philebus* (1014d-e), the *Critias* (1017c), the *Sophist* (1013d), the *Republic* (1017c), and the *Phaedo* (1013d). Still treating the *Timaeus* in the second and eighth of the *Platonic Questions*, he brings in the *Symposium* (1000f), *Phaedrus* (1001a), and *Republic* 6 (1006f). The *Sophist*, to which the tenth and last of the *Platonic Questions* is devoted, is closely related to the *Philebus* in the essay *On the E at Delphi* (391b-d), and other *Questions* are devoted to *Theaetetus*, *Republic* (books 4 and 6), and *Phaedrus*.

It is easily seen from this that Plutarch builds up his picture of Plato's philosophy primarily on the foundation of what we now refer to as the middle and late-period dialogues. The others are used and alluded to occasionally, but not in the same interpretation-building manner. Even our customary distinction between middle and late groups of dialogues would have been understood as helpful by Plutarch, though not because of any chronological assumptions which he holds. For instance, at the *Eroticus* (764a), when 'Plutarch' is asked to explain similarities between Platonism and Egyptian religion, response highlights *Symposium*, *Phaedrus*, and books 6 and 7 of the *Republic* – the three works most relevant to the upward striving of the soul. And again, one may feel with some justification that the 'late' works – *Timaeus, Critias, Sophist, Politicus, Philebus*, and *Laws* 10 – are seen as a kind of unity, even though the only one that

Plutarch knows to be late is *Laws* (*De Iside* 370f). It is interesting that a generation later his follower Taurus, arguing for a less literal interpretation of the creation-process depicted in the *Timaeus*, insists that there is no support for the literal interpretation from the *Critias*, the *Politicus*, or the *Republic*.[30]

We can see from Plutarch and from Taurus' fragments how natural it was to be supporting one's interpretation of one dialogue with reference to others, a tactic connected with the assumption that it is ultimately the *corpus* which the Platonist must interpret; Plato grows in stature if he is represented as always offering the same message. The anonymous *Theaetetus*-commentator likewise has a group of dialogues in mind as being relevant for the interpretation of the *Theaetetus*; they are *Meno*, which allegedly supplies the answer to the question posed by the *Theaetetus* (columns 3 and 15), *Phaedo*, which is likewise important for the Theory of Recollection, and probably *Republic* books 6 and 7.[31] Today we should be wary of seeing a *chronological* relation between the four, but, apart from the fact that this is never the anonymous' intention, it is certainly clear that the *Theaetetus* approximates less to the style of the late dialogues as measured by stylometry than do the later books of the *Republic*; while the *Meno*, though regarded as early, is generally seen as one of the last members of this group.[32]

When writing *against* Plato, Aristides adopts the opposite tactic of showing how all sorts of other passages in Plato are in disagreement with things said about oratory and orators in the *Gorgias*.[33] If the Platonist's task is to show how Plato's works are in mutual agreement, then it is natural for an opponent to adopt the reverse tactic of showing how Plato's other works give a radically different picture from the one in hand: works that Aristides uses to demonstrate a contradiction include *Phaedrus*, *Laws*, *Menexenus*, *Politicus*, *Apology*, and *Euthydemus*.[34]

It is worth pointing out here how the groupings of dialogues which tend to be employed for the practical purpose of interpretation by the Platonists of the early Roman Empire are not obviously related to the groupings that were used by Thrasyllus and others to determine a reading-order for the dialogues, or to classify them by purpose. We never find an appeal to a particular dialogue which depends upon its position vis-à-vis another in the corpus. There are only two ways in which the scholars' groupings are relevant to Plutarch, for instance: (i) he might not have looked so closely at the *Critias* when interpreting the *Timaeus* if it had not so obviously been its sequel (something that he knew independently of Thrasyllus); and (ii) his favoured dialogues ordinarily belong to those that the classification treats as offering positive doctrine – but that is a necessity forced upon him by the nature of his task.

Chronological considerations are virtually absent from ancient treatments of Plato, and chronological groupings (other than those based on the dramatic dates of dialogues) are therefore virtually unknown. There was a firm tradition of the lateness of the *Laws*,[35] and a weak tradition concerning the earliness of the *Phaedrus* and *Lysis*,[36] but other than this there was simply an appreciation that certain works were sequels to certain others: most obviously the *Critias* to the *Timaeus* and the *Politicus* to the *Sophist*. The lateness of the *Laws* and the earliness of the *Phaedrus* were thought to be indicated by Plato's manner rather than anything distinctive about his doctrine. And if Plato said things in different ways this was not important. It was the message of Plato that was sought, not the terms used to convey or conceal it. The message was not simply the prerogative of Platonism, but was there, deep down, in all of us, understood in different terms but nevertheless transcending the individual. It was sought because there was a widespread belief that it was important: that it was a higher authority which humans beings ought to listen to.

iv. Which parts of a dialogue should I be concerned with?

Plato's readers are often frustrated with the slowness with which he seems to get down to business – when he gets down to business at all. Some works such as the *Menexenus* and *Critias* might seem to have little relation to philosophy. The *Symposium*, if containing useful insights into the historical Socrates, might seem virtually devoid of philosophy, except during Socrates' contribution at 199c-212c, which constitutes only a quarter of the dialogue, providing one prominent modern commentator with the opportunity to excuse himself from taking much interest in the philosophy of the work at all.[37] Works with a greater percentage of philosophical argument may still make considerable use of myths, allegories, images, mathematical illustrations, and the like. With our modern notion of philosophy that gives such prominence to argument it is all too easy to feel that the contents of a dialogue should be graded on a scale of relevance. With a broader conception of philosophy the ancients seldom undervalued most of this material, and of course gave greater attention to the quasi-mythical narratives, colourful descriptions, and bold mathematical material of the *Timaeus* than to any other dialogue. Plutarch actually finds the need to remind his readers, in the light of previous commentators' enthusiasm for mathematical analyses, that:

> It is not the case that Plato is dragging in arithmetic and geometric means into the plot of a work of physics that doesn't require it for a display of his mathematical studies; he introduces this discussion rather as something particularly relevant to the construction of the soul. Yet some seek the ratios we've mentioned in the speeds of the planetary spheres, some in their distances, some in the size of the heavenly bodies, and some who try to be too ingenious in the diameters of epicycles – as if this were the reason why the demiurge had fitted the soul into the mechanics of the heaven.[38]

So far from receiving cursory treatment, the mathematical passages could apparently become too dominant in interpreters' minds. From our point of view Plato's myths could also become too dominant, encouraging a considerable use of new Platonising myths in Plutarch, and occupying a great deal of Neoplatonist time.[39] Both mathematics and myths could be viewed as parts of Plato's Pythagorean heritage,[40] and this would certainly have helped assure interest, since it is highly likely that much of the interpretative activity preceding Plutarch, and quite a bit thereafter, sprang from Pythagorean motives and a desire to return in time to the very roots of Greek religious philosophy, if not beyond them. A significant number of those who interpreted Plato in Middle Platonist times did in fact see themselves as Pythagoreans.

In spite of a broad approach to the content of the dialogues in antiquity there was one area which they were often inclined to dismiss as of no real philosophical import, and that was the introductory part of a dialogue. An anecdote about the first words of the *Republic* strongly suggested that Plato was viewed as having put a great deal of effort into getting his introductions right, but was his effort philosophically or stylistically motivated?[41] In recent times the *Laches* has regularly worried scholars because its philosophical subject (assuming that to be the nature of bravery) is only explicitly introduced when we are already into the second half of the dialogue (190d). Other works may have quite long introductions that seem at first sight to do nothing but set the scene and introduce the characters. The relation of introductions to the philosophic material that follows is often problematic, but few interpreters would now reject the notion that a connection should be sought.

It is Proclus who provides us with the clearest insights into ancient debates about Plato's prologues. There is material on the correct approach to the prologue of the *Timaeus* within his *Timaeus*-commentary,[42] and a useful summary of the issues in the *Parmenides*-commentary (658-9). Proclus recognises three basic attitudes to the prologues: (1) that they are irrelevant to the interpreter's task, (2) that they are concerned with dutiful behaviour and perhaps loosely related to what follows, and (3) that they are an integral part of the dialogue and contribute towards its principal aim. Dillon (1987, 47) is correct in supposing that Proclus has in mind Middle Platonists, Porphyry, and Iamblichus as the respective proponents of these three views, though the actual historical situation must have been somewhat more complex. For one thing there is a significant question of how one defines a prologue, for many dialogues might be thought to contain *at least two* separate layers of introductory material. If one takes the anonymous *Theaetetus*-commentator (column 4), one finds him unequivocally dismissing that part of the introduction which is set at a different time and place, and spoken by characters who do not participate in the main discussion. Yet the majority of dialogues would not have a prologue of this type, but would begin with the kind of pleasantries that we meet at 143d-144d, which the commentator does indeed interpret, and considers as an appropriate occasion for a discussion of Platonic practical ethics, thereby anticipating the position taken by Porphyry. Moreover we find a detailed allegorical interpretation of Parmenides' prologue in the second century sceptic Sextus Empiricus,[43] an interpretation which reads a variety of philosophic symbolism into the young traveller's journey; what was a possibility for one philosopher was also a possibility for another. Without more examples of Middle Platonic commentaries we are scarcely in a position to say that they ignore all introductory material, especially when Crantor's pioneering interpretation of the *Timaeus* had things to say about the status of the Atlantis story,[44] which is clearly not part of the main body of the work. And besides Crantor, other Platonists prior to or independent of Plotinus had expressed views on the Atlantis story, including Atticus,[45] Numenius, and Origenes.[46]

It may seem somewhat absurd to claim that no material prior to the introduction of the chief question of a dialogue can be relevant to the interpreter, for this would mean that Plato wasted both effort and expensive writing materials on irrelevant pleasantries, but it seems little less absurd to find the kind of relevance that Proclus does in the *Parmenides*-commentary. Commenting on the very first sentence (659-62) he finds in the reference to Athens a symbol for the intermediary between nature (signified by the mention of Ionian Clazomenae) and intellectual being (signified by Italy whence come Parmenides and Zeno). In the same sentence he sees the departure from Clazomenae as indicative of divine activity transcending the natural realm, and the meeting with Glaucon and Adimantus in the market-place the rule of the dyad within unified plurality. Proclus sees Plato's narrative as so loaded with symbolic meaning that the whole of Book 1 of the commentary in fact covers only three Stephanus pages. To the modern reader Proclus' ingenuity will probably seem like a *reductio ad absurdum* of the view that prologues are significant, but this hides a very real interpretative problem. If we admit that prologues are relevant then it is difficult to discern at what level this relevance ceases.

In the same way myths may be complementary or they may hide the author's deepest thoughts; mathematics may be present for the sake of comparison, but the very essence of Plato's metaphysics may be mathematical; digressions may throw additional light on the main topic, or they may remind us that the putative main topic of the dialogue is important because of still greater corpus-wide concerns. Few would want to give every page of Plato equal weight, but the task of deciding which should be given priority is a Herculean one. These issues tend to lead back to the questions that we first discussed: is Plato to be read as literature or philosophy? Literature seems to presuppose a literary unity, but philosophy demands rather the unity of doctrines, or at least of approach, within a corpus.

The internal literary and philosophic unity of each dialogue was force-fully affirmed by the later Neoplatonists, for whom a dialogue was a miniature cosmos, containing within itself matter, form, nature that combines them, soul, intellect, and good.[47] Of these, the last three relate to its strictly philosophic side, whereas its form is its diction, construction, and everything else stylistic, and its matter is its characters and setting. The analysis was not employed for the sake of separating the literary and philosophic, but for showing how perfectly they may combine. For Proclus, however, it is clear that the literary aspects served the philosophic, for they contributed to the philosophic aim. Introductions are thus not explicable purely in terms of literary charm, nor can they be reduced to the level of newspaper reporting. They are literary; they may have some basis in historical fact; but they always contribute to the ultimate goal, which is philosophic.[48] Literary concerns are important, but those who seek to divide the dialogue according to its literary *topoi* take these concerns too far, and remain 'at the third remove from the truth' as Plato would have it.[49]

Proclus, following the overall strategy of Iamblichus, is to be commended for his efforts to evaluate both literary and philosophic elements and to show how they interlock in contributing to an overall purpose. For him all aspects of all parts of a dialogue were relevant to its goal. At times he was too devoted an advocate for Plato's skills, at times too ingenious, but he had the correct overall strategy. The ancients did not eschew the task of saying what they thought was relevant in a dialogue and justifying their position, and neither should we today.

PART TWO

4

Defending and attacking Plato's work

i. When could an interpreter arise?

It is debatable whether the activities of interpretation can be fully realised by those who have some insight into an author's mind and into the circumstances confronting that mind when a written work was produced. Interpretation at its most profound implies a return journey, an attempt to recover what has been to some extent lost or forgotten. It implies far more than the mere use or misuse of a written or oral text; more than satirising, or criticising, or defending, or explaining. There would, however, be no bar to anyone who lived in Plato's lifetime interpreting his writings, provided that they had no prior access to the truths that provided the key; but for most who were so inclined it might have been far more attractive simply to study with Plato, and to find out through their studies the philosophic mind underlying the writings.

Plato did his best in the *Phaedrus* to discourage the book-collector from supposing that he had upon his shelves the key to unlock the treasures of Platonic philosophy, and up until his time literary interpretation within the Greek world seemed to confine itself to revered figures of the past. Homer was the key figure who demanded interpretative and scholarly activity, and Hesiod also attracted attention; Plato's character 'Protagoras' extends such critical activity to poets such as Simonides and Pittacus (*Prt.* 339a ff.), and 316d implies that there are hidden depths behind the works of Homer, Hesiod, Simonides, Orpheus, and Musaeus. Interpretation and evaluation of revered poets of the past was perhaps typical of the sophists, however different they may have been in other respects; the latest poet to receive anything like an interpretation in the pages of Plato would be Pindar as interpreted by 'Callicles' at *Gorgias* 484b-c, whereas contemporary poetry was subject to little more than the mocking lines of the comic dramatists. Euripides is much *used* by Plato, but the intentions of the playwright are left unexplored.

It is interesting that Protagoras himself, who lived for less than a decade after Plato was born, was probably the latest thinker whom Plato could be said to have 'interpreted' in the course of his own works, for the *Theaetetus* has a great deal to say about his theory that 'man is the measure of all things'; other thinkers discussed there, such as Parmenides and Heraclitus, do not prompt an attempt to understand them on their own terms. The *Parmenides*, perhaps, tries to tell us something about the nature of Zeno's work that is read at the beginning, but there is no in-depth interpretation; the message, in fact, is rather that any effort to find a deep message would be misplaced (128b-e). *Presocratic* philosophy, like the activities of the sophists, is usually treated satirically by Plato. There is, in fact, just one figure whom Plato consistently tries to interpret, and that is Socrates: not a text, but rather a vast and variegated body of striking memories and shared anecdotes which cried out to be understood, if only because of the promise that understanding Socrates would be the key to human happiness.

When is it, then, that Plato himself could first be said to be 'interpreted'? Much depends on how obscure an impression he and his work made upon his contemporaries. Did he clarify the meaning of his works for his close associates, or did they too have to fathom the depths of the texts that he made available? How far, in fact, were all these texts available? Did pupils also acquire knowledge of unwritten doctrine that was denied to outsiders, or did they have to operate on the assumption that the key to reading Plato resided in doctrines to which *nobody* had access? These questions are secondary to my present purpose, but some observations may be made. The obscurity of a certain public lecture on the Good by Plato was famous in antiquity, and was used against the lecture-giver by Aristoxenus the musical theorist as well as being reported by Platonists.[1] The notion that certain key elements of his system, particularly of his late system, were not revealed in writing before his death is entirely understandable if we bear in mind how certain features of supposedly 'middle period' works such as the *Republic* seem to be foreshadowed in supposedly earlier writings like the *Euthydemus*.[2] Those who doubt that doctrines were much discussed orally before they were expounded with any clarity in writing should perhaps consult *Phaedo* 100b, where, in what is probably the first dialogue openly to discuss the Platonic Ideas, the Ideas themselves are already referred to as 'much-discussed' (*polythrulêta*): they are already well-known. Thus readers would have expected to enhance their understanding of individual dialogues by material imported from elsewhere, and perhaps from private conversation or hearsay.

It is possible that we have in the *Seventh Epistle* (341b-c) Plato's own attack on the promulgation of misunderstood versions of his metaphysical doctrines by the Sicilian tyrant Dionysius the Younger, briefly his pupil; if not from Plato, it seems certain that the attack emanated from somewhere within the Academy. The *Epistle* tells us that Plato thought some doctrines of central importance unable to be captured in writing, though, if they had to be written at all, they would have been better written by himself that by others. Yet those who wrote down doctrines that Plato nowhere recorded included Aristotle, the principal source of the unwritten doctrines;[3] and also another of his pupils, Hermodorus, who is said to have introduced Platonic doctrine to Sicily, and 'traded' in his theories.[4] He explained Plato's theory of matter (nowhere explicitly a concept of the dialogues) in terms of the 'great and small', and did so in terms of his likewise unrecorded theory of three categories.[5] Interestingly, those who directly reported unwritten doctrines do not include (as far as we are aware) Plato's two immediate successors as Head of the Academy, Speusippus and Xenocrates.

Speusippus (head, 348/7-339/8 BC) seems to have been more interested in explaining the principles of the Pythagoreans, but explaining them, no doubt, in a manner calculated to shed light on Plato.[6] Xenocrates (head, 339/8-314/3 BC) probably resorted himself to a rather simplified Platonist system, making use of figures from myth and religion when he wanted to communicate deeper doctrine.[7] Obviously their teaching had some claim to be 'Platonic', but that did not make their task an interpretative one; their goal was the investigation of the truth, and they felt no more obligation to stay behind with Plato than Plato had felt to stay behind with Socrates. Where interpretation did enter into the reckoning was where it was necessary to defend Plato against unfriendly readings, just as Plato had had to defend the work of Socrates against its detractors. We do not, therefore, expect subtle readings of the dialogues supported by constant textual references; we expect authoritative statements from the privileged successors about the true meaning of texts that were allegedly misunderstood.

ii. An early dispute over interpretation

Differences soon arose about the real beliefs that underlie the dialogues. The most obvious of these concerned the picture of the creation of the universe in the *Timaeus*. Aristotle, who had studied in the Academy for the better part of twenty years, simply assumes that Plato meant what he wrote, so that he did conceive of a creation-process completed over a period of time.[8] Whether he did so out of a belief that this was Plato's conviction, or out of the desire to criticise what his own pupils had supposed Plato to be saying, is unclear. Everything points to Aristotle's having avoided in depth exegesis of his predecessors, and to his need to understand all of them within his own, often unsympathetic, conceptual framework, a framework that could only take account of firmly fixed doctrine. Hence his doxographies attribute unequivocal, and often contrasting, positions to his predecessors. By contrast both Speusippus and Xenocrates,[9] who are represented as undertaking the defence,[10] denied that Plato ever envisaged a creation in time, not simply because Plato spoke of time as coming into being only when the heavens were created (37c-39e), but because there never was a beginning in, or of, time. One might quote the account of Simplicius:[11]

So these people, saying that the world was both generated and unperishing, say that one must understand 'generated' not as from a given point of time, but as hypothetically expressed: for the sake of teaching the order of things more primary and things more composite. For since, of the things in the universe, some are elemental and some are the products of the elements, it was not easy to realise their difference, nor the fact that compounds come from what is simpler, for anybody who has not, at a theoretical level, analysed the composites into their simples, and examined how, if the simples were on their own, the composites would originally have come about from them, ...

Simplicius goes on to suggest that Xenocrates compared the use of the creation-narrative with the use of geometrical diagrams as expository devices in mathematics. Whatever the validity of our information here, it is clear that for Xenocrates and others like him Plato's story of the creation, and to this extent the figure of the creator himself, were mere expository devices, and the story was utilised in order to show more clearly how the universe *operated*. One receives from Plutarch, who has mentioned interpretations of Xenocrates and Crantor (*c.* 336-276/5 BC), the impression that this was the view of the entire Old Academy (to around 265 BC, and in some cases beyond):

All these [interpreters of the psychogony of the *Timaeus*] are uniformly of the opinion that the soul has not 'come to be' and is not 'generated', but that it has a plurality of 'powers', into which Plato, as a logical exercise, analytically divided its substance for study's sake and imagined it being mixed together and 'generated'. [They say] he had the same intention concerning the universe too; he understood that it was everlasting and ungenerated, but, seeing that it would not be easy to learn the manner of its composition and governance if one did not initially imagine its generation and the coming together of its generative principles, he resorted to this path. (*De An. Proc.* 1013a-b)

The view of the Old Academy is consonant with Plato's representation of the account of the universe in the *Timaeus* as a myth (29d2).[12] It is well known that in order to capture the opposing forces that perpetually confront human beings myth resorts to a narrative that speaks of entities representing those forces as prior and posterior in time. It is in its own nature narrative, and must utilise a temporal sequence, even though it may deal with eternal truths. This function of myth is not modern, but was well known to Platonists of late antiquity. When dealing with the myth at the end of the *Gorgias* Olympiodorus, who believes his comment applies to traditional (poetic) myths (cf. 4.3, 46.8) from Hesiod and others as well as Platonist ones, writes as follows:

In this way the myth, moving forward like a story, does not preserve the simultaneity of things that are contemporaneous, but divided them into earlier and later, ... (*On the Gorgias* 48.1)

The meagre evidence does not allow us to claim that this approach to myth in general would have been shared by the Old Academy, but it should be said that Plato would have been following established Presocratic practice by trying to show something of the workings of the universe and its creatures through a story of their generation.[13] Plato himself knew this; when in the *Sophist* he discusses those predecessors who have sought to discern the *number and nature* of things (non-temporal!), he writes as follows:

> Each appears to me to be telling a kind of myth to us as if we were children, one how there are three things, and some of them somehow *sometimes* make war on each other, and *then* they become friends, and produce marriages, births, and the raising of offspring. (*Sophist* 242c-d)

Other 'stories' follow, most with a recognisable temporal sequence, which only the Heracliteans are held to avoid (e2-3). He complains of the obscurity of the meaning of these stories (243a-b), much as others, including Galen and Calcidius,[14] have complained of the obscurity of the *Timaeus*. And though the debate over how *we* are to understand the creation-process in the *Timaeus* continues, Dillon (1997) has now made a careful study of the clues within the text which warn us against taking its temporal machinery seriously. So the chances are that the Old Academy was justified in taking Plato's creation story as a mere expository device.

Even so, one should reflect on the motives of the Old Academy. At very least it is improbable that Plato could have written the *Timaeus* if he had had a strong conviction that the universe was ungenerated, for he was bound to be taken to believe the opposite. A much disputed text at 27c5 might easily suggest that he did not wish to affirm either view, and it is difficult to see how Plato could have written any proposed version of the text if he had wished it to be known that he felt strongly about either the generation or the eternity of the world. Perhaps this was the kind of issue that would be discussed in detail within the Academy. In these circumstances it may be that the Academy was just as concerned to defend Plato against unfriendly over-literal readings of his work, as it was to record accurately the intentions of Plato the author. The unfriendly reading that would have been taken most seriously was clearly Aristotle's.

iii. Aristotle on the written 'Socrates'

That Aristotle imported the 'unwritten doctrines' into his understanding of Plato, and used them as a basis for his criticisms, need not much concern us here. We are dealing here with the interpretation of texts, and though it is becoming clear that the supposed unwritten doctrines, or something rather like them, have exercised an *influence* on at least *some* dialogues,[15] particularly the supposedly latest group, Aristotle never treats the texts as if they implied much more than could be found openly in them.

One might look briefly at Aristotle's treatment of Plato's writings in three areas: politics, Socratic ethics, and psychology (this last alongside the treatment of the Old Academy). The first eight chapters of book 2 of the *Politics* are given over to the criticism of systems of political organisation which, while not practised anywhere, are nevertheless found in writings. Of these, the first six relate to Plato, five to the *Republic* and one to the *Laws*. Clearly, we must now be dealing with written dialogues rather than oral doctrine, and reference to Plato's *Republic* itself at 1261a6 establishes this. However, Aristotle is not 'commenting upon' passages of Plato, as has been suggested,[16] since nothing suggests that either Aristotle or his audience will have a text of Plato before them; rather we have Aristotle's own response to ideas within a work read widely among his students. Moreover Aristotle speaks as if it is the theory of Socrates, notably that on the community of wives and property, which is under investigation: it is not a philosophic work, but a theory present in a small part of it which is investigated, and like the denial of incontinence (*EN* 7.3) and the equation of the virtues with knowledge (*EN* 3.6, 6.13), Aristotle clearly associates that theory with Socrates; this may be contrasted with his treatment of the Athenian Stranger in the *Laws* (*Pol.* 2.6.4-5; *EN* 2.3) and 'Socrates' in the *Philebus* (*EN* 10.3) who are treated as Plato himself. According to the rather dubious requirements of 'Fitzgerald's Canon',[17] inclusion of the article with the name of Socrates here means that Aristotle is dealing with Plato's rather than the historical Socrates. This is to my mind far too great a burden to place on such a small detail, and accords poorly with ordinary Greek practice. Yet, even if it were correct, Aristotle is plainly not identifying Plato's Socrates directly with Plato. It is, perhaps, some intermediate hybrid.

The most obvious feature of Aristotle's treatment of the political theory of Plato's Socrates is that it is a partial view. There is little that does not depend on book 5 of the *Republic*, a book where 'Socrates' is following through the consequences of his earlier conclusions, and recognising constantly the lack of credibility that they will have among his contemporaries. Aristotle is not interested in the crucial underlying analogy between the state and the soul of the individual, nor in establishing that it is the political element of the *Republic* that matters to the author. He is interested instead in the picture painted of a novel form of political organisation that denies private property and a personal spouse to the guardians of the state, and in rebutting the reasons offered in the *Republic* for preferring such a system. Plato's own views are not an issue, for, even if this had accurately reflected Plato's position at one time, it had probably not done so during the years that Aristotle studied at the Academy. Socrates' views are also an irrelevancy. All that matters is ensuring that readers are not more tempted by the arguments of 'Socrates' than they should be.

One feature of Aristotle's treatment is particularly worth noting: he concentrates to a considerable degree on what he sees as the motive behind the measures of *Republic* 5, the achievement of the greatest possible *unity* in the state.[18] Though the need for internal harmony is stressed at 462a-e, the overriding importance of unity is hinted at in the *Republic* rather than emphasised. However, the close connection between goodness and unity was implied by the alleged tendency for Plato to identify the supreme Good with the One: an identification again hinted at by the timely oath by Apollo when the Good is unveiled at 509c1.[19] It is difficult to resist the assumption that Aristotle had insights not available to the lay reader of the text – not necessarily as a result of having details explained to him, but as a result of long familiarity with the way that Plato's mind worked. Aristotle could probably have been a serious candidate for the Headship of the Academy on the death of Speusippus;[20] and if, by Plato's death, he had already composed a number of significant works in the school's defence as is usually supposed,[21] then he must have been by now quite close to his mentor, regardless of the age-difference which Kahn appears to see as such an obstacle to their effective communication.[22]

Kahn's questioning of Aristotle's insights arises in relation to his knowledge of Socrates. It is Kahn's view that, since so many of Aristotle's comments about Socrates can be linked with particular 'Socratic' writings of Plato and even Xenophon, he has no knowledge of Socrates independent of the *written* tradition. This seems hasty. If Aristotle is reconstructing what Socrates was like on the basis of writings of a genre now accepted as fictional, as Kahn seems to suppose,[23] then he is either naive or curiously misinformed. The key point is that however much Aristotle heard orally about the themes of Socrates' philosophy, he would naturally recall passages in the written literature, usually by Plato, when discussing these themes. If one takes the *Nicomachean Ethics*, one finds Socrates referred to in three distinct passages. The best known of these discusses the famous denial that incontinence can be used to explain lapses of human conduct (7.2-3), and there is clear allusion to Plato's *Protagoras*.[24] Shortly before this, at 6.13 (1144b17-21), he had discussed Socrates' alleged view that the virtues were all types of practical wisdom, accepting only that they *were* *accompanied by* wisdom. This is closely related to the denial of incontinence, which goes hand in hand with the theory that knowledge is sufficient to ensure virtuous conduct. The third passage is at 3.8, which recalls that Socrates thought courage was (some kind of) knowledge, because experience seems to generate courage regarding particular cases. This is but another instance of a virtue being equated with some kind of practical wisdom, so all three Socratic themes from the *Nicomachean Ethics* are interrelated, and all in fact can be linked with a single dialogue: the *Protagoras*. It is reasonable to assume that he took this dialogue to be exploring the principal themes of Socratic ethics; his treatment is always of themes here, never of anything necessarily tied to the context of a single text, but he took the text to illustrate the themes well enough. Yet one thing which Aristotle does not do is to assume that every position that Socrates sponsors in the *Protagoras* is automatically Socratic doctrine; the name of Socrates is pointedly absent from the discussions of pleasure at 7.11-14 and 10.1-5, something unlikely to be the case if Aristotle saw the equation of 'the good' and 'the pleasant' at 351-60 as being a Socratic theme.

Something should also be said here of the *Eudemian Ethics*, where Socrates is again twice associated with the view that courage is knowledge, and specifically knowledge of things fearful as in the *Protagoras*;[25] likewise the *Protagoras* is in Aristotle's mind when he talks of the Socratic theme that nothing is stronger than knowledge.[26] Another passage clearly recalls another of Plato's anti-sophistic works, the *Euthydemus*; Aristotle is talking of the possible consequences of attributing all success to experiential knowledge, one of which would be that all branches of knowledge would be cases of success.[27]

Of the remaining two references to Socrates in this work, one (1216b2-10) treats the notion that knowledge of virtue is sufficient for virtue, and appears to be a general reflection on why Socrates asked 'what is V' questions, as opposed to 'how does V come', or 'what are the constituents of V'; the remaining one relates rather to Xenophon.[28] Strangely, both of these references which do not relate to specific Platonic texts speak of Socrates as an old man, giving some credence to the belief that one should distinguish between phases in Socrates' career. The dramatic date of the *Protagoras* is very early, and it is undoubtedly this earlier Socrates that Aristotle finds most useful in his ethical works. Certainly the *Protagoras* sees Socrates at his most contentious, trying to impose strange views on the company by skill in argument. Aristotle takes these views which Socrates sponsors rather more vigorously than usual, and not unreasonably supposes them to represent Socrates' true position. When he draws on the *Euthydemus* it is from the part of the work where Socrates seems to be openly instructing Cleinias in the principles of ethics, and hence where his opinions seem to be emerging more clearly.

So the *Eudemian Ethics* confirms the centrality of the *Protagoras* to Aristotle's picture of Socratic ethics, and also gives the equally vivid *Euthydemus* a place. Other works of Plato that elsewhere seem to enter into the portrait are *Meno*, *Menexenus*, and *Apology*.[29] But it is actually in the *Rhetoric* that we find material relating to *Apology* and *Menexenus* – the two works of Plato likely to be in the young rhetorician's mind, while the apparent reference to the *Meno* in *Politics* 1.13 might equally be recalling book 5 of the *Republic* when it refers to Socrates' denial that there are separate virtues for men and for women. It is hard to resist the conclusion that Aristotle draws any 'Socratic doctrine' referred to *in ethical works* from those 'Socratic' works of Plato most likely to be familiar to students of ethics, and hence that *Protagoras* and to a lesser degree *Euthydemus* conform with this criterion.[30] Aristotle was prepared to use them, like *Republic* 5, for an indication of Socratic rather than Platonic moral theory. The key question is whether he did so because he knew them to be Socratic, or because this was a widespread belief among his audience, or for both reasons. Where he criticises what he finds, he does so not because of any animosity towards Socrates, but because he wants to refute positions taken by respected predecessors. The exercise is therefore not an interpretative one, and it always concerns doctrine to be found in a part of the work, never the work as a whole.

iv. Aristotle and the Old Academy on Plato's psychology

While there is strangely little surviving evidence for Old Academic views on Socratic or Platonic ethics, we are once again able to contrast the Old Academy and Aristotle concerning their response to Plato's psychology. Speusippus and Xenocrates are known for having sponsored strange definitions of soul: 'the idea of the all-extended' and 'self-moving number' respectively.[31] Regardless of how they would have chosen to define soul for themselves, it is reasonably clear that both of these definitions are connected with the Platonic *Timaeus*, and that Xenocrates at least is explaining the very strange picture of the construction of soul in that dialogue in terms of some kind of tradition.

The two recent editors of Speusippus agree on relating his definition to the interpretation of Plato.[32] Tarán rightly points to the fact that the definition 'idea of the all-extended *breath*' appears as a *Platonic* definition at DL 3.67, and that the Speusippean words are incorporated into Posidonius' explanatory formula for the *Platonic* world-soul at Plut. *Mor.* 1023b. We have also a passage from Iamblichus which refers (without naming the authors) to the definitions of both Speusippus and Xenocrates along with another attributable to Moderatus the Pythagorean;[33] it is significant that Moderatus' definition 'a harmony established in *logoi*' is also plausibly taken as a definition of the Platonic world-soul – or of Pythagorean 'soul' as evidenced by Plato.

The evidence for Xenocrates is itself quite clear, in that Plutarch implies that it was the central plank of his interpretation of the nature of the Platonic world-soul (*Mor.* 1012d-e). But Xenocrates did not only use the definition in relation to Plato, as can be seen also from a variety of sources. To begin with Plutarch somehow blends into his discussion of Xenocrates' interpretation 'Zaratas, the teacher of Pythagoras', and in a *Platonic Question* discussing individual souls, ascribes the Xenocratean definition to 'the ancients', where it is unlikely that he is thinking of Xenocrates and Plato alone.[34] Secondly, the definition is ascribed in doxographies to Pythagoras and only then to Xenocrates.[35] And thirdly, in a quotation of Xenocrates from Themistius[36] it is said that *they called* soul number, going on to give reasons, so that it seems that Xenocrates was trying to *defend* a numeric conception of the soul encountered more than once in his predecessors. It was being associated with Plato's Pythagorean predecessors, if not Pythagoras himself, and the number-like nature of the soul in the *Timaeus* was being explained in historical terms.

Aristotle also clearly sees the construction of the soul in the *Timaeus* as being indebted to earlier theory. Having discussed thinkers who had founded their psychology on the assumption that soul was first and foremost an agent of motion, he moves on at *De Anima* 404b7 to discuss those who treated it as primarily a cognitive agent, and claims that they compose the soul out of the first principles of the world in order that it should be able to comprehend the world – on the assumption that like comprehends like. Empedocles is discussed first, and then comes Plato. The theory is that the constituents of the soul in the *Timaeus*, by which Aristotle presumably means Divisible and Indivisible, with or without Sameness and Difference, are of the same nature as the constituents of the universe. What follows shows that Aristotle had explained such matters quite fully in his lost *On Philosophy*, though quite how much of the explanation relates to Plato and how much to the Pythagoreans and others is unclear. There seems to be no polemic intended here, but rather a genuine attempt to put a very odd theory of Plato in context. At any rate Crantor explained the construction of Plato's soul along the same broad lines as Aristotle, as we read in Plutarch:

> Crantor's followers, on the assumption that the particular job of the soul is above all to judge things both intelligible and sensible, as well as their differences and similarities both in themselves and in relation to one another, says that the soul has been mixed together out of all things in order that it may get to know all things. And there are four of these things, the intelligible nature which is always in the same stable condition, and the malleable and changeable nature to do with bodies, and also that of the same and that of the other, on account of the first two participating in otherness and sameness. (Plut. *De An. Proc.* 1012f-3a)

The *theory* behind Plato's picture of the soul's construction was perhaps most fully spelt out by Crantor, but what has been lost, so far as we can tell, is the connection with Presocratic philosophy.

If one reflects about the tactics of the Old Academy and Aristotle in explaining the strange mathematical construction that is the 'soul' of the *Timaeus*, one sees that they are working with some significant assumptions. The historical assumption is one of these: Plato's 'Timaeus', while clearly voicing *Plato's* theory as all of them suppose,[37] nevertheless is not a typical Platonic spokesman; he operates within the traditions of earlier thought, particularly that of the Pythagoreans. Hence it is to earlier thought that one should turn, *rather than anything else written in the dialogues*, in order to interpret it. Moreover, *it does need interpretation*. The obscurity, perhaps a feature of its remoteness from fourth-century thought patterns, and perhaps of Plato's willingness to depict rather than explain, gives legitimacy to a reading of the text which says far more than Plato says. Moreover, in the case of this passage of the *Timaeus* at least, *mathematics provides the explanation*. Finally, we are being helped to understand the *nature and not the origins* of reality, in spite of the way that 'Timaeus' presents his material, so that it is legitimate to ignore as unintentional or unplatonic many of the claims that 'Timaeus' makes; so that in another sense one's reading may say far less than Plato says.

This leads to a further contribution that Speusippus and Xenocrates seem to have made to the interpretation of Platonic psychology. The *Timaeus* tells the story of how the younger gods built on a mortal part of the soul to the immortal entity that they received from their maker (69c ff.). The implication would seem to be that there can be a kind of soul that is not immortal, but that stands in conflict with the superficially clear statement at *Phaedrus* 245c5: 'All soul is immortal.' It should by now be clear that the *Timaeus* was inclined to be taken at something other than its face value by those to whom it fell to defend Plato, and that such a conflict would be settled in favour of the *Phaedrus*. Though the evidence is late, occurring in Damascius' commentary on the *Phaedo*, there seems good reason to believe the claim that Speusippus and Xenocrates 'made the soul immortal right down to the non-rational part'.[38] Since the whole context concerns the views adopted by earlier interpreters, we may I believe take it for granted that here too it is their interpretation of Plato which is at issue rather than their own views – and indeed any who ventured to explain the nature of soul in the *Timaeus* were likely to have to tackle the extent of the individual soul's immortality.

It is a curious paradox that the late Platonic work that made most impact and earned most respect through virtually the whole of antiquity, and the one that was most regularly subject to interpretation, was probably also the one that started off being taken least literally of all the major dialogues of Plato's maturity. Being respected, it was likewise the most desirable work for an opponent to attack; alternating between profound obscurity and a naive simplicity that is suggestive of a deeper meaning, it needed more defence than many other works; and being in need of defence, it needed to be interpreted in a way which would anticipate a variety of objections. Here defence and interpretation are interwoven. With Speusippus and Xenocrates, defence probably dominated. With Crantor, described by Proclus as 'the first commentator' (at least on the *Timaeus* – but what dialogue would have been commented on earlier?), the balance probably moves towards interpretation. For Academics who never knew Plato interpretation became a personal goal, something that one was actively engaged in, not something that one did for the benefit of others.

5

The struggle for Socrates and Plato

i. Crantor and the Academy

The death of Xenocrates brings us to a period when we have little useful information about the doctrines, tactics, or Platonic interpretation of the Academy. Under Polemo, who was scholarch for well over forty years from 314/5, our sources suggest that there was little change. Most of the information about Polemo connects him with doctrines attributed to Xenocrates and the rest of the Old Academy. Information that has reached us through Cicero is usually written from the point of view of Antiochus of Ascalon, who was claiming to revive the Old Academy as it was under Polemo. Polemo is chosen as being the last major scholarch of the Academy who did not lean in the direction of scepticism, and also as being the teacher of Zeno the founder of Stoicism. Antiochus wished to draw on Zeno too at times, particularly in relation to the criterion of truth. Polemo was succeeded briefly by a colleague, Crates of Athens, of whom even less of relevance is known, and under him worked the important figure of Crantor of Soli, who probably played the dominant role in determining the Academy's reading of Plato during Polemo's years as Head.

It is highly likely that the Stoics were influenced by a number of works of Plato from the beginning. Certainly they always held Socrates in great respect, and sometimes looked up to him as a pre-Stoic figure who had fulfilled their requirements for the title of 'sage'. Plato's portrait of Socrates is likely to have been influential here, and hence some of Plato's works involving Socrates were likely to have been studied. We have seen how Aristotle seems to have drawn much of his portrait of Socratic ethics and politics from *Protagoras*, *Euthydemus*, and *Republic*. Zeno (c. 334-262/1 BC), who wrote a *Republic* of his own, even more radical in its concept of the ideal city than the Platonic original, must certainly have derived some inspiration from what Socrates had proposed there.[1] And there has been recent discussion of the part played by the *Euthydemus* in determining the Stoic view of Socrates.[2] The more Zeno used Plato to support or illustrate theory of his own, the more an Academic reaction would have been inevitable. Unauthorised accounts of Plato's meaning were attacked as early as the *Seventh Epistle*, and needed to be answered.

Crantor's work now puts what must surely have been the Academic perspective. We do not know how extensive his response to Stoic use of Plato was, only that he treated several passages of the *Timaeus*, and could be described by Proclus as the first interpreter. There is no evidence of commentaries on other works, and it is probable that Crantor, like others known to Galen,[3] did not treat the human physiology at the end of the work. Moreover, since he thought that the Atlantis story had no philosophic content, it is likely that he said little about anything prior to the presentation by 'Timaeus' of his cosmology.

It is worth looking briefly at Proclus' report of his treatment of Atlantis, since it has sometimes been put to questionable use.

> This whole account of the Atlantinians has been supposed by some to be a bare narrative, like Crantor, the first interpreter of Plato, who says that he was even being ridiculed by his contemporaries for not being the author of his constitution, but a transcriber of the laws of the Egyptians; and such was the attention[4] that he paid to the mockers' charge that he attributed to the Egyptians the story of the Athenians and Atlantinians, implying that the Athenians had once lived according to this constitution. And the Egyptian prophets too, he says, witness this, saying that these things are recorded on *stelae* that are still preserved. (Proclus, *On the Timaeus* 1.75.30-76.10)

One should begin by distinguishing the question that is of most interest today from those which concerned Crantor on the one hand and Proclus on the other. We are keen to know whether Plato's account is being offered as the historical truth. Crantor seems to have wanted to explain, in a favourable light, why Plato wrote a story so far from his normal interests. But Proclus wants to know whether Plato intended us to read it literally or allegorically. Hence in this report Crantor is being contrasted not with those who see the Atlantis myth as a lie, but with those who find in it some higher truth.[5] Even so it is legitimate to ask whether he supposed it to be historically true, and while no sensible commentator could have claimed the truth of the whole Atlantis story as presented in the *Timaeus* and the *Critias* (for it is told in such graphic detail that it clearly goes beyond the scope of any Egyptian records), it was possible by the time of Posidonius, about two centuries later, to think that the overall story *might* be true, as against the conviction (possibly Aristotle's)[6] that it was invented.

Crantor claims that Plato had written the story in response to those who mocked him for stealing his ideal state, as found in the *Republic*, from the Egyptians. The charge is less likely to be one of lack of originality, but of proposing a foreign and in many ways unsuccessful political system as a replacement for the proper Greek polis. So, in the *Timaeus*, a work whose introduction clearly flags it as a sequel to the *Republic*, Plato rebuffs the plagiarism charge with reference to Egyptian records confirming that *Athens* had once been organised on similar political lines and enjoyed great success. So far Proclus' report actually gives Plato a distinctly unhistorical motive for writing, and there seems to be the implication that attributing the Atlantis-tale to the Egyptians was a stroke of genius rather than a scholarly footnote. However, since 'he says' in the final sentence should grammatically refer to Crantor rather than Plato, it would seem that Crantor made reference to Egyptian priests *in his own day* who could point to inscriptional evidence for the story (though Proclus may have been misled by his own source for Crantor). Such a point could indeed be made in support of its historical truth, but it could also have been a satirical observation about Egyptians who were only too ready oblige inquirers[7] by confirming the *true Athenian character* of Plato's ideal state when it suited them. If we assume that Crantor's motives in writing were still linked with the defence of Plato,[8] then he would surely have made use of any corroborative statements of contemporary Egyptians, without necessarily believing in what they had to say. It may not have been in Crantor's interests to confirm the fictional character of Atlantis, but he was not working within an established tradition that postulated historical truth, and he is no more likely to be seeking to defend the literal meaning of the Atlantis-story than the literal meaning of Timaeus' creation-story which is framed by it.

Yet our present purpose is not to assess the historicity of the Atlantis-story, but to find out what one can about Crantor as an interpreter. Here one may point out that he is providing an *explanation* of some of the great puzzles concerning the *Timaeus*. Why did Plato find it profitable to frame his cosmology within an account of the exploits of ancient Athens? What is the connection between the *Timaeus-Critias* and the ideal state described in the *Republic*? And why did he find it necessary to connect the story with Egypt in particular? But in addition to explaining, Crantor seems also to be *defending* Plato's originality and his Greek cultural credentials, and showing how he cleverly turned the tables on those who questioned it. He was, after all, a senior member of the school that Plato founded, and the reputation of its founder was a key factor for the school's success.

Regarding the cosmology of the *Timaeus* Crantor persisted with the Old Academic view that there was no time when the world was not there, and his explanation for Plato's seeming to call it generated is that its being is always dependent on an anterior principle beyond it, without which it could not be.[9] He made the generation of the soul just as fictional, and subscribed to the Old Academic view that it was included as a substitute for analysing the soul into its powers.[10] Plutarch regards such theories as forcing the text in any way whatever so as to avoid the unthinkable hypothesis of generation,[11] so it is clear that he had little respect for the surface meaning of the *Timaeus*, however it may have been that he interpreted the *Critias*. Other than this, Crantor the exegete is only known from his contribution to the discussion of the mathematics of Plato's world-soul, interpreting its base number as 384, and arranging its harmonic divisions in a lambda-shaped diagram rather than a straight line. Here details are less relevant than the fact that, on each issue where his interpretation is known, several others followed him. He is the link between the Old Academy and the commentary-tradition of a later age.

ii. The Stoic bid for Socrates – and Plato

If Stoic philosophy before Seneca (*c.* 1 BC – AD 65) is fragmentary, then this is all the more true of the Stoic picture of Socrates. Nevertheless, it is clear that the Stoics were interested in claiming that Socrates was part of their own heritage. Firstly, Socrates was usually recognised as a sage by Stoic philosophers, which was an honour often denied their own founder Zeno. A.A. Long has done much to show that Socrates was almost common property among Hellenistic philosophers,[12] and that this was because a whole generation of intellectuals, from hedonists to antihedonists, from men of subtle argument to men of unsubtle actions, had been in some sense followers of his. Zeno had studied with the Cynic Diogenes, who had himself inherited the mantle of Antisthenes, the senior follower of Socrates, and hence he could claim to be just as much a successor as his rivals in the Academy. Furthermore, he had himself studied in the Academy with Polemo. The life and death of Socrates, by now the paradoxical paradigm of human happiness through unyielding dedication to virtue, could serve just as easily to represent the ideals for which Stoicism strove as the ideals of Platonists or Cynics.

What the Stoics had to do if they were to make full use of the Socratic paradigm is to ensure that the right image of Socrates was circulated. While evidence is lacking for the earliest Stoics, it was in this context that Panaetius (*c.* 185-109 BC) undertook a review of the Socratic literature in general, and decided on what should be accepted as depicting the authentic Socrates. Four authors were generally accepted as giving a true picture: Plato, Xenophon, Aeschines, and Antisthenes (fr. 126). This was a considerable range, bearing in mind that scholars now have difficulty even in reconciling Plato with Xenophon. Furthermore, apart from the *Phaedo*, there is at first sight no reason to think that any Platonic dialogues that employed Socrates as a protagonist were excluded from consideration: the *Republic* and even the *Philebus* may have been afforded a certain Socraticity. Hence Panaetius was willing to learn about Socrates from a commendably wide range of literature, though he had much more to choose from than us. He was in doubt as to whether he should exclude Socratic works ascribed to Phaedo and Euclides, and he did reject all others. We know nothing of the grounds on which his choice was made.

It may be in this context that Panaetius is said to have regarded the *Phaedo* as spurious. The story is known only from later Neoplatonism,[13] first attested in Syrianus' short poem of two elegiac couplets (fr. 128), and its reporting is thus unlikely to be reliable. Panaetius is said to have regarded the work as spurious because Socrates affirms the immortality of the soul, and while this was probably just a denial that it represents *Socrates* correctly,[14] that is certainly not what the sources are saying. For them, Panaetius denied that Plato was the author, and this extreme thesis would logically follow from (i) a denial of Socraticity together with (ii) an acceptance that Plato always represented Socrates accurately. The close of the *Apology* represents Socrates as uncommitted to any view about the soul's afterlife, and this does pose questions for anybody who would wish to see the *Phaedo* as equally Socratic. Even so, these questions remain for anybody regarding the *Republic* as Socratic also. No informed philosopher could deny that this was the work of Plato, but they could deny its Socraticity.

For these reasons I prefer to interpret Panaetius' investigation of Socrates as an attempt to discover which works accurately represented facets of Socrates' life and death: dialogues with a biographical element. This element is strong in the *Phaedo*, so that it seems in part to be making historical claims about Socrates, but it is virtually absent from the *Republic*. It may also be a problem that the central story of the work was narrated by the Socratic Phaedo, since Panaetius did not accept Phaedo or Euclides (the 'source' of the conversation recorded in the *Theaetetus*) as reliable reporters. Panaetius also expressed doubts as to whether things said of Socrates late in Aristophanes' play *Clouds* could have applied to Socrates the philosopher (fr. 134), and appears to have gone to some trouble to defend Socrates against the oft-repeated charge of living with a second woman in the role of a wife (frs 132-3). Hence his interest in the real Socrates was wide-ranging.

This did not mean that he had no interest in Plato. His predecessor Antipater had already written a work in three books to demonstrating that Plato shared key Stoic ethical doctrines, and above all that virtue was the sole good – sufficient in itself for happiness.[15] He must have relied on passages in Plato that emphasised the potential harm of all other so-called goods when separated from correct use, such as *Euthydemus* 280d-281e,[16] which concludes, 'Surely of other things none is either good or bad, whereas of these two wisdom is good and ignorance bad.' Similar material is found at *Meno* 87e-88d, and to the extent that wisdom is seen by Stoics and Plato alike as an integral part of developed virtue (under-developed 'virtues' still being potentially harmful, 88b), one might conclude that this true virtue which embraces knowledge is alone an unequivocally good thing. Since the *Euthydemus* then goes on to regard this as the sole cause of happiness (282c) and tries to discover the particular type of wisdom responsible for happiness, this text provides what Antipater needed; his task now would have been to argue that it is in such passages that the true views of Plato emerge, and that other passages should be read in their light. From his point of view it was probably an advantage that it is Plato's Socratic writings which are most helpful to his case: if the Academics were building *their* picture of Plato principally on these works, then he could best undermine Academic authority by reinterpreting them. Here, in a polemical work that on one reading seemed to suggest the epistemological anarchy sought by the Academy, was a Socrates openly teaching Stoic virtue.

If the details of such a reading of Plato are lost to us, we must nevertheless accept that it was sufficiently attractive to make the Stoic reading an issue. It was hereafter a matter of importance whether Plato did make virtue sufficient for happiness, and whether virtue is the sole thing that he deemed unequivocally good. Our extant Platonist handbook, Alcinous' *Didascalicus*, did promote a view of Plato's ethics that was not so far from the Stoic view.[17]

If Antipater could enthuse over Plato as well as over Socrates, then so could Panaetius, and several passages bear witness to his love of Plato and indeed of Aristotle (frs 55-7), including one in which the Neoplatonist Proclus actually refers to him as a Platonic, apparently meaning an interpreter of Plato (F59). He is one of those who told the story of how the opening of the *Republic* had been discovered written in many different versions (fr. 130). Yet any details of his reading of Plato have also been lost with time.

iii. The Academic counter-claim

It was not long after the earliest Stoics mounted their challenge to the more remote philosophies of the Academy and the Peripatos that the Academics ceased to confront other philosophies with competing doctrine, and moved into the realm of dialectical scepticism. The initiator of this phase of the school's history was Arcesilaus (316/5-241/0 BC), who is said to have been the boy-friend of Crantor, but who in his Headship of around twenty-five years took a contrasting attitude towards the promotion of the Academy's expertise. This certainly did not entail the abandonment of Plato, to whom Arcesilaus seems outwardly to have expressed allegiance,[18] and whose books he was well known to have acquired,[19] but it would certainly have meant an end to the attempt to teach any Platonic message *directly*. The Academy now became known for its ability to argue against any thesis. Its leaders invited their audience or pupils to make statements against which they could argue, and any preferred position could only be deduced from an experienced appreciation of those theses against which they argued with least conviction.

There is now a degree of consensus that Arcesilaus emphasised the Socratic side of Plato, and the role of Socrates himself as a professor of ignorance. There is every reason to suppose that this tactic would have been effective against attempts by other schools to claim the authority of Socrates. Nor did he have to turn his back on dialogues that would not be regarded as Socratic today. Works like the *Phaedo* and *Republic* could be regarded as bold challenges to orthodox ideas rather than as attempts to prove a philosophic thesis. The *Phaedo*'s apparent confidence that the soul is immortal could be contrasted with the agnosticism of the *Apology* (40c), and the *Republic*'s occasional suggestion of semi-seriousness about the proposed political order might seem to undermine its authority, particularly if its differences from the *Laws* were brought out. The *Menexenus*, *Gorgias*, and *Phaedrus* could be seen as polemical attacks on established funeral orations and against rhetoric more generally, for these works are known to have been interpreted in that way at some period of antiquity.[20] The *Cratylus*, *Theaetetus*, and *Parmenides* might be held to argue both for and against central theses, and once again as polemical,[21] while the *Sophist* and *Politicus* might at very least be regarded principally as lessons in logic given by a character not wholly representative of Plato. The *Timaeus* can be seen as a non-dogmatic document because of the modest claims that it makes: to likelihood rather than to truth. The obscurity of the *Philebus* might support a picture of a Plato anxious to avoid giving too clear an idea of the basis of his ethics, and the *Laws* might be seen more as a practical document than a vehicle of doctrine. Hence the sceptic interpretation of Plato's Socrates *could* be argued to be compatible with the rest of the corpus as well, and it was easy for Arcesilaus to argue that there was a fundamental difference between the truth-claims made by Plato within his dialogues and those made by the Stoics (or Epicureans for that matter) in their treatises, handbooks, and propaganda.

It has been emphasised by Long (1988) that Arcesilaus' interpretation of Socrates is, as far as we can tell, a new and rather radical one, but this did not make it difficult to argue. At very least one can insist that Socrates would never have sanctioned uncritical use of his own authority rather than the student's own mental effort. The Academy was provided with a pedigree for its new dialectical tools, capable of serving it for nearly another two centuries. Little is known of the school under Arcesilaus' successors until Carneades (214-129/8 BC), who dominated the history of the Academy in the central years of the second century. Even under him we cannot point to any new reading of Plato. It may be that Arcesilaus had used the obscurity and esotericism of some of Plato's works to fuel the belief that the Academy did have a position which might be revealed to the initiate, but the rumour of esotericism seems not to have extended to the school of Carneades.[22] It would have been uncharacteristic of Carneades to have wished to make too much of Plato's authority rather than that of the argument.

Carneades' dialectical activities were preserved for a while by his pupils, most notably Clitomachus, who seems to have compensated for his mentor's refusal to write. But another, less rigorously sceptic, version of Carneades was promoted by Metrodorus of Stratonicea. On Clitomachus' death in 110 BC the school passed into the hands of Philo of Larissa (158-84 BC, while the senior figure of Charmadas continued to have influence and teaching responsibilities within it. We find the latter using Plato's *Gorgias* as a text to lecture on, and the influence of both *Gorgias* and *Phaedrus* can be seen in his attack on non-philosophical rhetoric.[23] The writings of Clitomachus and Philo, together with his personal studies with the latter, must have provided most of the source material for Cicero's picture of the Academic-Sceptic versions of Socrates and Plato which we find in his *Academica*, composed, like most of his philosophical writings, in the final two years of his life (45-44 BC). Here no detailed *interpretative* issues are discussed from the Academic-Sceptic perspective, and in a sense this absence follows from the basic Academic attitude. Why should one discuss details of interpretation that are just as hard to solve as philosophical issues, and what point would there be if Academics have no intention of trusting Plato's authority? They needed above all to argue against the interpretative approach taken by their opponents. In this case, however, it would also have made sense to emphasise the polemical element throughout Plato, and late evidence discussed in Chapters 9 and 11 shows that one early and important group of interpreters did just that. To judge from Cicero's account of Charmadas in the *De Oratore*, he was among them.

One problem in assessing the contribution made to the study of Plato by the Academy of Carneades and Clitomachus (sometimes known as the 'Third' Academy), and more especially that of Philo and Charmadas (sometimes known as 'Fourth'),[24] is the possible gulf between public, written stance and private, orally taught approaches. If Charmadas could be reading Plato's more high-profile works with his pupils, then it is likely that Philo did so too. For he was accused of being a radical (at least in his Roman books),[25] implying some significant weakening of allegiance to scepticism, and he maintained that there had always been a single Academy, implying open allegiance to Plato. He clearly had a profound influence on the Plato-loving Cicero. It has long been recognised that Philo's so-called division of moral philosophy, known to us from Stobaeus (*Ecl.* 2.39.20 ff.), owes a debt to *Sophist* 230b-e. There we have (i) a comparison between medicine and philosophy, and (ii) the notion that Socratic elenctic activity is actually a purgation that prepares the way for the application of healthy learning (*mathemata*, d2). The application of first the purge and then the health-giving doctrines corresponds to the double stage two of Philo's education-programme, the first stage being protreptic and again having a double task – encouraging the pupil to come to philosophy and countering the advice of its detractors.

One may also note that this double stage is compared with the need of the doctor to have the patient (i) persuaded to take the cure, and (ii) immunised against the advice of those who advise against it. This may relate to passages in the *Gorgias* that focus on the need of the doctor to persuade his patients to take the cure. At 456b 'Gorgias' tells how his rhetorical expertise has been required to persuade his brother's medical patients. At 464d it is observed that in a debate among the young and foolish about whose medicines should be taken, the pastry-cook would beat the doctor and get his own 'remedies' accepted. This theme returns at 521-2, with Socrates imagining the pastry-cook as a *false-accuser* of the doctor, and imagining his own tough medicine for the soul being the cause of his condemnation just as fools might condemn the true doctor on the cook's advice. Socrates here is the soul's equivalent of the body's doctor, while the soul's counterpart of the sycophantic pastry-cook is assumed to be the flattering orator (cf. 522d7): the orator who looks to the gathering's pleasure rather than its benefit. Hence an important message of the *Gorgias*, the one text we know to have been studied in Philo's Academy, is that the Socratic philosopher will fearlessly recommend his harsher discipline in the face of challenges from orators who fail to prescribe the medicine that the soul needs. The dialogue in fact sees Socrates fighting hard to get his message across and to undermine the attractive claims of rhetoric to offer a better life.

This is very like what Charmadas was doing in Cicero's *De Oratore* (1.84-92). He was handling the Academy's protreptic and apotreptic, turning people towards philosophy and countering critics who prefer empty rhetoric. So in this regard Charmadas performs the first task of Philonian education. Then there would follow the expulsion of false opinions and preparation for the healthy ones through a programme of moral philosophy that dealt with the topic of things good and things bad. This would lead into the third stage, where the long-term health of the soul would be promoted by further questions, about ends and about types of life, in both the public and the private context. Presumably Philo, at least as much as any late Hellenistic philosopher, thought of himself and his associates as doctors of the soul. Charmadas might simply have been his master of protreptic, playing for Philo the same role that Gorgias had once played for his own brother Herodicus. Philo himself, perhaps, would prefer the Socratic role depicted in Plato's *Sophist* and *Gorgias*. This in turn suggests that Plato's dialogues were not only being interpreted, but being used as models for the philosopher's true role. That role would be such as to justify polemic against one's critics and genial criticism of the pupil's beliefs, thus justifying the elenctic role of the Academy, which was now traditional. But it would henceforth be richer and more complex than anything that the Academic Sceptics had previously been found to have on offer. Still largely Socratic, it draws for its picture of Socratic activity on dialogues that seem serious – neither comic nor merely dialectical. The Socratic heritage could no longer be seen as an excuse to avoid the Platonic.

iv. The mathematical Plato

A little ought to be said about one strand of Platonic interpretation that was being pursued somewhat independently, so that it made comparatively little impact on inter-school rivalry. The scientist Eratosthenes, who flourished in the second half of the third century BC had specialised in the interpretation of mathematical passages in Plato, passages often easily wrenched from their context and examined in isolation. Before this Crantor had certainly taken a keen interest in the mathematical parts when commenting upon the *Timaeus*, but his fellow Solian Clearchus had paid them some attention in isolation, and one Theodorus of Soli, known to us from Plutarch, had also made a contribution, examining such matters as the harmonic theory and the construction of the regular solids in the *Timaeus*.[26] A specialisation on the mathematical side of Plato may readily be attributed to Theon of Smyrna, active by the late first century AD, in his *Exposition of Mathematics useful for Reading Plato*, and he draws on the Platonic mathematics of Thrasyllus and Dercyllides; the former wrote on harmonics,[27] and, as the end of Theon's work shows, the latter devoted either a work or part of a work to the mathematical significance of the spindle and whorls of the Myth of Er in *Republic* 10 (616c ff.).

Since the interpretation of mathematical passages in isolation from the rest of the corpus need not have involved these figures in the kind of interpretative tasks which we are here most concerned with, I do not wish to dwell upon their contribution in isolation. Yet any reading of the platonising parts of Plutarch's *Moralia*, where developed interpretation first appears, shows that mathematical problems had received a disproportionate amount of attention among his predecessors and were still live issues.[28] Thrasyllus and Dercyllides are not mentioned by Plutarch, and it would be fair to suggest that he and Theon had inherited different mathematicising traditions. This in turn shows how pervasive was the feeling that Plato's mathematics was crucial. Anecdotes concerning Plato's love of geometry in particular were popular,[29] and an interest in the Pythagorean background to certain parts of the dialogues was ensuring a special place for anything approaching mathematics.

v. Posidonius' Plato

Another influence on Plutarch and Theon was an interpretation of aspects of the *Timaeus* stemming from Posidonius, which has also left a mark on Sextus Empiricus' account of Pythagorean epistemology. All this material is related to the psychology of the *Timaeus*, so that it is difficult to be sure that Posidonius wrote a commentary; he may rather have written an interpretative work on soul in the *Timaeus*, or in Plato more generally, or in Pythagoreanism more generally. In fact the passage in Theon makes it clear that the seven numbers employed by Plato for the construction of the world-soul at *Timaeus* 35b-c were read by Posidonius as having a connection with the significance of the number seven in nature (a sure sign of a Pythagorising reading),[30] while Sextus Empiricus is treating the epistemology of the Pythagoreans when he uses material on like-by-like cognition used by Posidonius in interpreting the *Timaeus*.[31]

What is certain, however, is that Posidonius was an interpreter of Platonic passages in the *Timaeus*, and that he undertook his interpretation with due regard for the interpretative tradition thus far. The most informative discussion is found in Plutarch, who is giving the interpretation of 'those who follow Posidonius'.[32] Though sometimes such expressions are little more than a polite way of avoiding direct criticism of the author of a view, or perhaps an indication that one is not citing the material directly, Plutarch probably does have a plurality of persons in mind, as also in the case of Xenocrates and Crantor (*Mor.* 1012d-f).

The Posidonians are said to call the Platonic world-soul 'an Idea of the all-ways extended constructed according to a number that incorporates a harmony.' This is strange stuff, but we know that the first component (Idea of the all-ways extended) is indebted to Speusippus, who, since he rejected the Platonic Ideas, probably meant 'Idea' in some other sense: perhaps as a kind of abstract blue-print, though not just as a kind of three-dimensional grid. One needs to remember that the Platonic soul was indeed a kind of mathematical entity extended through the physical world. Posidonius followed Xenocrates to the extent that he worked number into his account. And it is also plain that he followed Crantor (1012d), firstly insofar as he utilised the Presocratic principle of like-by-like cognition,[33] and secondly insofar as he emphasised the composition of soul from intelligible and opinable substances, for Plutarch explains how Posidonius regards it as an essentially *mathematical* substance, composed of intelligible substance and the substance proper to the (two-dimensional?) limits of physical bodies, and hence intermediate, like other mathematicals, *between* the first intelligibles (Ideas) and sensibles. Mathematical intermediates are associated with Plato by Aristotle, and so this is another case of Posidonius drawing on material found in one or more of Plato's pupils. Merlan (1960) recognised long ago the importance of Posidonius as an intermediary between the Old Academy and Middle Platonist exegesis; Posidonius could interpret Plato with more concern for historical accuracy, not having the same propaganda needs as one who traced his authority back to Plato. He supplied the interpretative tradition with the scholarship that it needed if it was to thrive and develop. The consequence of this, perhaps, is that Plato tended to fade into philosophic history, becoming not so much an inspired figure as a step along the road between Pythagoras (with the Presocratics) and the Old Academy – and so on to Posidonius himself.

We know thanks to Galen that Posidonius appealed to a different element of Plato's psychology, employing the tripartite soul of the *Republic* for what Galen takes as anti-Chrysippean polemic.[34] Unfortunately Galen's partisan account of Chrysippus and Posidonius is increasingly being questioned, and Gill (1998) now argues that 'Posidonius' modification of Chrysippus' psychology consists in a relatively minor shift: namely, from developing Socratic (early Platonic) thinking to developing middle and late Platonic thinking'. Such a shift, if it could be established, would be of major interest to us. It agrees well with Posidonius' high praise for Plato (not Socrates – F150a), with his keen interest in the *Timaeus* (a non-Socratic text), and with his readiness to attribute tripartite psychology to Pythagoras (T91 = F151EK), who was now being viewed as the main non-Socratic influence upon Plato. He no doubt assumed that Timaeus' account of the lower parts of the soul was essentially Pythagorean, noted that they agreed broadly with the *Republic*, and inferred that the psychology of the *Republic* too was indebted to the Pythagorean rather than the Socratic tradition. It so happens that the *Timaeus*' account of separate functions of the soul (69-72) played a large part in Galen's discussion of the issues, and a significant one in Chrysippus' too,[35] so it would be surprising if Posidonius had not given it a high profile in his evaluation of Plato's position.

Posidonius did not always praise Plato. We find him positively attacking Plato's readiness to write prologues for legislation in his *Laws* as totally inappropriate to the work of an inspired law-giver.[36] This shows that his references to Plato were not always detached and scholarly, but served his own ends. Most interesting in this context is his reading of statements made about the soul at *Phaedrus* 245c-246a, where Plato declares, and indeed tries to prove, that 'All soul is immortal'. Posidonius, perhaps because of his Stoic affiliations that should have led him to deny total individual immortality, was among those who took the passage to be speaking of the cosmic soul, i.e. the Soul of the All, rather than about all (individual) souls.[37] Certainly the arguments work more easily when applied to soul as a whole, and the Posidonian interpretation was supported with reference to d8-e2 which speaks of the 'whole heaven and whole earth' collapsing into one stationary mass. Probably the interpretation would have involved also 246b6-c2, which again speaks of 'all soul', its care for 'all body', and its governance of 'the whole cosmos'. It does not seem that these interpreters ever denied that Plato believed that the individual soul was immortal, only that such claims were not being made in this text. It is entirely possible that the interpretation derives from Posidonius' discussion of the world-soul of the *Timaeus*, and that the *Phaedrus* was being used to flesh out the picture of universal soul that figures there, without any strong desire to force the text into saying what Posidonius himself believed. Close attention to details of the text and a degree of cross-dialogue interpretation are present, and they indicate a mature reading of Plato. Posidonius was fully a philosopher, and may like others have had a philosophical agenda behind his reading of these dialogues, but if so we are largely unaware of it. Ironically, the beginning of serious interpretation is coming from the Stoa rather than the Academy.

vi. The Fifth Academy: a naive reading?

Before we proceed to the Middle Platonist commentators we should return
to Cicero's *Academica* and consider briefly the picture of Platonic philosophy given by Varro, which is written largely from the point of view of
Antiochus of Ascalon.[38] Antiochus is considered principally as a product of
the Academy under Philo of Larissa, though he also studied with the Stoic
Mnesarchus, and must have thoroughly understood the Stoic system. He
had written works from the non-dogmatist perspective while working in
the Academy, but eventually seceded, claiming that he was reverting to the
views of the Old Academy. The rift became open in 87 BC when he read
certain 'Roman Books' of Philo at Alexandria. Thereafter he set up his own
school at Athens in the Ptolemaeum at a time when the Academy itself had
ceased to function.

Antiochus wanted to be regarded as a Platonist, following in the tradition of not only Plato, but also Aristotle and the Stoic Zeno. Most of their
differences, he believed, were in fact disputes over terminology rather
than substance. One may well ask what it could have been that prompted
Antiochus to interpret Plato in such a manner that he could be reconciled
with *both* Aristotle *and* the Stoics. The historical answer was that he saw
in Polemo a distinguished representative of the Academy who understood
both Plato and Aristotle, and inspired the young Zeno: so there was
continuity of tradition. The philosophic answer is that he could reconcile
the schools *on the issues that he judged most important*. For instance, if
Plato and Zeno thought virtue sufficient for the happy life, while Aristotle
denied it, then this could be explained by Aristotle's having used 'happy'
as a kind of superlative: for it was not sufficient for the *happiest* life
according to the Antiochean account in Cicero's *De Finibus* 5. Finally, the
interpretative answer is that he could reconcile the schools by interpreting
expressed differences as principally a matter of terminology (Cic. *Acad.*
2.15), interpreting their diverse statements in terms of his own understanding of the issues. He believed that, if they had had the benefit of
hearing his case, they would all have agreed with its fundamentals.

If one searches for Antiochus' interpretation of Plato, considered alone,
one is disappointed. Varro offers a doctrinal summary in Cicero's *Academica* (1.15-34) on the basis of which Antiochus can claim to have
inherited the mantle of Plato. It is particularly interesting that no similar
claim is made for Socrates' authority, *Acad.* 1.15-17, so that one must
believe that he was more interested in what Plato did not inherit from
Socrates than in what he did. It is Plato himself who is held to have
initiated the still living tradition of a tripartite philosophy (19), composed
of ethics, physics, and logic. The Old Academy, of course, would have
remembered principally the later Plato, and it would have interpreted
Plato's views in the light of the less paradoxical, less transcendental views
of its leaders. There is in fact scarcely any distinction between the Pla-

tonic, Old Academic, and early Peripatetic positions, though (i) Aristotle's fifth element is recognised as a new contribution (1.26), and (ii) there are strong claims that Theophrastus and more particularly Strato had abandoned matters central to the Lyceum's original stance (33-4); in contrast Old Academics down to Polemo, Crates, and Crantor are said to have remained faithful to Plato (34). This is in fact the kind of 'history' that the Academics of Polemo's generation could have profitably promoted against the remnants of the Peripatos, a kind of foundation-myth. Meanwhile no Platonic work is cited, as if this were not the appropriate way of establishing Plato's position; we are simply told what *they said* in the plural, and Plato is given individual credit only for naming objects of thought 'Ideas' (1.30). Hence this account does not constitute an interpretation of Plato, let alone particular Platonic dialogues, or the Platonic corpus; it is an account of Platonically inspired philosophy over a particular period.

As Varro is the one who speaks, an overall proximity to Antiochus' position should be presumed; that its continuation, the theory of Zeno's 'corrections' of the Old Academy (1.35-42), is Antiochus' is remarked upon at 1.35 and 43. However, not only Varro, who is no puppet of Antiochus', but also Atticus (and perhaps tacitly Cicero) give their assent to this picture of short-lived Peripatetic and longer-lived Academic fidelity to Plato. In the *Lucullus*[39] Cicero, speaking *in propria persona*, seems content to accept this general picture. So this aspect of Antiochus' historical theory may be less innovative, and the passage might be indicative of later Old Academic claims rather than anything newer. The lack of appeal to the written Plato is indicative of an age when documented ancient authority was not yet as issue. By Cicero's day things were changing.

If one considers the difficulties that Antiochus would have experienced if he were claiming Plato's authority today, the hardest task would be to reconcile the transcendent metaphysics of Plato with Aristotelian immanentism and Stoic materialism. The trust that he placed in the senses would also be seen as a problem. To be seen as returning to the later Old Academy, however, was less unlikely: the transcendental features of Plato, and the Ideas in their Platonic conception at least, had been dropped already by the Old Academy. Some moves were made by Speusippus and Xenocrates towards re-establishing the authority of the senses.[40] Cicero, usually in contexts where Antiochus would have been expected to have an influence, acknowledged that Plato had a Theory of Ideas and a Theory of Recollection.[41] Antiochus was surely aware of both a metaphysical and an epistemological role for them in Plato, but that did not mean that he attached any importance to those aspects of them which would conflict the priority of the senses. The talk of *Academica* 1.33 is of a rather quaint and excessively other-worldly theory. Hence Plato's authority did not matter; what mattered was the Platonic heritage.

It was not in fact through his interpretation of Plato that Antiochus set an example, but rather through his interpretation of philosophy. The techniques that he had applied to minimising the differences between schools could equally well be applied to Plato himself. If for Antiochus philosophy could be always saying the same thing (cf. Pl. *Grg.* 482a-b), then surely for some interpreters Plato could be understood as always saying the same thing.

vii. Cratippus, Platonic recollection, and dream-divination

Even if serious interpretation of Platonic texts does not need to be attributed to Antiochus, it is certainly to be found at some time before Cicero's great burst of philosophical activity in the closing two years of his life (46-44 BC). Here we find signs that a more genuinely Platonic philosophy, involving religious aspects, the immortality of [the] soul, and elements of non-empirical epistemology, had already made its mark. Glucker (1999) has shown the relationship between *De Divinatione* 1.115 and *Meno* 81c-d, which explains the core of the recollection theory. When this is coupled with the fact that Cicero refers to the paradigmatic role of Ideas in his *Orator* (8), that there is evidence of the 'Thoughts of God' interpretation of the Ideas in his contemporary Varro,[42] and that he himself utilises accounts of the Recollection Theory from both *Meno* and *Phaedo* in the first book of his *Tusculan Disputations* (1.57), we may see that already by about 45 BC there existed a movement towards taking the transcendental aspects of Platonic metaphysics and epistemology seriously. We should begin with the passage in the *De Divinatione*:

> viget enim animus in somniis liber ab sensibus omnique impeditione curarum, iacente et mortuo paene corpore. qui quia vixit ab omni aeternitate versatusque est cum innumerabilibus animis, omnia quae in natura rerum sunt videt, si modo temperatis escis modicisque potionibus ita est adfectus, ut sopito corpore ipse vigilet.

> [For the soul flourishes in sleep, free from the senses and from all hindering cares, while the body lies there and is almost dead. Because it has lived from all eternity, and has associated with countless (other) souls, it sees everything that is in the nature of things – just as long as it is so affected by restrained eating and moderate drinking as to be awake itself while the body slumbers.]

This is strange stuff indeed, combining, as Glucker has shown, various Pythagorising elements in Plato. It is explaining divination by dreams in particular in terms of this stock of recollectable knowledge open to the soul, here apparently expanded by our access to everything that other souls know too. An ascetic life contributes to the maximum possible level of separation of the soul from the body in sleep, so that the knowledge available to us produces clear images. One possibility might seem to be that the knowledge available must consist of insights into the nature of the universe, plus an appreciation of the situation that now prevails, so that the future can somehow be subconsciously worked out from the present. This kind of prophecy turns out to be similar to a scientific prediction, of an eclipse for instance, except that none of the processes are actually conscious.[43] The theory is not represented as Plato's, but the allusion to the *Meno* is unmistakable. The same stock of recollectable knowledge that allows the slave-boy to draw geometrical conclusions, initially in a dream-like fashion, is allowing the ascetic to predict the future in a process that is even more dream-like simply because he is asleep.

If there were any doubt that the *Meno* is closely connected with the argument here one should reflect that one of Cicero's two primary sources here, the so-called Peripatetic Cratippus who is committed to the case for 'natural' divination by both ecstatic experiences and dreams, uses as the climax of his argument (1.71, 2.107) an argument inspired by a reading of *Meno* 81d2-4: one completed act of sensation confirms that one has the power for acts of sensation in general, hence one clear-cut completed act of divination is enough to confirm that one has the power of divination in general. The *Meno* was claiming, on one natural reading at least, that one completed act of learning by recollection is enough to confirm that one has the power of learning by recollection in general.

Cicero's pro-divination sources have clearly been involved in exegetical activity, though here they are not trying to communicate their interpretation, only to mine Plato (as they understand him) for material that will be help to explain their case. The way in which they utilise themes and ideas merely *suggests* an underlying interpretation – an interpretation that is both imaginative and challenging. Unlike Glucker, I do not believe that there is any bar to regarding *De Divinatione* 1.115 as Cratippan, and it is clearly attractive to regard both passages in the work that depend on *Meno* 81 as the work of the same author. We might better understand Cratippus' approach to interpretation if we can establish his position on the wider philosophic issues behind it.

Cicero is a great admirer of Cratippus, whom he sees in the *De Officiis* as the foremost teacher currently at Athens; he sees his own differences from Cratippus, a nominal follower of Plato from a nominal follower of Aristotle, as being slight. A little later in the same work (2.8) Cratippus is seen as the foremost representative of the 'most ancient and noblest philosophy', and to be personally very like its founders. The talk of a plurality of founders is surely enough to identify this philosophy as Plato-nism and Aristotelianism, conceived of as being one, and it is spoken of as the oldest philosophy by virtue of its being the oldest still flourishing, older at least than the hellenistic philosophies popular at Rome. Cratippus had in fact been a pupil of Aristus, the brother and successor of Antiochus. Aristus also professed to be 'Academic' in the Old Academic tradition, and would presumably have seen this, like his brother, as virtually identical with the Peripatetic legacy, and little different from Stoicism. For some unknown reason both Cratippus and another school-member, Aristo, declared themselves Peripatetics (Index Acad. Herc. XXXV), but we cannot identify a doctrinal switch that would have brought this about. The result is that a moral philosophy that shows the basic characteristics of Antiochus is regarded as the *Peripatetic* position in the fifth book of Cicero's *De Finibus*. It seems safe to conclude from this that Cratippus would not have differed much from Antiochus on ethical principles, and one might therefore expect that any significant difference involved the other main issue promoted by Antiochus' school – that of the criterion of truth.

Here it is noticeable that the position attributed to the Peripatetics in Cicero's *Academica* (2.112) seems to involve a firm cognitive grasp *without involving a criterion of truth such as the Stoics proposed*.[44] Furthermore, Cicero claims that he has no quarrel with Peripatetic epistemology at *De Finibus* 5.76, and this ought surely to apply to the position of Cratippus as the leading 'Peripatetic' known to him. That Cratippus was the antithesis of a sceptic is suggested by his very sponsorship of divination, and particularly from the passage in which he compares the first completed act of divination with the first completed act of sight. Yet to appeal to epistemological ideas distinctly reminiscent of Plato suggests an attempt to find a foundation for his confidence that was (i) different from the Stoic foundation supported by Antiochus, and (ii) better suited than the Stoic criterion to the explanation of religious knowledge.[45]

Let us recall what we know about Cratippus' theory of knowledge from the *De Divinatione*. He not only puts his trust in the senses as Antiochus had done; he also supports the notion of divination by two methods: by ecstatic prophecy and by dreams. These were jointly known as natural divination, and contrasted with any imagined sciences of divination (1.34), all of which Cratippus rejected (1.113). As such he must have been keen to find a basis for knowledge that was altogether unlike sensation, for it could predict what was not yet there to be sensed. How could the soul draw upon non-sensory knowledge? The basis of Cratippus' position appears to be given at 1.70, and relies upon the close relationship between the human soul and the divine soul that spawned it. Normally this relationship is impeded by the body, so that in order to access the available knowledge we need to be immune to the influences of the body: to be soul alone insofar as that is possible, either in ecstatic frenzy or during our sleep. Human souls are meant to share the privileged knowledge of other souls in these circumstances, and that is what is supposed to go on in dreams. Cicero mockingly sums up the argument as follows at 2.119:

> They think our souls are divine, and that they are drawn from an outside source, and that the universe is packed with a multitude of souls that share one another's intuitions (*animorum consentientium*). Because of the mind's own divinity and its contact with other souls the future is foreseen.

If we unpack this a little we realise that the theory depends upon the following:

1. All souls are able to share one another's intuitions
2. The future is known to at least one soul.
3. Divinity is somehow involved.

Presumably the souls who know the future will include that very providential soul which arranges the future and from which we are sprung. Even our own souls are able to share in the knowledge available to divine souls, and as long as one divine soul can foresee the future so can we.

Here I believe we can see the way in which Cratippus was interpreting the troublesome sentence of the *Meno*'s recollection-passage that refers to the kinship of all nature, and begins *hate gar tês physeôs hapasês syggenês ousa kai memathêkuias tês psychês hapanta* (81c9-d1). We ourselves might translate 'Because all nature is akin and the soul has learned absolutely everything nothing prevents one, once one remembers just one thing, from discovering all the rest.' Whether or not they were using a different text, Cicero's supporters of dream-divination were interpreting this rather as 'because *its* entire nature is akin, and all things have been learned by soul, nothing prevents one, after recollecting just one thing, from discovering all the rest.' The emphasis is on the total stock of knowledge available to soul as a whole, and the lack of any non-removable barriers that distinguish one soul's private knowledge from another's.

This early use of the Theory of Recollection to explain quite unexpected types of cognition will be helpful in explaining how the theory became so crucial in the anonymous *Theaetetus*-commentator,[46] for the nature and extent of innate recollectable knowledge can seem surprising there too. Another similarity is that the *Meno* and *Phaedo* have been read in conjunction. Whereas this approach will have been suggested by the overlapping treatments of Recollection, the latter work has been found relevant to epistemology in that it emphasises, more than anywhere else in the corpus, the epistemological hindrance that the body represents. In one key respect the Cratippan approach to Platonic interpretation is reminiscent of Posidonius: it seems that the non-corporeal life of soul does not have to be an individual life, as in Posidonius' interpretation of the *Phaedrus*,[47] but the loss of individuality may even be an ideal. If we were to lose our individual identity in that existence, it would involve us in losing also what separates us from divine knowledge.

There is no doubt that the paucity of evidence for this early period permits some steps in our argument above to be challenged. However, the theory is sufficiently important to demand our attention and to make the probable connection with Cratippus worth exploring in full. His status as a 'Peripatetic' has caused him to be neglected as a possible source of revived Platonic doctrine, but his pre-eminence during Cicero's later years, and Cicero's own feeling of affinity to him, mean that he was the last great influence upon his work. Hence we should explore briefly the possibility that he is the chief source of new non-empirical strains in Platonic interpretation.

If our kinship with the soul that steers the universe gives us the chance to share its capacity for foreknowledge, then it gave us the chance to share other types of divine knowledge as well. If it explained the prophet's correct predictions, then it could surely also explain the correct opinions of the habitually successful politician who is compared so closely with the prophet in the *Meno* (99b-e). To judge from the *Phaedo*, which was used in close conjunction with the *Meno*, then knowledge of Ideas would be included in our innate recollectable knowledge; this too could be simply explained in terms of reunion with a divine soul that was itself able to contemplate the Ideas. In these circumstances the Platonic Ideas need have been no more than patterns present in a divine mind, that seemingly strange doctrine of the early Platonist revival found in authors such as Philo, Seneca, Nicomachus, and Alcinous.[48] Hence too the path towards wisdom for human beings need involve no more than seeking to revive this inner awareness of knowledge shared with the divine, whether through recollection of past contact or ecstasic contact or death itself. In short, we realise our cognitive goal by assimilation to god in the sense of reawakening divine thoughts within us. This assimilation, the goal for mankind throughout Middle Platonism, was an assignment made easier by our souls' being closely related to the divine soul in question. Assimilation in this life would be partial, and our share in divine wisdom imperfect. Assimilation in a world beyond might involve far more, and be the source of that lingering vision of the Plain of Truth that spurs the soul in this life on to love and to philosophy.

If Platonic recollection had come, already by the time of Cicero, to be explained in terms of our earlier share in the thoughts of a divine mind, then the basis of early Middle Platonic interpretation of Plato was already established. There was a place for the Ideas, and Platonic goal of human life, assimilation to the divine, was already established.

6

The re-establishment of
Platonic philosophy

i. Eudorus of Alexandria

Alexandria was the home of ancient scholarship. Scholarship invites commentaries. Commentaries in general demonstrate a level of seriousness about interpretative issues. Eudorus called himself an Academic, yet what this meant in the middle to late first century BC is not at all clear. The influence of Antiochus is not in evidence; the influence of Philo of Larissa cannot be proven; only the allegiance to Plato is unquestionable, and for Platonic interpretation he gave cautious approval to certain of the ideas of the Old Academy. In Plutarch (*Mor.* 1013b) he is found in partial agreement with both Xenocrates' and Crantor's interpretation of the basic construction of the cosmic soul of the *Timaeus*. This would seem to suggest that he thought that its arithmetic, motive, and epistemological aspects all had some role to play in determining the structure that Plato had given it. Strangely, however, Eudorus' own view goes unstated, perhaps because he is being included among 'all these' at 1013a:[1] interpreters in the Old Academic mould who deny that the creation-story was any more than an expository device, and therefore equating the materials out of which the soul was constructed with its on-going ingredients. The other main possibility would seem to be that he broadly adopted the Posidonian interpretation, seeing that as a refinement of Xenocrates and Crantor, but this is less likely. Plutarch is probably indebted to Eudorus in several respects, and thus reluctant to criticise more than Eudorus' own reluctance to chastise the Old Academics. At any rate he is ready to praise Eudorus' explanation of the arithmetic and geometrical means relevant to the soul's construction (1019f), and apparently content to follow him until he is again thought to show too much deference to Crantor (1020c). It is interesting that, when disagreeing with Eudorus, Plutarch appeals to the standards of probability and reasonableness (*pithanon, eulogon*) employed by the Academics of the Sceptic period, as if Eudorus were *his own kind of Academic* paying lip-service to the entire Academic tradition. Certainly, one feels that Eudorus has been partly responsible for shaping the interpretative tradition to which Plutarch, and probably his teacher Ammonius, belonged. In fact Eudorus should probably be regarded as the first Middle Platonist commentator on Plato, and if this is the case then his importance is considerable.

The difficulty in seeing Eudorus as Plutarch's kind of firm, *but cautious and undogmatic*, Academic instructor lies in his evident interest in Pythagoreanism, whose principles of physics and (probably) ethics he discussed.[2] Thereafter Pythagorean leanings are usually associated with the kind of Platonic interpreters who are dedicated to dogmatic instruction, though there is plenty of discussion of the Pythagoreans in Plutarch too. It is certainly of relevance here that according to the Eudoran view Plato in the *Timaeus* speaks *in a Pythagorean vein*, if a variety scholars are correct in supposing Stobaeus *Eclogues* 2.49.8 ff. to be a continuation of the Eudoran material on the division of philosophy. Eudorus' exegesis of the *Timaeus* may have attempted to explain many of its doctrines with reference to Pythagorean themes, such as are in fact brought in by Plutarch,[3] and this would certainly have ensured a sympathetic treatment for them.

As an interpreter of Plato, Eudorus was surely a figure of some importance, and it may have been he who first forged an important principle: 'Plato is a man of many voices, not of many views.'[4] That Stobaeus is continuing to follow Eudorus as he embarks upon an exposition of Platonic (and related) views on the goal of human life has been denied by Göransson,[5] and it is clear that Stobaeus is shifting, though shifting *naturally*, away from material on the division of moral philosophy and towards a doxographic account of Platonic and related ethical views: a doxography influenced by the Eudoran order of topics. It is quite probable that Stobaeus' immediate source had begun with a section on the division of moral philosophy, for which he drew on both Philo of Larissa and Eudorus, and then proceeded to tackle the principal Platonic ethical doctrines. I believe that Göransson is indeed correct in assuming that the latter material does not come from Eudorus' little book on the division of philosophy (which is not specifically a work on ethics!), but the doxographic material, *which must come ultimately from early Middle Platonist sources*, is still likely to come from an author with Platonist credentials who is respected by the doxographer. It is a reasonable supposition that the author is again influenced by the much-respected Eudorus. Only a significant interpreter is likely to have expressed strong views about the way in which Plato should be interpreted, and I shall persevere cautiously with the view that Stobaeus' doxographic source continues to express a *broadly* Eudoran approach to Plato. That it has something to do with Eudorus is in any case a great deal likelier than that it has something to do with the doxographer Arius Didymus to whom the wider context has almost constantly been ascribed from the days of Diels and Meineke until Göransson established the non-existence of the original case.[6]

The limitation of disagreements between dialogues to Plato's differing *voices* entails that, when he divides goods into two at one point, into three at another, and into five at another, it does not signify *vacillation* about their correct division, but one division is into their kinds, another into their locations, and another into their species. Similarly the goal of assimilation to the divine has been treated from a physical and Pythagorean aspect in the *Timaeus* (90a-d), from an ethical point of view in the *Republic* (608c ff.), and from a 'logical' (epistemological?) point of view in the *Theaetetus* (176b), as well as being expressed in a different way at *Laws* 716a-c. If the Eudoran source was correct, then an interpreter could reconcile what seem to be conflicts within the corpus, and Plato ought always to be able to be credited with a single position on all important issues of philosophy. The source pays most attention to works where it cannot easily be argued that a given viewpoint is that of Socrates rather than Plato. In fact, when illustrating Plato's position, the Stobaeus passage refers more often to the *Laws* than to any other work except the *Timaeus*;[7] neither use Socrates as protagonist, and the Athenian Stranger in the *Laws* was often seen as the thinnest of guises for Plato himself. That explains the affirmation that *Socrates* and Plato followed Pythagoras in making assimilation to God the goal of life; Stobaeus' Platonist found the doctrine in both the *Republic* and the *Theaetetus*, and, without denying a Platonic contribution, he probably regarded all dialogues in which Socrates is protagonist as building on Socratic foundations. That would not be so different from the attitude that Plutarch seems to take, in giving priority to the late and non-Socratic dialogues when discussing the *Timaeus*.

Another figure whom Eudorus appears to have influenced was Philo of Alexandria, who interpreted Jewish scripture in the light of Greek philosophy, and often showed Platonist inclinations. It might in fact be said that Philo *interpreted* the *Timaeus*,[8] though other Platonic works tend rather to be alluded to. Philo's task was the interpretation of the Jewish scriptures and in particular the books of Moses, and his use of Plato largely subservient to this task. Another whom Eudorus may have influenced was Potamo of Alexandria, who belonged to the time of Augustus. He called himself an Eclectic philosopher, as we hear from Diogenes Laertius 1.21. He would not be mentioned here, if he had not written a *Commentary on the Republic*, a fact preserved by the Suda. It is the earliest datable case of a commentary on a dialogue other than the *Timaeus*.

Even so, Eudorus' influence on Plutarch, and directly or indirectly on other Middle Platonists, was more important. A recognisably Middle Platonist version of Plato's ethics with a Middle Platonist goal is present in the supposedly Eudoran passage in Stobaeus, together with an emphasis, confirmed perhaps by the pattern of allusions to Plato in Philo, on the same group of supposedly late dialogues that Plutarch preferred to use.

ii. Doxographic sources

We are now dealing with an age when there seems to have been a widespread desire to find out the basics of various philosophies, without spending too long absorbing any of them. To meet this need it seems that a variety of authors may have engaged in either a listing of the opinions of different philosophers and schools on the set topics of philosophy, or outline summaries of the principal tenets of one philosophy at a time. The doxographers (opinion-listers) were so masterfully treated by Diels in the nineteenth century, that it is only recently that a thorough examination is beginning to confirm some and seriously question others of his findings.[9]

Clearly two doxographies, that of Ps.-Plutarch and one layer of material in Stobaeus, are related to a major work by an otherwise unknown Aetius which probably stemmed from the same period in which the interest in the interpretation had been rising; the latest authors whose views are catalogued come from the first century BC. From the present point of view the following points may be noted. Material in Aetius seems to have been arranged *diaphonically* – so as to give prominence to contrasting views (*diaphoniai*). This may suggest some influence of scepticism, for *diaphoniai* gave the Sceptics one of their principal reasons for suspension of judgment. However, it would be premature to suppose that Aetius must therefore have been a Sceptic, for diaphonic material might reflect a literary policy rather than a philosophic one. Material, which on some issues is influenced by doxographies in Aristotle and Theophrastus, often treated quite obscure figures, and among them the Old Academics Xenocrates and Speusippus featured regularly. The picture of Plato that emerges again shows signs of influence from the Old Academy, but there are occasional hints of Middle Platonist doctrines not otherwise known from before the first century AD.

The basic principles of the Platonic universe according to the Aetian tradition are three, (i) a god who is the world's intellect, 'that by which'; (ii) matter, that which underlies change, 'that out of which'; and (iii) the Ideas, immaterial substances in the thoughts and imaginings of god, 'that in relation to which' the world is made.[10] The transcendent intellect-god is also the One, the Single-Natured, the Monadic, the Really Real, and the Good;[11] underneath him are the Idea-paradigms, forces that pervade ether, air, and water, the heavenly bodies, the earth and the cosmos itself.[12] These texts do not in themselves show much concern for interpretation, but it is clear that some interpretation – at least of the *Timaeus and possibly much more* – does lie beneath the surface. The doxographic exercise was not ordinarily an interpretative one, and the author of this compilation was presumably not a Platonist either, but that did not prevent him having some knowledge of who might currently be offering the most attractive picture of what Plato's doctrines were.

There is also a general tendency, not uncommon in Middle Platonism, to link the name of Pythagoras with some of the views being attributed to Plato, or at least with similar views. Pythagoras is seen as a precursor of the Platonic theory of Ideas, finding them 'in numbers, their harmonies, and the so-called geometricals, inseparable from bodies'.[13] This may involve an attempt to find a *Pythagorean* theory of Ideas behind the mathematical construction of the *Timaeus*, for Pythagoras' view of the generation of the world, that it is generated conceptually but not temporally, looks like another *Timaeus*-inspired attribution.[14] Certainly the attribution to Pythagoras of the relation between earth, air, fire, and water (plus the whole) to the five regular solids comes directly from the *Timaeus*, 53c-55e, being followed in Ps.-Plutarch with the claim that 'Plato is pythagorising in these matters too'.[15] Later Pythagoras is given *Xenocrates'* definition of soul.[16]

The general principle that mathematical aspects of Platonism may be traced to Pythagoras seems to have been applied. Plato's originality is seen to be in the postulation of transcendent Ideas, with which Platonism ceases to display a simple Pythagorean dualism. Pythagoras himself is here credited with the contrast between god and the sensible world or, more Platonically according to some reports, between the Monad and the Indefinite Dyad; but Plato is seen as adding the Ideas to this dualist system, and so making it triadic. Without the Ideas the 'Aetian' Plato comes close to being a Pythagorean.

Another doxographer largely unrelated to Aetius and those who draw on him was Didymus, once called Arius Didymus, and therefore usually identified with Augustus' court philosopher Arius, who came from Alexandria. This identification has recently and rightly been questioned,[17] though not to the extent of disproving it or removing some of the attractiveness in accepting it. The fact that he tends to be called by one name in sources relevant to Augustus, and another in doxographic sources is not an insuperable problem, as Augustus himself is evidence that persons might take on a different name at a given stage of their career if it served some purpose. To exchange the less dignified Didymus for another which, though Greek in form, related to a god far more prominent in Roman life, might have been a shrewd move. If we discount the Platonic ethical doxography following Göransson,[18] there is only one passage of this doxographer which is of particular interest to our subject, and this is a passage preserved by Eusebius (under the name of 'Didymus') and Stobaeus, which talks at some length of the Platonic Ideas, and which is close to the wording of Alcinous at *Didasc.* 12. Significantly, the *Timaeus* is once again the dominant Platonic source, and the overlap is with the account of Ideas in Alcinous' physical chapters rather than that in his more original metaphysical section.

In general the doxographic material on Plato seems to stem mainly from *Timaeus*, and this can be said also of the doxography which Diogenes Laertius appends to his account of Plato's life and works (3.67-80); furthermore it tends to see the *Timaeus* as largely a Pythagorean document apart from material which deals with Ideas. In these respects it could be related to the work which Posidonius had done on the *Timaeus*, simplified, contaminated, and generally popularised. Fortunately moves against the Timaeocentric reading of Plato were already under way.

iii. Thrasyllus, Diogenes Laertius, and corpus-organisation

With Thrasyllus, usually identified as Tiberius' astrologer and court-intellectual (d. AD 36), we come to the consideration of somebody who was a Platonic scholar rather than a Platonist. Thrasyllus arranged the 36 works[19] of the Platonic corpus that he accepted as authentic into nine 'tetralogies', gave them second titles, and almost certainly composed an introduction to reading them.[20] Though his polymathic activities seem to have extended to developing some Platonising metaphysical theory reminiscent of Philo of Alexandria's *logos*-doctrine,[21] he was not, as far as we know, an author of Platonic commentaries, but engaged in this organisational task with which others of the time were also associated: Dercyllides, Theon of Smyrna, to an extent Albinus, and authors who wrote summaries of the dialogues. The task was to create a vision of the corpus as a whole, a vision that would explain differences between works in terms of the different roles they had in a programme of Platonic education. This was an important exercise in the light of the partial and relatively unsuccessful interpretative exercises reflected in Cicero, the incomplete arrangement of fifteen works into trilogies by Aristophanes of Byzantium, and the excessive importance attached to the *Timaeus* by many others, including the unidentified author whom Diogenes Laertius uses for his summary of Plato's philosophy (3.67-80).

It is Diogenes who has preserved most of our information about Thrasyllus' arrangement, including the precise order of dialogues and the second titles, which usually aimed at describing the principal subject of a dialogue: and hence seem already to constitute an interpretative exercise except where based on traditional alternative titles. In my view most of 3.48-66 derives from, and gives a reasonable but condensed picture of, Thrasyllus' introduction to the reading of Plato – though many will disagree with this and postulate another, unnamed source. I have no problem with the view that Diogenes is using an intermediate source, but would in that case stipulate that the source is itself inclined to follow the basics of Thrasyllus' approach. Certain clearly-marked snippets of Favorinus are added, presumably by Diogenes himself, but the rest makes a reasonably coherent whole. The passage as a whole gives what might be seen as offering an advanced anti-sceptic reading of Plato, by showing the positive contribution which seemingly aporetic dialogues could make towards a Platonic teaching programme, by discussing the nature of Plato's doctrinal teaching (52) and adapting requirements for interpretation to provide for the recognition of key doctrine (65),[22] and by explaining variations in Plato's expression as a means of concealing his approach from the ignorant rather than as an indication of uncertainty. Here too Plato's many voices do not imply many opinions.

The most hotly contested issue concerns the classification of the dialogues by 'character' at Diogenes Laertius 3.49-51, according to which all dialogues are allocated one of two basic types (instructional or inquisitive), both of which are subdivided into two species and four sub-species. I associate this with Thrasyllus, believing that it was not intended to form the basis of a reading order. Many others believe that it cannot have been intended to be used alongside the tetralogies – which seem to have been put together with little or no regard for 'character'.[23]

I see the 'character'-classification as an attempt to explain the differences within the Platonic corpus, continuing the work of Eudorus, and believe that it evolved principally from the concern to show that major differences between dialogues are not a sign of doctrinal vacillation but rather a matter of the function or approach adopted in each case. Eudorus, or somebody following Eudorus, had seemed to distinguish between the *manner* of presentation of the Platonic goal, calling the treatment 'ethical' in the *Republic*, 'logical' in the *Theaetetus*, and 'physical' in the *Timaeus* 'in accordance with the three-fold division of philosophy'.[24] Even here, where the division is made out to be one of manner, there seems to be more attention paid to the wider subject-matter of the dialogue than to the approach within the passage concerned; but since the *Republic* is not given an ethical *character*, nor the *Theaetetus* a logical one in Diogenes' character-classification, Eudorus seems uninfluenced by it.

The major division offered by the character-classification is between works that aim to instruct (*hyphegetic*) and works which aim to inquire (*zetetic*). That basic division does almost certainly antedate Thrasyllus, and is presented in slightly different terms by authors between Quintilian in the first century AD and Proclus in the fifth.[25] We gather from Albinus that the instructional works would be those composed with a view to the demonstration of the truth, while the inquisitive class would be aimed rather at a careful critique terminating in the refutation of falsehood. The instructional class is then divided into theoretical (physical, logical) and practical (ethical, political) according to the subject-matter of philosophy, but the inquisitive class is divided rather according to the requirements of the interlocutors.[26] Those directed towards younger persons and friends of Socrates are thought to be *gymnastic* – mental training; those directed towards rival intellectuals are thought to be *agonistic* – essentially polemical. The former class is then divided into those which merely make trial of the interlocutors (*peirastic*) and those which make them aware of the common notions deep within them by the exercise of Socratic 'midwifery' (*maieutic*). The latter has as its subdivisions those trying to trip up the opponent (*anatreptic*) and those merely trying to lay open the truth about him (*endeictic*), which would seem an unnecessary division were it not for *Theaetetus* 167e-8a:

> It is to be unfair in such a matter, when somebody fails to keep *competitive* and *dialectical* activities separate in his conversations, and to have sport and *induce as many slips as possible* in the former, but to take dialectic seriously and try to correct the interlocutor, only *laying open (endeiknumenos) those slips* which he was led into by himself and his previous associations.

According to this passage the difference between *anatreptic* and *endeictic* dialogues ought to be the desire to induce errors in the former, and the desire to bring to light existing errors in the latter. Since the distinction is put into the mouth of Protagoras, it is hardly surprising that Protagoras is the only sophist thought to have been treated in the *endeictic* manner.

It is quite significant for the history of interpretation if this distinction has been built upon a passage from the *Theaetetus*, and we should bear in mind that this dialogue is also the only one in which Socrates' maieutic skills are mentioned. In fact another passage might easily be read as distinguishing between *peirastic* and *maieutic* procedures. After Socrates has given a long exposition (or parody) of a secret Protagorean theory of sensation (156a-7c), Theaetetus cannot decide whether Socrates is giving his own view (the function of the instructional mode), or making trial of him (*apo-peirâi*); Socrates (157c) says that Theaetetus is forgetting that he has no doctrine himself, but that he is practising midwifery upon him by giving him this to taste. The implication would appear to be that the maieutic activity is different *both* from teaching *and* from trying somebody out. Hence the *Theaetetus* can supply us with some authority for all species of inquisitive activity.[27] Not only does the division of these 'characters' of discussion imitate Plato's own dichotomic methods in the *Sophist*; it is founded upon a reading of another Platonic text that uses the same interlocutor. And there is more: this text may itself have been seen to employ every 'character' itself: first *peirastic* to test Theaetetus' aptitude, then maieutic when it is established that he is 'pregnant'.[28] Then the initial refutation of Protagoras would begin *anatreptically* but become *endeictic* when Protagoras calls for greater standards of fairness. The so-called 'ethical digression' clearly employs a new didacticism indicating a shift to instructional style, beginning at 172b with an emphasis on the political consequences of ethical Protagoreanism, but shifting to the moral needs of the individual at 176a. After the refutation of the theses previously under examination it could very plausibly be maintained that the discussion of false opinion (187d-200c), with its 'opining what is not', interchange of knowledge objects, wax-tablets for the memory, and even aviaries in the mind, employs the type of approach characteristic of physics, while the later material which looks at the claim of true belief plus an account (*logos*) to be knowledge contains much more material which would be recognised as *logical* by interpreters. I conclude that it is highly likely that the *characters* were modes of discourse inspired first and foremost through close study of the *Theaetetus*, and that they had less to do with classifying whole dialogues than with classifying all separately identifiable sections of dialogues.

For a corpus-organiser, however, the temptation to classify whole dialogues by character must have been considerable. Ultimately there is no doubt that it is dialogues that are classified in this way by both Albinus and Diogenes, but there is no proof that this is how things began. From Thrasyllus' point of view, it would have been quite legitimate to divide through dichotomy Plato's modes of discourse, relating *some* to particular dialogues, and still others to interlocutors who in most cases had given their names to dialogues. It would have been unhelpful, however, to produce another way in which dialogues could be arranged and presented, in competition with his tetralogies.

Thrasyllus seems to have had two separate lines of influence. On the one hand his name was linked by Porphyry and Longinus with those of the Pythagoreans Moderatus, Numenius, and Cronius, as contributors to the literature on the metaphysical principles of Plato and Pythagoras;[29] this would naturally put him among those who wanted to use selected doctrinal content in the dialogues as evidence for early Pythagoreanism. But questions of corpus-organisation were taken up by one Dercyllides (assuming that he followed Thrasyllus), by Theon of Smyrna, and Albinus. The key figure upon whom Thrasyllus leaves no mark perceptible to us is Plutarch, which is perhaps not surprising in view of the fact that Plutarch continues to value the quasi-sceptical heritage of the Academy, while Thrasyllus had no time for it. Again, as corpus organisation lost its appeal while commentaries became more popular, there seems to have been no influence on Neoplatonism either. Yet arranging the corpus, like the assignation of second titles, was certainly an activity involving interpretation, and probably contributed considerably to the feeling that Plato's works constituted one interlocking educational programme.

iv. Seneca at Rome

From one court intellectual, we move to another. Seneca (1 BC – AD 65) was a Stoic, and close to the Emperor Nero for some time before his accession until their differences became irreconcilable in AD 62. Like most of those who did not have to earn their living by teaching philosophy and representing themselves as the authentic product of a given tradition, Seneca did not have to speak exclusively for his chosen school, and his *Epistles* demonstrate his interest in Plato. In particular *Epistles* 58.16-24 and 65.7-10 contain material on Plato that reflects recent developments in Platonism, so that one would wish to know their origins. In 58 we meet an

account of Plato's alleged six-fold 'division' of 'what is',[30] most easily seen
as deriving (with the acknowledged help of his servant Amicus, 58.8) from
a commentary or other interpretative exercise on *Timaeus* 27d6 ('What is
that which is always ...?'). In 65.7-10 we are given an account of five
Platonic causes, which takes Aristotle's four (motive, final, formal, material) and adds the exemplar or paradigmatic cause, no doubt as being an
essential explanatory factor in Plato's account of how the world came to
be, again in the *Timaeus*. A similar origin to that of 58.16-24 seems certain,
since they overlap in significant respects, above all in making a key
distinction between transcendent and immanent form, both of which are
seen as key elements in Plato's metaphysical machinery.

While Seneca somewhat unexpectedly provides crucial insights into the
path of Platonic interpretation, we cannot know whether the chief influence was Posidonius, Eudorus, somebody like Thrasyllus who would have
been known at Rome more recently, or a relative unknown. The five-cause
system sounds rather like an attempt to outdo Aristotle in a way that takes
note of the third cause that Aetius or his source had added to an earlier
two, for common to both Seneca and Aetius is this quasi-Aristotelian use
of prepositions to describe different types of cause, and both seem to use
the same expression for the paradigmatic cause: 'that in relation to
which'.[31] As for the difference between transcendent 'Idea' and immanent
'form' it does seem to be implicit in Aetius, the latter being what matter
receives,[32] while the former is defined in such a way that it remains a
paradigm.[33] Moreover, the Idea in Aetius is to be found in the thoughts and
imaginings of god's intellect,[34] which is where it is found in Seneca (65.7),
though he describes them in terms that make their *mathematical* nature
more prominent. In fact a god with a mind full of *figurae* reminds one more
of the mathematical patterns that go to make up the world-soul and its
intellect in the *Timaeus* than of anything else in Plato, the overriding
importance of the *Timaeus* to Seneca's version of Platonism matching that
of Aetius.

v. Plutarch on the Greek mainland

Plutarch (c. AD 45-125) provides us with the largest body of Middle
Platonist writings. The great biographer was also an accomplished Platonist, who wrote philosophical works in a variety of forms, manifesting a
general hostility to the Epicureans and Stoics, and showing loyalty to
Plato himself and to the New Academy. His attitude to Aristotle was more
ambivalent, but generally positive. A man of great religious conviction,
who became a Delphic priest and apologist, he shows no inclination to that
kind of scepticism which required the adherent to suspend judgment, but
advocated caution and attention to the common notions, which were now
becoming widely accepted as the source of those truths which philosophy
could reach. He was taught by one Ammonius who seems to have been of

the same philosophic persuasion and belonged to the same Delphic environment; his Egyptian name may or may not indicate that he had received his training in Egypt, but must indicate some kind of Egyptian connection that might explain how Plutarch had come to know the detailed work of Eudorus. It also explains Plutarch's own strong attraction to Egyptian religion, at least when Platonically interpreted, as in the treatise *On Isis and Osiris* and elsewhere. As priest and as Platonist Plutarch was an interpreter, seeking hidden meaning to which he, as a human being and as a Greek, could relate. As a Plato-interpreter he did not write commentaries on extended parts of Plato's works, but rather selected short passages which he felt needed explaining, but many of his best philosophic works go forward from Plato rather than going back to him. He tries to build creatively on Platonic materials, utilising Plato's literary forms including direct and narrated dialogue, and also symposia, and leaving much of the message for the reader to interpret. To those used to reading Neoplatonic texts Plutarch will perhaps appear as rather an unimaginative interpreter, thoughtful but inclined to dwell too much on the details of what was said rather than on the wider Platonic enterprise. He is one who insisted on taking the *Timaeus'* picture of a temporal creation literally, and he wants to find some explanation of every word that Plato wrote. Yet one has to acknowledge that Plutarch stands early in the interpretative tradition, at a time when the text was probably still much used with a view to supporting one's personal position than with any consideration for historical truths. A cautious picture of Plato was by no means inappropriate at the time.

vi. The *Theaetetus*-commentator

From Plutarch we move to a figure who is likewise convinced of the essential unity of Academic philosophy from Plato's day to his own, a belief that must have been based on a picture of *both* critical activities *and* instruction, as in Philo of Larissa. Much of what has been said about the appropriateness of Plutarch's caution could also be said of this anonymous Theaetetus-commentator. The papyrus text, with handwriting from the middle of the second century AD, is scarcely a glamorous document, with too much paraphrase for modern tastes, but it would have attracted a great deal more attention if only we had been able either to identify its author or to fix its date with precision. Until 1983 the tendency had been to date its composition close to the date of the handwriting, having the work fall in the middle of the second century AD; I then argued that its overall nature and stance would make better sense if located at the beginning of the Middle Platonic period, at around the end of the first century BC. Recent editors have agreed with me, for rather different reasons,[35] but doubt remains owing to our limited knowledge of early commentaries.[36] What one might claim with some certainty, however, is that the interpreter's world seems closer to that of Plutarch than to that of subsequent Middle Platonism. Prior to Plutarch, there are so many gaps in our knowledge that comparison is simply not possible.

The commentator is a moderate, clearly dissatisfied with interpretations that deny Plato doctrines, but equally convinced of the value of procedures in the dialogues which do not aim at or result in doctrine. He is largely prepared to let the natural message of the dialogue emerge for itself, but it is surely no accident that he is commenting on the *Theaetetus* in the first place: some might have preferred to confine themselves to commenting on dialogues which are more didactic. He is insistent that the work is about knowledge (as it seemed to be!), not about the criterion (as Platonists desiring a Platonic statement on this topic had apparently wanted it to be). More will emerge about this author when details are examined in Chapters 10 and 11.

vii. Theon of Smyrna

Theon was a contemporary of Plutarch, and an inscription records him as a Platonic philosopher. He would scarcely qualify for that title today if we were to judge from his surviving *Exposition of Mathematics Useful for Reading Plato*, but an introductory work on the background to Platonic mathematics is not likely to be a source of great insights into Platonist philosophy. Furthermore, Theon lifts whole slabs of material from a number of named sources including Thrasyllus, Dercyllides, Eratosthenes, and the Peripatetic Adrastus. The introduction is strung together fairly artlessly from Platonic passages illustrating the importance of mathematics, and only an extended comparison between philosophy and a sacred rite (pp. 14.18-16.2) tells us much about Theon's approach to Plato. I have discussed previously the way in which this passage relates to the Seventh Book of the *Republic*, already much utilised by Theon, and how this probably preserved not just Theon's but also Thrasyllus' theory behind the ordering of the dialogues.[37] It would be an advantage for any proposed reading order if it could be seen to be in accordance with the sequence of the education of Plato's guardians.

In this context, we should also note the last four words of the title: 'useful for reading Plato'. Like Thrasyllus Theon was concerned to facilitate the encounter with Plato through Plato's works, and understanding the nature and function of mathematical passages would certainly assist. Like Thrasyllus, Theon had written on the ordering and the titles of Plato's dialogues, with a little material being available in the *Fihrist* of Ibn al-Nadîm (pp. 591-4 Dodge), and Theon too would appear to have worked with tetralogical groups, some of them identical with Thrasyllus'.[38] It is interesting that Dercyllides, whose study of the spindle and whorls from the Myth of Er in *Republic* 10 is quoted at length in the *Exposition*, is another of those who worked with tetralogies,[39] so that they seem to have shared a particular approach to *reading* Plato.

viii. The Neopythagorean Plato

We come now to an obscure and controversial area, where there are a number of tantalising texts, most often too isolated for their meaning to be properly assessed. There are often problems about the degree to which an author's views have been correctly represented by a source, and hence the use of Platonic texts that they imply is less than clear. Besides the Pythagorising element, these figures are linked by dogmatic attitudes that imply a rejection of the Academy's more 'sceptical' activities, which Numenius at least, in contrast with Plutarch and others, regarded as a betrayal of its Platonic heritage.

We begin again with a contemporary of Plutarch, Moderatus of Gades, an obscure but tantalising figure who is best known for interpretations of *Pythagorean* metaphysics which seem to be based as much on the interpretation of Platonic texts as on any hard evidence for early Pythagoreanism. Moderatus was shown by E.R. Dodds (1928), with as much success as might be expected for such an unexpected thesis, to have been influenced to some extent by a reading of the *Parmenides*, certainly the first hypothesis, probably the first three, and conceivably, as I have argued,[40] all of them. It is often claimed on the basis of perfectly acceptable evidence in other authors that the Middle Platonists interpreted the work as a contribution to logic rather than metaphysics, but the 'Middle Platonists' were far from a homogeneous group and display widely divergent views on key interpretative issues, and the Neopythaoreans, especially Moderatus, did not see themselves as part of a Platonist movement at all. Moderatus, in fact, saw Plato as somebody who plundered the Pythagorean tradition and tried to conceal the fact,[41] and the better-known Numenius, who followed in the mid-second century, believed that Plato's main fault was his *reticence* about Pythagorean doctrines. All this suggests the belief that Pythagorean doctrines are *hidden* in Plato, who for one reason or another is reluctant to reveal them, and *that true Pythagoreanism can be teased out of Platonic texts by in-depth interpretation.* Like Thrasyllus, Moderatus, Numenius, and Numenius' friend Cronius were all supposed to have written on the first principles of Plato and Pythagoras in such a way that they had somehow anticipated Plotinus.[42] This must mean that they found Pythagorean metaphysical principles *within Plato*, and that these principles were of a different kind from any principles that ordinary Platonists (not anticipating Plotinus) saw operating in the Platonic corpus.

One way in which Moderatus did anticipate Plotinus was in detecting in the ancient Pythagoro-Platonic philosophy a One *above* Being, subtly different from Speusippus' doctrine of a One *not yet* Being. This is a degree of transcendence which is seemingly not found in Numenius, for Numenius calls his first god (and One), among other epithets, Being-Itself.[43] Nevertheless Numenius' theology extends to the discussion of the extent to which his divinities are one, and there is a distinct chance that he too is influenced by some metaphysical reading of the *Parmenides*. From our point of view it is disappointing that Proclus, often a good source for pre-Plotinian Platonism, seems to have been not particularly familiar with the Neopythagoreans,[44] though they had clearly been important in Porphyry's day.[45] It is legitimate, at least, to suspect the influence of the *Parmenides* on the negative theology of Alcinous 10.3 as well as on Clement of Alexandria.[46]

Though working in a tradition, Numenius was clearly an original thinker and interpreter, and the work *On the Good* from which the majority of the metaphysical fragments come involved interpretation of various Platonic works including the *Republic*, *Timaeus*, *Politicus* myth, and *Epistle ii*. It is probably because he did not write commentaries of the normal type on Platonic texts that he does not receive fuller treatment in later commentaries. For instance, in spite of his postulation of a separate principle of evil, an evil soul, it is to Plutarch and Atticus that Proclus chooses to refer when discussing this kind of doctrine.[47] When Numenius does receive special attention in the *Commentary on the Timaeus* it is in relation to doctrines which were influential with Porphyry, Theodorus, Harpocration, and Amelius respectively,[48] and in the two latter cases Numenius is found detecting more than one metaphysical entity in phrases of Plato, at 28c and 39e, which any casual reader would assume to be speaking of one only. Plato's 'Creator and Father of this world' becomes a double reference to Numenius' second and first gods, while when god plans to create those natures which intellect sees in the Animal-Itself, the latter is associated with the first god, and intellect and the planning god are distinguished too. As for the anticipation of Porphyry, this concerns the story of Atlantis, which Numenius pioneeringly interpreted as a story about a conflict between *souls*.

So it would seem safe to say that something quite esoteric is regularly being detected beneath Plato's text, concealing details of the allegedly Pythagorean metaphysic that Pythagoreans, almost as a matter of faith, supposed to exist there. And clever interpretation did not stop with Plato: as far as their long-term influence on Neoplatonism is concerned, it is perhaps Numenius' and Cronius' allegorical interpretation *of Homer* that was most important, though even this had a bearing on the interpretation of (e.g.) the Myth of Er at the close of the *Republic*.[49]

An unknown quantity is the extent of Numenius' influence on Calcidius' later (perhaps fourth-century) Latin *Commentary on the Timaeus*, which makes extensive (acknowledged) use of Numenius and (unacknowledged) use of the Peripatetic Adrastus. All this might readily be explained by postulating an ultimate source, probably Greek, which stood in the Numenian tradition, acknowledged Numenius whom it names because of his acknowledged originality, and fails to acknowledge Adrastus because what comes from him is now assumed to be a standard view. Calcidius is concerned mostly with standard interpretative problems within the *Timaeus*, which he views as a particularly difficult work to interpret; the broader issues concerning the interpretation of a corpus do not arise, and indeed he himself makes it plain that he does not find anything of philosophical interest in the introductory part of the work up to 27b. On this issue he agrees with Severus,[50] but Severus was hardly alone, and the attitude would most be appropriate among those who were mining the *Timaeus* for Pythagorean doctrine – which would not be expected outside Timaeus' grand monologue.

Another Pythagorean not so far discussed but from a time between Thrasyllus and Numenius is Nicomachus of Gerasa, who is known from an *Introduction to Arithmetic*, a *Manual of Harmonics*, and extracts and summaries of a range of other works. There is little in Nicomachus of relevance to this study, and he probably stood apart from the more metaphysical tradition embracing Moderatus and Numenius. He is, however, one Neopythagorean mentioned by Proclus in his *Parmenides*-commentary, and it is significant that he is said there to have regarded Parmenides and Zeno as members of the Pythagorean school. This provides all the excuse a Pythagorean would need for mining the examination of the One in the second part of the *Parmenides* for Pythagorean doctrine, making this and the *Timaeus*, along with anything which looks promising in the Eleatic Stranger's teaching in the *Sophist* and *Politicus*, the key sources of Pythagorean doctrines in Plato.

ix. More Middle Platonist commentators

Second-century Platonism after Plutarch saw no further major figures (none to compare in influence with Numenius, for example), but several whose contribution to interpretation was remembered in Neoplatonist days. Once again, there was no homogeneity, no basic Platonist creed that required allegiance. Rather it was Plato who required allegiance, for pupils approached them as representatives of Platonic philosophy, and it was up to individuals to promote their own versions of Plato as the authentic one.

Still indebted to Plutarch, though capable of taking an independent line (as on the generation of the universe),[51] was Taurus of Beirut, the teacher of Aulus Gellius, whose memories of him are preserved in the *Noctes Atticae*. Taurus was a painstaking and analytic interpreter, who did seek for a deep inner message in passages of Plato which might not have been thought to contain one,[52] although not such an imaginative message as that searched for by the Neoplatonists. Among works on which he commented were the *Timaeus* and the *Gorgias*.

Apparently a little later came one Atticus, something of a literal reader of Plato[53] who followed Plutarch in taking the creation story of the *Timaeus* literally, as implying a creation at a given time out of forces hitherto in chaotic motion.[54] He was a fierce champion of an aggressively *Platonic* Platonism, and a critic of Aristotle and of Platonists who tended towards Aristotelian doctrines. He is referred to a number of times in Proclus' *Commentary on the Timaeus*, once in connection with comments on the *Phaedrus*.[55] His reading of the *Timaeus'* theology is fairly straightforward for the time in making Plato's Demiurge into the supreme god, identical with the Good.[56] In general it lacks dynamism, and is innocent of exegetical finesse, to the extent that one wonders whether Atticus was not reacting *against* the ingenious speculations of Numenius and others. Certainly one may take his comments, as reported by Proclus,[57] on the absent guest at the beginning of the *Timaeus* as an attempt to kill speculation by sticking closely to a literal reading of the text.

Harpocration of Argos was a pupil of Atticus,[58] but late enough to be strongly influenced by Numenius, particularly on questions of psychology and theology. Rather than a number of exegetical works on individual dialogues, he produced a *Commentary on Plato*, which suggests a unified reading of the corpus. So often is Harpocration linked with another thinker in our sources, that I believe it difficult to say very much at all about his manner of exegesis, other than that it was not among the more original. Much the same could be said also of the even more shadowy Severus, whose attested interests likewise included the exegesis of the *Timaeus* and of aspects of Plato's psychology. However, he is the figure named by Proclus as a champion of the view that the whole introduction of the *Timaeus* (up to 27b) does not need any interpretation. Clearly, in order to be singled out for this not unusual view, it required that one should do far more than fail to interpret it: one had to be taking a stand on the issue, and it is likely that Severus was reacting against others who did try to read a lot into the introductory passage – most likely against Numenius or some of his adherents.

On the coast of Asia Minor the Platonism of Gaius and Albinus was of some repute in the middle of the second century. The 'School of Gaius' was once a central part of any account of Middle Platonism, but as the anonymous *Theaetetus*-commentator, Apuleius, and Alcinous have been detached from the school we are left with very little. Next to nothing is known of Gaius except insofar as he is linked with Albinus; Albinus' *Prologus* is either a clumsy epitome of a rather ordinary original, or a careless and amazingly brief introduction to the reading of Plato that does no credit to its author. Other fragments of Albinus are useful, certainly, but rather unhelpful on the wider issues of Platonic interpretation. The main exception here would be the claim that Plato teaches doctrine (*dogmatizei*) in two ways, in a knowledge-producing way and in a probabilistic sort of way. The latter was clearly supposed to include those doctrines of the *Timaeus* which had been designated a 'likely account'. On balance, this amounts to a claim that even in the *Timaeus* and presumably in the myths of other works Plato is handing down teaching in spite of a degree of uncertainty.

The final Greek Middle Platonist author with whom we shall deal here is Alcinous, the otherwise unknown author of the *Didascalicus* or *Handbook of Platonism*, which, though in a sense an introductory work, does assume a given stance on several interpretative issues, engages in some fairly straightforward interpretation of the *Cratylus* in chapter 6, and varies from being directly indebted to Plato at one point to being a spokesperson for contemporary Platonism at another. Of course the very fact that the author feels that a compendium of Platonist doctrine can be written, and will not violate any educational precepts of Platonism, does itself presuppose answers to some of the most important interpretative questions. He assumes that Platonic doctrine exists, is communicated through both Socrates and Timaeus, and can be usefully delivered to the new recruit in written form. He assumes that the dramatic aspects of the dialogues are largely irrelevant, and that the theses for which Plato argues are not context-dependent. He assumes that Plato has an intricate epistemology that will provide adequate justification for his views. He presumes that this epistemology is supported by a general understanding of syllogistic argument. He seems to assume (uncontroversially) that the treatment of physics works according to rather different and less certain principles, and operates as if the theology and metaphysics of Plato's physical dialogue, the *Timaeus*, should be treated without any attempt to bring it into direct alignment with the more general treatment of metaphysics and theology. He assumes that some aspects of Plato's work are important, while others, such as politics, can be much more fleetingly treated, and others still, such as rhetoric, can be omitted. He seems also to have views about distinctly different purposes for different dialogues, leading to the use of different kinds of logical figures depending on whether the aim is doctrine, exercise for the pupil, or refutation of opponents. One imagines that he does not himself write commentaries on Platonic works, because he shows no signs of preparing his readers for a deep analysis of the dialogues, and he does not refer to any commentaries as he writes.

The importance of the *Didascalicus* is that it is the only contemporary Greek document which covers most aspects of Platonic doctrine to some extent, and hence gives a more complete picture of the Platonism that one might have learnt in the second century AD, if scholars are correct in giving it such a date. It may not be typical of this Platonism, but Apuleius' work *On Plato and his Doctrines* seems to confirm that such handbooks were actually in demand, and that their production could actually enhance an author's reputation. To condense Plato into a single book, or into two in Apuleius' case, was in itself a challenge. A confident handling of Plato would enhance one's intellectual image, and many writers of the second sophistic era were certainly keen on maintaining that image. Apuleius himself, though thinking of himself as a Platonist and capable of making much creative use of Platonic themes,[59] is more naturally regarded as a representative of the 'second sophistic' and an intellectual all-rounder. There are no signs that he ever earned his living interpreting Platonic texts for small groups of philosophy students, or that he had any special interpretative flair beyond what one would expect of an accomplished man of letters. Nor can we be sure that Alcinous was a practising teacher of Platonic philosophy, though that would perhaps be the likeliest guess for he does not share Apuleius' literary skills. But even if he did teach Plato, then there is no guarantee that he did not do so more in the manner of that other hybrid sophist-philosopher, Maximus of Tyre, whose sermon-like Platonising speeches lend themselves to the theatre rather than the school-room, and show no interest in issues of interpretation.

Scholars used to make much of similarities between Apuleius and the *Didascalicus*, promoting the idea that they were products of the same 'School of Gaius', yet, even before the once accepted identification of Alcinous with Albinus had been found to built on straws, the differences between Apuleius and the *Didascalicus* had been given some prominence by Dillon, who spoke of 'a common stock of dogma' dating back to the first century BC and elaborated by successive 'schoolmen'. Certainly it could well be that handbooks more generally were not ordinarily composed afresh, but arose out of the modification of such earlier materials as were to hand.[60] Furthermore there was a long tradition of Latin authors modifying Greek originals, and Apuleius certainly did this in the case of the *Metamorphoses*. It is interesting that in this work the author-narrator is a member of Plutarch's line, and the influence of Plutarch is plain at times in other works, such as the treatise *On the God of Socrates*.

Apuleius reminds us that there are many intellectual types who could lay claim to Platonic philosophy. Maximus of Tyre does likewise. The principal influence of Middle Platonism over Neoplatonism came from the exegetical works of those dedicated to explaining Plato within Platonist schools. The principal remains of Middle Platonism which have come down to us – other than as fragments embedded in the work of Proclus – are not of this kind. There are huge gaps in our knowledge, and it is dangerous to assume that details and attitudes found in Alcinous and others are representative of Middle Platonism as a whole. Even more dangerous is the argument from silence: it means very little that interpretations known from Neoplatonists are not found in extant Middle Platonism *unless* it can be shown that extant Middle Platonism would have mentioned them if they had existed. In view of the heterogeneity of extant Middle Platonism such a case can seldom be made.

7

The principal Neoplatonist interpreters

i. The Plotinian influence

Since my main purpose here is to discuss the earliest approaches to the interpretation of Plato, I am less concerned with the Platonism of the third century AD and beyond. This is particularly so in view of (i) the powerful influence of first Plotinus and then Iamblichus, which meant that doctrinal loyalties to figures other than Plato may have had a marked effect over early Neoplatonic interpretation, and (ii) the much more accepted and widespread use of allegorical interpretation that did in fact give an interpreter a task of a different order. The result of this combination of additional loyalties and allegorical interpretation was a system of philosophy which saw itself as instantiated within Homer, Pythagoras, and often Aristotle as well as in Plato, and where the system was more important than any single instantiation.

With Plotinus (AD 204/5-270) we meet a figure who was clearly more worried by the philosophic problems themselves than by historical and interpretative issues. The *Enneads*, so-called because of Porphyry's arrangement of the corpus into six groups of nine, are meditations on philosophic topics, not on Plato's meaning. He takes into account the views of other major philosophic schools, though the ultimate message is clearly Platonic, and often supported by reference to Plato. The works of Plato that Plotinus finds important are mostly the same as seem to have been important in Plutarch or Numenius, with a strong emphasis on the *Timaeus, Republic, Phaedrus, Sophist, Politicus*, and *Philebus*; but the *Parmenides* and *Second Epistle*, both of which may possibly have been important for Numenius too, are now clearly classic texts. There is no sign that this is a new development, and, while others will disagree, I do not believe that Plotinus' innovation is much in evidence in the realm of Platonic interpretation, and I should certainly resist any suggestion that Plotinus' philosophy is simply the product of a reading of Plato in a particular way. It is entirely possible that much of his overall reading of

Plato came from his notoriously esoteric but very influential teacher, Ammonius Saccas.

ii. Amelius and Porphyry

Amelius is perhaps the most consistently devoted pupil of Plotinus, who served him during the period AD 246-69, though he is known to have been influenced by Numenius too. He interpreted the principal Platonic works (at least *Timaeus*, *Parmenides*, *Republic*, and *Philebus*), and traces of these interpretations survive in later Neoplatonists.

Far more important for us today is Porphyry. A pupil of Longinus at Athens, he joined Plotinus' circle in AD 263, where he studied, contributed, and wrote philosophical works until leaving in 268. This period of a mere five years seems to have had a profound influence on Porphyry, whose works he arranged and published together with his own introduction some thirty years after Plotinus' death. He also wrote the *Sentences*, which attempts to capture briefly the essence of Plotinus' philosophy. Besides moral works and discussions of the philosophic significance of religious beliefs and practices, he wrote much that involved interpretation. The *Life of Pythagoras* contains much that is interpretative, *On the Cave of the Nymphs* discusses the allegorical interpretation of a well-known passage of Homer, and there is a commentary on the *Harmonics* of Claudius Ptolemaeus. Though he wrote an introduction and commentaries on Aristotle's *Categories*, and commented on other Aristotelian and Platonic works, only the popular *Categories*-introduction (*Isagoge*) survives in anything more than fragments. The remains of a commentary on Plato's *Parmenides*, attributed to Porphyry by Hadot (1968) may be mentioned here, but there is no guarantee that the commentary is either by or connected with him. It is even possible that it is an essentially Middle Platonist document.

As an interpreter, Porphyry was clearly inclined to seek for in depth metaphysical meaning behind Platonic texts, seeking to see Plotinus' kind of Platonism in the writings of Plato himself. This did not, however, entail that every corner of a dialogue should be related to the overall metaphysical purpose as it did for Iamblichus.[1] What remains is enough to convince one that it is a pity that so much of this work of Porphyry is lost.

iii. Iamblichus

The next key figure had an early career that is something of a mystery, and there is room for much doubt even about the decade in which he was born.[2] The present tendency is to assume an earlier date (*c*. AD 245) than that indicated by the Suda's report that he flourished under the emperor Constantine (AD 306-37). His main teacher seems to have been an Anatolius, and he seems not to have known Plotinus in person. He was apparently acquainted with Porphyry, but the evidence does not show that he was his pupil. At times, it is clear that there were substantial religious and philosophical disagreements between them, and yet there is no Platonic interpreter known to us who had as much influence on Iamblichus as Porphyry had.

His surviving works contain contributions to a grand Pythagorean project, and a substantial treatise directed against Porphyry's *Letter to Anebo* whose usual modern name is *On the Mysteries*. Hence there are reasons for suspecting that extant works may give an excessively Pythagorean and an excessively religious picture of Iamblichus' Platonism, but it is certain that this picture is not wholly incorrect. Iamblichus was interested above all in those aspects of the dialogues that might be suspected of having religious or Pythagorean connections. It is to him that the Platonic curriculum of the later Neoplatonists should be attributed,[3] and the twelve chosen dialogues give an excellent indication of what he found important in Plato. They include all those in which Pythagoreans or Eleatics take a leading role, all those with a myth about the nature of the soul or the universe, and all those in fact with a strong didactic element – except for the *Republic* and *Laws* which were apparently not regarded as dialogues according to the Iamblichus' strict criteria, but were certainly read and taught. Largely absent are those dialogues with a markedly 'Socratic' appearance, particularly those that did not seem to move on to unveil significant Platonic teaching.

Each dialogue was considered to have a single aim or target (*skopos*), and this is precisely why the curriculum could not include works of an exploratory nature that seemed *aimless*. All facets of the dialogues were thought to contribute towards the unveiling of some mystery that one should learn about, resulting in a kind of literary and philosophic microcosm. Characters and setting assumed a metaphysical significance, and even the philosophic content was often seen to be merely hinting at some much deeper truth. What might strike the reader as arbitrarily chosen words, and particularly names, would take on some symbolic association: standing for something else without actually resembling it.

The result of this hermeneutic approach is at first sight quite strange and unfamiliar. It may, I believe, be best illustrated from selected quotations from the fragments of the Platonic commentaries. First in the curriculum came the *Alcibiades*. *On the Alcibiades* seems to have argued that this dialogue contains the germ of the whole following series (fr. 1). Its aim is to teach us the nature of us human beings, and to turn us inwards towards our true selves. To achieve this it includes a section which purifies the reason, another which exhorts us to perfect virtue, and a third which helps us to 'recollect' our inner selves (fr. 2). Now for the modern reader the initial words 'O son of Cleinias' seem totally unremarkable, but not so for Iamblichus (fr. 3):

The address by the father's name is an indication of the manly appearance of true erotic attraction, and of how it is awakened from matter and goes into action.

Every word must count for Iamblichus; perhaps the first words in particular. At any rate, Iamblichus certainly took part in the debate on the puzzling first phrases of the *Timaeus*:

> Soc: 'One, two, three, ... But where, good Timaeus, is the fourth of yesterday's diners and today's servers?'
> Tim: 'He's met with some illness, Socrates, for he wouldn't willingly have missed today's meeting.'

Whereas Porphyry finds here an indication of correct philosophic behaviour, how one must only miss philosophic discussion for reasons of physical incapacity, and how one must make the noblest excuses for a friend's absence, Iamblichus (fr. 3) explains that the absent fourth person, being familiar with the brightness of intellectual contemplation, is in fact unsuited to discussion of the murkier physical world, so that his absence in fact indicates a kind of intellectual superiority.[4]

In spite of the attention that was probably afforded regularly to first words, it is clear that Iamblichus' *Alcibiades*-commentary continued in the same way as it opened, selecting seemingly small points of detail and making much of them. In conformity with Iamblichus' religious interests, much attention was paid to the workings of Socrates' divine sign (frs 4-5), and to the relative distance from the divine of Socrates and Alcibiades (fr. 7). His commentary on the *Phaedo* was noticed by Olympiodorus chiefly for the thesis that the various arguments for the immortality of the soul are all capable of standing independently.[5] The later commentator prefers to emphasise the limitations of each argument, and makes an interesting observation about Iamblichus' manner of exegesis:

> This is characteristic of the ardour of Iamblichus, uttering this as if from his contemplative vantage-point in a trance, though it does not accord with what we read. (fr. 1)

We are invited to think of his exegesis as the prophetic utterances of some religious devotee, who, like the fourth person in his own *Timaeus*-commentary, is hindered by his own higher contemplation from seeing the text as it is.

The inherent strangeness of Iamblichus' interpretations might be seen in his account of the overall target of the *Sophist*, which sets out ostensibly to define through the method of division what a sophist is, and in the course of the investigation tackles the question of how 'that which is not F' can exist and be meaningful. There is no hint of theology in the dialogue, yet the scholiast reports as follows:

According to the great Iamblichus the target in this case concerns the demiurge of the sublunary world. For he is (1) a creator of images, (2) a purifier of souls who always separates them from views which are an impediment,[6] (3) one who changes his guise,[7] and (4) a fee-taking hunter of rich young men (in as much as he receives souls full of reasoning-principles as they descend from above and receives payment from them in the form of their rational animation of mortal things). He is embedded in Not-Being as creator of material things, and he takes delight in what is supremely not-Being, i.e. Matter. But he looks towards what is supremely Being. He is the many-headed one, projecting the guise of many natures and many lives, through which he devises the variety of generation. This same [divinity] is also a wizard, enchanting souls with the principles of nature, so that they become hard to wrench from the world of generation. ... So here he wants to teach us the sophist in all his forms; for (i) the philosopher too is a sophist, insofar as he imitates not only the demiurge of the heavens but also the creator of becoming, and (ii) the craft of division imitates the procession of entities from the One, and (iii) the creator of becoming imitates the demiurge of the heavens. Hence he is a sophist too. Even the actual sophist, the man that is, is called 'sophist' on account of his imitating many things, and that is why Plato spoke of a 'many-headed sophist'.

Thereafter Iamblichus relates the various characters of the dialogue to his scheme, the Eleatic Stranger to the transcendent Father of Demiurges, Socrates to Zeus, Theodorus to Hermes, and so on. What is clear is that Iamblichus has united in his own vision of the dialogue all its principal elements: sophists, philosophers, division, Being and Not-Being, likeness and imitation, its characters and even the order of its progression. In so doing, he has seemingly imported much theology and metaphysics that is alien to this dialogue. He has in fact divorced the ultimate purpose of the dialogue from the issues surrounding its immediate subject-matter, making the target (*skopos*) of a dialogue not something which that work proposes to discuss, but rather something which it intends to illuminate – for the true devotee – from a plurality of angles. His interpretation seems at first sight bizarre, yet it is somehow attractive and challenging, and one can readily understand the powerful influence which such a vision, 'as if from his contemplative vantage-point in a trance', had upon his immediate followers.

It is beyond my present purpose to understand the detailed workings of Iamblichus' theology and of its relation to traditional mythology. Yet it may not be superfluous to examine his comment on the reference to the mythical figure of Prometheus at *Philebus* 16c:

Prometheus reveals the paths of the gods into nature, Epimetheus their return paths as they ascend to the intelligible world – or so Iamblichus said, in the footsteps of Pythagoras.

The *Philebus* mentions neither Epimetheus nor Pythagoras, but Iamblichus seems to have imported the first for mythical completeness (though in a role that bears no relation to known myths),[8] and the second as part of the essential background for understanding Plato. Both mythology and Pythagoras are not only key elements in a highly imaginative interpretation of Plato, but they themselves stand in need of such interpretation in the course of his total project.

Thanks to the extraordinarily full account of prior interpretations which Proclus provides in his *Timaeus*-commentary, without begrudging us the names of the interpreters as he often does, we know most about Iamblichus' *Commentary on the Timaeus*, which provided a model for Syrianus and Proclus after him. One question of importance is the nature of the link between the *Timaeus* and the *Republic*, and the reasons for Socrates' summary of the Platonic ideal state before Timaeus embarks upon his cosmology. In fr. 5, on 17b-c, it is said that, while Porphyry considered this an ethical lesson of how one must enter upon our observation of universal order only after achieving a moral order within us, Iamblichus emphasised the way in which the images of psychical and political organisation can function as introductory images of the divine order of the universe. This commencement with images is said to be a Pythagorean tactic, leading on to a symbolic presentation of the same order through the myth of Atlantis, and so on to the revelation of the cosmology itself. Hence Timaeus' cosmological order that the dialogue sets out to examine is already being foreshadowed in Socrates' account of the political order of the ideal state and in Critias' account of the myth of Atlantis. This does not make Iamblichus question the historical truth of the Atlantis story (fr. 7),[9] but he feels that the conflict which it describes mirrors a conflict which may be found in among the basic principles of the cosmos too, between One and Dyad, Same and Other, Motion and Rest. Symbolic meaning does not cancel out literal meaning (this being a philosophic rather than a poetic text),[10] but causes it to diminish in importance. The historical example, as Iamblichus understands it, has been chosen with a view to a symbolic purpose.

The fragmentary evidence shows that Iamblichus was a figure of great importance in the history of Platonic interpretation, combining depth, detail, and originality. In spite of the impression that Proclus conveys of many substantial differences between Iamblichus and Porphyry, it must surely be said that Iamblichus' own reading of Plato could never have arisen but for the influence of Plotinus and his immediate followers. The trends which they had set reached their logical conclusion in Iamblichus, but they did so at an enormous cost: the cost of taking all judgments of interpretation out of the realm where an ordinary educated person could make a contribution. Without the lecturer, in whose quasi-prophetic words one trusted until one's own insight could grow to maturity, Plato's words could never mean to the pupil what Iamblichus helped them to mean. The lecturer's authority lay in the claim that the vision that inspired

Pythagoras, Plato, and others had been recreated within his own spirit. The interpretation was an interpretation of a vision rather than a text.

iv. After Iamblichus

Iamblichus influenced an army of followers, who ranged from the Emperor Julian to philosophers such as Dexippus and Theodorus of Asine. Even so, his legacy has come down to us rather through Plutarch of Athens (d. AD 432), his pupil Syrianus (d. AD 437?), and the latter's pupils Hermeias and Proclus (AD 412-85). Proclus, who had heard Plutarch in person, seems principally to be indebted to Syrianus' interpretation of Plato. All will have had their own insights, but they were surely refining the work of Iamblichus, eliminating its more bizarre features but adhering to his principles of unified, in-depth exegesis, directed towards a single target, and making liberal use of symbolic interpretation. We know of their work on Plato principally through Hermeias' *Phaedrus*-commentary and the commentaries of Proclus on the *Parmenides* (extant to 142a only),[11] *Timaeus* (extant in five books to 44d), the *Republic* (interpretative essays rather than a running commentary), the *Alcibiades* (again partial), and the *Cratylus* (abridged and again incomplete); to these should be added the important and extensive interpretative work entitled *Platonic Theology*. Proclus commented on other authors, and wrote treatises on various set topics, but his Platonic interpretation is best illustrated by the commentaries. Proclus is the giant of later Neoplatonism, a figure of wide influence who was equally at home with philosophic and with interpretative issues. Since space precludes my tackling him properly here, I must reserve this task for a later contribution.

After Proclus we have Platonic commentaries from two authors, Damascius and Olympiodorus. Damascius is perhaps best known as a leader of the Athenian School when Justinian brought its operations to a close in AD 529. At this stage he was already quite old, around sixty-seven, and he survived a decade or so afterwards. We have from him two works on the *Parmenides* (a *Commentary* and *On Principles*), two records of lectures on the *Phaedo*, and one on his lectures on the *Philebus*. This is clearly the oeuvre of the devotee of the Athenian School, with its intricate metaphysics, and a first principle so transcendent that apophatic methods must be employed, yielding a very unsatisfactory understanding. It is demanding, remaining essentially beyond the grasp of the ordinary reader of Plato, as Iamblichus and Proclus had been.

Damascius may be contrasted with Olympiodorus (c. AD 505-70), a pupil of Ammonius and one of the pillars of the Alexandrian Platonist School. Our impression of Olympiodorus may be distorted by the fact that we have records of his lectures on the first three works in the curriculum only: *Alcibiades*, *Gorgias*, and *Phaedo*, of which the last and deepest set of lectures is a lacunose fragment only, and treats just a small portion fairly early in the work (61c-79e). The impression is of a more elementary treatment, requiring less sophistication in philosophy, literary appreciation, linguistic expertise, and historical knowledge. One feels that he is both addressing the issues needed to present Plato to a less sophisticated Alexandrian audience, and deliberately avoiding the theological excesses of the Athenian professors. Presumably these would have been (i) little appreciated, and (ii) somewhat dangerous owing to the political difficulties for pagan Platonist teachers in Christian Alexandria. Though there are recognisable Neoplatonist features to his Platonic commentaries (he lectured on Aristotle), the ardour of Iamblichus has given way to a more controlled commitment to his author. This signals a new willingness, comparatively speaking, to let the text speak for itself, without trying to impose upon it any vision from outside. The result may seem dry and bleak at times, but we may feel the strong concern for the moral and intellectual development of his listeners, and recognise that we are dealing with a genuine teacher and a genuine Platonist tackling a practical as much as a theoretical job.

The enormous difference in tone should not lead one to forget that Olympiodorus still adheres to the fundamental principles of interpretation found already in Iamblichus. The curriculum is still Iamblichus' curriculum, devised for a Pythagorising project, but without the same commitment to Pythagoras. The target or *skopos* of the dialogue remains of fundamental importance, though it is now related more directly to the subject-matter of the dialogue and the questions which it *openly* asks. Furthermore, the unity of content, character, and plot is observed as strictly as ever. The principles of his school's interpretation of Plato are recorded in the anonymous *Prolegomena to Plato's Philosophy*. The most important difference from Iamblichus lies in the refusal of Olympiodorus' school, ever since Ammonius, to treat Plato's words as something which have to be (in some sense) right. In *On the Gorgias* at 41.9 we are told that even if Aristotle disagreed with Plato at times, it was only because he had learnt a fundamental lesson from the *Alcibiades* (114e) and *Phaedo* (91c): that one should not trust excessively in a teacher, but inquire for oneself.

> That is surely why Ammonius said 'I may have been wrong, but when somebody once said something, adding "Plato said so", I answered "That's not how he meant it, and anyway (forgive me Plato!) even if he did mean it I am not persuaded without his adding a demonstrative argument." '

Plato's authority no longer stems from his vision or his inspiration, but from his rational arguments, without which the former cannot be entirely trusted. These sentiments are to be found in an author that may seem to us today to dote upon the words of Plato, so that they certainly do not colour the commentaries unduly. Olympiodorus' successor Elias (*In Cat.* 122-3) records rules for the interpreter, which include greater commitment to the truth than to the target author. If Plato was fallible, then one did not have to fall head over heels in the attempt to extract a deep and believable meaning from everything. Finally, Elias requires that, while one interprets one work at a time, one does so with a view to the whole corpus. The dialogue continues to be part of a greater whole, a single great philosophy; but that greater whole does not involve more than one author, and Plato no longer needs to be interpreted in the light of Homer, Pythagoras, the Chaldaean Oracles, nor even Aristotle. All these parallel sources may be helpful, but it is within the Platonic corpus that a consistent message must be found.

PART THREE

8

The so-called early dialogues

I now deal briefly with the reception of most dialogues that are generally held to be among Plato's earliest and, in some sense, most 'Socratic'. These include (i) those that share the intention of exploring the nature and teachability of particular virtues or of virtue as a whole: *Charmides*, *Euthyphro*, *Laches*, *Meno*, *Protagoras* (*Republic* 1, though a part of a larger whole, being also allied with this group); (ii) those that share the intention of undermining the professional status of others: *Ion*, *Hippias Minor*, *Hippias Major*, *Euthydemus*, *Gorgias*, and again *Protagoras*; (iii) certain works that purport to explain Socrates' conduct relating to his trial and acceptance of death: *Apology*, *Crito*; and (iv) certain less easily classifiable works: *Alcibiades I*, *Theages*, *Lysis* and *Menexenus*. Of all these only the *Gorgias* will be treated in detail, chiefly because it offers the best opportunities. The *Cratylus* will be treated in Chapter 12.

i. Groupings

The dialogues listed above were never seen as a group in antiquity. However, apart from group (iii), the unusual *Menexenus*, and the part-dialogue *Republic* 1, all were seen as 'inquisitive' according to the character-classification. This marked them as concerned principally with the exercise of the young or the refutation of false beliefs, not with the establishment of the truth. They all belonged to the first, fourth, fifth, sixth, or seventh tetralogies of the Thrasyllan arrangement, tetralogies into which only one other work of undoubted authenticity intruded:[1] the *Phaedo* in tetralogy 1. In fact the first tetralogy (*Euthyphro*, *Apology*, *Crito*, *Phaedo*), with only the one 'inquisitive' dialogue and one that was clearly seen as a vehicle of Platonic and even Pythagorean doctrine in antiquity, deserves separate treatment.

It was seen as a paradigm of the philosophic life and death. This obviously involved the lack of concern that the philosopher would have for dying as exemplified in all but *Euthyphro*, the concern he would give to matters of justice and piety (the latter plausibly seen only as a sub-division of justice at *Euthph*. 12d), and how the whole of the philosopher's life could plausibly be seen as 'practising death': as withdrawing from the concerns of the body and sensation so that the concerns of soul and intelligence might take control. The appreciation of the fact that the philosopher practises death seems to have been for Albinus a more important purpose than the establishment of the immortality of the soul.[2] We are not told that this tetralogy only shows what *the end* of the philosopher's life should be like, and this is probably quite deliberate. Although the earliest dramatic date for the conversations depicted here is when Socrates has to make an initial appearance before the King Archon to answer the charge of Meletus that will lead to his death, all these dialogues inform us of the ordinary philosophical practices that Socrates had been pursuing for years. The 'practising death' of *Phaedo* is supposed to be an integral part of philosophy, and not something for one's final days only; *Crito* goes back to the principles of Socratic ethics with which 'Crito' the interlocutor had been long familiar; *Apology* describes the philosophical practices of Socrates which had long led to his unpopularity, links them with the Delphic oracle, and pictures them as a kind of cross-examination of those who professed some knowledge; and *Euthyphro*, which seems at first sight to be misplaced here according to ancient principles, is giving an example of this process of cross-examination which somehow sums up the philosophic career of Socrates, explains how it led to unpopularity, and tackles the most important question that the reader of the *Apology* must keep in mind: what is the nature of holiness. The *Euthyphro* provides a theoretical framework crucial for the reading of the whole tetralogy, and it asks a question that can only be answered after we have received various unfamiliar lessons on holiness in the *Apology*, been treated to a picture of somebody approaching blessedness in the *Crito* and *Phaedo*, and finally glimpsed the blessed abode reserved for the exceptionally holy and the philosophers at the end of the *Phaedo* (114b-c): holiness is the work of philosophy.

As a kind of paradigm of philosophy it is only reasonable that the first tetralogy should include a work that raises the important questions of life, others which show the philosopher confronting practical situations, and another which expounds and argues a clear view of what we humans really are and what this implies for the behaviour that is appropriate to us. Seen like this the *Phaedo* is a less problematic dialogue, for the exact analysis and evaluation of its arguments is less critical if its purpose is not so much to prove logically the immortality of the soul as to convince others that the path of Socrates was a fine and honourable path towards a well-founded hope of blessedness hereafter. The *Phaedo* was in fact regularly known in antiquity by the title *On Soul*, which suggests that its purpose was conceived as being much wider than to prove our immortality.[3] All this does not amount to an argument for the *Phaedo* having been *written* as an integral part of a group of works illustrating the philosophic life and death; the most that could be plausibly claimed – and indeed seems to have been claimed by Thrasyllus – was that Plato had *presented* his dialogues in tetralogies.[4]

The *Phaedo* will be discussed further in Chapter 13 ii, but what of *Apology* and *Crito*? These were well enough known, but little used by ancient Platonists; their importance was chiefly for the study of Socrates, not as a source of Platonic doctrine. Plato's doctrines concerning justice and law, it seems, were better studied through his three largest dialogues, *Gorgias, Republic*, and *Laws*. Neither *Apology* nor *Crito* rate a mention in the index to the Budé edition of Proclus' *Platonic Theology*,[5] which is clearly dedicated to a specifically *Platonic* investigation, while both feature in the corresponding index to his *Commentary on the Alcibiades*,[6] which has much more relevance for the study of Socrates. Here it is plain that both works are being used as evidence for Socrates, his divine sign (79-83), his 'big-talk' (*megalêgoria*, 155.22), his lack of shamelessness (309.21), and his tendency to soften the impact of the elenchus by introducing the criticism through another voice such as that of the 'Laws of Athens' in *Crito* (289-90).

Back at the beginning of the imperial era both had been seen as belonging to the dialogues of 'ethical' character, and that is consistent with them having been regarded as a portrait of Socratic morality; it may mean that the discussion of the relationship of the individual to his *polis* and its laws did not constitute such an important part of the *Crito* as it does for us, since in that case we might have expected it to have been labelled 'political'. Next, Middle Platonism afforded neither work an important place in the determination of Platonic doctrine – no place at all if we are to judge from the extant handbook of Alcinous. There the *Crito* is of insufficient importance to feature in Whittaker's full index,[7] while the only reference there to the *Apology* is to the phrase 'political virtue' (189.5) that does not need to be rooted in the text of Plato. If we looked for authors for whom the *Apology* had been of special relevance, we should include intellectuals like Apuleius and Maximus of Tyre, but it is their interest in Socrates that is shown by their composing works on Socrates' divine sign. Apuleius also took pains to cast himself in the role of Socrates in his own *Defence to the Accusation of Magic*. The *Apology* was occasionally used as a starting-point of the curriculum, but the implications are unclear, since other starting-points included short and little-studied works like *Euthyphro* and *Clitopho*, as well as works of major importance.

ii. Virtues and definitions

This leads us back to the *Euthyphro*. Given the expected second title *On Holiness*, there is no sign of its having risen to any importance in what was an intensely religious age. Though Proclus will make some use of it in the same discussion of Socrates' divine sign referred to above, it finds no place in the *Didascalicus*, and, having been classed as 'peirastic' or 'tentative' in the character-classification, it was not regarded as a dialogue designed to instruct us, as both *Apology* and *Crito* were. Dillon does find a little use of *Euthyphro* in two authors seemingly on the fringe of Middle Platonism, Philo and Apuleius,[8] and one could discover its influence on Plutarch or Maximus of Tyre,[9] but nothing points to its having been a work that rated interpretation.

Similar things could be said about two other dialogues from our group (i), *Laches* and *Charmides*, both of which share the same 'What is this virtue?' question, and the same aporetic structure, and of the two related 'What is x?' dialogues, *Hippias Major* and *Lysis*. It seems likely that the aporetic structure of them all, and the lack of any clear doctrinal statements in general, was a considerable impediment to them being studied seriously by later Platonists – and hence a ticket to relative obscurity. None of these dialogues is mentioned in Dillon's index to *The Middle Platonists*, though their influence has been suspected in Alcinous.[10] Maximus Tyrius does make fairly wide use of them, but as part of a corpus that scarcely has the establishment of Platonic doctrine as its main purpose, and is more interesting in proving the philosophic versatility of its author. In later times Libanius will use them a lot. But only the *Lysis* finds more than the rarest of mentions in the works of the Neoplatonists. Even here the spectacle of Socrates arguing firstly that friendship is between things similar, and then that it is between things dissimilar (214a-216b), had provided an argument for those who championed the sceptic view of Plato: Plato argues for both sides of the question.[11] The *Charmides* had given the same impression. The authoritative messages that most Platonists wanted to find were too elusive in all of these works, which, for the most part, seemed to explore issues rather than find conclusions.

An issue that the ancients would have considered of importance here is the degree of relevance to the education of the young. Educational importance is most obvious in the case of the *Lysis* where none of the interlocutors is of mature years, and still clear in the *Charmides*, where the reader is acutely aware of the struggle about how Charmides may make progress in virtue. But even in the *Laches* we are experiencing a conversation vitally concerned with the future of two young men who are present on the scene, and with how they may best acquire courage. This contrasts with the *Hippias Major*, where the young are only relevant insofar as Hippias purports to be a teacher, so that this last is regularly seen as a polemical work in contrast to the others which are exercises in philosophic inquiry.

Antiquity took a more ambivalent attitude towards the *Meno*, which was not considered a particularly useful contribution to the overall issue of whether virtue can or cannot be taught (the question that is *explored*), but which was assumed to offer excellent insights into the nature of the learning-process and the means by which fleeting opinion may be turned into stable knowledge. In this way it seems to conform with what the anonymous *Theaetetus*-commentator says about Platonic *investigations*, that there is no open pronouncement on the main topic investigated, though we are often offered doctrines about other issues (58.39-59.2). Since epistemology had been such a hard-fought issue in Hellenistic and Roman Republican times, there was little chance that philosophers would ignore the Theory of Recollection, which occupies the centre of the dialogue, between unsuccessful attempts to define virtue and an unconvincing discussion of its teachability. When 'Socrates' shows 'Meno' how his slave can sensibly discuss geometry, in spite of his never having learnt any (81-6), this is taken by a later age to demonstrate that all individuals have within them shared concepts, present from birth and a source of basic human truth, which, while normally dormant, will return to consciousness when somebody uses skills in the art of questioning to awaken them and clarify the truths within them.

While it is likely that the *Meno* had been influential in the early days of Hellenistic philosophy, in helping the Epicureans and Stoics to develop their own theories of the *prolepsis* (pre-conception) and *koinê ennoia* (common notion) respectively, authors instrumental in the revival of Platonism who utilise the passage include Cicero, Plutarch, the anonymous *Theaetetus*-commentator, Albinus, and, less obviously, Alcinous.[12] That this passage is viewed with an almost solemn seriousness, more seriously than it is sometimes taken today, *even though it is part of an inquisitive dialogue*, is quite understandable when one considers that the Theory of Recollection is also discussed in the *Phaedo*, a dialogue that was widely agreed to expound Plato's philosophy. The *Phaedo* actually seems to make reference to this passage of the *Meno*, singling out its conclusions as something that remained important for Plato. While there are important differences between the passages, above all the identification of the objects of this 'recollected' knowledge with the Ideas in the *Phaedo*, this was simply taken to be the same kind of challenge for the interpreter that is constantly recurring. Further, the inquisitive status of the *Meno* would certainly have absolved Plato from any obligation to reveal his *whole* theory there. The main use that the theory is put to in the *Meno* is to justify our continuing to *be inquisitive* even though we may not seem to have the answers at hand; it justifies the process of inquiry without any investigation of the nature of the knowledge which may be 'recollected'.

A second, apparently minor, contribution of 'recollection' to the dialogue occurs at 98a, where, at least according to received texts,[13] the process of binding correct opinion by 'reasoning of cause' is identified with the 'recollection' that had previously been discussed – reasonably so, since both processes represent what is normally referred to as 'learning'. The notion of 'binding by reasoning of cause' is picked up by a variety of authors, including the *Theaetetus*-commentator, Albinus, Galen, Atticus, and Neoplatonists, and it generally signified for them the addition of

logical demonstration to what was being said or believed.[14] Even in the
Theaetetus-Commentator where this is not the case, it was compared to
Aristotle's insistence that we know *that* P only when we know *why* P (e.g.
APo. 94a20). Facts must be supported by reasons if we are to be convinced
that they are indeed the facts. Since Platonism increasingly sought to
speak with conviction, any passage which might seem to offer a justification of that conviction was welcomed; we shall return to it when we discuss
the *Theaetetus* and Platonic epistemology more widely.

Since a principal object of Platonism was to discover as rational a basis
as possible for human life, it would be particularly welcome if virtues or
excellences were founded firmly on knowledge. Over the question of
whether virtue or its constituent parts are identical with, or founded
firmly on, moral knowledge, Plato's 'Socrates' seems to waver, not merely
from one dialogue to another, but also *within* dialogues, chiefly in the
Protagoras and *Meno*. The ultimate response of the Platonism of antiquity
will be to postulate a *plurality of levels* of virtue,[15] and even in early Middle
Platonist times the virtues proper were being distinguished from natural
predispositions towards laudable conduct such as bravery and self-control.[16]
Interpreters would have been well aware that Aristotle had reported
Socrates' view of the virtues in general and of bravery in particular as
tending to turn them into knowledge, but they would likewise know the
concepts of temperance, justice, and bravery in the fourth book of the
Republic, and there is no doubt that the *Republic* would be given precedence over most other works in the determination of the true Platonic view
of virtues, especially when the Socratic view had never been presented
unproblematically in Plato's work.

Here the *Meno* was especially ambivalent. Immediately after the 'recollection' passage, at the very time when the Middle Platonist would expect
Plato to be trying to base his inquiry upon the 'natural notions' present in
the recesses of the mind, he conducts an inquiry founded on the notions
that virtue is an unequivocally good thing (87d), and that anything which
turned out to be knowledge would be a teachable thing (87c), and goes on
to argue that all things which are good for us are in fact dependent on some
knowledge: hence virtue, being good, is founded on knowledge, and is
teachable. However, when Socrates, after consultation with Meno and
Anytus, concludes that there are no teachers of virtue, this leads to the
natural conclusion that any virtue that does occur is not taught and is not
knowledge (96b-c). The end of the dialogue then explores the further
possibility that human success depends only on correct opinion, not on
knowledge proper. It suggests that it is founded on an unstable judgment
that does not derive from teaching (for teaching teaches knowledge), and
is in a way like prophecy. For prophets can consistently be right without
knowing why they right, but only so long as the divine voice speaks
through them. Similarly, those known for their virtue operate through
some kind of divinely sent inspiration – for as long as they are successful.

What can it mean that virtue, or at least the virtue of the politician, is something that depends on correct opinion arising from a 'divine allocation' (99e)? Is it being given a high or a low status as a result, and how serious is Plato about this comparison with the seer?

It is not easy to say precisely how ancient Platonism responded to these questions, but a general dislike of appeals to irony meant that some kind of genuine message was likely to be found here. Alcinous at first sight offers us little guidance. The discussion of virtue in chapter 29 begins by calling it a divine thing, strongly suggesting that its origin from divine allocation is taken seriously. Yet in chapter 31 the author insists that virtue is something *depending on ourselves*, and he denies that it would be praiseworthy if it was the product of our birth or a divine gift. That it belongs to its possessors by birth is indeed ruled out by the *Meno*, but its divine allocation is affirmed at 99e. Does the author not take this seriously, or is he trying to qualify what Plato says by claiming that the allocation can only follow some considerable effort on our own part? Must we *want* to be virtuous, in much the same way as most prophets would want the voice of the god to speak through them, and might strive for closeness to the god? Could it be that the divine gift relies equally upon the god and upon ourselves?

Alcinous is less than clear, but the complications on this particular issue vanish when one realises that he does not even acknowledge that the end of the *Meno* is discussing true virtue. The same word, he believes (30.1), is also given to natural good qualities and dispositions manifesting progress towards virtue. Certainly he would have detected the use of secondary senses of virtue-terms like 'temperance' and 'courage' at *Meno* 88b, where it is thought that these dispositions can have harmful effects if accompanied by folly, though in these cases it is clear that not even correct opinion would be present. These potentially harmful qualities could be regarded as the gifts of nature, but qualities that are linked with correct opinion would be something different again: while they lasted they would have as good an effect on our behaviour as knowledge-based virtues (97b-c), but they would still fall short of that virtue which is guided by the wisdom of the soul's rational faculty: they would remain imperfect, and hence they could apparently be present even in the absence of other virtues, if one is to judge from *Didasc.* 29.4 and a parallel passage in Apuleius (*Plat.* 2.6.228). So the 'virtue' under discussion as the *Meno* closes is something intermediate between mere natural inclinations to a given type of behaviour and the total subservience of the irrational faculties to a fully reasoned mind: intermediate between what nature does for us, and what we achieve through mental powers that can transcend nature.

The tripartition of virtues followed by Alcinous, in which situations involving moral progress are distinguished from natural dispositions and also from complete virtue, is found for instance in Philo of Alexandria and Arius.[17] It is evident that Alcinous is anxious to establish the existence of something analogous to virtue in those who are making progress, and the very concept of progress seems at odds with the idea that these quasi-virtues could be the good qualities that one is born with (30.2). Given that the virtues associated with respected politicians, such as are in the fore-front of Meno's mind throughout the dialogue which bears his name, will inevitably lack something in Plato's eyes, and given too that a basis in innate gifts is specifically ruled out as late as 98c-d, it must have been quite natural to attribute them to moral progress. This, I submit, is what Alcinous does: the virtues that come by divine allocation are for him the intermediate 'virtues' marking moral progress. If this sounds odd, seem-ingly attributing to the divine what the individual achieves of his or her own accord, it is only because we fail to see what this 'divine allocation' really is in Middle Platonist theory.

No reader of the *Meno* in its totality could afford to be misled by the satirical tones of the dialogue's conclusion into forgetting the epistemologi-cal issues. Virtue in the *Meno* was attributed to divine dispensation only because it was found to be dependent on a facility to arrive at correct opinions that could not be explained by the fully reasoned process of coming to *know*. When human beings arrive at correct opinions it is obvious that they have certain basic natural abilities, and probable that they have made a serious effort to address the issues. Yet an element of chance, such as would be excluded by firm knowledge, seems to remain. How could one be repeatedly guided to the correct conclusions without ever mastering the considerations that justify them? The anonymous *Theaetetus*-commentator has an answer. Knowledge is for him dependent upon the awakening of our innate ideas, as demonstrated in the scene with the slave boy, *and their clarification (diarthrôsis)*. Before this the innate ideas may operate beneath the surface and have some bearing on our understanding of things without our being properly aware of them.[18] We do not have to have clarified our innate ideas in order to act in accordance with them; they can influence us subconsciously. Plato himself had already shown that the recollection process may lead to *either* knowledge *or* correct opinion, and carefully described the slave-boy's condition as involving the latter (*Meno* 85c-d). He has *knowledge* within him, but he has not yet recovered so much. It was not difficult for the Middle Platonists to see this dream-like awareness of innate knowledge as the basis of 'political' virtue too, and to give political virtue an epistemological foundation not sug-gested by the phrase 'divine dispensation'. In fact the 'divine share' (*theia moira*) was nothing other than the portion of divine knowledge, allotted potentially to all human beings, and actualised sufficiently by some of them to guide them subconsciously towards the correct conclusions. If this seems far-fetched, one only has to recall the way that this same body of recollectable knowledge had even been held responsible for divination by dreams in Cicero's *De Divinatione*. Perhaps, then, the parallel between politician and seer *was* taken seriously.[19]

The availability of an epistemological foundation for the imperfect virtue displayed by politicians helps to explain various features of Alcinous' discussion of the virtues in chapters 29-31; it must be said, however, that the key detail of the subconscious functioning of the natural notions has to be imported other authors. Is there evidence, even, that Alcinous and his contemporaries were giving close thought to the 'divine dispensation' at the close of the *Meno*? In fact there is evidence of this kind, and it is found in Clement of Alexandria. At *Strom.* 5.83.4 he preserves an apparently deliberate emendation of *Meno* 99e6 by which 'divine dispensation without understanding' becomes 'divine dispensation *not* without understanding'.[20] I strongly suspect that this is the text that Alcinous would have known and read, as it fits the view that the politician's virtue is something different from the natural good qualities (*euphuiae*); the good qualities of *Meno* 88b could have bad results if exercised without intelligence, and good results if exercised with it. Hence the politician's virtue, which has been agreed to have *good* results, must surely not be the same as natural good qualities without intelligence, whose effects are bad. But does the emendation have the effect of bringing the politician's virtue too close to perfect knowledge-based virtue? Rather, I believe, it is what was required to distinguish the hidden operation of some innate intelligence within us from knowledge that is openly available for us to grasp.

Alcinous himself associates human intelligence with the natural notion (4.6), 'an intellection stored up in the soul',[21] and hence with the Platonic theory of Recollection, so that no process involving the influence of innate notions could accurately be described as 'without intelligence'. He also makes considerable epistemological use of the phrase 'not without' at 4.7;[22] scientific reason, *not without* intellection, judges ordinary forms in matter, while intelligence, *not without* this scientific reason, is the judge of the Ideas, etc.[23] One of the principal uses of the phrase during this period, a use influenced by Stoic theory, was to indicate contributory factors, which, while not being *causes* in the full sense, are nevertheless necessary for something to take place. What Alcinous needed, therefore, was to have the politician's virtue come 'not without intelligence', indicating that a kind of intelligence is a necessary *background* factor, linked with the natural notions. These notions themselves constituted the 'divine portion' by which this arose: a kind of divine element within us.

Those displaying political virtue, then, would be dependent upon a kind of intelligence (as all would imagine), and this 'intelligence' would be concerned with the extent to which they could access the natural notions common to all human beings. The *Theaetetus*-commentator insists that we cannot all access these notions within this life (47.23-42), for some remain barren in soul as the *Theaetetus* teaches (151b).[24] And several centuries later Olympiodorus will be explaining the differences between the characters of the *Gorgias* in terms of their distance from the common notions. The better the character, he thinks, the closer he stands to the common notions,[25] and the link between them and one's public conduct is made clear at *In Grg.* 7.1, 30.2, and 39.6.

What kind of a reading of the end of the *Meno* do these findings imply? They show that the irony has not gone entirely unnoticed, but that the effort is still made to extract from the passage a sense in which it would have been true. Socrates' suspicions of those politicians usually regarded as virtuous does not mean that his attribution of their 'virtue' to a divine apportionment is a flippant comment or simple untruth. Pericles' divine apportionment would indeed have to differ from that of some seer, but he is not being deprived of all merit, and in a sense the special gift which he possesses (and which enables him to act for the better) is a divine gift, brought with him from his disembodied existence into this corporeal life, and guiding his conduct in a manner which he does not fully understand and has not fully reasoned through. On this interpretation Plato's Socrates appears honourable, because there is no outright deception behind his words, and Pericles and those like him also appear honourable, because there is a genuine explanation of their political success, and this explanation is to be associated with something commendable within their souls – however far it may fall short of knowledge.

iii. Irony

I have dwelt at some length over the interpretation of this passage because it illustrates the standard tactics adopted by the ancients in relation to passages exhibiting Socratic irony – i.e. on Socrates' utterances that seem deliberately to conceal relevant considerations or expertise of his own. Irony is an important issue in the interpretation of the dialogues with which we are currently dealing, because it is hazardous to write off some of the remarks made by Socrates as non-serious, or exhibiting false modesty or other pretence, if one expects others to agree to take seriously all the passages to which one does wish to attribute serious intent. Appeals to irony would have to be disciplined, and there would have to be criteria by which irony can be distinguished. Even then one would have to be able to justify the irony if it involved any potential deceit, for interpreters were usually trying to promote Socrates as some kind of moral paradigm. During the period when those of Stoic sympathy disputed over the heritage of Socrates with Academics of sceptical inclination, it is clear that the latter took Socrates' various professions of ignorance at face value,[26] while the former were inclined to regard them as ironic, as we have seen.[27] Moreover, in the works of Cicero, there was interest in irony as a rhetorical device that tended to cloud any moral doubts about when it should be used.[28]

For professional interpreters it was not at all satisfactory to claim that, in a given passage, 'Socrates' is being ironic *and therefore does not mean what he says*. Plutarch and the anonymous *Theaetetus*-commentator are insistent that the familiar appeal to Socratic irony cannot be used as an excuse for ignoring Socrates' claims of intellectual barrenness in the midwifery section of the *Theaetetus*. These authors would actually reject modesty as an explanation of the alleged irony here, for they observe that Socrates is holding the god responsible for his activities (150c), and even comparing himself with the god (151d). The latter author, commenting on 151c-d, makes the following observation:

> Look what he says about himself, this man they say[29] speaks ironically! He is comparing himself with a god in his benevolence towards humans; and, just as important, that he doesn't agree to falsehood or obscure the truth – in which both the fact of his knowledge and the fact of his goodness are made clear .... (anon. *Tht.* 58.39-52)

The task of the interpreter, according to them, would have been to find some sense in which every statement made by Socrates would be true, and would not involve promoting falsehood or deliberately hiding the truth in the manner forbidden by *Theaetetus* 151d. To ignore statements on the assumption that they were ironic was to fail in one's interpretative duty.[30]

There are a number of cases, even outside the ranks of the Platonists, where straightforward appeals to 'Socratic irony' are rejected. One is to be found in Julian, who argues against neglecting *Philebus* 12b4-6 simply because it sounds ironic, and compares a passage from the lips of the non-ironist 'Timaeus' (40d-e):

> I have used this comparison so that Socrates, by his being a natural ironist, does not offer you the pretext to dishonour the Platonic position (as it does to a number of Platonists apparently). (*Against Heracleius* 24)[31]

Another appears in the Peripatetic Aspasius:

> People say that Socrates was an ironist, but this certainly was not the case; a proof of this is that none of his companions call him by this name, only ordinary persons who misunderstand him, like Thrasymachus or Meno. He used to say he knew nothing, apparently, when comparing human wisdom with divine, ..., and perhaps also, to guard against making boastful and vexatious claims, and not because of any allegiance to falsehood, he underestimated himself, which is not irony. (*On Nicomachean Ethics* 54)

Proclus is more inclined to see irony in Plato's Socrates, and builds on the same observations concerning references to irony in Plato in order to draw rather different conclusions. Talking of *Timaeus* 19c-d, where Socrates laments his inability to picture the inhabitants of his ideal state at war, he notes that some think that a straightforward point is being made: a military encomiast should have military expertise; but others thought that Socrates had plenty of military experience, and is in fact being ironic and pretending not to know. Proclus, perhaps prompted by the talk of the difficulties of imitating things alien to one's own proper upbringing at 19d, thinks that Socrates is actually trying to avoid sinking to a level twice removed from the paradigm that he had presented. But the important point is that he rejects the notion that Socrates would use irony *when talking to men of wisdom*; it is only used, he believes, when addressing sophists and young men (*in Tim.* 1.62.21-5). Sophists would include Thrasymachus, and perhaps Callicles with whom Olympiodorus thinks Socrates uses the occasional irony;[32] young men would include Meno and also Alcibiades from the *Symposium*, who does indeed makes remarks about Socrates' irony (216e).

This passage of Proclus actually comes quite close to associating irony with the *agonistic* and *gymnastic* parts of the corpus, designed to tackle intellectual rivals and to train young men respectively. Together these parts comprise the inquisitive (*zetetic*) parts. Hence Proclus may well be following a tradition concerning irony based on the earlier division of the dialogues, according to which Socrates did use irony in the *inquisitive* works, but refrained from it in the *instructive* ones.[33] Such a division would come close to, though not mirror exactly, the popular modern distinction between 'Socratic' and 'middle' or 'late' dialogues; hence an equivalent modern thesis might be that one finds Socratic irony in Plato's 'Socratic' works but not in others. This correspondence appears particularly plausible when one takes into account the fact that some had detected irony in the words attributed to Socrates by other writers, and that Olympiodorus denies that Plato himself is ironic.[34]

Olympiodorus is alone among commentators in having left us commentaries on two inquisitive works, the *Alcibiades* and the *Gorgias*, and he finds harmless cases of Socrates being ironic in both works.[35] Yet he will not admit to the kind of irony that would turn Socrates into a dissembler, and finds some truth or valid moral purpose in every case. For instance, on *Gorgias* 489d7-8, he makes the following observation:

> He may be speaking ironically, but at least he is making an honest point. For he is teaching him not to be rough but mild.[36]

As may be seen from *In Alc.* 88, Olympiodorus will always look for a sense, a deeper sense if necessary, in which Socrates is telling the truth:

> One must inquire how, if even the ironic utterances of the philosopher must be true, Socrates who knows what justice is now says to the young man, 'Tell me who it was from whom you learnt justice, so that I can study with him.' Either we claim that the lover must share the ignorance and the cure with those he loves, and so qua lover Socrates couldn't understand justice because the young man couldn't, whereas qua teacher he did know; or, as an alternative solution, that Socrates would either study with somebody better and be helped, or with somebody worse and help him, or with an equal, and 'the property of friends is shared'.

Both solutions actually make Socrates' wish a reality, so that the invitation to reveal the teacher's name is genuine, and both seem to give a visit to this teacher a moral purpose. But it should be noted that the first solution, that of having Socrates, qua lover, share the ignorance of youth who needs educating, could have had a wide application among the dialogues in which the young men whose education is currently Socrates' concern witness contradictory arguments from a seemingly ignorant Socrates. It explains not only why Socrates should sometimes *express* ignorance, but also why he should *appear* ignorant.

By Olympiodorus' day the issue of irony was no longer pressing. It had long been assumed that the interpreter's task is to tease out the meaning of what Plato has written, and to show in what manner it is true or suggests a moral lesson. Hence to write off anything which is said by any spokesman-like character in a Platonic dialogue, whether as irony or as non-serious in some other way, is to back away from the proper task of the interpreter. Furthermore the nature of the Neoplatonic curriculum, with its strong emphasis on dialogues where Plato was clearly expounding doctrine and its neglect of most of the works which we might be tempted to describe as 'Socratic', actually meant that they had to wrestle with few problems associated with Socrates, including problems of irony. But reverence for Plato's admired teacher ensured that they continued to adopt an attitude to his irony comparable with that of the Middle Platonists earlier.

iv. Socrates and Protagoras

This seeming digression on irony was necessary before discussion of the *Protagoras*, a work in which almost every position that Socrates seems to be adopting could easily be held to be presented either for the sake of the argument or in a manner so contentious that his commitment to the truth has been suspended. The two theses which he seems to adopt early in his discussion with Protagoras are (i) that virtue cannot be taught (319b-320b), and (ii) that all five parts of virtue, one of which is 'wisdom' or 'knowledge', are all identical (330b ff.). Yet he observes at the climax of the work (361a-b) that knowledge would be that thing most likely to be teachable, and to make all virtues one would be to make them all knowledge, so that his two theses are scarcely compatible. Again Socrates' exposition of Simonides' poem at 342a-347a involves a number of counter-intuitive claims, among them that the Spartans are intellectually superior, that the only way to fare well or badly is to have or to lack knowledge, that no educated person could *imagine* anybody doing something base or bad willingly, and that Pittacus had been making the *grossest of blunders* in saying that it is hard to be good, when he should have said that it is hard to become good, and impossible to be good. The following argument for courage being knowledge (349e-350c) can easily be taken to be flippant in the light of Protagoras' subsequent claim that Socrates had argued wrongly. And the further attempt to show that courage is knowledge is based upon the notion that we all have to pursue those courses of action which involve for us the greatest possible balance of pleasure over pain, which seems at odds with the anti-hedonist attitude taken by Socrates elsewhere, and is usually taken to be an example of *ad hominem* argument.

How then do later Platonists respond to the rather eristic, and perhaps even dishonest Socrates of the *Protagoras*? Very few could have taken the theory of a hedonistic calculus propounded at 353-7 seriously, for it would have brought their own philosophy too close for comfort to that of the arch-enemy Epicurus.[37] Though later Platonists may recognise and value a higher pleasure, perhaps even one associated with god(s),[38] any thought that pleasures were all qualitatively the same (so as to be able to be measured against each other) would be resisted. But was the hedonism passage so special? What of the other positions for which Socrates argues?

For the most part they certainly would not assume that the theses with which he had been operating were true. It is standard Middle Platonic doctrine, seemingly from the time of Antiochus of Ascalon through to that of Plotinus and beyond, that the virtues are one in the sense that anybody possessing one will possess them all, at least in the case of the *perfected* virtues.[39] Yet this doctrine of *antakolouthia* or mutual implication makes only a small concession to the Socratic theme of the unity of the virtues in the extravagant form that it takes in the *Protagoras*. Common sense resists any notion that the virtue-terms are simply five names for the one thing (329d1), or are parts of the one whole in the sense that the parts of a lump of gold were parts: without employing any differences of property or function (d6-8). At least in the argument concerning temperance and wisdom (332a-333b) it is the stronger identity thesis that is argued for, but Platonists gave precedence to the theories of *Republic* 4, whereby the virtues are separately defined, and have their own roles to play both in the city and in the constitution of the individual soul. Later Platonists would mostly have given the same answers to Socrates' questions at 329d that Protagoras gives, and on the further question at 329e2-4, as to whether the same individual would always have all the virtues, some of them at least would distinguish between stronger and weaker senses of the virtue-terms, and not insist on mutual implication for anything other than perfected virtue.[40]

As for the teachability of virtue, which Socrates in the *Protagoras* seems inclined to deny, a Middle Platonist was most likely to compromise along the same lines as Alcinous: the virtue proper to the rational part of the soul would be teachable, but not the virtues that belong to non-rational parts (*Didasc.* 30.3), or only in the cases where these latter are perfected.[41] Progress towards their perfection will be brought about by other means. This means, in fact, that the path towards the acquisition of virtue is a highly complex one. Middle Platonists would not deny the relevance of (i) natural good qualities, (ii) practice and habituation, or (iii) teaching to its successful fulfilment. Alcinous is quite specific that all three contribute towards our final goal of assimilation to the divine (28.4), a goal which is for him achieved through the acquisition of virtue: since it is a virtuous god to which we assimilate ourselves (28.3). What this means is that he and his fellow-Platonists would recognise the account of virtue-acquisition which the character Protagoras offers in this dialogue, involving as it does natural abilities (327b), and more especially practice and teaching (323c-d), as being extremely close to the truth.

At this point it should be becoming clear that later Platonists actually have at least as much regard for the positions adopted by Protagoras in this dialogue as those seemingly adopted by Socrates. Protagoras' theory is most clearly put in his long speech (320-8) which begins with the myth of the origins of humans and of the social virtues, and we frequently find all or parts of this speech being treated as if it reflected the thought of Plato himself. The most obvious case is Proclus' treatment of the myth as a key text for the study of Plato's theology,[42] and in the Plutarchian essay *On Chance* (*Mor.* 98d) the account of the creation of humans seems to be taken as Plato's own.[43] Protagoras' eloquent attack on punishment as revenge rather than as a cure and deterrent (324a-b) must also have been noticed,[44] and of course his views on the origins of virtue, as we have seen.

Where does this leave those who are committed to finding truth in the words of Socrates? Where does it leave the anti-ironists who are committed to acknowledging the basic honesty of all his declarations? They would surely have been struggling to find such truth and frankness in some parts of the literary digression, such as that which proclaimed the proud philosophical heritage of Sparta, but there was no special problem with the main philosophical themes simply because Socrates only appears to adopt certain positions, but never finally commits himself. Again, just as an anti-ironist could claim in respect of the *Alcibiades* that Socrates qua lover somehow shared in the ignorance of the young man who was his concern, so too it could be claimed with some justification that Socrates was trying to put himself in the position of the young Hippocrates on whose behalf the interrogation of Protagoras takes place.[45] Moreover, Socrates' purpose here is less the discovery of the truth than the testing of Protagoras' credentials to advance the moral education of Hippocrates, and Socrates is trying to ensure throughout that the true value of Protagorean education is revealed. Finally, the comparative youth of Socrates in this work, as revealed chiefly by the final prophecy of Protagoras that he *will become* renowned for wisdom (361e), could easily be used to excuse his inadequacies.

Although ancient ingenuity might save the Socrates of this dialogue from condemnation, it remains a fact that much of value was found in the words of his eminent opponent. It is significant, then, that though antiquity acknowledged that the work had some kind of polemical purpose, placing it in the 'agonistic' or competitive species of the inquisitive class of dialogues, it did not place it in the same sub-species as the *Euthydemus*, *Gorgias*, and two *Hippias* dialogues. These four were seen as 'over-turning', i.e. as setting out to throw Socrates' opponent, but the *Protagoras* is unique in being seen as 'endeictic', a word whose meaning is less than clear, but which may have the milder meaning of 'exposing' since it is associated with a verb of showing. I have discussed the meaning of the term elsewhere,[46] but the key issue is the nature of the *distinction* between over-turning and endeictic method. That distinction is surely to be found at *Theaetetus* 167e, quoted in Chapter 6 iii. Protagoras himself is found in Plato demanding a more serious level of debate, which involves showing up any errors in the other's reasoning, but avoids trying to lead them into making mistakes or fallaciously drawing unwelcome conclusions. Hence, when Plato has Socrates argue with Protagoras there should be an effort on the part of both speakers to tackle the true position of the other, and to point out any problems with that position. Does this requirement pertain to the *Protagoras*? Does it pertain any more than to the *Gorgias* and *Hippias Major*?

Here we must leave our own answers aside, and ask ourselves what reasons the ancients might have had for answering these two questions in the affirmative. The behaviour of Socrates does not seem any more exemplary here than in other polemical works, and Protagoras even says towards the end (360e), 'It seems to me, Socrates, that you are being contentious in claiming that I am the one giving answers.' What we can point to, I believe, is a number of cases where Protagoras politely points out places where Socrates gets things wrong. The long speech contains various passages where Protagoras turns to Socrates and shows what it is that he has not taken into account;[47] he makes various good points in response to Socrates simplistic notion of resemblance;[48] and even when annoyed he can make valid points.[49] Finally, at 350c6-351b2 he can explain carefully what he thinks has been fallacious in Socrates' reasoning. Socrates himself is quite correct in pointing out the inconsistency of Protagoras' recent admissions at 333a-b, and at 335a-b Protagoras' dissatisfaction with his own earlier answers might be taken as a sign that Socrates had asked his questions and drawn the consequences fairly. At no point is there much doubt that some kind of contest is taking place between the two, but there is constant engagement with important issues that lifts the main discussion above the level of eristic quibbling.[50] As in the part of the *Theaetetus* to which he is relevant, much of the credit for lifting the tone of the conversation must go to Protagoras, who is treated by Plato with more respect than other sophists.

This higher level of discussion is some justification for the *Protagoras* having been put in a special category: inquisitive, and hence exposing falsehoods rather than establishing truth; competitive, and hence involving debate between rivals; but not over-turning, and hence not making its principal purpose the undermining of the very practices in which the rival engages. Protagoras is in fact treated as a *philosophic* rival, which cannot be said for Gorgias, Hippias, or Euthydemus. While I doubt whether the

endeictic character, or any characters, were originally meant as descriptions applied to dialogues rather than passages, and I suspect that
'endeictic' was meant to apply to conversations between Socrates and
Protagoras anywhere in the corpus, it remains clear that it would always
have been closely bound up with this most important and extended
engagement with Protagoras, and that important figures in the history of
the organisation of the corpus had no difficulty in seeing the work itself as
unique in its approach. The special 'character' which Middle Platonist
times allotted to this dialogue agrees well with their ability to find at least
as much moral philosophy in positions adopted by Protagoras as in those
preferred by Socrates.

This stands in sharp contrast to the *Euthydemus* and *Hippias*, dialogues that, though read and alluded to widely enough, seem never to have
become a major source of any Platonist thought in antiquity. That they
were seen as polemical works, which made the overturning of one's opponent a priority, would not have assisted in establishing their importance.
The *Euthydemus*, of course, was often seen as Plato's work on sophistic
refutations, and something of a repository of fallacious arguments and
strange syllogistic. This is clearly the case in Alcinous (*Didasc.* 6.8) and
Alexander refers to it a number of times in the commentary on Aristotle's
De Sophisticis Elenchis. It is also interesting that Galen's compendia of
Platonic dialogues, as known to the Arab world, included this work in a
single book of epitomes of *logical* dialogues: after *Cratylus*, *Sophist*, *Politicus*, and *Parmenides*,[51] though we cannot of course be sure of the
rationale behind this. Deeper content was probably detected in the sections that bypass the sophists, but the *Didascalicus* only makes any
obvious use of 281-2.[52] Material from 280-1 is also noted by Olympiodorus,[53] who, like Clement,[54] also notices 290b-d and 291d-e.[55] One reason
why such passages in a dialogue like the *Euthydemus* would attract
attention is that they have links with other works such as the *Meno* and
Republic, and can thus be used rather more confidently than most of the
content: some of which degenerates into farce.

The most serious in tone of the polemical works was clearly the *Gorgias*.
This could never be treated so lightly by Platonists, and material illustrating the history of its interpretation abounds. Moral teaching seems to be
far more closely bound up with the polemical content than it does in other
comparable works, and it will therefore be to the *Gorgias* to which our next
chapter turns. But there are other issues concerning the interpretation of
the early dialogues that should be dealt with first.

v. The Socratic elenchus

Talk of the Socratic elenchus is now routinely part of scholarship concerning Plato's portrait of Socrates in all or most of the so-called 'early'
dialogues. This used not to be the case until Gregory Vlastos' pioneering

article of 1983, in which he complained that Socrates' principal tool of philosophic discovery had been rather neglected. Whether *Plato* ever credited Socrates with a truth-yielding armoury accurately described as an 'elenchus' is debatable, for it is easily observed that the terminology of *elenchos* is sparsely used in the relevant dialogues *outside the Gorgias and the Euthydemus*. When it is used, it is generally in conversation between Socrates and his sophistic opponents rather than his friends. Whether Plato saw Socrates as having his own special elenchus, or simply as having practised elenchus in a slightly different way from orators and sophists, is again unclear.

What we must discuss here is whether the ancients saw in Plato's Socrates special reasoning processes, different from those of his opponents and from those of Plato, and if so whether they interpreted these processes as making progress towards the truth. Plutarch (*Mor.* 999e) speaks of Socrates employing his elenctic *Logos* rather like a cathartic drug. His words suggest that *elenchos* constitutes a straightforward description of Socratic activity, while *catharsis* is a mere metaphor: one of a number of medical metaphors for this same activity. Yet Plutarch had been reflecting on *Sophist* 230b-d when treating *Theaetetus* 150 without reference to our putatively early dialogues, and ancient Platonism works without any clear notion of a Socratic *elenchos*. We might have had some expectation of discovering the notion of Socratic *elenchos* in various authors: in anon. *In Theaetetum* (which uses the term *zetesis* rather than *elenchos* to charac-terise Socratic activity); in the Olympiodoran and Proclan commentaries on the *Alcibiades*, which identify (at 11 and 14 respectively) the earlier part of the work only to 119a as 'elenctic'; and in Olympiodorus' *In Gorgiam*. Once in Olympiodorus (*In Alc.* 87) we meet the phrase 'Socratic admonitions and *elenchoi*', but is has a decidedly untechnical ring, unlike the modern 'Socratic *elenchos*'; while in his *Gorgias*-commentary, which seemingly draws on a long tradition,[56] and where he is conscious of the importance of *elenchos*, he never suggests that the term means anything special when applied to the activities of Socrates.

Olympiodorus finds in the *Gorgias* a debate between rival parties, *both* of which try to examine and refute the other, and both of which utilise elenchus in their own customary way. He does not discern here two different elenchi, Socratic and rhetorical, but finds a single elenchus used differently by philosophers and rhetors: well by the former, badly by the latter. The absence from Olympiodorus' *Gorgias*-commentary of any clear concept of a Socratic elenchus, as distinct from a correct philosophic manner of elenchus, is interesting given that Vlastos built much of his theory of the elenchus on this dialogue (even while seeing it as the latest dialogue in his 'early' group). While Olympiodorus has actually anticipated many of Vlastos' claims about Socrates' arguments, in particular about the presence of true moral beliefs residing within questioner and interlocu-tors, he explains this with reference to one's awareness (conscious or unconscious) of common notions, which are the foundation of *philosophic demonstration in general* – not just of Socratic elenchus.

A passage that nicely illustrates Olympiodorus' treatment of an elenchus conducted by Socrates can be found at *In Gorgiam* 10.1-2, where the refutation of Gorgias himself is discussed (460a-461b). The author discovers four premises in a demonstrative elenchus. That the orator knows about justice (A) is granted by the interlocutor, on the basis of the 'common notion' that each craft knows its subject matter (11.2). That one who performs just deeds is not unjust (D) is universally granted. Two further premises have to be established: that one who knows about justice wants it (B), and that one who wants it does it (C). These premises are strung together syllogistically in order to show that the orator will not commit injustice; that in turn is in contradiction with Gorgias' expressed view that the orator can in fact be unjust. Hence Olympiodorus fully believes that the elenchus has shown a contradiction in Gorgias' set of beliefs; he also realises that the same set of arguments cannot be used to defeat Polus, who does not grant A. So elenchus functions on a personal level, unlike ordinary demonstration.

All this sounds fairly familiar, picking out Socrates' habit of eliciting from the interlocutor two or more premises which do not agree with each other, and going on to demonstrate the contradiction between them. Would it be wrong, then, to claim that the ancients saw nothing special about the way in which Socrates argues in the so-called early dialogues? Olympiodorus is aware of *tactics* used by Socrates to keep the interlocutor responding, including changes in the natural order of the argument (9.3), and a non-combative approach (8.1). But he does not seem to be aware of any formal features of the argument that would set it apart from philosophical argument in general. Socratic arguments can be syllogised like any other, and they are likely to appeal to common notions or *endoxa* like any other. Socrates simply employs elenchus philosophically. Philosophic elenchus is contrasted with a baser form at 8.1; the contrast is probably inspired by (i) the contrasting picture of eristic in the *Euthydemus* and (ii) the distinction put into the mouth of Protagoras between serious dialectic and attempts to trip up an opponent regardless,[57] rather than by the contrasting views of elenchus that emerge in discussion with Polus (470c-472c) and that attract little attention in lectures 18 and 19.

Also worth mentioning at 8.1 is the view that philosophers in general are committed to using the elenchus cathartically to drive out false opinions from the soul, much as doctors must drive out harmful physical substances from the body. The ultimate source of the medical analogy is *Sophist* 230b-e, where it is applied to an especially noble form of sophistry, though generations have thought these words to have been inspired by Socratic practice. For Olympiodorus, this cathartic-elenchus is simply a part of proper philosophic practice, but note that it is seen as expelling false opinions only. There is no hint here that properly conducted elenchus will lead to the truth, and indeed one should recall that in Middle Platonist times dialogues aiming at elenchus, i.e. inquisitive dialogues in general, aimed at the refutation of falsehood; only the instructive dialogues aimed at the establishment of truth.[58] Elenchus was associated by antiquity, just as it is by us, with certain of the dialogues in which Socrates was protagonist; but it was not because the group was conceived of as uniformly early or Socratic, but rather because it was uniformly concerned with inquiry rather than teaching. Middle Platonism also recognised the cathartic-elenchus as the Plutarch passage referred to above shows, and Albinus associated this with a sub-species of the 'inquisitive' dialogues: the 'peirastic' type that began the philosophic programme of *Prologus* 6.

So one may conclude that the ancients (i) could work adequately without a concept of a specifically Socratic elenchus, (ii) saw elenchus as a part of inquiry, and (iii) did not see it as a truth-giving process in its own right. I shall discuss elsewhere the limited implications this may have for our own view of elenchus.

vi. Starting the curriculum

We have yet to tackle an important dialogue for later Platonism, which is usually placed in this early group, when it is not held to be spurious: the *Alcibiades I*. Its importance lies in the existence of two Neoplatonist commentaries on it, a fragment of papyrus commentary, and a prominent position at the head of a number of reading-programmes: that of later Neoplatonism in general, that of Albinus in *Prologus* 5, and that of the anonymous corpus-arranger in al-Farabi.[59] It had not always been so favoured, for it was absent from the arrangement of Aristophanes of Byzantium, and heads the *fourth* tetralogy of Thrasyllus, leading the four tetralogies in which the education of the young and the refutation of sophists are a primary concern. Diogenes knew of further works with which educators chose to begin: *Theages, Clitophon, Timaeus, Phaedrus,* and *Theaetetus*; Albinus would apparently begin elsewhere with certain pupils; but in time the *Alcibiades* certainly came to be the accepted introductory work, and Proclus is able to defend this with some quite elaborate theory (*In Alc.* 1-11).

In a sense this position of prominence has quite a simple reason: this work best teaches us to know ourselves: to know that we are really soul, and rational soul at that. Soul is the true 'self' (*auto*) that remains the same and remains the true subject of our actions. Body is relegated to the position of an instrument, utilised by the soul for its own purposes. As such it cannot have been much used by Antiochus of Ascalon, who seems to have emphasised the *double* nature of the human being, specifically choosing to attack the Stoics on the ground that they make us soul alone.[60] In fact, it would have better suited the Stoics themselves to give prominence to this work in their treatment of Plato. Insofar as it was Socratic it could be treated as their heritage as well as any other school's, and insofar as it was Plato it served to enlist his support for their emphasis on the well-being of the soul even if the body suffers.

The interpretation of the *Alcibiades* is for us such a problem that there are a great many scholars who dispute its authenticity, and many others who, while not convinced that it is spurious, nevertheless fail to make any significant use of it in their portrait of the Platonic Socrates. It divides naturally into two parts, which are separated by a laudation of the educational advantages of the Kings of Sparta and of Persia (121a-124b). The first part seems very Socratic, asking all sorts of questions about expertise and demonstrating to Alcibiades that he does not have the knowledge required for leadership of the type that he seeks, using both the theme of the *Meno* concerning the inconstancy of mere opinion and the theme of the *Apology* that the worst ignorance is thinking one knows what one does not know. There is a handbook-like quality which makes us painfully aware that Plato is not writing a research document in any sense, nor trying to focus on any single aspect of Socratic philosophy. Following this the interlude on the royal education of Athens' enemies seems too generous towards those systems, though the praise may be interpreted as ironic, and the final section, designed to show that we should take care of our true selves, i.e. our souls rather than our bodies, seems to say rather less well what is said in the *Phaedo*, and to use language which *sounds* Platonic rather than Socratic, but which is still not used in a routine Platonic sense. The conclusion of the work sees Alcibiades deciding, like a good pupil, to devote himself to Socrates, and does not have any of the *tension* that one expects from Plato. Indeed Alcibiades, in spite of an abundance of material underlining his natural gifts, had been throughout a rather lack-lustre interlocutor, with none of the natural brilliance that one expects to see in him, slow to learn, unable to contribute significantly to the discussion, and content in the end to meekly follow Socrates.

Now what are difficulties for the modern interpreter could easily become advantages among those of a different period. It suited them well if Socrates' themes could be reduced to a handbook-like format and still somehow find room for the important place that the exposure of culpable ignorance plays in a Socratic education programme. It suited them well that there should be a blend of Socratic and Platonic content, with the Socrates who induces *aporia* eventually transformed into an effective teacher. It suited them well if the argument can been seen persuading one destined to be an inspiring politician that he first needs a Socratic education, and it suited them well that the new follower should behave in a surprisingly cooperative manner. The Alcibiades of the dialogue is at the beginning independently minded, well endowed in body and soul, wealthy, of noble birth and with powerful connections (104a-c). He is also bent on glory and determined to succeed (104e-5c). He is precisely the kind of pupil that a philosopher determined to gain widespread fame would wish to have as his pupil. The Alcibiades-type would best see the advantages of Socratic-Platonic philosophy by experiencing a work in which Socrates tailors his questions to the young Alcibiades himself.

It is therefore not surprising that our earliest evidence for this work heading a Platonic education-programme makes it quite specific that such a programme is designed for the *ideal* recruit. Albinus (*Prologus* 5) recognises five significant areas in which his pupils might differ: they might have great natural aptitude or none, they might be of an ideal age or beyond their prime, they might be studying philosophy with philosophic or non-philosophic ends in mind, they might have a good general education or none at all, and they might have the leisure for philosophy or be impeded by the distractions of public life. Ideally, they will be endowed with natural aptitude, of the correct age, studying with a view to achieving excellence, educated in the preparatory disciplines, and free from political distractions. This fits Alcibiades sufficiently well for Albinus' picture of the ideal pupil to have been drawn *directly* from this dialogue. He has aptitude in abundance; he is not too young because the god had not permitted Socrates to converse with him at a time when the message would have been wasted (105e); he strives for excellence in public life; he has studied everything expected of an Athenian except *aulos*-playing which would be irrelevant; and he is not yet quite of an age to be occupied with public affairs (106c). The *Alcibiades I* is thus being marketed by Albinus as an ideal introduction for those who had the attributes of Alcibiades as portrayed within the dialogue. This has considerable interpretative significance, for it shows him working according to the general principle that dialogues are designed for persons who have the same attributes as the principal interlocutors.

Albinus thought that the *Alcibiades* would assist the pupil to 'change direction, turn inwards, and recognise what it was that he should be caring for', the latter clearly being his soul.[61] This leads naturally on to the next dialogue in the programme, the *Phaedo*, where one might learn what the philosopher is, what he practises, and how this practice is linked to the belief in the soul's immortality. The *Republic* will then show our pupil how education in excellence must proceed, and the *Timaeus* will provide insights into theology. One might note that the *Phaedo and Republic* both largely employ interlocutors who can be seen as gifted auditors of Socrates, and hence are used for the education of persons with Alcibiades' main attributes *after they are already committed to looking for philosophy's guidance*. If one may see Timaeus' long speech as being addressed to Socrates himself, then that work might be seen as designed for one who had already achieved the status of an accomplished moral and political philosopher.

Since a great deal of speculation has been devoted over the years to the status of this education-programme in *Prologus* 5, and to its relationship to the order of dialogue-groups in chapter 6, this would be an appropriate place to say a little more about these matters.[62] It is quite clear that the reading-order of chapter 5 is *only an example*, but it is an example that would apply to the *preferred pupil*. Hence it is the order that the teacher would wish to be using, and presumably an order commonly employed by Albinus and perhaps also by his teacher Gaius. There must have been a small selection of texts which were regularly lectured on, and we should have expected them to include the works most regularly commented upon: since the rise of the commentary clearly relates to the institution of new text-based classroom practices. All major Platonist commentators would surely have left commentaries on all or part of the *Timaeus*, and most on the *Phaedo* as well.[63] The *Republic* seems also to have attracted commentaries in the Middle Platonist period, from such figures as Potamo of Alexandria, Taurus of Sidon (?), and (at least in part) Dercyllides. A fragment of commentary on the *Alcibiades* also survives. So it is not unexpected that Gaius or Albinus should have been found lecturing on all these works. Similarly, there are several works in the Platonic corpus that they are most unlikely to have been lectured on regularly. This makes it likely that the reading-order of chapter 5 is mentioned simply because it conforms with the normal practice of the school. Modifications might have been made to allow for other groups, but any suggestion that there should have been 32 different reading orders, beginning with any of 32 approved dialogues, is clearly outrageous.[64]

The order of dialogues encountered in chapter 6 concerns the appropriate way to order the dialogues themselves *in accordance with Platonic teaching*,[65] and has nothing to do with the order of any prescribed education-programme. Nobody, in fact, was going to read all dialogues of one group, followed by all of another, and all of another after that. However, because Albinus *denies* the existence of a fixed order of dialogues in the instruction of pupils, he is now adding some thoughts about how the dialogues might nevertheless best be arranged. The best *arrangement* will be based on *theoretical* steps in Platonic education, which does of course relate to programmes of reading designed for the individual, but does not have to be identical with any. The separation of reading order from the arrangement of the corpus might perhaps be an innovation of Albinus.

Albinus cannot be left before we take note of the *character* or type of dialogue to which both he (3) and Diogenes Laertius (3.51) assign the *Alicibiades*. It is said to be a *maieutic* dialogue, that is to say one which draws out and clarifies the individual's inner ideas so that they may be come to light, according to the theory that Socrates is a kind of midwife of ideas (*Theaetetus* 149-51). Albinus (6) thinks that these inner ideas are the 'natural notions', commonly regarded as true and dependable source of knowledge by Platonists and other philosophers of the period, so that there is the implication that Alcibiades is made to 'give birth to' some *truth* within himself which is subsequently made clear by Socrates. This inner truth is of course the doctrine of the final part concerning the soul being the true self, and it is no accident that the Neoplatonists found in this part and this part alone the *maieutic* content of the dialogue.[66] According to them at least there were two further parts of the work, the first (to 119a) being elenctic, and the second (to 124b) protreptic. So the education of Alcibiades here culminates in the emergence of the natural notions, but begins rather with cathartic elenchus. Cathartic elenchus is associated by Albinus with the *peirastic* dialogues rather than with *maieutic* ones, so that there is every chance that he did not conceive of this work as purely *maieutic*, but rather as some kind of combination. This can explain for us why the order of dialogues in chapter 6 places *peirastic* dialogues before *maieutic* ones even though Albinus' preferred educational programme began with the allegedly *maieutic Alcibiades*. Dialogues did not have to be homogeneous in character, and this work actually began with a *peirastic* section, so that the favoured pupil did not miss this stage, but passed over it in half a dialogue. For committed dogmatist teachers of Plato the *Alcibiades* in fact constituted sufficient coverage for the Socratic activities of elenchus and midwifery to lead up to the philosopher's main purpose: the delivery of doctrine.

A rather different programme that used the *Alcibiades* as a starting-point is known to us only from the Arab philosopher al-Farabi, but stems nevertheless from some Middle Platonist source.[67] Here each work in the standard corpus seems originally to have been listed[68] in a manner supposedly reflecting Plato's own order of inquiry, but clearly meant to suggest an appropriate reading-order for Plato's pupils. The programme begins with a series of five dialogues pointing to the existence of a life-science, related to our status as human-beings (*Alcibiades I*), the object of discussion in the *Theaetetus*, leading to true happiness (*Lysis*?), able to be achieved (*Protagoras*), and achieved by inquiry (*Meno*). One should note that all these dialogues, if *Lysis* is correctly identified, are of the so-called zetetic group and are looking forward to what humans might achieve rather than making any great steps along that road. The *Alcibiades* is recognised as a work that deals with the importance of knowledge for human happiness, and as one that actually asks what a human being really is. In this latter respect the arrangement seems influenced by the subtitle afforded to the dialogue by Thrasyllus (DL 3.59), 'On the Nature of a Human Being', and to give absolute preference to self-knowledge over knowledge of any other kind.

While the *Alcibiades* tells us little that is not also able to be derived from other dialogues, it did rise to fame in antiquity, perhaps because its prominent position in curricula ensured that it became well known to teachers and pupils alike. Before Albinus, however, there is virtually no sign of its importance in Plutarch, and there is a similar lack of direct influence over the pages of Alcinous.[69] Odd allusions in Maximus of Tyre and Clement do nothing to alter the picture of a dialogue that had been somewhat neglected in circles uninfluenced by Gaius and Albinus. In the second century the author using it most regularly in extant work is Aristides,[70] and we shall see in Chapter 9 that his anti-Platonic works are directed specifically against their school, and employ the dialogues in a way which would reflect Albinus' use of them.

From false art to true

A Neoplatonist history of the interpretation of *Gorgias*

For our first detailed case-study, we look at the *Gorgias*; the work is particularly rich because of its employment of three chief interlocutors, its rich uses of myth and analogy, and the breadth and variety of its subject matter. At first sight there seems to be a tendency for the subject to broaden or shift as the dialogue progresses and as one interlocutor takes over from another. Any shift is not such as to compromise the literary or philosophic unity, but it contributes to the diversity of the work, which might be represented in the following schema:

	Interlocutor	*Subject*
1.	Gorgias	Rhetoric and its *dynamis*
2.	Polus	Justice superior to injustice
3.	Callicles	The best life
[4.	(The Myth)	Rewards of justice]

McAvoy (1999, 221) writes of the work as follows:

> This must surely strike most readers as the darkest and most tense of the dialogues, building up from the skirmish with the urbane Gorgias, then the battle with the petulant Polus, to the all-out war with the vituperative Callicles. Socrates too seems aggressive and angry, and especially when we consider the horrors of his final myth. It is tempting to see the melancholy passion of Plato here imposing itself, or some relation of the Athenian Stranger.

The same division is present here, but there is little else in this powerful image that can be matched in ancient testimony. The *colour* of a dialogue was not of great interest, whether as a device promoting literary unity or a source for insights into the author's mind. Cicero suggests they were more struck by the work's paradoxical eloquence (*De Oratore* 1.47). The thought that the author's passions might emerge, or that Socrates gives way to anger and aggression, would have reduced the status of both in the eyes of commentators who turned both into paragons of virtue. The sinister reference to the Athenian Stranger would have been totally lost. Where then did the ancients find interest in this work? Where did they find its unity, if not in its moods and in the mind of the author?

Unity in late antiquity was determined by the dialogue's *target*, the ultimate goal to which it is designed to bring us closer. All facets of the work, literary and philosophical, are to be explained with reference to this.[1] Olympiodorus, author of the sole surviving ancient commentary, who himself rightly demands that the dialogue should have this kind of single overriding purpose, gives an account of the positions of earlier interpreters:

> As for the *target* of the dialogue, different views have been taken of it. Some say that *its target is to discuss rhetoric*, and they give it the heading '*Gorgias, or On Rhetoric*', but wrongly so. For they describe the whole on the basis of a part. [Socrates] speaks with Gorgias about rhetoric, and it is from this that they derive the target of the dialogue, even though that discussion is not extensive. And others say that it *discusses justice and injustice*, because the just are happy and the unjust unlucky and wretched; the more unjust somebody is, the more wretched he is too; the more chronic his injustice, the more wretched still; and if it is immortal he is far more wretched still. These people too extract the target of the dialogue from a part of it, i.e. from the arguments against Polus. Others say that the *target is to speak about the creator*, since in the myth [Socrates] speaks of the creator as we shall learn. Their view too is strange and highly selective. We say that the target is to speak about *the ethical principles that lead to constitutional well-being*. (Olymp. *In Grg*. proem 4)

There is similar discussion of them in an anonymous author from the same school, who is illustrating a long list of methods for ascertaining the target of any dialogue:

> And again we criticise those who say that Plato's target in the *Gorgias* is to speak about whether it is better to act justly or unjustly. For he teaches about this in a small part of the dialogue, but about the moral principles of happiness in the whole dialogue. ....
> [We also discern his target] on the basis of superior and inferior, so that we choose the superior aim over the inferior. Hence we do not accept them telling us that he [Plato] has the target of criticising the rhetoric of Gorgias and Polus in the *Gorgias*: for that's a base and sophistic thing; his proposal is to discuss true rhetoric, which is better and admirable. ....
> [We also discern his target] on the basis of harmonious and discordant, so that we choose what is in harmony with his words over what does not accord [with them]. Using this rule, we refute those who say that the *Gorgias* has as its target to discuss the Self-Seeing Intellect. For this is altogether alien, and not in accord with what he says there. (anon. *Proleg*. 22.8-12, 39-58)

Our two sources are agreed that each group of these interpreters build their account of the work's primary subject upon a single part of it only. Some saw the basic target as deriving from the discussion with 'Gorgias' where the question concerns the nature of rhetoric itself, and regarded the work as a polemic against both Gorgias and Polus. Others thought that it was in fact more constructive, and was intended to convince us that justice is altogether better for the person who practises it than injustice. A third group, whom I have argued to be Iamblichus and his immediate followers,[2] want to make the work tell us about some kind of creator-god who is also a self-seeing intellect. They belong to a time when allegorical and symbolic interpretation had become an art-form, so that not only Plato, but Homer and Hesiod were thought to be hinting at deep Neoplatonic doctrines about theology and the like. The subject or 'target' of Plato's *Sophist*, which others interpreted variously as concerned with sophists, true being, or what is not true being, becomes the Creator of the world beneath the moon. This appears strange indeed, but can be easily understood.

The initial task is to compare the account of earlier interpretation against what we know from other sources. Throughout we must bear in mind certain key questions which were bound to affect an interpreter's stance from the outset. Was the author of an exegesis a philosopher committed to finding *truth* in Plato? Were these people *users* of rhetoric of not? Were they trying to make sense of just *one* dialogue, or a whole corpus? Were they committed to any *principles* of interpretation? Did they resort to *allegorical* interpretation? Did they regard the dialogues as *divinely inspired*? In general, of course, the more highly they regarded Plato the more ingeniously they had to set about reconciling one passage with another in order that all difficulties should be resolved, and Plato would eventually be found to be philosophising in a manner with which they themselves could agree. Ideals of exegetical impartiality were not prominent: it was quite common for people's livelihood to depend upon their manner of handling the texts of Plato. They had to put up a plausible case for Plato being broadly in agreement with what they now stood for.

ii. Pre-Neoplatonic interpretation of *Gorgias*:
(1) on rhetoric

The earliest known arrangement of Plato's dialogues, that of Aristophanes of Byzantium, did not include the *Gorgias* in its five trilogies, perhaps causing it to be less widely read than it deserved. But Cicero, who is familiar with the work, as one would expect of a writer whose interests included both philosophy and rhetoric, makes it clear in the *De Oratore* that under the guidance of Charmadas the *Gorgias* was read in the Academy at the end of the second century BC, in close conjunction with the *Phaedrus*.[3] The focus here suggests that it was regarded principally as a text about rhetoric, though it is possible that we are receiving a rather unbalanced view from reports in a theoretical work about oratory. We are told that Crassus (*De Orat*. 1.47) studied the *Gorgias* with the Academic Charmadas, and he appears to regard it as a *critique of oratory*: a direct attack on Sicilian rhetoric designed to overthrow its claims to fame. As we know from Proclus, there were in fact a number of Platonic works which had once been seen primarily as dialectical attacks on opponents including *Parmenides* (attacking mainly Zeno the Eleatic, and his 40 *logoi*), *Theaetetus* (attacking Protagoras, perhaps throughout the dialogue),[4] *Phaedrus* (attacking Lysias), and *Menexenus* (attacking the funeral oration of Pericles in Thucydides).[5] Since this interpretation of the *Parmenides* appears to have been the earliest known to Proclus, it is quite likely that these interpretations also go back to the Academy's use of Plato in its sceptical era. Since the Academic Sceptics engaged in attacking the views of others while concealing their own beliefs, they welcomed the chance to claim that Plato was doing the same thing.

Cicero's Antonius had heard the prominent Academic Charmadas utilising the *Gorgias* for an attack on rhetoric in those circumstances where it is divorced from philosophy, and consequently picking a fight with non-philosophic rhetorical teachers at Athens (1.84 ff). It is likely that Charmadas' *Gorgias*-related activities were connected with the Academy's claims to be able to improve speaking and arguing skills quite as much as other teachers could.[6] Yet the very unwillingness of the Academy openly to reveal its opinions meant that too strong a case for *their own* rhetorical guidance could not be made – therefore the alternative tactic of undermining the claims of rhetoric to be a craft and to be acquired by teaching were employed. Rhetoric as normally conceived was the product of natural impulses towards flattery, self-defence, and justification of one's beliefs, benefiting from experience, but never rising to the status of *technê* because of the lack of knowledge on both sides (*De Or*. 1.90-2). In the course of his attack, Charmadas uses selected themes from the *Gorgias* as a kind of launching-pad for an updated attack on traditional enemies. We can already see here in Cicero two important links with *Gorgias*-interpretation over six centuries later: (i) the strong suggestion that there is a *genuine philosophic rhetoric*,[7] and (ii) the use of *technê*-definition (here a stoic-peripatetic synthesis) to test rhetoric's claim to the title of *technê*.[8]

Charmadas is associated with much the same anti-rhetorical role in Sextus' *Against the rhetoricians* (*Math*. 2.20-43), where his name is coupled with that of the better known Academic-Sceptic Clitomachus. Sextus is interested in how they set out to prove that rhetoric was not a science, but it is clear that some of the material ultimately derives from Plato, and the passage most reminiscent of Plato's *Gorgias* is at 2.41: 'Indeed, not even the demagogic orators proceed for the benefit of their cities, but demagogues have the same relation to the politician as the drug-seller does to the doctor.' Again, we see the implication that there are two types of rhetoric,[9] but it is the analogy that is of most interest. It is not the same as Plato introduced in the *Gorgias*, but it is likewise concerned with the relation of rhetoric to statesmanship, and likewise uses the doctor as a point of reference. The *demagogic orator*[10] has the same relation to the *statesman*, as the *drug-seller* (who just wants to make a sale) has towards the doctor. The drug-seller's relation to the doctor will appear a number of times in Olympiodorus' *Gorgias*-commentary in due course (1.13, 32.3-4, 42.1).

I shall reflect briefly on Sextus' own use of Plato's *Gorgias* at this point, as it takes little obvious consideration of recent debate, and, like much else in Sextus' discussion of philosophic history, shows an interest in those thinkers most discussed in the first century BC, in this case using second-century Academic and Peripatetic authors known to Cicero: Clitomachus, Carneades, Critolaus.[11] The rhetorical authors mentioned, Aristo friend of Critolaus, Athenaeus, and one of those with the name Hermagoras, seem to belong to the same period. This marks this doxography as heavily dependent upon Sextus' predecessors, and probably Aenesidemus himself;[12] the doxographic material is quite compatible with a date of around 50 BC. In sharp contrast to his second-century contemporary Aristides, Sextus (*Math.* 2.2) pieces together[13] a Platonic definition of rhetoric from the arguments *with Gorgias* rather than those with Polus, where it did look as if Plato's 'Socrates' was giving his own view of rhetoric. Sextus' definition runs 'rhetoric is a producer of persuasion through words, having its means of control in the words themselves, persuasive rather than instructive.' Thus he allows the part of the dialogue concerned directly with rhetoric to take precedence over later discussion, when matters of ethics begin to take over.

We move now to the early first century AD. The tetralogical arrangement of dialogues attributed by Diogenes Laertius to Thrasyllus couples the work with the *Euthydemus*, *Protagoras*, and *Meno*, seeing it as part of a series of works designed to tackle rival educators. It also gives it the subtitle *On Rhetoric*, which implies that rhetoric is still the chief interest of the work. The tetralogies stand in an unknown relation to a classification of dialogue *character*: together with the *Euthydemus* and the *Hippias*-dialogues, the *Gorgias* was regarded as 'anatreptic', concerned to *overturn* the position of Socrates' opponents. It belonged to the genus of 'zetetic' dialogues, implying that it was aimed more at the refutation of falsehoods than at the establishment of the truth, and to the species known as 'agonistic', seemingly because Socrates is in competition with the interlocutors.[14] Other pre-Neoplatonic arrangements of the dialogues seem to have afforded the work a similar role. Al-Nadîm appears to preserve the arrangement of Theon of Smyrna, which puts the work in similar company – in a group consisting of *Euthd.*, *Grg.*, *Hp.Ma.*, *Hp.Mi.*, *Ion*, *Prt.*;[15] while al-Farabi is following a Middle Platonist arrangement when he places the *Gorgias* among those dialogues which are supposed to illustrate the crafts that *fail* to provide the desired human happiness[16] – *Euthph.*, *Crat.*, *Ion*, *Grg.*, *Sph.*, *Euthd.*, and *Prm.*, dialogues said to be concerned with the inadequacies of religious science, linguistics, poetry, rhetoric, sophistry (x2), and dialectic respectively. This suggests that the author of this reading-arrangement was identifying the central thesis of the *Gorgias* with the inadequacy of rhetoric to bring *eudaimonia*, giving the dialogue a more constructive purpose and a moral message; no longer is it mere polemic.

iii. Pre-Neoplatonic interpretation of *Gorgias*: (2) on justice

At this point, some discussion of Quintilian is pertinent. The rhetorical theorist seems in some respects to belong to a transitional stage in the interpretation of the *Gorgias*, and he tells us something about its readers and the principal issues of interpretation. Naturally, it is views of rhetoric that are the principal content of the dialogue in which he, and apparently many another reader, is interested. He is aware of two distinct views of rhetoric there, one adopted by 'Gorgias' in the arguments with Gorgias and the other expounded by 'Socrates' in the arguments with Polus. *Neither* of these views is associated by the writer with Plato himself, as may be seen at *Institutio Oratoria* 2.15.5 and 24-7. 'Gorgias' is seen as admitting *under pressure*[17] that rhetoric is 'a manufacturer of persuasion' (2.15.5), that it operates in the law-courts and other assemblies, and that it treats matters just and unjust by mere persuasion rather than by teaching (2.15.18). 'Socrates' is seen as arguing *ad hominem* against 'Polus' that rhetoric is an 'image' of an art and a 'flattery'.

Quintilian obviously does not want a respected figure like Plato, or indeed Plato's 'Socrates', to be committed to such a low view of rhetoric, but it is clear that many were now, by the later years of the first century AD, of the belief that he was (2.15.24). Their impression is attributed to their having read what are represented as inferior epitomes of the work.[18] They had neither read the *whole work* nor *other works* of Plato, either of which might have saved them from committing a grievous error, involving as it did the view that Plato withheld from rhetoric the status of an art. Quintilian of course resorted to the already standard technique of appealing to the *Phaedrus* as a source for the belief in a true rhetoric, which is scientific and does not flatter (2.15.29-31); but he also appealed to the conclusion of arguments with 'Gorgias' (460c) and 'Callicles' (508c) for the unrefuted view that the true rhetorician cannot help acting justly.

Quintilian, however, is also able to appeal to the widespread division of Plato's works into those which expound doctrine and those which do not: the latter being known to him as 'refutational' (*elenktikoi*). No dialogue is more permeated by the vocabulary and theory of exposing and refuting (*elenchein* and *exelenchein*) than the *Gorgias*, so that the choice of this term (rather than Sextus' 'aporetic' or Albinus' 'inquisitive')[19] naturally places the *Gorgias* in the non-dogmatic group. Quintilian's opponents assume

that because it is 'Socrates' who introduces the view that rhetoric is a
flattery, and 'Socrates' is the spokesman for Plato's views, Plato must think
rhetoric to be a flattery rather than an art. But Quintilian does not accept
that Plato's views are communicated in the 'refutational' works, whether
through 'Socrates' or any other (2.15.26). The argument is *ad hominem*,
and the quarrel is with a particular type of rhetoric common in Plato's time
(2.15.27).

As Quintilian shows, Plato was an author much read in the early
imperial period by non-Platonists and non-philosophers as well as Platonists. Despite its length and the power of its argument, the *Gorgias* seems
not to have been specially influential with Quintilian's contemporary
Plutarch of Chaeronia, although it was well known to him;[20] this may well
be connected with the now popular view that such a dialogue is not a
vehicle for doctrine. But the work was studied seriously by Plutarch's
successor Calvenus Taurus in Athens in the second quarter of the second
century.[21] Gellius speaks of a multi-volume commentary on the work in
which Taurus discussed the reasons for punishment in Book I. Since there
is no material *early* in the *Gorgias* to justify a treatment of punishment,
the discussion probably belonged to Taurus' general introduction; this
seems to be confirmed by Gellius' failure to understand why Plato does not
accept *revenge* as a reason for punishment, which would certainly have
been explained by Taurus in his comments on Plato's own remarks about
punishment, including 525a which Gellius quotes. If we are looking at
introductory material, and if introductions were concerned with major
themes, then we see further reason to believe that the work is no longer
being treated as devoted to rhetoric alone: it is seen to concern the place of
punishment in our lives, and the limited use of rhetoric for achieving or
avoiding it. Like other Platonists of his day, Taurus would have been
turning away custom if he had adopted an unqualified anti-rhetorical
attitude – certainly when he called young Roman friends like Gellius
rhetorisce – so that emphasis falls now on the *moral content* of the *Gorgias*
rather than on any polemical purpose.

Gellius himself is interested in the *Gorgias*, and at 10.22 there is some
subtle use of Callicles' attack on Socrates' philosophising to illustrate the
unmanliness of childish delights in tricky argument. Whereas recent
introductions to reading Plato had talked of Plato expounding his views
through the figures of Socrates, Timaeus, and the two Strangers, and been
content to see the more sophistic interlocutors as there as mouthpieces for
views which are to be refuted,[22] Gellius, probably following Taurus, sees
Plato as one who has lessons hidden behind the words of the unphilosophic
characters: certainly Taurus adopts this approach to the rather sophistic
figure of Pausanias in the *Symposium*.[23] Such lessons again suggest a
moral reading, and lessons on the lips of Callicles suggest a more sympathetic reading of Socrates' opponents that accords less well with reading
the dialogue as polemic.

We should recall now how Olympiodorus treats the moral reading of the *Gorgias* as coming after the view that it is a critique of rhetoric (*In Grg.* proem 4). We have now seen signs in Gellius and even in the al-Farabi corpus arrangement that interpreters are swinging towards a moral rather than a polemical reading. It is clear that a moral reading of the work is assumed in the circles in which Aelius Aristides moved in the period AD 155-65.

By the second century AD the *Gorgias* was regularly studied by orators,[24] and Aristides, in a group of works whose impact on Neoplatonism is highly visible, makes Plato look most ungracious in his handling of oratory and of the orators.[25] In speech 3, *In Defence of the Four*, where 'the Four' are the Athenian statesmen Miltiades, Themistocles, Cimon, and Pericles whom the *Gorgias* treats severely, section 174 briefly sums up the essence of the work in such a manner as to give clear precedence to matters of justice and injustice, and of the superiority of the former. We are expecting the orator to see oratory as the subject, but in fact it seems that oratory is assumed to have been a secondary concern, so that Plato could perfectly well have achieved his purposes without being rude to orators at all!

> Surely you [Plato] are saying in the course of the whole discussion that justice is a fair thing, and that whatever one does should be done with its assistance, and that rhetoric should be used always for what is just? And if somebody strikes me, you say, there is a difference in whether he does so justly or unjustly, and if he banishes me and does so unjustly he is wretched, and in all cases we should employ these qualifications, stating whether the act is just or unjust. And you consider what's done justly is done honourably, and its opposite is done badly; and the one, justice, is the mark of the prosperous man, and the other, injustice, the mark of a wretch; and one should pursue the one to the greatest extent possible, and flee the other as quickly as one can. Are not these your themes? Don't you praise everything that is done justly, and find fault with everything done in the opposite way?

This no doubt reflects the interpretation of the work that Aristides had encountered around the Platonist schools of the coast of Asia Minor where he was now functioning: for it had probably been in response to the view of rhetoric encountered among Platonists at Pergamum and Ephesus that Aristides had set pen to paper in the late 150s.[26] More importantly it was certainly a local Plato-enthusiast, Capito, who had taken up the argument with Aristides, and prompted him to pen the second of his replies to Plato, *To Capito* in 157, and this work already sets the agenda for *In Defence of the Four*, hence even here, in spite of a more vigorous anti-cynic polemic, Aristides has contemporary Platonists in mind.[27]

Platonism in the eastern Aegean seems now to have been dominated by the pupils of Gaius. Nothing is known of him as an interpreter independently of his Smyrna-based associate Albinus, but Proclus regards the latter, along with the Platonist Atticus, as being excessively literal in his treatment of Plato:[28] with Atticus we are reaching an era of Platonic fundamentalism, and it may be that the school of Gaius had adopted a similar approach. It is thus very probable that local Platonists around Pergamum were taking seriously the ironic picture of rhetoric as an un-scientific knack of audience-flattery painted by Socrates: falling into what *Quintilian* regards as the error of failing to notice that what 'Socrates' says in such works is not intended to convey doctrine. With the work being now regarded as a source of *positive moral theory* rather than as a purely polemical document, it follows naturally that 'Socrates' must contribute towards genuine moral lessons in the course of refuting his opponents.[29]

It is Quintilian's non-serious passage (463a-465c), quoted at length, that is taken utterly seriously and becomes the launching pad for Aristides' speech two, *In Defence of Oratory*. Aristides (2.20) actually mentions that some particularly admire the passage, giving credence to the notion that the real objects of attack are contemporary Platonists in or around Perga-mum. This work evoked the anger of one Capito, who counter-attacked on behalf of the Platonists, and this in turn caused Aristides to pen his speech 4, *To Capito* – a work in which Plato is censured also for the ungracious-ness towards Parmenides and Zeno (37), Protagoras, Hippias, and Prodicus (44-5), and Aristophanes (50-1).

We can learn more about the interpretative assumptions of Aristides' opponents from Aristides himself. Firstly, I make a point which is con-nected with the over-literal approach that Aristides always adopts,[30] and Proclus finds in the Gaius-school: we meet the assumption of Quintilian's allegedly naive opponents that whatever Socrates says, *Plato is stating*. If Aristides takes this for granted, then for the criticism to stick the oppo-nents must come close to holding this view too. The view of Plato's Socrates as a mere mouthpiece for Platonic doctrine is occasionally backed up by the observation that Aeschines, a less innovatory witness, gives a different view of Socrates, and that Plato makes Socrates espouse doctrines on topics which, *by general agreement*, Socrates never even discussed.[31]

Secondly, Aristides adopts the tactic of showing how all sorts of other passages in Plato are in disagreement with things said about oratory and orators in the *Gorgias*.[32] We can see from Plutarch and from Taurus' fragments how natural it was to be supporting one's interpretation of one dialogue with reference to others,[33] a tactic connected with the assumption that it is ultimately *the corpus* which the Platonist should be interpreting; Plato grows in stature if he is represented as always offering the same message, and that would be particularly true with a work which actually speaks of philosophy *always saying the same thing* (482a-b). If the Platon-ist's task is to show how Plato's works are in mutual agreement, then it is natural for an opponent to be adopting the reverse task of showing how Plato's other works give a radically different picture from the one in hand: works that Aristides uses to demonstrate a contradiction include *Phdr.*,

Laws, Menex., Plt., Ap., Euthd.[34] He also tries to demonstrate that the *Gorgias* is not even internally consistent, something easily achieved with Platonic texts by those taking an over-literal approach. It is also significant that Aristides feels obliged to cut off one avenue of defence of Plato that one would expect from a Platonist in particular, for he insists that, while Plato did recognise a better and a worse form of oratory, there is no such distinction in the arguments with Polus (3.537-8).[35] He claims that its absence actually tends to make Plato seem unnecessarily uncharitable, and to be concealing craftily his opponents' line of defence.

The *Gorgias* was thus still viewed during this period as a work with much to say about rhetoric, by Platonists and orators alike, but there was a clear movement towards giving it an important moral message about wrong-doing.

iv. Second Sophistic distortions or philosophic restructuring?

The movement away from the polemical interpretation of the *Gorgias* towards an interpretation that gave the moral message priority was clearly a welcome trend for those second-century second-sophistic chameleons who are *both* Platonists *and* orators. Obviously they cannot welcome the idea that the *Gorgias* is a polemical attack on rhetoric, with no more profound purpose and no mitigating factors. Apuleius (assuming as one should that he is indeed the author of *De Platone*) therefore resorts rather more obviously to the tactic detected in Charmadas, associating the *Gorgias* with the more optimistic *Phaedrus*, and separating off the higher and nobler rhetoric, which does indeed aim at the good, the *disciplina contemplatrix bonorum* that is in total agreement with the statesman, from the lower, unscientific art of flattery with an eye for plausible arguments (2.8).[36] The true rhetoric is here indistinguishable from statesmanship, and hence is assimilated to a true art by being absorbed into the twin craft-status roles of the statesman: *sôphrosynê* and *dikaiosynê*. The false art which must be substituted for Plato's 'rhetoric' – in the baser sense according to Apuleius – is now that of the mere lawyer. Other than this Apuleius' chief use of the *Gorgias* would again seem to derive from the arguments with Polus, and relates particularly to the themes of moral responsibility for one's actions and the superiority of justice over injustice (2.8).[37]

In Maximus Tyrius we find a philosopher who writes short performance-speeches with a strong moral content. The opening of speech 17, with its story of Mithaecus the cook coming to Sparta with his new-fangled pleasure-focussed 'craft' and the Spartan refusal to accept his physical flatteries and pleasures, draws creatively on the *Gorgias*' craft/flattery theme, but scarcely comes close to interpreting it. This is typical of a moralist who wants to seem learned but has no intentions of faithfully reproducing Plato. Two passages make rather more direct use of the analogies involved in Socrates' classification of crafts and flatteries,[38] one at 14.9 and the other at 20.3:

> One may see types of flattery in practices and crafts, resembling the crafts in outward appearance, dissimilar in what they do. A bastard music has flattered people .... A bastard medicine has also flattered people, when [healers] left the remedies of Asclepius and the Asclepiads, and showed 'the craft' in no way different from fancy cooking, a debased flattery for debased bodies. And the false advocate plays the flatterer to the orator, setting up one account against another, fortifying injustice against justice and the foul against the fair. And the sophist plays the flatterer to the philosopher: he is a flatterer in the most precise manner of all. (14.9)

> The drug-seller imitates the doctor, the false advocate the rhetorician, the sophist the philosopher. In every area you could find an evil grafted onto a good, with a considerable admixture of similarity to it, either differing in policy, as orator differs from false advocate, or in purpose, as the doctor differs from the drug-seller, or in excellence, as the philosopher differs from the sophist. Policy, excellence, and purpose are recognized by few. (20.3)

The remarkable thing about this passage is that rhetoric is no longer a flattery or pseudo-art, but a true craft, whose false counterpart is now false-advocacy, which sets speech against speech, injustice against justice, and disgracefulness against uprightness. So it is no longer the orator who argues for either side of a question, let alone purely for causes which are either unjust or disgraceful: that job is now called false-advocacy, so that rhetoric itself can take over the role of the craft which Plato had called *dikaiosynê* (the judicial art) in the *Gorgias*. Furthermore, philosophy has now taken over the role that Plato had given to the legislative art. The false advocate (not very well translated by Trapp as 'professional prosecutor') now becomes the poor imitation of the orator, the sophist the poor image of the philosopher, and orator and philosopher take over from Plato's twin crafts of statesmanship, judicial and legislative. Maximus of course is both orator and philosopher, so Maximus is also the complete statesman. One is tempted to view his own machinations here as an exemplary piece of sophistry, though he would no doubt claim to have accurately translated Plato's thoughts into the language and the social milieu of the second century.

The creative reworking of Plato's schema of arts and flatteries is not confined to our hybrid philosopher-orators. The same tendency leaves its mark on their contemporary Clement of Alexandria, who, being uninclined towards oratory himself, retains *both* sophistry *and* rhetoric as false arts, but makes them correspond to the true arts of philosophy and dialectic respectively (*Strom.* 1.44.2). This adaptation of the schema by an erudite and seemingly unbiased author should, I believe, remind us that the interpreter's task was not considered to be one of simply reproducing

Plato's words. Plato's intentions were assumed to lie deeper, and there was some agreement that they could be teased out by paying attention to other Platonic passages and divorcing what was being said from its immediate polemical context. The presence of a true art of rhetoric in the *Phaedrus* made authors look more circumspectly at the notion of rhetoric as a flattery in the *Gorgias*, and to ask themselves what it was that was being treated as 'rhetoric' at that point, and what other 'rhetoric' there might be which served statesmanship rather than pretending that it could do better. That Plato was attacking Polus' rhetoric could be because of the close link between Polus' pursuits and the practices of injustice. To attack amoral rhetorical knacks did not undermine the value of those speaking skills that were employed by persons with genuine insights into, and concern for, the well-being of society. Hence the tampering with Plato's schema of arts and flatteries could be seen as a valid act for the Platonist, and even as an act of interpretation: translating a Platonic insight from its original polemical context into terms more accurately reflecting the interrelation of arts and their false counterparts.

v. *Gorgias* and *Theology*

The strangest interpretation reported by Olympiodorus and his anonymous colleague identified the target or *skopos* of the work with the Demiurge:[39] seemingly implying that it was intended to reveal to us the Demiurge's nature, though it is difficult to be certain of the exact meaning that *skopos* had here without being able to identify the interpreters concerned. The anonymous *Prolegomena* tells of those who made the target 'the intellect which sees itself',[40] which is usually assumed to refer to the same interpretation in different terms. But since we do not know whether the phrase belongs to the interpreter himself or (more likely) to his anonymous critic, it is easier to give precedence to Olympiodorus' report.[41]

Olympiodorus says that this view was based on a single passage, the final myth concerning the judgment of souls, 'which mentions the Demiurge as we shall learn'. The myth, for Olympiodorus, is concerned with the paradigmatic cause (46.7) of constitutional happiness, whereas the target is to locate *all* the causes. He says nothing to *identify* this paradigmatic cause with a Demiurge or intellect of any kind, and for him the paradigm is rather his creation: the cosmos itself (cf. 35.15). He does however see Zeus in the myth as a demiurgic figure.

The origin of the strange, myth-based interpretation of the *Gorgias* is not a primary concern. It is usually assumed to be Amelius, on the strength of an unconvincing similarity between the report in the *Prolegomena* and Amelius' 'Intellect which sees', detected at *Timaeus* 39e.[42] I have argued that it was Iamblichus, noted for making a particular demiurge the 'target' of the *Sophist*.[43] Elsewhere (1999b) I use Proclus' *Platonic Theology* to shed

light on the reasons behind this interpretation, for related theory about
the theology of the myth appears to have influenced him too. The myth is
the only part of the *Gorgias* which he used in the *Theology*, and while this
is not surprising (since it is the sole part to openly treat divinities), it does
help to show how a brief passage of a dialogue can come to dominate the
Neoplatonic exegesis of the whole. Proclus in fact (6.9.43-6) detects in the
myth two Zeus-figures, a transcendent one, and the senior of a triad of
three further demiurges (Zeus, Posidon, Hades in mythology). In Proclus'
eyes the *Gorgias* is the work which gives most insight into the triad of
demiurges (6.6.29.6-23), and which makes it clear that Zeus the universal
Demiurge is not identical with either Cronus or the other Zeus. Hence it
clarifies above all the position of the higher Zeus, the Demiurge of Plato's
Timaeus.

Proclus' interpretation shows how important the myth of the *Gorgias* is
for Neoplatonism's view of the Demiurge. But in what way could one justify
ignoring all the ethical and political content, and passing over a host of
interpreters who have seen the principal subject as being rhetoric or
justice, in favour of a single brief passage when determining the dialogue's
target? Proclus (5.24.89.1-3) says that Plato linked Zeus with 'the paradigm of political science'. Zeus is the one who first established the
constitution (*politeia*) of the whole (9-14), and this comes close to making
Zeus himself the *paradigm* of the statesman. Though Proclus is here
dealing with the *Protagoras*, such a paradigm could also be detected in the
Gorgias, and would serve to link the myth with earlier passages that focus
on the nature of true and false statesmen. Proclus does in fact seem to
make his higher Zeus into the complete statesman according to the craft-
classification of the *Gorgias*, for the latter makes legislative and judicial
crafts the twin parts of statesmanship, and the Zeus of the myth organises
both laws/constitution (see 6.9.43.23-4) and judgment-processes. He is the
paradigm of the legislator and the judge, hence of the statesman. This
does not lead Proclus to claim that the *Gorgias* expounds theology, and
he himself knows well that the myths of *Protagoras*, *Gorgias*, and
Republic are subservient to the moral 'targets' of these works.[44] What
he does claim is that Plato sometimes ascends to the principles, as if to
an observation-tower (*skopia*), for a better view of his subject (1.7.30.24-
31.2). The term *skopia* sounds like a correction of *skopos*, Proclus is
saying that these theological glimpses which intrude into the *Gorgias*
and other works are not 'targets' that one aims *at* so much as vantage-
points that one aims *from*. Almost certainly he is correcting those who
believed that the this-worldly ethical and political material was studied
for the sake of the paradigmatic vision: instead Plato invites us to
glimpse the paradigm in order that we may be more aware of its
this-worldly implications.

vi. Constitutional virtues

The traditional role of the *Gorgias* within the Neoplatonic curriculum as instituted by Iamblichus was to introduce us to the 'political' or 'constitutional' virtues.[45] An attempt to reconcile various things said about the virtues in different dialogues, together with a range of remarks in various dialogues that suggest different *levels* of virtue, had, from Plotinus on, meant that the Neoplatonists schematised these levels. Olympiodorus, following Ammonius, identifies the 'constitutional' virtues as found in the *Gorgias* with those discussed in *Republic* 4,[46] hence they are the virtues of the *tripartite* soul; justice and temperance, of particular relevance to the *Gorgias*, are viewed as the qualities necessary for the proper unity-in-diversity of such a soul. This is contrasted with the purificatory virtues of the *Phaedo*, where such divisions of function in the soul disappear as the influences of the body are purged away.[47] The existence of divisions within the soul is suggested already by the Water-Carriers myth at *Gorgias* 493, and it leads to the situation at 507a-c where the various virtues are distinct though interrelated (or co-implied),[48] not all one thing as suggested by arguments in the *Protagoras* or *Laches* (199d-e), nor totally subservient to wisdom as suggested in the *Phaedo* (68c-69c).

Any Neoplatonic interpretation of the *Gorgias* since Iamblichus would have been expected to acknowledge the role it had of promoting the constitutional virtues within the curriculum; hence the view that the Demiurge is its 'target', unless it had preceded Iamblichus, ought to be compatible with the view that its *subject-matter* involved the constitutional virtues. But Zeus in the myth, like the Demiurge of the *Timaeus*, establishes a constitution; he even presides over a tripartition that mirrors the tripartition of the soul. Not only does the myth contain the paradigm of the happy constitution, it contains the paradigm of its organiser. An Iamblichus could readily find Plato promoting the constitutional virtues within the myth, which is after all talking of the rewards for virtue and the punishment of vice, for the divine Statesman is the regulator of the constitutional virtues.

There was a time, then, when making the Demiurge, and the whole demiurgic order, into the 'target' of the *Gorgias* was making them the paradigm of the statesman and the true inner constitution respectively. The 'target' seems to have signified the paradigm employed for the discussion rather than the 'subject' in our sense. So there was originally nothing perverse about the view that the *skopos* of the *Gorgias* was the Demiurge and his paradigmatic constitution of the myth. It came to be seen as perverse by the time of Olympiodorus, but this is because the distinctive meaning of *skopos* shifted slightly, and became again a work's principal object of inquiry.[49] Other Iamblichan *skopoi* may well have been equally difficult to comprehend.

What happens at this point is that the traditional view that the work is about the 'constitutional virtues', because it was in fact securely rooted in the text, comes to dominate, and the work is found to be about the principles of constitutional virtue. These are as follows:

Type of cause	Rejected candidate	Actual cause
1 material	living body	tripartite soul
2 formal	luxury	justice/temperance
3 creative	rhetoric	philosophic life
4 paradigmatic	tyranny	cosmic order
5 instrumental	persuasion	habits/education
6 final	pleasure	the good

The scheme, relying on the Neoplatonist expansion of the four Aristotelian causes,[50] is carefully worked out. Any reader of the *Gorgias* will appreciate its relevance, and none will see it as related to only a part of the work. The way the causes of constitutional happiness are supposed to relate to the constitutional virtues and the soul in which they are found is clear from 1 and 2. We have advanced to what is probably the most thorough and sensible reading of the *Gorgias* in antiquity. When spelt out in detail it is inclined to seem a little dull. It is a sad feature of the interpreter's task that thoroughness and plausibility seldom make exciting reading.

Before we leave Olympiodorus, however, it would be well to take a brief look at how the *Phaedrus* is read into the *Gorgias*, for though this is a late author his material is often traditional and he paints the fullest picture. In search of a scientific rhetoric he fastens on 271c-d, and notes that it must be able to identify how many types of soul there are, and the nature of each. Each type of soul must then be correlated with the types of speech to which they are most susceptible. At 46.6 Olympiodorus speaks of demonstration being for those ruled by the intellect, *endoxa* for those swayed by opinions, and myth for those dominated by the imagination. However, at 1.13, though still using the tripartition of individual souls, he correctly realises that it is whole persons not parts of persons that have to be persuaded by the rhetorician. Hence he correlates the five different types of individuals, and more importantly the five types of constitutions from *Republic* 8-9, which do indeed owe their different characteristics to the manner in which the tripartite soul functions, to five types of rhetoric. Of these the type relating to aristocracy will in fact be the only true rhetoric, and it will operate in accordance with the directions of the true statesman, while the other four kinds are false.

It seems odd that the true rhetorician will know how to affect all kinds of soul, but will in fact be confined to operating in an aristocracy. However, the overall nature of the polis cannot determine the nature of all its citizens; the true rhetorician will be able to discern separate arguments that should be employed for separate classes of person, such as the doctors, the soldiers, and the labourers. Here it seems that the tripartition of the soul is once more influencing the activities of the rhetorician. It is clear from 6.11 that persuading those in different occupations with different remedies is *Phaedrus*-dependent.

As for the inferior kinds of rhetoric, their four kinds are soon dropped in favour of two, according to whether they serve honour-loving or pleasure-loving regimes. The honour-loving one is concerned simply with the salvation of the city, and this is said to be the rhetoric practised by Demosthenes, Pericles, and Themistocles. This kind is opposed to the flattering kind, as practised by Python for instance, that aims only at the pleasure of those addressed. This results in practice in a three-fold division of rhetoric, true, city-serving, and flattering. Consequently, where Plato seems to be telling us at 517a that prominent fifth-century Athenian statesmen were neither true orators nor even successful flatterers, Olympiodorus salvages their reputation by drawing the conclusion that their failure to flatter is a sign that they used a *higher* rhetoric than most (33.3, 41.18), taking care of the better desires of non-aristocratic regimes. In fact their willingness to function in a non-ideal society seems all that is held against them!

Another passage of importance to Olympiodorus is 270b-c, in which Plato uses the analogy of medicine to determine what true rhetoric should be like. This is used to support the idea that there is a rhetoric that is the exact psychical counterpart of medicine in the body (14.13; 40.10), occupying the same ground as justice in the *Gorgias*. But where in the *Gorgias* does Olympiodorus find this true rhetoric? He certainly found it somewhere here, as 9.4 shows, and 41.11 draws attention to the occurrence of the concept at 517a6. He cannot point to anybody whom Plato includes in the category of true rhetoricians, but the term is there. Had he been less concerned to separate the role of rhetorician from the controlling role of statesman, he would perhaps have made more of Socrates' suspicion at 521d that he is himself the only true user of statesmanship, for the statesman is here presumed to be a speaker too. However, there would still have been problems, for this true statesmanship is true in virtue of the true welfare of the citizens that it seeks. The true rhetoric of the *Phaedrus*, on the other hand, was true because of the scientific approach that it took towards the achievement of persuasion. Nobody would credit Socrates with *that* kind of true rhetoric.

The initial attractiveness of the popular tactic of reading the *Phaedrus'* treatment of true rhetoric into the *Gorgias* thus turns out to involve its share of problems. Unitary readings of the corpus are nice for as long as they work.

Recollecting Plato's Middle Period

i. Intuiting related dialogues

It is a fact often forgotten that the modern notion of a Middle Period in Plato's work is an artificial construct that has no stylometric basis.[1] 'Late' dialogues are more readily spoken of as a coherent group. There is a group of works that have by-passed Plato's previous protagonist 'Socrates', and which show some obvious stylistic differences from all others except the *Philebus* – notably the avoidance of hiatus and of certain poetic rhythms at the end of sentences. Some of these works are structured as a sequence (*Timaeus-Critias*, *Sophist-Politicus*), and there are a number of concerns in common between them and the *Philebus*, whose 'Socrates' is sufficiently different from that of other works to be set apart. Hence this latter is reasonably included within the same overall group, and there was a persistent ancient tradition that one of its members, the *Laws*, was Plato's last work. Hence the term 'late' seemed a reasonable designation for the group, even though there can be no proof that work on other dialogues had ceased when the first of this group (probably the *Sophist*) was begun.

Scholars frequently connect the *Parmenides* and *Theaetetus* with this group, principally on account of the 'developmental' hypothesis of a shift away from the so-called Theory of Ideas, which is questioned in the former and avoided in the latter. It is usually supposed that the *Theaetetus* must be placed after 369 BC because the preface refers to events in that year, but this argument is quite unable to justify the confidence with which it is habitually used – for two reasons.[2] One can also appeal to links between dialogues: the cast-list of the *Theaetetus* links it with the *Sophist*, whose introduction places that conversation on the previous day,[3] while a passage at 183e looks as if it is intended to refer to the meeting between Socrates and Parmenides depicted in the *Parmenides*. Yet these links are not chronological indicators.[4] A later work can be represented as a continuation of a very much earlier work, just as thematic connections can simply mean that old interests are being revived. Stylistically both the *Parmenides* and *Theaetetus* belong with the rest of Plato's works, and some linguistic features strongly suggest that if another division is to be made, then the *Theaetetus* and at least the latter part of the *Parmenides* would be placed in the same group as books 2 to 10 of the *Republic*. The earlier part of the *Parmenides* looks earlier still.

The principal books of the *Republic* in turn have been seen as very different from those works in which 'Socrates' examines young men, intellectual rivals, and their ideas. He now examines his own ideas, usually taken to be Plato's ideas rather than those of the historical Socrates. There is a strong didacticism which had not always been present, and a strong desire to communicate more difficult ideas through myth, allegory, metaphor and simile – so that Plato seems to have achieved his peak as an inspiring writer. His politics move in an interventionist direction, and his ethics towards psychological, epistemological, and metaphysical foundations. He builds up theories, including that of the immortality of the soul and the Theory of Ideas itself. Some of these features are shared with the *Phaedo*, *Symposium*, and *Phaedrus*, and so these have been grouped along with the *Republic*, and referred to as 'Middle Period' works. The assumption is that they represent the first clear move away from Socrates, and openly make 'Socrates' a mouthpiece for Platonic theory, notably the Theory of Ideas. Where exactly they stand in relation to dialogues like the *Euthydemus* and *Cratylus* is a matter of some controversy among those for whom chronology matters; *Theaetetus* and *Parmenides* are usually assumed without question to follow the *Republic*. Insofar as stylometry suggests anything, it strongly suggests that both works were begun far earlier than the *Republic* was finished.[5]

My present purpose is not to offer a critique of the modern construct of a Middle Period, but rather to show that it is unnecessary. An ancient response to some of the issues that are behind this construct may be independent of any *chronological* hypothesis. For Gregory Vlastos the initial shift away from the legacy of Socrates had come with the advent of an epistemological foundation for inquiry, notably with the *Meno*: a work which also introduces mathematical theory and practice, and which outwardly relies upon the notion of a soul that can exist apart from the body. If Vlastos were correct on this point, then Plato's epistemological development begins with the transition from 'early' to 'middle', and reaches its fullest expression in the *Theaetetus*, so that epistemology would be primarily a 'middle' activity. That certain works here have distinctively Platonic epistemological foundations is something well appreciated in antiquity. I now discuss an interpretation of Plato's epistemology that is based primarily on *Meno*, *Phaedo*, *Republic*, and *Theaetetus*, with input from other 'middle' dialogues such as *Symposium* and *Phaedrus*.

There is no suggestion, of course, that this epistemology represents any shift away from Socrates, or something characteristic of one phase of Plato's work. Rather the demand that all of Plato's dialogues should be in agreement has ensured a broadly unitarian approach to a given issue. It is the author's judgment about which texts are relevant that has tended to exclude other works. Furthermore, there is no suggestion in this interpretation of any development within the relevant dialogues. Interpreters assume that they are dealing with a complete educational system in which nothing has ever been totally superseded, and where all apparent anomalies have their explanation. The author of this interpretation has appreciated the coherence of a group of works that we should suppose to be *chronologically* linked, but he did so by an intuitive grasp of what was relevant. It will be seen that a unitary view of these works could be based on a scrupulously detailed reading of the texts, and could result in interpretation that was both plausible and philosophically attractive.

ii. Two Middle Platonist interpreters

As I showed in 1984, the anonymous *Commentary on Plato's Theaetetus* and a *Commentary on Plato's Republic* by one Taurus, said to be from Sidon but perhaps identical with the Platonist from Beirut, used the same doxography on an epistemological topic, with similar wording.[6] The author of the *Theaetetus*-commentary (henceforth TC) might plausibly have been understood by the reader of column 15 as offering three definitions of geometry (this is more easily understood as the antecedent of a demonstrative pronoun than is 'simple knowledge' [*epistêmê haplê*], which is also crucial to the context). It is clear, however, from column 3 that the definitions were intended to be of this same 'simple knowledge', and they do indeed sound like some kind of knowledge-definitions. Yet the fragment of Taurus, preserved in Ps.Hero by a circuitous course, runs quite simply as follows:

> Plato defined geometry in the Meno as follows: right opinion bound by calculation of a reason; Aristotle as assumption with demonstration; Zeno as a condition in the reception of impressions rendered inalienable through reason.

The Platonic text upon which one of the 'definitions' is based, at *Meno* 98a3-4, reads: 'until one binds them (i.e. true opinions) by calculation of a reason.' The Aristotelian definition seems at first sight to be little more than a translation of the supposed sense of this Platonic definition into Aristotelian terms, and the Zenonian definition appears elsewhere either as a definition of knowledge by Herillus,[7] or as a general Stoic definition of one kind of knowledge: again contrasted with 'systematic' knowledge.[8] The three definitions ascribed to Plato, Aristotle, and Zeno could be interpreted as definitions of a particular kind of knowledge applicable to mathematical and related sciences, of which geometry was a prime example.[9] The *Meno* itself had approached epistemology via geometry,[10] and geometry would have been the most obvious example of a discipline which proceeds from certain assumptions ('Let AB be parallel to CD,' etc.) and demonstrates the conclusions which would follow. Even so, there is nothing in these 'definitions' which could possibly isolate geometry or even mathematical science in general.

As an eminent Platonist, who appears to have thought deeply about Platonic texts, Taurus of Beirut cannot have thought Plato was trying to define geometry at *Meno* 98a. We should therefore assume that a subsequent scholar had mistaken what he had been trying to define – in exactly the same way as one might mistake what TC was trying to define. Though Ps.Hero purports to be giving Taurus' exact words, and has indeed recorded them sufficiently accurately to enable the reconstruction of some lines of the papyrus of TC, one cannot insist 'geometry' had appeared here rather than a simple 'this', which Ps.Hero or his source has *interpreted* as referring to geometry. It would have been possible to mistake these definitions as descriptions of geometry if Taurus had been introducing them in the same way as TC had introduced them. Bastianini and Sedley (p. 500)[11] suggest that Ps.Hero or an intermediate source has indeed mistaken the word to which 'this' refers at an equivalent point of Taurus' text. In this way the confusion could have occurred in exactly the same way as it could occur in TC.

It would be well now to record TC's words:[12]

> For his discussion is not about complex knowledge, that some people call 'systematic', but about the simple kind. That is the kind of cognition that applies to particular theorems of geometry and music, but from these individual [acts of cognition] a single complex knowledge is accomplished. So the simple is prior to the complex, and this is what he himself [Plato] defined as
> ....

TC is commenting upon the phrase 'some bits of geometry' at *Theaetetus* 145c8. He appears to mean that Plato's phrase has been deliberately chosen so as not to suggest the whole science of geometry, which would be a systematic knowledge (a science). Rather it makes clear that 'Theaetetus' is learning certain individual theorems, which amount to simple knowledge only.[13] Where he finds this distinction elaborated in Plato is not entirely clear, though he must surely have found it somewhere. Had he too found it in the *Republic*, like Taurus in Ps.Hero, and if so where? We should attempt to clarify the fragment of Taurus' *Republic*-commentary in Ps.Hero by establishing its context too: if possible the precise phrase of Plato which has prompted this string of definitions.

iii. A context in *Republic*

Relating comments to the text commented upon is nearly always the appropriate methodology when examining ancient commentaries. So as to explain the overlap between a commentary on the *Theaetetus* and one on the *Republic*, we require similar reasons for a comment of this kind to have been made – some similarity in the two lemmata. To explain the confusion between knowledge and geometry we require a lemma to which both of these were obviously relevant. Furthermore we require that Taurus' words should have been extremely close to those of TC in the passage which led up to the definitions.

One asks therefore whether there is a passage in the *Republic* that could have attracted almost the same comment, and for similar reasons, as the comment about 'some bits of geometry' in TC. One does not have to look far. Mansfeld[14] has already identified passages of Republic 6 and 7 in which the epistemological status of geometry is sufficiently important to have warranted this kind of comment, and the book 6 passage was 510c-e. Here, at 510c2, at the first mention of geometry we read:

> For I believe you know that people who deal with geometries and calcula-
> tions and the like, postulating in the case of each treatment, ...

The important point here is that the term geometries (*geômetrias*) is plural, suggesting individual geometrical problems again, while the singular of the term is normal. The phrase 'in the case of each treatment' confirms that Plato has in mind single mathematical problems, rather than any branch of mathematics as a whole. He is at pains to avoid giving the impression that what he is saying applies to geometry conceived of as a single science, since at 511b1 we again meet the plural.[15] The singular is in fact not used during this passage at all,[16] even though it comes to be used regularly in Book 7 (526c10, d8, 527a2, c2, c7, 528a7, d3, d9, 529e3, 530b6). However, when in Book 7 Plato returns to the material of 510c-511b, he again uses the plural: 'geometries and those [crafts] that follow the same pattern', 533b7-8.[17] Some commentator, whether Taurus, TC or their common source, has recognised that there is method in Plato's careful choice of singular or plural. He has interpreted the plural, quite naturally, as referring to separate geometrical problems rather than the science of geometry as a whole. We shall call this commentator Ur-C.

Ur-C has done more than find in Plato's use of singular and plural the basic distinction between simple and complex knowledge. He has assumed that separate geometrical problems yield a different kind of knowledge from that which we associate with the science as a whole. Again this is not surprising, since (i) the context is one in which Plato is trying to explain the difference in cognitive status between what we normally think of as discursive reasoning (*dianoia*) and the intellectual insight called *noêsis* or *nous*, and (ii) the Stoics also inclined towards attributing a different status to systematic knowledge from that afforded to individual acts of unwavering cognition. Certainly they perceived a need to distinguish the two.[18]

Leaving the Stoics aside, we may observe that there is good reason why a *careful choice* of the plural in relation to geometrical problems as promoters of *dianoia* should be thought to help explain the distinction between *dianoia* and *noêsis*. The precise interpretation of this distinction remains a matter of considerable debate today, but the fact that geometers leave basic assumptions unargued is one factor leading Plato to consider the geometry of his own day[19] inferior to dialectic: apparently the major factor.[20] The other factor is geometers' use of visible diagrams – even when it is not about the diagram that they demonstrate something, but rather about some intelligible entity.

The assumptions that the geometers make could in theory be one of two kinds: *either* the postulation of specific data, a line of four feet here, a right-angle here, a circle of two-foot radius here, and so on, *or* the basic machinery of geometry, lines, angles, shapes, and so on, without any attempt to understand exactly what these basic materials are. In fact we find Plato pointing to the latter sort of assumption: odd, even, shapes, three kinds of angle, etc. (510c3-5), and saying that geometers give no account of them as if they were obvious to everyone (510d1, 511a7). It is as if the visual had ousted the intelligible at this basic level, and this may be what has led him to emphasise the geometer's inability to dispense with his diagrams. Instead of going further back to a rational explanation of his principles, explaining them in terms of principles still more basic (hence 'higher' in Plato's eyes), the geometer has fallen back on the 'lower' visual world (511a5-9). This is contrasted with dialectic as Plato envisages it.

When speaking of dialectic, Plato describes a moral science that is integrated and internally consistent, with the less fundamental explained in terms of the more fundamental and vice-versa. By contrast geometry, as he there depicts it, fails to explain the most fundamental things, so that it no longer has that same coherence. Euclidean geometry was of course a remarkable attempt to trace geometry back to first principles, and hence to render it 'systematic' to a high degree. After the systematising activities of Euclid, two generations after Plato, we do not expect the Divided Line of *Republic* 6 to be explained in terms of the cognitive inferiority of the mathematical sciences. This is particularly so because many commentators approached the *Republic* from the point of view of mathematics.[21] Rather we expect two types of 'knowledge' within the mathematical (and perhaps other) sciences, one systematic, another more limited. The Platonist, at least, was under strong pressure to accept the need for knowledge-elements because of the rejection of Socrates' so-called 'Dream' in the *Theaetetus*.[22] The Stoic would have to assume that the infallible sage, who never errs and never repents, would also have cognitive experiences of a totally secure type,[23] contributing to the totality of his knowledge. As we have seen, he would be able to distinguish the system of knowledge from the cognitive act that qualifies for the title of knowledge.[24]

The overall effect, then, of interpreting the *dianoia*-stage of Plato's Divided Line in terms of simple (as opposed to complex) knowledge, is to link it with individual acts of cognition as opposed to the mastery of a whole science. Such an interpretation is not compelled to distinguish between *dianoia* and *noêsis* in terms of different objects, as might be encouraged by 511e. Instead, it concentrates on a distinction between methods. It makes no direct use of the dependence of *dianoia* on illustrations from the senses, though it does not exclude the possibility that sensation could fill gaps left by one's failure to grasp a complete cognitive system.

There seems to be no trace of this theory outside Ps.Hero and TC, although the Divided Line was an important passage for Middle Platonists and Neoplatonists alike. The third of Plutarch's *Platonic Questions* is given over to the general issue of the relation between the Line itself and the cognitive activities that correspond to it. Plutarch assumes without argument that the *dianoia*-stage of the Line concerns 'the mathematical' (1001c, 1002a), and there is no contrast between cognitive procedures.[25] Theon of Smyrna uses the Line and Cave passages extensively when trying to establish the importance of mathematics, but the effect is rather to emphasise a genuine gulf between mathematics, however it is practised, and dialectic. Mathematics has a cathartic and preliminary role in the philosophical process. Alcinous does not alter this impression.[26] In Numenius there seems to be some hypostatic gulf between *noêsis* and *dianoia*, though not necessarily between their objects.[27] The Divided Line passage continues to be of importance in Neoplatonism, where the emphasis usually falls on the distinction between objects of cognition rather than cognitive processes.[28] Thus Ps.Hero and TC are witness to a well-informed interpretation that runs counter to late Platonist trends, particularly as it is less concerned with establishing ontological hierarchies than with elucidating cognitive procedures.

iv. Cross-dialogue interpretation (1) *Meno*

What implications does this interpretation of the Divided Line passage have for other dialogues? It was linked in Ps.Hero, as we have seen, with the notion of a right opinion's becoming knowledge in the *Meno*. The *Republic* had been keen to avoid calling the result of the *dianoia*-process knowledge or intelligence,[29] yet it is being equated with something that Plato is willing to call 'knowledge' in the *Meno*, something which TC calls 'simple knowledge'. In an age when the variations in Plato's terminology were notorious (DL 3.63-4), it is not to be wondered that commentators should be prepared to identify two otherwise similar concepts, one of which was labelled F and the other ~F. They merely needed to say in what way it was F and in what way it was ~F, and there are examples of this in TC.[30]

The implications for the *Meno* go beyond the identification of true opinion bound by reasoning with elemental knowledge, for epistemological themes keep recurring within this dialogue, whose subject might reasonably be described as the relation between excellence and cognition. In particular it follows from this interpretation of 98a that the important concept of learning as Recollection also pertains, to some extent at least, to the acquisition of this simple knowledge.[31] This is a natural enough conclusion within the context of this theory, since the passage in which the Theory of Recollection is demonstrated (82b ff.) is concerned with a particular geometrical problem illustrated by a visible diagram. The slave boy is being led with the help of the diagram to the point where correct opinions emerge naturally, and it is foreshadowed that these opinions can eventually be transformed into knowledge. All that is required is a questioner who employs the tactic of repetition with variation (85c9-d1, 86a7-8). Strictly speaking, it is not when the right answer has been first given, but when this knowledge has been arrived at, that Recollection is said to have occurred (85d3-7). The process is one of opinions (plural) being converted into knowledge-pieces (plural), as 86a makes clear.[32] At 97a-b the illustration of the similar results of right opinion and knowledge, using the example of the road to Larissa, involves a knowledge so straightforward, not to mention empirical, that a reader would take it as simple rather than systematic, unrelated to any science of map-reading or the like.[33] In fact there is little suggestion in the *Meno* that Plato's concern is with any knowledge-system.[34]

There is one other factor supporting this treatment of the *Meno* in relation to the *dianoia*-segment of Divided Line, and that is its introduction, immediately following the Recollection-episode, of the notion of arguing from hypotheses *as the geometers often do* (86e4-5). If the dialogue, insofar as it as an epistemological study, concerns simple knowledge, then an ancient commentator would have expected it to be employing (if only for illustration's sake)[35] the methodologies applicable to simple knowledge. In this case a hypothetical methodology, comparable with that associated with the *dianoia*-stage,[36] is seen as characteristic of a geometer's method. Again Plato's words do not preclude the possibility that there exists a systematic geometry that rises above hypotheses.

The hypothetical method is subsequently applied to problems in the realm of ethics (87b, 89c), suggesting to our interpreters that mathematical problems are not the only ones that can be objects of *dianoia*. The principal hypothesis here applied is that if excellence is knowledge then excellence is teachable (*qua* recollectable). This hypothesis is never doubted (89d3-5), but does not permit one to rise to an understanding of reality so long as it remains a hypothesis.[37] The method used by Plato here is to test the truth of the condition according to essentially empirical means, and it is here that difficulties arise. At first it seems established, but then empirical evidence seems to question the conclusion, which in turn leads to the condition being questioned, and then new empirical evidence explains how the original empirical evidence could have been wrongly assessed. Reliance upon this empirical evidence does not undermine the validity of the hypothesis, but it means that the apodosis cannot be established with any greater certainty than a protasis established solely by observation will allow.

Given that Ur-C had ample scope for interpreting the *Meno* as a dialogue about the relationship between virtue and *simple* knowledge, an obvious question must be asked. How exactly did he interpret the 'definition' of simple knowledge that he encountered at 98a: what text did he know and what did it signify to him? It seems clear that TC did not have our text ('until somebody binds them by calculation of *aitia*'),[38] but an aberrant one. The scribe who has prepared our copy[39] appears twice to have written '*aitia* of calculation', thus making it likely that TC had not reproduced the Platonic text known to us. Either his text was different, or he had actually chosen to vary it slightly.[40] Ps.Hero however, and hence *perhaps* Taurus,[41] used the same reading as modern manuscripts. Still, his version may have made little difference to his interpretation, for in spite of the variation TC seems to interpret the passage much as if he had our text. The addition of calculation/*aitia* to right opinion is regarded as the equivalent of adding awareness *why* a thing is so to an awareness *that* it is so (3.3-7). There is also a strong suggestion at 3.21-5 that the *aitia* rather than the calculation is the key ingredient in the binding-process, since it is of 'the bond of the *aitia*' that we hear, not 'the bond of calculation'. Calculation (*logismos*) is presumably already involved in 'right opinion plus an account (*logos*)', which falls short of simple knowledge, while 'right opinion bound by *aitia* of calculation' suffices. TC sees a natural progression from right opinion, to right opinion plus a *logos*, to right opinion plus *aitia*/*logismos*, so it seems that he has in mind the need to possess not just an account of one's correct opinion, but also a reason *why* that account holds.[42]

These details TC hoped to clarify in the course of his commentary on the *Theaetetus*, as 3.25-8 shows – for it seems fairly clear that he neither had written, nor intended to write, a commentary on *Meno*. Clarification would surely have involved explaining how the various attempts to define knowledge in terms of 'right opinion plus an account' failed to capture what was distinctive about simple knowledge. The *Meno*'s 'definition' had to offer more than:

(i)   right opinion set out in words (206d-e),
(ii) right opinion cataloguing the parts of the thing opined (206e-208b), and
(iii) right opinion noting a distinguishing mark for the thing opined (208c-210a).

More difficult, TC ought surely to have clarified how the binding of right opinion by an *aitia* of the *logismos* could avoid the objection at 210a7-9 that it is silly for one searching for a definition of knowledge to say that it is right opinion plus knowledge: plus knowledge of anything at all. Could he claim that this *aitia* was something other than *knowledge* of the *aitia*?[43]

Correct opinion about the *aitia* seems quite inadequate to turn another opinion into knowledge.

However, any of these commentators who read the *Meno* into the *Theaetetus* would be familiar with the use of the Theory of Recollection to avoid vicious regresses (80d ff.). They would not hesitate to think of our acts of getting to know something in terms of prior, albeit unrecognised knowledge. It is not unthinkable that an act of knowledge-acquisition, i.e. knowledge-recovery, should consciously or unconsciously involve prior knowledge that can supply the ground upon which one's calculation of an answer is based. Recollectable knowledge is sufficiently different from the kind of acquired knowledge discussed in the *Theaetetus*, yet of sufficient cognitive stature, to offer hope of avoiding the problems posed by the closing pages of that work. Indeed one would be at least free to argue that recollectable knowledge is not 'simple' but 'systematic'.

Clues as to TC's solution are available to anybody willing to give the same unitary reading of the commentary that TC gave to Plato. We have established that he did not want an *argument* to explain the argument that justified the right opinion: for the *Theaetetus* had discouraged one from believing this could yield knowledge. What he needed was rather some *truth* to found that argument upon. A prominent source of truth in TC are the common or natural notions, his epistemological equivalent of the Platonic Idea and an acknowledged starting-point of demonstration in early imperial philosophy.[44] There is no better candidate for identification with the binding *aitia*, for TC at least, than the natural notion upon which the reasoning is grounded. Consider the following: (i) the binding process of the *Meno* is seen as the acquisition of simple knowledge (15.16-23, cf. 31-3). (ii) the acquisition of simple[45] knowledge (learning, 16.14-17.32) is conceived of as Recollection (46-57). Finally Recollection is nothing more than the awakening and unpacking of those natural notions (47.37-48.7, cf. 46.43-9).[46] Binding = acquisition of simple knowledge = learning = recollection = awakening & unpacking of natural notions. This equation should occasion no surprise. *Meno* 98a explicitly identifies the binding process with Recollection, and Middle Platonism in general explains 'recollection' in terms of a new awareness of the natural notions.

There are welcome consequences of such a theory. First, it turns Plato's Socrates into somebody who actually leads people forward to knowledge; although he is not a teacher in the sense of an *implanter* of new knowledge, the very practice that is found to be most characteristic of him, the 'midwifery' by which he unfolds the natural notions, can be viewed as a process of *teaching* (47.33-8), that is to say of knowledge-production. Socrates' educational methods are thus elevated to a stature where they can serve as a *complete* education rather than as an initial purificatory process.[47] This would mean that the very practices that can result in knowledge are being dramatically *demonstrated* in the *Theaetetus*, even though they do not in this case achieve success.[48] Second, it is in broad agreement with an important aspect of Alcinous' *Didascalicus*; here chapter 4 is quite specific that intellection is the starting-point of 'knowledge-giving *logos*', meaning by 'intellection' the acquisition of recollectable knowledge in our pre-carnate existence (155.28-32). Those intellections are reawakened in this life by Recollection, and function as natural notions in our present life. Natural notions are given various alternative names, one of which is 'simple knowledge', and it is stated that 'from these knowledges that are simple arises 'natural and knowledge-giving reason', naturally implanted in us (155.32-6). Slight differences from TC's theory will be discussed below, but should not be allowed to obscure the same close links between the common notions and the production of knowledge, together with a distinction between simple and complex.

There is, however, an immediate problem that may seem to diminish the ability of our natural notions to explain knowledge. If they are 'natural', and indeed 'common', how is it that we are not all of the same intellectual standing? How can they produce knowledge in some cases and not in others? The seeds of a complete answer are present in Plato, but they are clearer still in TC. To begin with many individuals seem to have the natural notions buried deep within them. To use the *Theaetetus'* terms (151b), they are *in a way* not pregnant.[49] This does not mean that they have no trace of the natural notions within them, but that they are unable to access them during this life (57.29-33). Theaetetus himself differs, being pregnant; his natural aptitude is explained by his being replete with natural notions, and having them not too far hidden (47.19-24). This 'pregnancy' has a positive effect, and makes him persist in inquiring what knowledge might be (47.7-18), but it does not bring him to the answer. Why does he fall short? Because the presence of natural notions is not in itself enough. They need unpacking, or 'taking-apart-at-the-joints' (*diarthrôsis*: 46.43-5), which is precisely what Socrates' midwife-like skills would ideally achieve (47.37-45). They do have a role to play in cognition before they are unpacked, when we are able to employ only their traces, but it is a comparatively shady one (46.45-9). That is why Theaetetus can neither offer nor hear from another a satisfactory explanation of knowledge (47.1-7).

So the degree to which we grasp the natural notions determines whether we have no clue at all, raw intellectual gifts like Theaetetus, or the proper knowledge that can be restored to us through Socratic questioning. These three conditions are firmly rooted in the *Meno* itself. They are characterised by the indifference, and even obstructionism, of Meno himself to questions of concept-grasping; the unreasoned grasp of some truths by intuitively-gifted seers, poets and politicians (99c-e),[50] which is comparable also with the unsure correct opinions that the slave boy arrived at, as if after a dream (85c); and finally the accurate geometrical knowledge that the slave might eventually achieve through further questioning (85d-86a), that seems to have no counterpart in the world of politics though theoretically possible (100a).

The surprising thing about TC's conviction that the *Meno* should be read into the *Theaetetus* is that it actually seems to have strong advantages for the interpretation of the *Meno*. The epistemological content within that dialogue begins to have a unity that modern interpretation seldom allows for. The Theory of Recollection, instead of being a quaint attempt to explain how discovery is possible, dependent in turn upon an earlier discovery that requires explanation itself, becomes a doctrine of innate knowledge (however acquired), that underpins other epistemological considerations in the *Meno* and the rest of Platonic epistemology too. We know that by Cicero's time some thinker had actually utilised the Theory of Recollection to explain dream divination, with the undisturbed soul recalling how it had shared visions of the future with other souls, including the divine.[51] With the slave-boy's new correct opinion being compared with the post-dream condition at 85c9, and the cognitive condition of prophets being compared with that of successful politicians at 99c-e, this is not totally far-fetched. If the success of prophets was attributed to subconsciously accessed recollectable knowledge, then it is likely that the 'divine portion' that inspired some politicians (99e) was explained in a similar fashion at this time.

The subconscious influence of recollectable knowledge is something that Plato himself utilised at times. In the *Phaedrus* the strength or weakness of our 'memory' of the Beautiful is said to influence our behaviour at the sight of beautiful young persons (250d ff.). In the *Phaedo* infants are said to appreciate the imperfection of physical instances of equality etc. as soon as they begin to see them (74d-75d), but in nearly all cases not even adults have fully recollected what perfect equality is (76b-c). Here subconscious recollectable knowledge is playing a vital role in cognition without ever being properly 'recollected'. In these circumstances it is not at all strange that early interpreters such as TC should have postulated the influence of our 'natural notions' upon matters of both behaviour and cognition long before we come to understand them well enough to be able to give an account of them and to use them consciously for the solution of philosophic problems.

v. Cross-dialogue interpretation (2) *Phaedo*

The place where TC will give his interpretation of the Theory of Recollection is his own *Phaedo*-commentary (48.7-11).[52] The *Phaedo* offers an allusion to the *Meno* as it introduces the Theory of Recollection (73a-b), and no interpreter for whom that theory is important will neglect it. It must therefore be significant that the kind of recollected knowledge that is discussed in the *Phaedo* involves the Recollection of the Platonic Ideas (74a-76e). While TC does not, in extant parts of the commentary, discuss the Theory of Ideas per se, there is no doubt that that the common (or natural) notions are the vital underpinnings of his version of the Theory of Recollection and of Socratic Midwifery.[53] Moreover, the terminology of the *Phaedo* actually encourages that link, as Cicero for instance had noticed.[54] It is therefore legitimate to pay special attention to this dialogue when discussing TC's interpretation of epistemological passages of the *Meno*.

When TC discusses Theaetetus' difficulties in offering an answer to the question of what knowledge is, he is attributing them to the fact that his natural notions have not been unpacked. At 46.45-9 we meet the following:

> Before this they notice (*epiballousi*) things (*pragmata*) by possessing traces of them, but not with clarity.

There are some unknowns here, including (i) the subject of *epiballousi*; which might be the natural notions or people in general; (ii) the verb's precise meaning, even given that it had a regular cognitive sense at this time; (iii) whether it is people or things that possess the traces, and (iv) whether they are traces of things or the natural notions. The context is concerned principally about what *people* can do as a result of the common notions, and 'things' are regularly objects of cognition (or of definition) in this commentary. I interpret the verb here and elsewhere as concerned with the *empirical* process of concept-formation from repeated experience,[55] and in an epistemological context rather than a metaphysical one I should expect that it is our own possession of traces of the natural notions that is referred to.[56] Hence I believe the passage means that people are able to build up concepts of things as a result of their retaining traces of subconscious recollectable knowledge. An inkling of the natural notions is guiding the way in which we come to conceive of things. This is a message that Ur-C could have taken directly from *Phaedo* 74-6. The theory of that passage, when read into the dialogue at hand, would mean that Theaetetus has had a subconscious awareness of what knowledge is from the beginning, and that this awareness had assisted him in classifying and evaluating instances of knowledge that he has observed – as indeed 146c-d suggests. Even so, there would be no expectation that he would be able to offer an adequate account of knowledge. Given that TC treated Recollection along with the *Phaedo*, it does seem highly probable that he is following the *Phaedo* on the *subconscious effects* of our innate *a priori* knowledge.

Besides its obvious relevance for Plato's epistemology, the *Phaedo* may be significant in offering both an elaborate passage on *aitiai* (95e ff.), and a discussion of a method of hypothesis (100a-b, 101d-e). The crucial hypothesis adopted there is the existence of Ideas (of the beautiful, good, large, etc.) in which particulars participate, and which are themselves the *aitia* of a thing being beautiful, good, big, etc. As with the objects of *noêsis* in the Divided Line section of *Republic* 6, there seems here to be some ordered series of 'hypotheses' that interlock and form what one might think of as a *system*. If a hypothesis is challenged one goes back to some more basic hypothesis. Hence the passage offers unitarian interpreters considerable scope for links with the two other works where hypotheses feature, *Meno* and *Republic* 6. The vital question, however, will be whether Ur-C used its theory of causes or reasons, unparalleled in the rest of the corpus, in explaining the *aitia* of *Meno* 98a.

The *structure* of the *Phaedo* may have been a key consideration. By an impressive group of arguments Socrates had convinced most of the gathering of the immortality of the soul by 84b. Simmias and Cebes remain unconvinced, and offer their famous challenges to Socrates' conclusion. Those who had previously come to a firm belief in personal immortality are thrown into a state of scepticism. They doubt their own judgment, and they doubt also that things are knowable (88c). Echecrates is brought back into the dialogue to echo their experiences, and to express his own sudden loss of confidence in previously convincing arguments. The *Phaedo* is here illustrating exactly what is wrong with unsecured correct opinion: that it may be rapidly overthrown. Socrates knows that he needs more than his previous arguments if lasting conviction is to be implanted in his hearers. It is not that he distrusts argument, though he does realise that skill and confidence in handling it is called for by all concerned (89d-90d). In fact, the defeat of Cebes is going to involve him in an account of the *aitia* of coming to be and passing away (95e). If the depiction of unsecured correct opinion had not earlier been fortuitous, then one would be correct in expecting the account of this *aitia* to be what finally secures it – at least for Cebes (107a). Soul must have certain properties as a result of its being, or bearing, the *aitia* of life, as fire bears the cause of heat. One of these properties is to be deathless itself (105b-e).

It appeared above that TC thought simple knowledge depended not just on an account of one's correct opinion, but something to explain *why* that account holds. How well does the postulation of this sort of *aitia* fit such a theory? Whether the major part is played by Plato's Ideas, as revealed through our natural notions, or whether the important part is played rather by those things that are naturally conceived as bearing a given Idea, the explanation of a correct opinion will depend ultimately on the implications of a concept. Plato can be depicted as teasing out in the *Phaedo* what is implied in the natural notion of soul: that its power is to cause life, just as fever's power is to cause sickness or the monad's to cause oddness. Knowledge-giving explanations are thus grounded in the store of recollectable concepts that had been with us from birth.

vi. Simple and complex in *Meno* and *Phaedo*

The distinction between simple and complex knowledge was evidently a crucial one for TC and Ur-C alike, more important than any similar distinction that we should make when interpreting Plato today. If it was read into the *Theaetetus* and the *Republic*, then presumably it could also be read into works thought to illustrate the same epistemology, such as the *Meno* and the *Phaedo*. Certainly, in so far as the *Meno* was being read as an epistemological work, it was seen as concerning simple rather than complex knowledge. But are there no hints in the text there that Plato recognised the existence of an integrated knowledge, perhaps one still more secure than right opinion bound by reasoning and cause? There are a few significant passages that deserve to be noticed even today:

(a) 76b2: the use of the plural 'geometries' would suggest that Plato works with the same distinction as in *Republic* 6-7.

(b) 81c9-d4: the notion that the kinship of all nature can explain our ability to build on our Recollection of just one thing so as to 'recollect' anything (or everything) else does suggest that recollected knowledge is an interlocking system, whether one regards the 'one thing' as (1) the recollectability of knowledge itself, (2) any single recollectable thing, or (3), in a unitarian's eyes, the Idea of the Good which is the supreme explanatory principle in *Republic* 6.[57] The first of these possibilities does not really demand the kinship of all nature anyway. The remaining two demand that adherence to one piece of (simple) knowledge will be a guide as one tries to discover others, *because knowledge is ultimately an interlocking system*.

(c) 85e1-3: The slave boy will be able to have the same recollective experiences 'concerning all geometry, and the other mathematical sciences in their entirety'. Our interpreters must surely have associated this language with what they called complex or systematic knowledge. It would naturally be contrasted with the slave-boy's being able to recollect one single piece of geometrical knowledge.

(d) 87b5-8, 87d2-3: The very different nature of the two types of hypothesis, one rendered by the conditional, the other confidently postulated, is strongly suggestive of two kinds of hypothesis to be employed in different epistemological processes: one securely founded upon some more basic tenet within a system, the other unable to be supported immediately by any independent confirmation.

(e) 87e ff.: The possible relationship now being explored between knowledge and excellence is suggestive of systematic knowledge rather than individual knowledge-items. The notion of *knowledge* as a guide to successful conduct gives way to the term *wisdom* (*phronêsis*) when popular notions of the virtues are introduced, suggesting a systematic awareness (88b4c2, c5, c7, d3, d6, e6, 89a1, a3).

(f) 98a: The notion that knowledge is in some way right opinions bound by something else is again suggestive of simple knowledge, unless one can have such a thing as *systematic* correct opinion.

(g) 98d10, d12, e7: The language of *phronêsis* rather than *epistêmê* figures in the recapitulation of the material on the link between wisdom and virtue. It is replaced by *epistêmê* when dealing with what can lead human action (99a2, a5, a7, b3), which might of course be presumed to be an individual piece of knowledge. The changing terminology may consistently reflect some distinction between knowledge-types on Plato's part.

(h) 100a: The truly excellent person (at the level of *polis* affairs), who could make another similarly excellent, is likened to Tiresias, who still has his intellectual faculties[58] while others flit aimlessly around. Like *phronêsis*, Tiresias' knowledge is presumably understood as some kind of intellectual complex. Indeed it is a complex of other-worldly knowledge that owes nothing to the ordinary source of empirical data, one's eyes. He is not just like ordinary seers, whose status is similar to that of ordinary politicians because they do not know any of the inspired truths that they utter (99c-d); he has some kind of systematic knowledge, some deeper understanding.

Thus, given that Ur-C, in interpreting Plato, is convinced of the importance of the distinction between simple and complex knowledge, there was ample opportunity for him to find it in the *Meno* too. What of the *Phaedo*? It may help to distinguish the following five elements of the dialogue's epistemology:

(i) a ground of knowledge that we bring into this world with us, and upon which our acquisition of knowledge is based;

(ii) triggers towards the activation of this ground, supplied here by sensation;

(iii) discursive reasoning processes (*dianoia*, *logismos*) aided at times by sensation;

(iv) conclusions which involve deduction from that initial ground, and which are now able to be described as cases of knowledge (*epistêmê*);

(v) realised fully only in the world beyond, a systematic knowledge of Ideas for which the mind should be independent of the senses (*phronêsis*).

Of these five factors only the first and last seem 'systematic', and the gulf between the fourth and fifth is crucial for the distinction in question. That the philosopher's goal in this work is *phronêsis* (wisdom) above all else is evident from various passages commencing with 65a9.[59] In the strictest sense *phronêsis* seems attainable only in the disembodied state after or before this life (68a7-b4, 76c12), or by a disembodied being (80d7). However, Plato is concerned initially with the steps that the philosopher may take towards individual truths rather than *phronêsis* as a whole,[60] and he talks in this context of our using discursive thought (*dianoia*) and reasoning-processes.[61]

There is then a considerable shift in terminology when we meet the discussion of learning as Recollection (72e-76e), and of the innate knowledge required to enable us to recollect. Here the language of 'knowledge' (*epistêmê*) is used freely along with other neutral terms that could in Ur-C's eyes refer either to simple or to complex knowledge.[62] This fits his interpretation well, since the passage begins with a discussion of the mechanics of Recollection in general, which focuses on individual cognitive acts, but moves on to postulate a more general awareness of the Ideas in the pre-carnate soul. The terminology most characteristic is that of bringing something to mind (*ennoia* etc.),[63] and here we are certainly talking of the Recollection of particular knowledge-items.[64] The terminology of *dianoia* and of *logismos* appropriate to the philosopher's search for higher knowledge is passed over.[65] Only at the end of the passage (76c12) does the term *phronêsis* occur, now as the complex of pre-natal knowledge which had already been referred to at 75d4 by the plural of *epistêmê*.[66]

Relevant terminology recurs on a smaller scale in the course of the argument from similarity between 79a and 84a. At 79a we are told that one can *only* grasp Ideas by the *logismos* of the *dianoia*, reintroducing momentarily the terminology of 65c-66a.[67]

Overall, the *Phaedo* does not *emphasise* a distinction between simple and complex knowledge, but it is natural for those who stress it elsewhere in Plato to employ it consistently and constructively as an analytical tool here too. Plato is viewing *phronêsis* as a condition of the discarnate soul in which it is conscious of an *interrelated world* of Ideas; accordingly *phronêsis* is the goal of the philosophic life. On the other hand, the incarnate soul characteristically works towards knowledge relating to *individual Ideas* through discursive reasoning processes. These processes, aided by sensation, ultimately jog one's memory and inspire cognition stemming from the Idea – even though it is no longer within the view of the soul. The recollected inkling of the Idea is what is being viewed as an *ennoêma* in the Recollection-passage, an internal reliving of the intelligible Idea beyond. Just as memory of things seen and heard is independent of any sense-organ, and is not in itself a 'grasp' of anything, so too there is no 'grasp' of the *ennoêma*, it is simply there within the womb of memory.[68] So Plato may say that *dianoia* and *logismos* alone can 'grasp' the Ideas in our present life (79a), for we can no longer have any direct experience of them.

This is not the place for a critique of such a reading of Platonic Recollection. What is important is that a relatively sophisticated approach, with attention to subtle changes of terminology, is compatible with the application to Plato's works in general of this distinction between simple and complex knowledge. The Recollection-passage of the *Phaedo* is critical because TC intended to explain his reading of Platonic Recollection, hence of the key elements in his epistemology, when commenting on it (47.43-48.11). It is vital that he would have been able to find there (1) a trace of recollectable knowledge, (2) a trigger to awaken it, (3) discursive reasoning processes, (4) knowledge-items, and (5) a wider wisdom – all the key elements of his own epistemology.

vii. Consistency

The distinction between simple and complex (or systematic) knowledge in TC was a straightforward one, not difficult for the layman to grasp. Geometry, music, and the like are complex or systematic *epistêmai* in the sense of 'sciences' or 'crafts'. Individual bits of geometry, however, are often treated as 'knowledge' even when they are encountered in those individuals who may not possess the craft as a whole. The slave-boy in the *Meno* is one (85c-d). Socrates in the same work claims only to know *a few things* (98b). Theaetetus has learnt only items of geometry from Theodorus (145c). In the Recollection passage of the *Phaedo* individuals draw on past cognition of the transcendent Ideas to the extent that they can appreciate how particulars fall short of them. But all that is normally possible is to approach Ideas one at a time.

The distinction must also work the same way when applied to *Republic* 6 and 7. A true science of geometry, of music, or of astronomy could not be the object of *dianoia* alone, but would rather be a legitimate object of *noêsis*, working within the realm of theory alone. In fact *Republic* 7 paints such an alien picture of the five mathematical disciplines that we can imagine Plato believing in such sciences.[69] Again, the process of coming to grasp a single Idea could not in itself be called *noêsis*, but would rather be an act of *dianoia* as it seems to have been in the *Phaedo*. This is acceptable interpretation, because Plato quite clearly sees the higher process of *noêsis* as working within the world of Ideas, from one to another (511bc), in a way that will obviously involve a complex grasp. The corresponding science of dialectic is not represented as one whose aim is to bring us to an awareness of just one Idea, not even of the Idea of the Good that is the greatest of them. In a nutshell, it may be said that *dianoia* transfers the mind into the world of Ideas, *noêsis* operates wholly within it.[70]

However, it was not simply a group of *Platonic* works between which Ur-C was attempting to find links. Ps.Hero and Column 15 of TC alike imply that a comparable theory of simple knowledge was held by Plato, Aristotle, and Zeno. They could not have attributed a theory of Ideas to Aristotle and Zeno, but then they felt more comfortable working with natural notions than with Platonic Ideas anyway. There was no need for our commentators to claim that Aristotle and Zeno would have sanctioned Plato's entire epistemology, and to take syncretism too far was to undermine one's distinctive claims, upon which one relied for an income, to teach a philosophy that understood the basics of the human cognitive condition. However, this still sounds like more than a simple doxographic insertion, being highly selective in its choice of philosophers and somewhat surprising in the definitions that it chooses for them. So what are they doing introducing Aristotle and Zeno at all? Are they in fact appealing to Aristotle and Zeno as secondary authorities, or making a point against contemporary Peripatetics and Stoics? Let us briefly consider the 'definitions' attributed to Aristotle and Zeno.

Aristotle was supposed to have defined simple knowledge as 'assumption (*hypolêpsis*) plus demonstration'. No such definition is extant, and, though it does not seem implausible,[71] we are probably dealing with an attempt to show how Aristotle *explained* simple knowledge rather than how he *defined* it. Ur-C may well have had well-known texts in mind when offering this explanation, and a passage mentioned by Mansfeld (p. 63) in this context may have been important. In one well-known location that TC knew,[72] *technê* is said to arise 'whenever one universal assumption (*hypolêpsis*) results from many *ennoêmata* of experience'. The close connexion between a *hypolêpsis* of this kind and *ennoêmata* makes it possible for it to be seen as the empirical Aristotelian equivalent of the natural notion. If one couples this with the common Aristotelian doctrine that *epistêmê* involves the ability to demonstrate, one can see him too as demanding the combination of natural notions and reasoning processes: simple knowledge will involve this appreciation of a universal concept or rule, and the ability to demonstrate it.[73]

We should now consider the case of the Stoics. Of the four definitions of knowledge which are attributed to the Stoics by Stobaeus (*Ecl.* 2.73.16-74.3 = SVF 3.112) two are of some kind of 'system', leaving two which could be referring to what Ur-C would have known as 'simple knowledge'. These are 'secure cognition (*katalepsis*), unchangeable by reason' and 'a *hexis* for the reception of presentations, unchangeable by reason'.[74] It is remarkable that the second of these has been selected to illustrate Zenonian simple knowledge, since the other seems the only one that unequivocally refers to single cognitive acts. However, if we bear in mind that Ur-C is really trying to *explain* rather than to define simple knowledge along Stoic lines, we see that this is the definition that does explain. Presentations have in this case attained the status of simple knowledge because they have been accompanied by a *hexis* unchangeable by reason. Why is the *hexis* unchangeable by reason? Surely because it operates without fail in accordance with universal reason, through which it gains access to certain fundamental truths, including the common notions.

We are not here arguing for the validity of such an understanding of Stoic epistemology, nor for the desirability of reconciling it with texts of Plato. What we are arguing is that such an understanding is reasonable, given the strong tendency of this era towards syncretism. It is not unlikely that Ur-C lived while Antiochus of Ascalon still had some influence, particularly his theory that Plato, Aristotle, and the Stoa (under Zeno at least)[75] had different ways of expressing their views rather than different doctrines.[76] It does appear to differ from the epistemology associated with Antiochus himself, for his natural powers of the mind that underlie sensation, concept-formation, reason, and then (when an appropriate state is apparently reached) cognition itself,[77] has been replaced now by natural notions.[78] However, in Cicero we can find one with a debt to Antiochus, who made important strides towards making the natural notions central.

viii. Recollection in Cicero and the logic of 'assimilation to god'

At this point we need to go back to an openly syncretist Ciceronian text that showed the clear influence of Platonic Recollection. We have discussed this passage, whose importance was indicated by Glucker (1999), in ch. 5.8, but it is worth reminding ourselves of Cicero's mocking summary of the argument at 2.119:

All souls are drawn from a single divine source.
Hence they are able to share one another's intuitions.
The future is known to at least one soul.
Hence the future is potentially known to all souls.

As a result of this we suggested at the close of Chapter 5 that *Meno* 81c9-d2, utilised by Cratippus, was being read as teaching that 'because its [the soul's] entire nature is akin, and all things have been learned by soul, nothing prevents one, after recollecting just one thing, from discovering all the rest'.

This early use of the Theory of Recollection to explain quite unexpected types of cognition, stemming in part at least from subconscious experiences, should be useful in explaining how the theory became so crucial in TC and Ur-C. It shows how our innate recollectable knowledge could be grounded not in *what we had seen* in a previously existence, but in *what we had been*. Socrates had, after all, been quite non-committal over the background details of the Theory of Recollection (*Meno* 86b6-7), and the slave-boy episode only showed what knowledge one had, not how it had originated. We had been, in fact, knowing beings by our very nature, suited by our divine provenance to sharing in those Ideas that belonged rightly in the divine mind.

Cicero agrees broadly with this in a more personal account involving the Recollection Theory at *Tusculan Disputations* 1.56-65. The overall theme is that of the divine element within our souls. He moves swiftly to the unlimited 'memory' that the *Meno* traces to an earlier life (57), and from there to the *Phaedo*, which is seen as the more detailed account of Recollection – an account involving notions impressed upon our minds in a non-corporeal world. The relevance of the Ideas is appreciated, and Cicero recognises that our prior state of knowledge removes any need to wonder at the extent of our cognitive powers now (58). The same power within us is responsible for discovery and for working things out (61); it is responsible for poetry, rhetoric, and philosophy (64). It is responsible for the fact that Archimedes could construct a model of the heavens in imitation of the creator-god of the *Timaeus* (63).

Here we see a further important step in the theory that explains Recollection as arising from our close kinship with a divine soul. The best of human activity imitates the divine. This is because the powers of soul owe everything to our unimpeded knowledge in a non-corporeal existence when we were more like that divine power. Hence, in order to maximise our present cognitive powers, we need to throw off the discordant influence of the body (cf. 58), and seek to return to our divine state. Take the case of Archimedes:

> Assuming [heavenly movements] could not arise in our universe without a god, so Archimedes could not even have imitated the same movements in his sphere without a divine intellect. (1.63)

Kinship with the divine is paramount. By assimilating ourselves to the divine mind during our earthly existence we can restore our remarkable cognitive and creative powers to a significant degree. Any such theory, that makes kinship with the divine (best experienced in a non corporeal state) the basis for human cognitive ability, would encourage the flight of the soul from this world to that, and assimilation to that same god insofar as is possible, as required by *Theaetetus* 176b. When we reach TC the goal of assimilation is already in place (7.14-20), and Recollection is fundamental to inquiry and learning. It is the contention here that their coupling is no accident.

Let us briefly reflect on the hermeneutical problems that the doctrine of assimilation to god would have posed for interpreters of the *Theaetetus*. Though it occurs during what is today regarded as an *ethical* digression, so that we are not usually inclined to afford it any role of epistemological significance, no ancient commentator would fail to notice that important things are said there about *wisdom*. To begin with 'Assimilation is becoming just and holy along with wisdom [*phronêsis*]' (176b2-3). Moral improvement is here tied to the (re-)acquisition of that body of knowledge that the philosopher seeks in the *Phaedo*, for which there too he dissociates himself with his physical surroundings. After a discussion of god's justice, and our need to imitate this, we read 'For it is the recognition of this that is true wisdom (*sophia*) and excellence, while failure to recognise is ignorance and outstanding vice.' This is followed by a dismissive attitude to other cases of so-called cleverness and wisdom, in the worlds of politics or industry. That wisdom (*sophia*) had been the same as knowledge had been argued long before at 145d-e, where TC strives hard to find to make the argument cogent (16.14-17.32). Hence Socrates' statement about true wisdom in the 'digression' seems to involve the answer to the principal question of the dialogue – the exact nature of knowledge.

It seems, then, that the doctrine of assimilation in the *Theaetetus* introduces something that must be seen as a kind of knowledge, and that ought to be considered when exploring the work's epistemology. Yet it also involves the philosopher in a flight to another world that is reminiscent above all of the *Phaedo*, so that the kind of knowledge needed can reasonably be identified with the kind that the *Phaedo* aims at. For the revived Platonism this is the overall body knowledge that belongs to us in a discarnate existence, and it is this totality of recollectable knowledge that opens up gradually to us as we liken ourselves to the being who most perfectly possesses it. Neither TC (7.14-20) nor Alcinous (*Didasc.* 28) makes the mistake of restricting this assimilation to our intellectual selves, but it is on intellectual likeness that the emphasis regularly falls. This is the case in Alcinous, in the source of Stobaeus *Eclogues* 2.49.8-25, and in Albinus (*Prol.* 5), for whom our intellect's imitation of a heavenly intellect at *Timaeus* 90b-d seems to be the key source.[79]

ix. Historical considerations

I hope that I have shown the existence of a sophisticated interpretation of Platonic epistemology, involving detailed interpretation of at least four dialogues, ranging from the 'early/middle' *Meno* to the 'middle/late' *Theaetetus*, no later than the time of the Platonist Taurus. We have called the originator of the interpretation Ur-C, and have not discussed in detail possible identification with either Taurus or TC who preserve the evidence for the interpretation. We are in a marginally better position to comment now, but it should be emphasised that our knowledge of Platonic interpretation during this period is slight, and one can expect only provisional conclusions. Furthermore, we do not know the extent to which commentators in this period might have been prepared to draw heavily on previous commentaries, as becomes the case with Alexandrian Neoplatonism. We are postulating an interpreter who fits the following pattern:

1. Believed that Plato had doctrines, doctrines that could be revealed, if indirectly, in the passages where a midwife-like 'Socrates' was operating.
2. Believed that he distinguished simple from complex knowledge.
3. Believed in the validity of cross-dialogue interpretation.
4. Made much use of the Theory of Recollection.
5. Though demonstrably a Platonist, was inclined towards, or influenced by, a syncretism embracing Plato, Aristotle and Zeno of Citium: precisely the syncretism associated with the school of Antiochus of Ascalon.
6. May have adhered to the aberrant text of *Meno* 98a3-4, hence giving priority to the *aitia* rather than *logismos* as a source of simple knowledge.
7. Declined to detect a separate class of mathematicals that constituted the objects of *dianoia*.
8. Commented on at least one and probably both of *Republic* 6 (Divided Line) and *Theaetetus*.

As we have seen, point 7 seems to make Ur-C atypical of Middle Platonism. Point 6 counts against Taurus, *assuming that* Ps.Hero faithfully preserves Taurus' reading. Point 5 counts against both Taurus and TC, though not decisively. From these details little can be said other than that our interpreter flourished some time between Antiochus of Ascalon and Taurus, a period of around two centuries. During this period we cannot even expect to know the names of all important Platonic interpreters, and only Eudorus, Thrasyllus, Theon of Smyrna, and Plutarch are known to us as significantly more than names. Points 5 and 7, and probably 8, count against Plutarch, but the epistemologies and other leanings of Eudorus and Thrasyllus are poorly documented. Material in Porphyry's *Commentary on Ptolemy's Harmonics* that might stem from Thrasyllus[80] shows only superficial points of contact, and (significantly) little direct debt to Platonic dialogues. Theon wrote some exegetical work on the *Republic* (*Expositio* p. 146.3-4 Hiller), but it is likely to have been limited to his own mathematical interests: in the same way as the work of Clearchus, Dionysius, and possibly Dercyllides had been.[81] Of other commentators on the *Republic* (or aspects of it) prior to Taurus, we know nothing of relevance about the work of Potamo of Alexandria or Onosander.[82] We have no evidence of Middle Platonist commentaries on the *Theaetetus* other than TC.

It is clear that we are unlikely to be able to identify Ur-C, but he was still influential. If both TC and the well-known Taurus could follow him closely enough to maintain nearly identical wording, then he is was a figure who seemed to them to be important. We now raise the possibility that another author has followed him on epistemological matters.

x. Comparison with *Didascalicus* 4

We have hitherto avoided discussing the relationship between Ur-C and the doctrine of simple knowledge which appears at *Didascalicus* 4 (p. 155.31-6 Whittaker). Despite the use of key terms such as 'simple knowledge', 'common notion', and *perilepsis*,[83] this at first seems very different.[84] But common terms are important: Alcinous is at this point obsessed with terminology, believes that he is giving Platonic epistemological terms,[85] and specifically attributes terminology to Plato at three points in the chapter.[86] Since he is often incorrect, it is likely they are in fact the terms by which some earlier interpreter, a direct or indirect source, had explained Plato. The question that now arises is whether Ur-C had been a source of Alcinous here.

Before examining part of chapter four in detail, we should see how far its material would be compatible with seven of the eight[87] observations that we have made about Ur-C:

1. There can be no doubt that the chapter reflects the belief that Plato

had doctrines, even where a midwife-like 'Socrates' was operating, for the *Theaetetus* itself is a significant source (155.41-155.13).

2. It distinguished simple from complex knowledge (155.32-6).

3. It utilised cross-dialogue interpretation, using *Tim.*, *Tht.*, *Phlb.*, *Phdr.*, and *Sph.*, and possibly *Rep.*, and *Phd.*[88]

4. It utilised the Platonic Ideas and the Theory of Recollection.

5. It shows an inclination towards syncretism embracing Plato, Aristotle (155.42-156.2), and Stoicism in general.[89]

6. Far from using a given text of *Meno* 98a3-4, the passage makes no explicit use of this dialogue. Memory of the Idea certainly explains simple knowledge, and, though cause-terminology is not present, it may be relevant that our discarnate vision of the Ideas is the origin of the (systematic) knowledge-producing reason (*epistêmonikos logos*).[90] For this suggests that the (individual) Idea is the *cause of the reasoning* needed to yield a single case of *epistêmê*.

7. It makes no mention of a separate metaphysical status for mathematicals, so cannot link them with *dianoia*. 'Second intelligibles' (155.40), or 'forms-in-matter', may be a substitute. The only process described by the term *dianoia* is internal mental debate (155.17-19).

None of these similarities is conclusive, but when combined they are such as to suggest some kind of link between Ur-C and *Didascalicus* 4. We should therefore examine the passage most relevant to the role of an Idea-trace in guiding the individual towards knowledge.

At 155.20 Alcinous defines intellection (*noêsis*) as the activity of intelligence contemplating the Ideas. Two kinds are distinguished, pre-corporeal and corporeal. The former is the source (*archê*) of knowledge (*epistêmê*, 154.32-3) or of scientific reason (*epistêmonikos logos*, 155.28-9). The present name of the latter kind of intellection,[91] when we speak of what occurs in this bodily existence, is said to be 'natural notion'. The sharp differentiation between original vision and present recollection found in the *Phaedo*, and the denial of anything approaching that vision to any human being other than the philosopher (as in the *Phaedrus*), have been discussed above. The natural notion is now said to be also called by Plato 'simple knowledge', 'wing of the soul', and 'memory'. Of these expressions the second relates to *Phdr.* 246e, and the third is connected by Whittaker[92] and others with *Phdr.* 249c5 and 250a5. Clearly the effect is to connect the natural notions with aspects of the Theory of Recollection, but I doubt that any Platonist really intended to allude to the *Phaedrus* by this last term, which in not prominent there. It is more logical, given Alcinous' well-known tactic of repeating Platonic words and phrases with variation,[93] to suppose that none of these expressions is supposed to be exactly what Plato used. Just as 'simple' has been added for clarification, and the order of terms changed in the memorable phrase 'soul's wing', so 'memory' (*mnêmê*) is nothing but a stylistic variation on the well-known Platonic term 'recollection' (*anamnêsis*). In this case the intention was to allude to the role played by our memory-trace of the Idea in learning, as well as in judgments and in love – or, to put it differently, in the *Meno*, as well as in the *Phaedo* and *Phaedrus*.

However, it is quite plausible that all these terms were prominent in the exegesis of a principal source of chapter 4,[94] which would be enough to identify it as somebody who conformed broadly with points 1-5. Of course Ur-C did not *identify* the 'common notions' with 'simple knowledge', but we have argued that he made them responsible for it; the common notions are the beginning, and simple knowledge the end, of a Recollection-process. Both would be involved in a full account of Ur-C's Platonic epistemology. But seeing that Plato had been ready to call the latent memory-trace 'knowledge' as well as the fully conscious memory,[95] Alcinous cannot in this case be blamed for any confusion. He now goes on to say that 'natural and scientific reason' is constituted from the simple knowledge-bits (using the plural *epistêmai*), a reason that belongs in us by nature. This provides confirmation that the term 'simple knowledge' had been deliberately applied to cover latent as well as actualised recollectable knowledge. For the natural and scientific reason that is comprised of it, being present in us by nature (155.35-6), belongs to ordinary human beings, not just those few who can recognise Ideas. Indeed it is this reason which, not without intellection, judges ordinary forms in matter; while intelligence, not without this scientific reason, is the judge of the Ideas (156.5-7).

Commentators agree on the relevance of *Timaeus* 28a here,[96] and it can also explain why Ideas should be grasped 'not without' scientific reason; but it cannot explain why immanent forms must be grasped 'not without' intellection.[97] The Platonic precedent for this is rather the fact that a grasp of the defective nature of properties immanent in particulars is said in the *Phaedo* to be necessarily dependent on some awareness of the Idea (74e-75a). The *Phaedo* also provides a second parallel for the intellection of the Idea being 'not without' the power that apprehends forms in matter, since it is this which triggers the process of Recollection. The *Phaedo* is also relevant insofar as it supports the basic idea that our innate cognitive powers include both 'knowledge' *and a logos* relevant to the Recollection of that knowledge in this world (73a9-10). The notion of two interlocking cognitive powers or processes being required for Idea-related cognition is easily detected in this dialogue so crucial to Ur-C's epistemology.

One should therefore return to TC, and recall how his interpretation of the *Meno* demanded that a grasp of the Idea (as seen in the natural notion) should be added to reasoning in order to produce simple knowledge. Or again, how he demanded that reasoning processes employing definition should be utilised before the natural notion itself could be properly explicated (23.1-12).[98] One could indeed suggest that, for him as for the source of *Didascalicus* 4, *logos* does not yield *epistêmê* without *noêsis*,[99] nor does *noêsis* itself give a grasp of the Idea without logos. His interpretation of

Meno 98a has right opinions becoming knowledge by securing one's reasoning in an explanatory natural notion, and only then when we are fully conscious of it. The author of the *Didascalicus* might speak rather of judgments involving *epistemonikos logos* plus *noêsis*. Behind TC and parts of *Didascalicus* 4 there is significant similarity *in the underlying theory*. The latter is much more formulaic, but that is in part a consequence of the type of work it is.

xi. Conclusion

This chapter has taken twisted paths. The intricacy of the problems has made this almost unavoidable, but that very complexity is in a sense what it is necessary to appreciate. There had been some deep interpretative thinking on epistemological matters, thinking that has influenced both TC and Alcinous. It is precisely by trying to hide the complexities that Alcinous has produced an account that is neither straightforward reporting, nor exegesis – a tendency that has often been the cause for our failing to respect him.

We began by observing that more could be learnt from a passage common to two Middle Platonists, one commenting on the *Theaetetus* and the other on the *Republic*. The key step was to isolate the lemma of the *Republic* on which the latter, Taurus, had been commenting. This allowed us to discover the way certain Middle Platonists were interpreting not only the *Republic*, but also the *Meno* (quoted in the common passage), and the *Phaedo* (to which TC related key parts of the *Meno*). A coherent epistemological theory, based on a clever cross-dialogue reading of Plato, eventually emerged. Unfortunately, it is impossible to isolate the origin of this interpretation of Plato's epistemology. Suggestive links with *Didascalicus* 4 were encountered, but that cannot solve the historical problem, given that the sources of Alcinous are so poorly understood.

I shall, however, venture to make this suggestion. Given the relevance of epistemological uses of the 'X not without Y' formula,[100] it is rational to look for the common source of the *Theaetetus*-commentator, Taurus, and the *Didascalicus* in Alexandria in or before the time of Potamo, an early exegete of the *Republic*. There at around the same time lived Arius, Augustus' court philosopher, who may or may not be the Arius Didymus whose material is duplicated in *Didascalicus* 12.[101] Just before this time lived Eudorus of Alexandria, to whom important features of Middle Platonism can be traced. There shortly afterwards lived Philo in whom the influence of Middle Platonism is evident, and who shows greater interest in epistemology than is easily detected in later Middle Platonists such as Plutarch, Atticus, and Numenius.

Finally it seems appropriate to make one last observation about TC's identity. If we did not otherwise know of a Middle Platonist called Taurus, who is generally agreed to have come from Beirut,[102] we should have no hesitation in giving a name to TC. That name would be Taurus of Sidon. Nor should we need to postulate an Ur-C, since TC shows every sign of being deeply involved in an on-going debate over the interpretation of Plato's epistemology, and he appears to be offering the views that he expresses as his own solution. It remains possible that a Taurus of Sidon could have flourished unnoticed in the period in which Ur-C must be dated. Could he not have been a Platonist relative of Taurus of Beirut? Even if this were so, it would not help us. We should still be working in a vacuum, and we should still be forced to understand the background to TC in terms of the information and clues offered in the mutilated text. For the overall topic of this book the question of TC's (and Ur-C's) identity is not critical.

11

The debate over the *Theaetetus*

i. The background to the *Theaetetus*-commentary

On a number of interpretative issues TC provides us with information concerning the state of the debate on the *Theaetetus* to which he contributes. Sedley's study of different interpretations has postulated three different ancient approaches overall. All of them may be found within TC, even though traces of them may still be found in the commentaries of Proclus and Damascius, as well as in the anonymous *Prolegomena*.[1] He distinguishes the Academic-sceptic reading from the reading of interpreters discussed in column 2 (of whom he considers Alcinous a late representative), and both in turn from the approach of the author. The most obvious area of debate is that concerning the proposed topic (*prothesis*) of the *Theaetetus*. Next is the debate concerning the validity of appeals to Socratic irony, particularly with regard to deceitful claims to ignorance.[2] Then there is the debate over whether Plato teaches doctrine.[3] Here I concentrate on the first topic, but it cannot wholly be separated from the others. The debate over the *prothesis* was clearly of crucial concern, and must have constituted the central theme of TC. It was 'simple knowledge' that he had made the theme of the dialogue, and though we have investigated the theory in the previous chapter (with respect to its objects and its relation to the theory of recollection), we have yet to examine in a historical context why he has been so careful to single out this particular knowledge. Why has the seemingly straightforward distinction between an item of knowledge and a system of knowledge become so crucial at this time? Let us examine the relevant passages.

ii. Column 2

The background to TC's view of the *prothesis* appears principally in column 2 and fragment D. We hear that some Platonists, seen from fr. D to be in the majority, thought that the work was about the criterion (the CR interpretation). The original edition had another view being added, which made the *Theaetetus* discuss those things of which there is no knowledge and the *Sophist* knowable things (the TS interpretation).[4] If there had been two *contrasting* earlier theories, then one would have expected the Greek to flag this contrast,[5] but it may have been that TS was meant to be a variant of CR, rather than an alternative. The new edition gives us a reading that makes the proponents of CR hold TS too, but the new reading faces a considerable difficulty. Those who contrast the *Theaetetus* with the *Sophist* acknowledge that Plato *proposes* to speak about knowledge (2.32-3),[6] but the strong implication of 2.11-21 is that CR interpreters did not do so. Furthermore, it is hard to see how any interpreters who see Plato investigating things of which there is no knowledge in the *Theaetetus* would have taken the initiative in identifying the criterion *of truth* as its main concern. A cognitive criterion will not exist for objects to which no knowledge belongs, so that CR and TS could readily be combined only by doubters: those who wanted to show that Plato had investigated a criterion of truth, and failed to discover one. Hence, while agreeing with Sedley that Alcinous does share features of both CR and TS, I am reluctant to believe that CR and TS had always been connected.

One should realise what is under discussion in column 2. TC has been tackling a problem concerning the subject of the *Theaetetus* that occurs to many a modern reader. Why, he is asking, does a work of 69 Stephanus pages go on for at least 45 pages, and perhaps even more, without making any serious attempt to explain knowledge, the concept for which a definition has been asked? There would have been increased difficulty for those familiar with Stoicism, insofar as Stoic knowledge is properly confined to the sage, in whom it will be present in a systematic way. What is sought in the *Theaetetus* is neither confined to the sage, nor of a systematic kind. To that extent the subject of the work would bear a greater resemblance to the Stoics' criterion of truth, the *katalêptikê phantasia*, than to their knowledge. These two factors lie behind CR.

TC, however, holds that the large section of the dialogue leading up to the refutation of Protagoras is present because Theaetetus must first be *purged* of the teaching of Protagoras (2.1-11). He needs this as the pupil of a Protagorean, and as one who has already been led astray by Protagoras' book *On Truth*. In contrast, the emphasis on the theory of Protagoras has led TS interpreters to propose that the *prothesis* is not meant to be constructively investigated until one reads the *Sophist*. Thinking rather like Cornford,[7] and certainly in a more Platonic manner, they considered that the *Theaetetus* must necessarily fail to give an account of knowledge, since it deals with things where no knowledge is to be found. They would have noted that the discussion had dealt largely with objects of the sensible world, paying some attention also to mere phantoms and to mathematical truths. They thought that it contrasted with the work that continues Theaetetus' education, the *Sophist*, owing to the latter's preoccupation with genus, species, and *logos* – seen perhaps as Ideas and propositional truths.

TC has an answer to both of these groups. It is because the *Theaetetus* is about simple knowledge, i.e. individual cognitive acts, that it cannot avoid occupying itself with questions of a criterion of truth. He is actually *agreeing* with CR to a degree, for to those of Stoic background the individual cognitive act *is* simply the assent to the criterion of truth. However, he gives a different analysis of that act of assent, one that makes it already a case of knowledge. Nor does he admit that there exists a 'criterion of truth' in a quasi-Stoic sense: the criterion that is relevant here is the criterion 'through which' [an instrument], something 'by which'[8] we may judge things. Plato, it is claimed, is concerned with the soul's cognitive faculties. The distinction owes much to *Theaetetus* 184b-c (for the greater precision of 'through which'), 185a (for the term 'instrument'), and 185e (for the soul's own agency). Consciously excluded here is the criterion 'by the agency of which' that Sedley discovers in fragment D,[9] which would include Protagoras' human measure. As fr. D shows, CR interpreters generally saw Plato's discussion of quasi-Protagorean theory at 152b-157c as a positive contribution towards a *Platonic* theory of the criterion 'by the agency of which'. However, TC maintains that they are refuted by Socrates' denial at 157c-d.

TC answers the TS interpreters by objecting to their emphasis on the *objects* of knowledge in the *Theaetetus*, as also in the *Sophist*. For him the *Theaetetus* is concerned with processes. TC in fact respects these interpreters, says that they have come near to the truth, and makes concessions when offering his correction. He seems to imply that the *Theaetetus* does deal mainly with things not strictly knowable, and the *Sophist* with knowable things. But this does not stop the *Theaetetus* being directly concerned with one kind of knowledge at least, and it is how we know and not what we know that Plato is tackling. The commentator is more positive about what the *Theaetetus* can tell us on knowledge, but there is qualification again when he specifies 'simple and uncompounded knowledge'. It seems that such knowledge can, in TC's view, apply to the sensible or mathematical objects generally encountered in the *Theaetetus*, and it was just this focus that had made necessary the subordinate investigation into the criterion.

It is clear, then, that TC uses this specific kind of knowledge to explain how the *Theaetetus* can be seriously investigating *epistêmê*. This is the kind of knowledge that (i) has to be investigated in conjunction with criteria of truth, and (ii) does not require Ideas as its object. Initially its requirements seem undemanding: accuracy within the faculty of judgment, the judging well done, and the stability of the final decision: the right kind of sensation, plus the right kind of *logos*, leading to unshaken confidence. It is clear from column 3 that TC does not think all cases of clear sensation plus good judgment yield knowledge, so everything will depend on what TC thinks we require if our judgment is to be permanent. The nature of the 'bond' will be critical.

One aspect of the current debate is clear from column 2. These interpreters are either unaware of, or unimpressed by, Thrasyllus' work on the corpus;[10] likewise, none seems to have influenced him directly.[11] Thrasyllus gave the *Theaetetus* the subtitle 'On Knowledge', perhaps the obvious subtitle for this work. This contrasts with the view that it is about the criterion, about unknowables, or about simple knowledge.[12] He also appears to have given 'characters' to the dialogues,[13] but TC gives no sign of any debate concerning the character of the *Theaetetus*. It is possible to link his statement that the young Theaetetus needed purging of Protagoras' influence with the *same overall approach* that causes Thrasyllus to label it *peirastic*.[14] However, the purificatory role of much material in the *Theaetetus* seems not to have been contentious.[15] Thrasyllus himself is not part of the background to TC.

iii. Column 3

Now TC offers a clearly Platonic view of knowledge, explaining what will be required for permanence in a manner that appeals to the *Meno*. The term 'simple' has temporarily been dropped, but 3.24 and column 15 can confirm that it is still simple knowledge that is at issue. *Meno* 98a is invoked, and we are made aware that knowledge must involve the binding of correct opinion, a process involving a cause and a reasoning, however one interprets the strange reading of *Meno* 98a. This process is further explained as telling us *why* P as well as *that* P. If Plato had introduced the bond of the reason, we are told, the account of simple knowledge would have been completed. Once again we are not being offered a definition of knowledge that would be likely to confine it to Ideas or the like, yet the use of the *Meno* implies that Recollection is somehow involved. The question is how. The obvious answer, given that the *Theaetetus* discusses only sensible and mathematical objects, is that it functions much as in the *Phaedo*'s account of our appreciation of the relationship between two 'equals' at 74-5, a passage that we have already had reason to link with 46.43-9. We recognise that they are would-be equals only because we have a prior grasp of Equality itself. Mathematicals are recognised in the sensible world only because of some prior, if latent, knowledge of the Idea.

Since this is still part of TC's answer to TS, he must be giving a view of the work that had been unavailable or unattractive to them. Its essential feature was the notion that knowledge is not after all confined to the Ideas, yet not possible without Ideas. The TS interpreters, then, had not seen the *Meno* and its Theory of Recollection as offering any solution to the question asked in the *Theaetetus*.

One further feature of TC's treatment should be emphasised. There is no use, either here or elsewhere in the extant parts of the commentary, of the terms 'Idea', 'Intelligible', or the like. TC apparently wants to convey his message without the use of such distinctively Platonic terminology, explaining things in terms more familiar to those used to the world of

Hellenistic philosophy. It is not eclecticism that non-Platonic material signifies, but an attempt to explain the hitherto less familiar philosophy in more familiar terms. It will become apparent that not all his rival interpreters are Platonists.

iv. Fragment D

Sedley's new reconstruction of fragment D,[16] and his discussion of its polemical content, have invested this half-column with a new importance, for the history of both the interpretation of the *Theaetetus* and the criterion 'by the agency of which'. Fragment D addresses 157c7-9:

> You are not remembering, my friend, that I neither know any such things nor claim them as my own. I am unable to give them birth, but I am practising midwifery on you, ...

TC wishes to distance Plato from the quasi-Protagorean theory that has been expounded, possibly from 152a on, and above all between 156a and 157c,[17] something clear also from Fragment B. Accordingly, he takes the lemma to be a welcome reminder of Socrates' indecision, at precisely the time when others have taken him to be revealing his view on matters relating to the cognition of the sensible world.

The fragment begins (lines 1-8) with what appears to be largely paraphrase of the lost lemma, but I believe that a little more is legible in lines 7-8 than was previously realised. It is likely to conclude 'concerning ourselves and the object'. This would clearly be referring to the 'Secret Doctrine' of Protagoras, to which the lemma refers back, and which made all sensation depend equally on object and perceiver. TC has recognised that what is special about this theory is its notion that each sensation is determined just as much by the perceiver's condition as by the object's. He is about to use this fact as an opportunity to discuss the notion of a criterion 'by the agency of which'. I now give the following translation, modifying that of Sedley:

> He made these remarks by way of offering a small reminder. But they are both absolutely essential and, perhaps, not untimely at this point.[18] They seem to me to be well aimed against the majority of Platonists, who say that the *Theaetetus* is about the criterion, ...

I feel I should draw attention first to the term for 'reminder' (*hypomnêma*) and the curious 'perhaps', for all this is inspired by a remark on timely reminders much later in the *Theaetetus* at 187e1: 'You were correct to remind me, for perhaps it is not the wrong time ...'.[19] TC characteristically notices details later in the text, and feels the need to speak Platonically himself without reproducing Plato's exact words.[20] The Platonic allusion adds irony to the remark, thereby contributing to an underlying polemic.

Reminders are there for a purpose, and indeed 157c-d has a very important purpose. The majority of Platonists, those who hold CR, are being criticised for not heeding this warning that Socrates does not offer his own theory. That must mean that they have taken the 'Secret Doctrine' as Plato's own, and are seeing this as part of *a positive contribution to Platonic criteriology*. For them, this is Plato quite as much as Protagoras.

Next TC goes on to make another comment about a reminder, which I interpret in a different way from Sedley. Without necessarily demanding a different reading of the papyrus,[21] I should translate 'What's been said is also reminding us to give a basic account of the agent of judgment.'[22] In my view TC then goes on to give an account of two or more views on Plato's criterion 'by the agency of which'.[23] Details are elusive, but an unusual past verb of saying reminds one that CR interpreters were referred to with an equally unusual past-tense verb of thinking in column 2. It therefore seems likely that CR interpreters who find a serious Platonic criterion 'by the agency of which' in Plato's discussion of Protagoras, are seen as belonging essentially to the past.

Since few could place Alcinous significantly earlier than TC, while Sedley regards him as a significant representative of anon.'s CR opponents,[24] some explanation is appropriate. Alcinous cannot be employed with confidence, partly because he may combine material of different origins,[25] but mainly because little of the epistemological chapter (4) is based *directly* on a reading of Plato. What we have is received Platonist wisdom, and like *Timaeus, Phaedrus, Philebus,* and *Sophist,*[26] *Theaetetus* is a source of doctrines without its being consciously interpreted. Two senses of the term 'criterion' are distinguished at 154.12-13, the judgment itself, and what judges. What judges is then divided into a criterion 'by the agency of which' and a criterion 'through which' (not the dichotomy of *Tht.* 184c ff.). These are identified as intellect and natural tool of judgment respectively; the latter is natural reason, while the former might also be said to be the philosopher or reason! These identifications ill accord with the *Theaetetus.*[27] At 154.41-155.13 the material on the interrelation of sensation, memory, and opinion ultimately derives from *Theaetetus* 191c-194b, but Alcinous has extracted little positive doctrine from the passage 152-7, either about sensation or about the judging agent. Granted, the term 'aggregate' (*athroisma*), which applies to objects of opinion such as fire or honey (156.3), is ultimately connected with 157b-c, while first and second sensibles may also be detected by the keen observer at 156e, as Sedley has acutely argued.[28] But Alcinous has not appropriated the theory of the *mechanics of sensation* offered at 156a-7c.[29] So what he sees at 152-7 are *traces* of Platonic epistemology.[30] Though he also thinks the *Theaetetus* contributes to the important topic of criteria, what we cannot know is whether he thinks the work is *primarily concerned with* the criterion, as CR holds.[31] We therefore search for a Middle Platonist theory that relates more directly to CR or TS.

v. Plutarch and Ammonius

There is only one Platonist within the period *c.* 50 BC – *c.* AD 150 of whom much is extant, and that is Plutarch of Chaeronea. It would be useful to examine his attitude to the *Theaetetus* and *Sophist*. We cannot build a full picture,[32] but the *Sophist* at least is one of the dialogues upon which he builds his picture of the Platonic universe.[33] The logic of the work is the subject of the last of the *Quaestiones Platonicae* (1009b-1011e), which ends with the observation that Plato calls the most basic unit of truth and falsehood *logos*. The *Megista Gene* of *Sophist* 254d-e have a key role in his ontology.[34] It thus becomes a work about things that are real and knowable, as Thrasyllus' subtitle suggests. As for the *Theaetetus*, it seems to be used in the first of the *Quaestiones* as a source for Socrates, whose non-dogmatic approach is taken for granted. Perhaps the most important feature of Plutarch's use of the *Theaetetus* is the way he takes 'Socrates' as a virtual representation of the critical faculty. Dealing with the divine ban of Socrates' 'conceiving', he takes the philosopher's own nature to be 'critical rather than creative' (999d), and shortly thereafter suggests that conceptions get in the way of judging (*to krinein*), which is something useful. To the extent that one has ideas of one's own, one is a worse judge of others (1000a-c).[35] This comes close to saying that the figure of Socrates *represents* the criterion 'by the agency of which'. Plutarch would not use this *language*, but he does speak of 'that which judges arguments in philosophy'. To the extent that the *Theaetetus* is about Socrates and his philosophic activity, then for Plutarch it is about the criterion, including the criterion 'by the agency of which'.

The following observations about Plutarch's approach are pertinent:

1. *Theaetetus* is not, and *Sophist* is, a work about objects of knowledge.
2. *Theaetetus* and *Sophist* may profitably be seen in conjunction.[36]
3. *Theaetetus* concerns Socrates, i.e. the criterion 'by the agency of which'.
4. Socrates is not expounding his own ideas in *Theaetetus*.
5. Positive Platonic ideas about epistemology do emerge in *Theaetetus*.

Numbers four and five are not in conflict since Plutarch sees the source of the positive ideas as being the common notions present in the mind of the interlocutor (and of course the author), not as anything of Socrates' own. *Plato* can offer us *his* epistemological ideas via the interlocutor, without *Socrates* deviating from his strict role as midwife. Here we have a plausible answer to fragment D of TC! If Socrates stands for the critical faculty, then he cannot also stand for Plato. Thus his disclaimer need not apply to Plato too, nor even to any total human being, all of whom are elsewhere considered productive in mind as well as body.[37]

Another thing should be noticed about Plutarch, which is of clear relevance to the interpretation of Platonic epistemology: he takes into equal consideration the *possibilities* that cognition (*katalêpsis, gnôsis*) does and does not exist, 1000c-d. That fits well with his continued allegiance to the New Academy as well as to Plato; yet he talks freely about Platonic intellection and intelligibles.[38] Doubts whether the *Theaetetus* ever concerns itself with genuine objects of knowledge might thus have involved a degree of scepticism without preventing discussion of our knowing intelligible Ideas. Reason and intelligence too have their limits. Plutarch uses the recollection theory in the *Quaestiones* (1000d-e) to suggest that Socrates was banned from acts of *this-worldly* discovery, as these are not to be valued highly. Instead, he is confined to progress in divine and intelligible knowledge, which cannot be generated or discovered by us – only recollected.[39]

While it would be hasty to conclude that TC has him in mind when discussing TS and CR, Plutarch has features in common with these positions, and was certainly a participant in the same debates as TC. He in turn had probably inherited many of his attitudes and interests from Ammonius, and the essay *On the E at Delphi* suggests that Ammonius in particular had learnt much from the *Theaetetus*. At 385c reference to inquiry as the beginning of philosophy, and aporetic amazement as the beginning of inquiry, alludes to *Tht.* 155d. At 393b reference to each of us being a multifarious conglomeration (*athroisma*) of countless different qualities that arise in our experiences is a clear reference to 157b and to the Secret Doctrine. Ammonius, then, is falling into what TC sees as the trap of supposing that Plato seriously advocates Protagoreanism and Heraclitism in respect of the physical world. The contrast is underlined with the help of the *Sophist* and its *Megista Gene*.[40]

On the E at Delphi is best known for the sharp contrast which Ammonius makes between god who 'is' and the things of this world which are in a radical state of flux and non-being. The contrast between stability and motion is matched by those between real and unreal, known and unknown. Likewise the Secret Doctrine tries to give an account of how sensation could occur within a world that is all motion. Its main emphasis falls upon how each sensation is the unique interaction of a perceiving motion and a perceived motion: i.e. how every sensation is relative to the perceiver. No doubt there were those who saw this teaching, that the human being is endowed with a clear grasp of the world of his sensations, as being about ourselves and our *infallible* grasp of our cognitive experiences. In this case Plato would be laying the foundations of a dogmatic philosophy. We can be sure that Ammonius rejects this view, since Xenophanes' doubts about firm knowledge of the physical world are constantly on his lips.[41] His reasons for finding Platonic doctrine within the Secret Doctrine passage are that it connects our subjective cognition of the physical world with a physical theory of flux. His Academic leanings find here an excellent justification for a sceptical attitude *towards sensation*.

That the epistemologies of both Ammonius and TC are essentially Platonist is clear, but there is a major difference between them. TC sees the physical world as initiating processes that lead to knowledge. He also finds a range of Platonic doctrine in the dialogues, even while admitting that Socrates' methodology requires him to conceal his view on matters under investigation. Another significant contrast between TC and both Ammonius and Plutarch[42] is that neither of these has great respect for those things which easily admit of the 'why' and the 'instruction of the cause',[43] preferring matters of a more mysterious nature. Nothing could be further from the case with TC, as column 3 shows in making the cause the foundation of simple knowledge.

Regarding the *Theaetetus*, Ammonius seems to have held views somewhat closer than Plutarch to those rejected by TC. He *both* regarded the work as a statement of Plato's own teaching on the criterion, *and* contrasted the *Theaetetus* with the *Sophist* as in the TS interpretation; he also found Plato's own voice behind the Secret Doctrine passage. The 'Academic' conjunction of CR and TS, which I shall call the CR-A interpretation, can thus be associated with the more 'Academic' of Platonist interpreters:[44] a group whose non-dogmatic picture of Plato TC rejects at 54.38-43. Unfortunately, we cannot plot this tradition prior to Ammonius with any certainty.[45] Still, it would be a mistake to think that Ammonius could have originated the idea that the *Theaetetus* is a dialogue 'On the Criterion'. The Plutarchian corpus uses the term 'criterion' remarkably sparely. Of its eight occurrences, half are from the *Quaestiones*, yet from the discussion of the Divided Line of the *Republic*, not from his treatment of the *Theaetetus*.[46] Three others are from *Against Colotes*, and concern other philosophies.[47] All seem confined to the criterion 'through which',[48] which was not the case with the original CR. None involves Ammonius. Theories of the criterion were not of sufficient importance to their own philosophy to be read into the *Theaetetus*.

vi. Alcinous and dogmata in *Theaetetus*?

We are searching, I believe, for interpreters who treated Plato's picture of Protagorean doctrine as *Platonic dogma* about the physical world – as a real contribution to a theory of how the world of our sensations work. We are also seeking those who recognised a criterion 'by the agency of which', regarding Plato's exposition of Protagoras' position as his own theory too. Did any who held CR interpret the *Theaetetus* as a genuine claim that we are the standard of judgment according to which this world must be judged, and that the senses really do give us information that is reliably true? Some had certainly attributed the view that sensations are in some meaningful sense 'true' to Xenocrates,[49] and it would then be a short step to crediting Plato with such a view. We shall call the detection, within the

Theaetetus, of dogmatist-style Platonic criteria the CR-D view. I return to Alcinous:

> Reason (*logos*) is of two kinds, one utterly incomprehensible and unerring, and the other free from error in the recognition of things. ... This too is two-fold, one kind concerned with intelligibles, and the other with sensibles. The one concerned with the intelligibles is knowledge and knowledge-producing reason, and the one concerned with sensibles is opinion and [= 'in the sense of'] opinion-giving reason.[50] Thus the knowledge-giving kind has certainty and stability, while the believable and opinion-giving kind has a great deal of (mere) probability, because it is not concerned with stable objects. (154.21-32)

Here we end with a description of a kind of *logos* which judges the world of the senses, and, as expected, terms like 'believable' (*pithanon*) and 'probability' (*eikos*) indicate the inferiority of our cognition of things susceptible to change. However, Alcinous can hardly share Ammonius' 'Academic' attitude to problems of knowing the physical world. He goes on to speak confidently about the role of senses and opinion as criteria, and this *logos* is a subdivision of human reason, which has already been declared to be 'free from error'.[51] The instability of our cognition of the world of flux would be readily admitted by Platonists in general; what is debated is its accurate apprehension *at the point of cognition*. Alcinous finds no error in opinion-giving reason, because he follows *Theaetetus* 192d-194b in attributing error neither to any *logos* nor to sensation, but to the mismatch of sensation and memory – a mismatch resulting in false opinion (154.40-155.13). But he creates a problem for the reader. The term 'opinion' is used at one moment for reasoning about the sensible world (a faculty, which doesn't lie),[52] and at the next moment (after re-definition!) for an opinion about the sensible world (a judgment that may be true or false). There is no reason why opinion-giving reason cannot be error-free in its own right for Alcinous as long as its concern is with appearances.

Now this same opinion-giving reason will later (156.8-10) be involved in the judgment of three kinds of sense objects. It is secondarily involved in distinguishing any sensible quality and also things so qualified, and primarily involved in distinguishing aggregates of such properties, such as fire or honey. As Sedley has astutely pointed out these three types are to be found at *Theaetetus* 156e-157b. But can some opinion-giving reason be found there too? Those used to detecting an immanent *logos* in the physical world, helping us to know it, such as Thrasyllus perhaps,[53] would have no difficulty finding such a concept in the Secret Doctrine passage. For it discusses the operations of the sensible world and the language appropriate to it, chiefly at 157a-b, *together with* use of the term *logos*.[54] That some such *logos*-theory was read into this passage is assured by Sextus' treatment of Protagoras at *PH* 1.216-19. Here this latter is given a theory of flux, of matter, and of the *logoi* in it, which derives from just this Platonic passage.[55] If 'Protagorean' *logoi* could be detected here, then Platonic *logos* could also be found by Platonists who saw the passage as Plato's contribution. Again, Plato's move from the mechanics of sensation to the language appropriate for describing our sensations would be relevant.

vii. Neoprotagoreans?

So Alcinous dimly reflects CR-D rather than CR-A. He is confident that various *criteria* are proposed with conviction by Plato, many of them within the *Theaetetus*. Yet few would accept that Alcinous masterminded such an interpretation. The view that Plato is serious about the Secret Doctrine theory would have been propounded by one who wished to promote that doctrine himself. The same individual would naturally have appealed to the authority of *Protagoras* too for the theories of flux, cognition, and language that are put forward there. Decleva Caizzi (1988) has linked such a view of Protagoras, assumed by Sextus at *PH* 1.216-19, with Asclepiades. This may be so, but Asclepiades is an unlikely source for Platonists.[56] For a plausible Protagoro-Platonist we must look elsewhere. The key concept must be that of the criterion 'by the agency of which', for Sextus understands Protagoras' 'measure' as the hellenistic 'criterion'. The criterion in that sense is to be discovered in TC, Sextus, Ptolemy, Alcinous, and the Eclectic Plato-commentator Potamo.

Something should now be said about the sources of chapter 4 of Alcinous. This author has traditionally been held to follow Arius Didymus, identified as Augustus' court philosopher from Alexandria. Göransson has now quite properly challenged the basis for our identifying Eusebius' Didymus (*PE* 11.23.3-6), whose wording Alcinous comes very close to in chapter 12, with Augustus' Arius.[57] Fortunately, there is a different route back to Augustus' Alexandria from chapter 4. There the phrase 'not without' has become both important and formulaic at 156.5-14; strangely the preposition 'without' is rare elsewhere in Alcinous, being found only at 5.157.3 and 14.170.3 (prompted by 'apart from' at *Tim.* 30b3). A negative is present in both of these cases. There are epistemology-related uses of the preposition in TC, and a negative is present in every case. The 'not without' phrase is prominent in three Alexandrian authors: Clement, *Strom.* 5.83.4 (in whom it is found 13 times) preserves an apparently deliberate emendation of *Meno* 99e6 by which 'without intelligence' (*aneu nou*) becomes 'not without intelligence'. This is an emendation of considerable epistemological relevance. Philo of Alexandria also uses 'not without' frequently,[58] usually not technically, but one epistemological passage should be mentioned: 'all that sensation experiences does *not* remain *without intelligence*', *LA* 2.41.

We come now to Potamo, again from Alexandria, a contemporary of Augustus and author of early exegesis of the *Republic* as the Suda indicates. Potamo apparently made formulaic use of the phrase 'not without' in his description of the moral goal at DL 1.21. Diogenes' brief outline of Potamo's 'eclectic' philosophy reserves a central explanatory role for *seven* very prominent prepositions, of which two appear in the crucial distinction between the criteria 'by the agency of which' and 'through which'. This alone gives us reason to examine his intellectual environment in conjunction with the pre-history of *Didascalicus* 4. Potamo's identification of the criterion 'by the agency of which' with the 'leading faculty' (*hêgemonikon*) is compatible with Alcinous' original identification of it with 'the mind in us'. This in turn is a short step from Protagoras' 'Man the Measure'. His criterion 'through which', 'the most accurate presentation', may have been conceived as a 'natural tool of judgment', also as in Alcinous' general description (154.15-17). Has Alcinous been updating Potamo, and was the latter a CR-D interpreter with sympathies for Protagoras?

Potamo did have reason to embrace a little of the legacy of Protagoras, because of the lack of absolute solutions within Protagoras' relativistic system. Relativism can lead in two directions, one towards scepticism, and the other towards a more encouraging attitude over the common man's ability to contribute to knowledge. The slender evidence that he did so begins with the name of his philosophy, too easily dismissed, owing to the questionable wider use to which the term 'eclectic' has often been put. To call oneself an 'eclectic' rather than accepting the authority of an ancient school must have implied the rejection of the notion of any authoritative vision. It suggested that no philosopher had provided the entire solution, and that several perspectives get nearer the truth than one. Hence one should pick from the range of available alternatives on every issue. This view differs substantially from that of Antiochus, which largely denied that one had to choose at all, since differences between respectable philosophers were mostly a matter of terminology.

Rejection of a single authoritative vision also involved the rejection of a sharp distinction between wise and ignorant in traditional terms (cf. *Tht.* 157a, *Prt.* 327e). For Protagoras, all humans are placed on an open-ended scale as regards cognitive power, for all are endowed with the critical faculty required for judgment. When they judge, he would surely have advocated use of the most accurate (or detailed) presentation, again representing a relatively high point on an open-ended scale. Hence his authority could be claimed for Potamo's two 'criteria', neither of which suggested the acceptance of absolute cognitive reliability.

What would such a Protagorean be doing commenting upon Plato's *Republic*, with its absolute standards and sharp distinction between those with good judgment and those without? Commentaries did not have to be sympathetic, as may be seen from Simplicius' treatment of work on the Aristotelian *Categories* by Nicostratus and others (Dillon, 1977, 233-6). Again, one doubts that Potamo discussed the work as a whole, and it is quite likely that his was a commentary rather on the Platonic republic – the socio-political system outlined in parts of books 2 to 5, which is presumably what had been intended when Favorinus claimed that almost the entire Platonic republic had a precedent in the *Disputations* (*Antilogiai*) of Protagoras (DL 3.57, cf. 3.37). It is plausible that Potamo was commenting on what some saw as Protagorean material in the *Republic*, stressing the influence of Protagoras over the Platonic Socrates.

As regards the *Theaetetus*, Potamo's combination of an interest in Plato, an acknowledged eclecticism, and a dogmatic epistemology that attached importance to the senses[59] is suggestive of CR-D theory. Furthermore, Potamo's physics, as outlined by this same passage of Diogenes, involved four physical principles (*archai*). The first pair resembled the familiar Stoic active and passive elements, matter (*that out of which*) and what creates (*that by the agency of which*), but they could perhaps be detected in the two principle motion-types, what creates (*to poioun*) and what undergoes (*to paschon*) found at *Tht.* 156a and 157a. The final pair are quality, clearly crucial to a Protagorean universe (*Tht.* 152b, 156c-e, and 182a) and place ('that in which'), which is vital for any system reliant upon perspective, including the Secret Doctrine.[60]

My suggestion is this: Potamo is impressed by the pictures of a universe in flux that generates sensations at *Tht.* 156a-157c. He chooses to use it to claim support both from Protagoras (who may already have been interpreted similarly by Asclepiades and Aenesidemus), and more importantly from Plato's Socrates, for analogous aspects of his own system.

As for Potamo's criteria, the notion that one is the ruling part in a human being is based on a modification of the notion of 'man the measure' in the light of Plato's idea that the soul is the ultimate organ of judgment (*Tht.* 184-6), while the other, the most accurate (or detailed) presentation might have been partly inspired by clarity or otherwise that results from the purity of the 'wax-tablet' at 194-5.

Does TC show any awareness of Potamo's proposed criteria? They do not appear directly in the discussion of Pyrrho at column 61.15-21: 'According to him neither is reason the criterion, nor true presentation, nor plausible (presentation), nor cognitive (presentation), nor any other such thing.' The three types of presentation specified belong to the Epicureans, Carneadeans, and Stoics respectively, but the reference to 'any other such thing' would allow for Potamo. This passage, giving an authentic picture of Pyrrhonism, would have special point if Potamo had somehow claimed Pyrrhonist support too for his doctrines, based on the Pyrrhonist theme that all things are relative. For at 63.1-40 TC feels obliged to show how the Pyrrhonist theme of relativity differs from some other unspecified use, presumably that which others attribute to Protagoras.[61] There is an excellent parallel for *non-sceptic* use of Pyrrhonist material just a little later in Alexandria, when Philo utilises a treatment of the modes of scepticism that presumably come indirectly from Aenesidemus.[62]

Another possible allusion to Potamo is column 2.23f:

> By criterion I now mean that *through which* we judge; for we must have
> something by which we judge things, then, *when this is accurate*, the perma-
> nent reception of things well judged becomes knowledge.

This could easily have been written in response to somebody who distinguished between the criterion *through which* and the criterion *by the
agency of which*, found positive ideas on both in the *Theaetetus*, and made
the criterion *through which* the most *accurate* presentation. Postulating
Potamo as an opponent gives TC's words added force: and perhaps nowhere more than in fragments B and C where he explains how Plato is
going on to *attack* Protagorean doctrines.

Identifying Potamo with the originator of the CR-D interpretation is
secondary to my purpose. Rather I have tried to give it a context in
Alexandria shortly after the influence of Antiochus' dogmatism was
brought there by Aristo and Dio. The CR-A interpretation might have
sprung up there in response to CR-D, among the forerunners of Ammonius
and Plutarch, one of whom was Eudorus. The epistemological debate there
occasionally surfaces in Philo, in such a way as to contrast Protagoreanism
with fallibilism, and scepticism with dogmatic faith.[63] Not far away in
space and time will be TC or Ur-C, ignorant of, or indifferent to, Thrasyllus, and unnoticed by Plutarch.

viii. Anti-Protagoreans

The existence of an interpretation that saw Plato *promoting* a version of
Protagoreanism in the *Theaetetus* might be expected to produce adverse
reaction among others. Among these we must number TC himself, since
Protagoreanism is something of which young Theaetetus must be purged
(2.1-11). He carefully interprets the phrase 'Let us follow him [Protagoras]'
(152b1, 64.28-36) as meaning only that *it follows from Protagoras' thesis*
that the same wind has contrasting properties and effects. At 66.11-43 TC
carefully distinguishes one premise of an argument, which can be attributed to Protagoras, from the next, identifying 'what appears to one' with
'what one perceives', which is said to be Plato's. At 67.47, on 152c2-3, he
contrasts Protagoras' claim that 'things are such for each as they appear
to him' with Socrates' claim. The papyrus fails here, but the key point must
be that Socrates has said 'may be such ...' (*kindyneuei*), quite enough to
show that he is not committed to Protagoras' doctrine. Further mutilation
of the papyrus cannot disguise the fact that TC resists taking the conclusion of the argument at 152c5-6 as Socratic dogma, because it is going to
be refuted (*a]naskeu...*, 67.18). That theme is developed in fragment C,
which sees the refutation commencing at 157e.

However, TC's efforts to *divorce* the Socrates of the *Theaetetus* from
Protagoras are mild in comparison with an interpretation that Sedley has
discovered in late Neoplatonism.[64] It can be seen from three texts that

there had existed an interpretation that saw the entire work as an attack on Protagoras,[65] including the investigation of false opinion and the refutation of Socrates' Dream (201d ff.). The former is easily regarded as an attempted attack on one who denied the existence of false opinions, whereas the Dream does in a sense echo the exposition of Protagorean theory – for it returns to the notion of each thing being in itself impredicable.[66] Moreover there is dialogue with an unnamed objector at 195c-e and 200a-c, while the Dream is easily taken as the theory of some rival of Plato's. In fact the notion that the work is a sustained polemic would not be so incredible to us today if it were allowed that Plato was attacking a Protagorean sympathiser in his own day rather than the long-dead sophist.

However, an interpretation, particularly in ancient times, needed more than justification in the text. It needed motivation. To regard the *Theaetetus* as a polemical work was unusual in the ancient world, and most sources treat it as being more concerned about helping the young Theaetetus (as a *gymnastic* dialogue) than about vying with Protagoras (as an *agonistic* one). This is evidently not the case with the interpretation hinted at by Proclus at *On the Parmenides* 631, and apparently associated with some who thought the *Parmenides*, *Menexenus*, and *Phaedrus* too to be competing with rivals such as Zeno of Elea, Thucydides, and Lysias.[67] Whereas *Euthydemus*, *Protagoras*, *Gorgias*, and the *Hippias* dialogues were regularly seen as competitive, this was not the case with the four considered here. In fact no Middle Platonist could write of the *Theaetetus* as essentially destructive polemic, because in one absolutely crucial way the work was central to all Middle Platonist attempts to reconstruct Platonic doctrine. At 176b it gave the clearest exposition in the corpus of the accepted Middle Platonic goal or *telos*, specifying the aim of assimilation to god.

The notion that competition can be pursued by *going beyond* rivals,[68] as well as by overturning them, has the effect of turning Plato into a willing sophist. He comes to resemble the erudite practitioners of display who flourished in the 'second sophistic'.[69] Dialogues are effectively stripped of any constructive purpose. Academic-sceptics may have inclined towards such a reading, but who among them would seriously propose this reading of Plato *as the correct one*? Early Pyrrhonists may have put forward such a view,[70] but then what had they to gain by arguing (hardly demonstrating!) that Plato was on their side? I suggest that sophists and Pyrrhonists would have had essentially the same motive in proposing such a view of Plato. They would themselves be taking on another well-respected view, and hoping to gain increased respect by arguing against the contrary thesis more glowingly themselves – just as they claimed Plato had done. Pyrrhonists might also be arguing for the sake of creating the balance that ends in indecision. But both motives would imply that a *directly contrary view* was already in existence. In the case of the *Theaetetus* it would mean that some respected philosopher was arguing that Plato was following Protagoras; in the case of the *Parmenides* that somebody was arguing that Plato followed the Eleatics. It is very difficult to believe, however, that any interpreter saw Plato as *following* Thucydides and Lysias in *Menexenus* and *Phaedrus* respectively; however, they may rather have been cited for the sake of illustration, as being works familiar to the target audience. If so, it should be noted that these are two dialogues that would interest the epideictic orator, and that Plato is seen to beat Thucydides by producing 'a much nobler discourse' and, 'by the grandeur of his words', to overwhelm the leanness of [Lysias'] style.'[71] This, I believe, betrays the interests of the sophists, at least some of whom practised in Alexandria in the age of Philo,[72] or of sceptically-inclined philosopher-sophists, such as Favorinus.

Although TC is clearly concerned to counter the excessively 'Academic' view of Plato, which denies that Plato has doctrines (54-5), he does not seem to have reacted against any interpretation of the *Theaetetus* as a non-constructive *polemical* work. I suspect that this is because it was not part of his world.[72] Perhaps that interpretation in fact *owed something* to TC or Ur-C, following their *scholarly* rejection of Platonic approval for Protagoras with a *polemical* one.

Here we must be ready to leave the *Theaetetus*. We have already allotted it a disproportionate space, but the early evidence justifies this. We have encountered interpretations to suit both sceptic and dogmatist agenda; interpretations that see it in hellenistic terms, and others that try harder to revive Platonic thought-patterns; interpretations that see Protagoras as an ally, and others that forcefully reject this. Its weakness on doctrine – apart from 'assimilation to god' – would have limited the extent to which it was cited, but this did not mean that it became less crucial overall. It generated lively debate, mainly because one's reading of this work depended so much on what brand of Platonic interpreter one was.

12

The 'logical' dialogues

i. The background

Sophist, *Politicus*, and *Cratylus* had appeared in the same grouping, with an obvious emphasis on dialectic, since the arrangement of Aristophanes of Byzantium (DL 3.62). They appeared together with the *Theaetetus* in the same Thrasyllan tetralogy, and were also among the four works classified as 'logical' in 'character': *Cratylus*, *Sophist*, and *Politicus*. The fourth, at the beginning of the next tetralogy, was the *Parmenides*. For the originators of the dichotomic character-classification, the 'logical' dialogues belonged to the theoretical section of the *hyphegetic* class. That is to say that they were seen as offering doctrinal instruction.[1] Whether this was instruction in dialectic, or in matters investigated by dialectic, is unclear. What is clear is that Albinus (*Prol.* 6) rejected the notion that they belonged to the *hyphegetic* class, classified them as *zetetic* instead, and so implied that they had little or no *doctrinal* teaching to offer, only instruction about logical method. Their purpose in his educational scheme was to provide the tools for securing doctrines that had already been communicated, not to offer further doctrines. While this view says something about the status of logic in Albinus' eyes, i.e. that it is more an Aristotelian *organon* (instrument) than a third part of philosophy proper (as for the Stoics), their conscious reclassification suggests a strong rejection of the notion that they are a proper place to look for philosophic illumination.

By contrast all of them feature in the late Neoplatonist curriculum, with the *Parmenides* being the most important of all for Proclus and the Athenian school. As we shall see, all of them are there seen as having metaphysical significance, and Proclus is undoubtedly in agreement with the view expressed at *On the Parmenides* 637 that none of Plato's works is principally a study of method. That view is perhaps Firmus' (see below), and sees the *Sophist* as aiming to discover 'the many-headed sophist', though orthodox Neoplatonists saw the identification of any human sophist as peripheral to its metaphysical or theological purpose. The Neoplatonist concentration on metaphysics and theology content has its strangest results in respect of the *Politicus*, which rarely rates a mention except for the myth, which is of constant importance to them.[2] It is remarkable that Olympiodorus' *Commentary on the Gorgias* constantly compares the *Republic* and regularly compares the *Laws*, but does not utilise the *Politicus* as a work of social and political philosophy at all![3]

The use of the 'logical' dialogues cannot be divorced from the question of why Plato chooses his speakers. Eleatics provide the chief speakers of three of them, and Cratylus the Heraclitan has provided much of the momentum for the discussion in the *Cratylus*. The anonymous *Prolegomena* uses a tradition which made Plato a pupil of Cratylus and of 'Hermippus' the Parmenidean.[4] That is clearly meant to signify that Plato *was indebted* to both of these philosophies, and this would give extra weight to Heraclitan and Parmenidean speakers and material in the relevant dialogues.[5] The theory that the Eleatic Stranger was a Platonic spokesman had long been maintained,[6] and we have seen in relation to the *Theaetetus* how Plato was seriously credited with Heraclitism in respect of the physical world.[7] The belief that Plato had acquired Heraclitan and Parmenidean doctrines naturally led to a view of the second tetralogy, whose order is still preserved in the Iamblichan curriculum. The *Cratylus* propounds Heraclitism in important respects; the *Theaetetus* rejects extreme Heraclitism and its conjunction with Protagoreanism, and finds no knowledge in the physical world; the *Sophist* and *Politicus* then find truth and reality in a Neo-eleatic intelligible world. A different view of Plato's relations with the great Presocratics might have given us a very much less positive picture of the doctrinal contributions being made by these dialogues.

ii. *Parmenides*

This dialogue produced the greatest range of interpretations in antiquity, and still generates a considerable amount of debate over the most basic of issues. It has little obvious unity, sees Socrates unsuccessfully defending the Theory of Ideas that many regard as central to Platonism, and then has Parmenides exploring the consequences of his own theory at great length and in a manner largely foreign to Plato. The thematic connection between the two parts, in which first Socrates and then Aristoteles answer Parmenides, is elusive. It is not clear whether Plato regards the difficulties in the Theory of Ideas seriously, and even less clear what we are supposed to deduce from Parmenides' self-examination. This is *presented* as a logical exercise that might have picked any thesis to investigate, but the detailed treatment of some parts of that exercise suggests a genuine Platonic interest in the subject matter. Its various sections sometimes seem to produce pictures that might mirror entities, and it is conceivable that the logic is masking metaphysics. The material relates to little material elsewhere in Plato's written works, except perhaps the One-Many problems of the *Philebus* and the construction of soul in the *Timaeus*. There may be a greater resemblance to Aristotle's picture of Platonic metaphysics: to the 'unwritten doctrines'. What can be bluntly stated is that anybody wishing to give a coherent interpretation of the whole dialogue has to read into it things which are never stated there. Literal interpretation is unsatisfying; in depth interpretation runs enormous risks.

We have already encountered facets of the ancient debate over the *Parmenides*, and a wide range of approaches to this work was known in antiquity. At least some of these approaches, and just conceivably all of them, may be traced to the Middle Platonist period. The difficulty is that little contemporary material has survived, and we are reliant largely on Proclus, whose doxographic material in the *In Parmenidem* (i) avoids commentator's names, and (ii) is too *schematic* to be readily believable. In book 1 he divides up the known 'ancient' approaches to the dialogue by dichotomy, and paints a picture of a development in interpretation that moved ahead in three orderly and well-reasoned steps. His purpose, however, is not strictly historical. He is rather showing how the reader may readily consider certain lines, and then see reason to reject them and move forward.

The story that he gives is as follows. There were two 'logical' interpretations, one treating the dialogue as a polemic against Zeno, and one treating it as a logical exercise for educational purposes. Then there were two metaphysical interpretations, one regarding it as a revelation of a Parmenidean One Being *in which the Platonic Ideas were founded*, and one taking it to deal with not simply this Being but all that derives from it. The final interpretation is then refined to yield not just any metaphysical series, proceeding from higher entities to lower ones, but a more intricate theological hierarchy. Of the four earlier stages in the dialogue's interpretation only the second and fourth are treated by Proclus in the *Platonic Theology*.

It is important to realise that all these interpretations have in mind, above all, to explain the long final part of the dialogue, which examines a series of hypotheses concerned with the One. It is an enormously complex exercise, occupying the bulk of the dialogue, proceeding in a manner uncharacteristic of Plato, and not leading the reader directly to any particularly illuminating conclusions. It must have been meant to encourage the reader to reflect rather than to conclude, and even then it is unclear what one is meant to be reflecting on. Was it examining Eleatic logic, or the One of Parmenides (supposedly under investigation), or the Ideas? Furthermore, what are we to make of the fact that Socrates is left entirely outside the exercise? Does this examination have any close relation to the other two works in which an Eleatic converses with a compliant interlocutor?

The second title system of Thrasyllus had labelled this work 'On Ideas', taking the obvious topic of the shorter first part, but the evidence suggests that he took the work as more complex than the subtitle suggests. To call the work 'logical' (if he did so)[8] suggested only that the subject was *approached* by an investigation employing logical tools, much like the *Sophist* and *Politicus*, not that logic was an end in itself. To label it 'On Ideas' did not make it clear whether its principal significance was for logic or metaphysics, but at least suggested *some* metaphysical significance. Again, to include it in the third tetralogy, alongside three works that had themes connected with a supreme 'good' or 'beautiful', is suggestive of a deeper, more metaphysical meaning. Further, to position it immediately before the *Philebus* would suggest that some connection was detected between the investigation of the One (etc.) in the final part and the One-Many problems that litter the early pages of the *Philebus*. Its position also makes it the last of a sequence of dialogues that contribute to epistemology and logic, beginning with the *Cratylus* and proceeding via the *Theaetetus*, *Sophist* and *Politicus*. There is no doubt that the seriousness of the content, as opposed to the method, had increased in the course of that tetralogy, and it would be strange if the work that already steps into the next tetralogy were seen as reverting to pure methodology: a methodology not employed in the works that follow. It is clear that with Thrasyllus a deeper meaning was already being sought, but there is no clear evidence that it was being found. One could accept the importance of the logical message, realise the importance of the Ideas, and still go on to suspect that the final part had some message concerning the supreme principles of reality. The sharply contrasting positions that appear in the doxography of Proclus give a false picture of exclusivity, and imply that all interpreters had been dogmatic about their interpretations. The remains of Middle Platonism suggest otherwise.

One would do well to mention Alcinous in this context. Chapter 6 affords the *Parmenides* a prominent place as a source for Plato's syllogistic and theory of categories. It was a fertile hunting-ground for all who want to show that Plato's logic was in fact just as well developed as that of Aristotle. This compares well with Proclus' account of the 'logical exercise' theory, which raise the final part of the work to a level above that of Aristotle's *Topics*, because it is allegedly more philosophical and leads to conclusions that transcend mere probability (635). Yet Alcinous' metaphysical section includes an account of the supreme god that uses the methods of negative theology, saying what god is not (10.4). It seems to reflect certain conclusions argued for (in respect of the One) by the first hypothesis of the final part of the *Parmenides*.[9] Whether Alcinous is aware of this or not, it certainly demonstrates some *theological* exploitation of the first hypothesis by some interpreter before him. However, one must note that theological exploitation no more guarantees an overall theological interpretation than logical exploitation guarantees an overall logical interpretation. Platonic texts were there to be exploited as an authority in whatever manner a philosopher found both convenient and plausible. If the *Parmenides* was used to illustrate Plato's system of logic then it would have been a brave opponent who denied that such exploitation was legitimate. If it was used to demonstrate Plato's metaphysical or theological principles, then it was up to an opponent to decide whether to challenge the validity of that use. After Plotinus no major interpreter in antiquity did.[10]

Of the 'logical' interpretations, we have dealt with the polemical one in Chapter 11 viii, claiming that it came from people who did not mind turning Plato into a sophist. I previously inclined towards associating it with Albinus on the grounds that he classified all 'logical' dialogues as 'zetetic',[11] but this strategy implies that Plato was investigating topics through logic rather than just teaching it: in the *Parmenides* as in the *Cratylus*, *Sophist*, and *Statesman*. These dialogues were credited with helping to render doctrines permanent, not with supplying the doctrines themselves. This is stage four of his education-programme, and in this respect they are distinguished from polemical doctrines which are reserved for stage five.

Steel (1997) has provided an illuminating account of the second logical interpretation. Undoubtedly this conforms better with regular Middle Platonist *use*, though it may have been somewhat extreme *as an interpretation*. Nevertheless, it was not as extreme as Proclus makes out, associating it with logical exercises for the young.[12] It is the interpretation of one who is preoccupied with method, and who is consciously rejecting both the polemical interpretation, and the notion of metaphysical content in the final part.[13] The rejection of the polemical interpretation, which had carefully avoided saying that Plato attacks Parmenides himself, concentrates on the closeness of Zeno to the respected Parmenides. But Parmenides himself is treated, like Zeno, as an abstract theorist with nothing to say about the nature of the cosmos (633): a clear parallel with the abstract and non-metaphysical approach to Plato's dialogue! Moreover, though the Idea of Human Being and the many particular humans are used as an illustration, one feels that it is purely in connection with logic, and nothing to do with metaphysics.

I have therefore associated this semi-Platonist logician's reading with Galen, whose views on the *Parmenides* were known to Proclus' school via his collection of *Compendia*,[14] which presumably came with some introductory material. Galen was both a formidable and dedicated logician who trusted securely in his methods, and somewhat agnostic over all questions of philosophy that involved immaterial entities. He is known to have spoken of the *Sophist* as a dialogue that employed *training* in methods of division, apparently borrowing the term itself from the *Parmenides*, which, along with the *Politicus*, was also treated as essentially logical.[15] He is also known to have grouped the *Compendium of the Parmenides* in a single book with other 'logical' compendia, but including also the *Euthydemus*. Why the *Euthydemus*? Surely because he saw it as Plato's equivalent to a different Aristotelian logical treatise, the *Sophistici Elen-*

chi. All were considered to be dialogues that illustrated (and hence in a
sense taught) Plato's logical methods.

I have claimed that the arrangement of the dialogues implicit in the
work of al-Farabi generally reflects the work of Galen, and all the companion dialogues except for the missing *Politicus*[16] feature there among works
illustrating arts that fail to supply the knowledge needed for happiness.
Cratylus shows that it is not name-science, *Euthydemus* and *Sophist* that
it is not sophistry, and *Parmenides* that dialectic, though useful, is not
sufficient. Thus, though the other three have some polemical element at
least, the *Parmenides* is thought to deal with the limitations of something
that is very much respected. If it does not supply the answers looked for,
then that is again because the dialectic with which it deals is devoid of
content: a framework for examining questions only.

The advantage of associating this interpretation, in this version, with
Galen is that we only have to assume Proclus' knowledge of a single Middle
Platonic interpretative work. If Favorinus, Galen's *bête noire*, had been
associated with the polemical interpretation, then Galen would certainly
have taken the opportunity to reject it forcefully: thus preserving peculi-
arities of the Favorinan version for Proclus. The problem that this involves
is that Proclus is supplying no real insights into any of the Middle
Platonists proper. As a pupil of Albinus, Galen would be *closer* to orthodoxy,
but no more is guaranteed.

There is at first sight a slight problem with our attribution. Proclus
begins his discussion of the non-metaphysical interpretations by stating
that the theory that the dialogue is intended only as a logical exercise
rejects the subtitle 'On Ideas' as pertinent only to the smaller part of the
work, and one that is aporetic rather than instructive. He appears to have
only the 'exercise' theory in mind, but Damascius states that Proclus'
successor Marinus had abandoned the theological interpretation of the
Parmenides and dragged down its study down to the level of Ideas,
drawing more on Firmus and Galen than on the insights of the blessed. At
first sight the implication is that Galen believed the work is 'On Ideas' as
its subtitle had suggested, and thus he could not be rejecting that subtitle
like Proclus' logical interpreters (630-1). This is a false inference, however.
The logical interpretation did indeed make method the goal; the metaphysical topic was chosen to illustrate it. But it admitted readily that this
topic was the One of Parmenides (634). For anybody of Marinus' background this One was the Intelligible World that comprised the Ideas.
Marinus could have taken the logical-exercise theme from Galen and the
Intelligible-World theme from Firmus (presumably the friend of Por-
phyry). Note that Proclus has introduced the 'logical exercise' theory of the
Parmenides by ascribing it to both ancient and contemporary interpreters.
Mention of contemporaries should remind us of Marinus himself.[17] After
Proclus' warning, and his protest that the theory conflicts with the subti-
tle, it was up to anybody continuing to sponsor it to show that there was

no conflict. The final part of the dialogue became a logical exercise *investigating Parmenides' One*; and, since Parmenides' One was an intelligible One embracing the Ideas, this part was just as closely concerned with Ideas as the first part had been.

The starting point for theories that reject non-metaphysical interpretations of the *Parmenides* comes from the account of Socrates' meeting with Parmenides given in the *Theaetetus* (636). It is claimed that Socrates' respect for Parmenides (183e), and his feeling that the man had hidden depth and unfathomable meaning (184a), implied that he offered a genuine treatment of Being, not just logical exercises.[18] This appears to agree with Parmenides' own intention at *Parmenides* 137b to examine his own postulate, even though it is there described as One rather than Being. For the interpretation in fact assumes that the work is about a One-Being, in which the Ideas are founded. It is metaphysical, but postulates nothing that transcends Parmenides' One-Being. Yet this was the theory that was needed to be grafted onto the exercise theory in order to give Marinus' version respectability. This then was the contribution of Firmus, more sensitive to Plato's methods than Galen, and able to give the dialogue a unity in the World of Ideas. He was unable to believe in the Plotinian school's claim that the One of the first hypothesis transcends the Intellectual World. It is no accident that this theory actually places considerable emphasis on the way in which logical method and metaphysical teaching go hand in hand, as in the *Sophist* too. The logical tool, it was claimed, could in fact only be claimed where there was need for it, and need only arose when important problems were unresolved.

Moving on to the fourth group of *Parmenides*-interpreters, we find that they do not deny that the final part of the work takes its point of departure from Parmenides' One. They claim, however, that the first hypothesis examines this One apart from Being and as a genuine One,[19] the second as a One-Being that generates the whole intellectual world, the third as a Being that is One. Then subsequent hypotheses examine things that do or do not participate in the One. Contradictory conclusions, as between hypotheses, must demonstrate that we do not always have the same entity in view but different ones.

Proclus' outline is strange for a number of reasons. No attempt is made to explain the relevance of the first part of the dialogue; the theory is explained as if the meaningful hypotheses were *five*, though this was not the case for Amelius, Porphyry, and Iamblichus; and it might be accused of compromising the transcendence of the One of the first hypothesis, in that its identity with Parmenides' One is still effectively affirmed. The concentration on five hypotheses has an easy explanation. Proclus will give the interpretation of Syrianus immediately afterwards, so what preceded has taken us up to Plutarch of Athens, whose schematic doxographic work Proclus admired (1061). He explains things in terms of five hypotheses only, because these are all that he saw as meaningful. The 'philosopher from Rhodes' (1057), from whom Plutarch learnt to see entities behind five hypotheses only, did not hold that the One totally transcended being and saw it also as the Good, perhaps compromising its transcendence. Finally, this Rhodian had no difficulties making the Ideas relevant, since his interpretation of the hypotheses was worked out in conjunction with the Divided Line of the *Republic*: the first hypothesis is now about the supreme Idea: the Idea of the Good.

These findings should worry the historian. If this is indeed Plutarch's account of the metaphysical interpretation, then Proclus has probably grafted his subsequent account of Syrianus' position onto a pre-existing doxography from his one-time teacher. A doxography that did not obviously include the positions of Porphyry and Iamblichus was clearly not presented for the sake of history, but rather for the clarification of interpretative issues. Again, if the third interpretation had been Firmus' then it had been no more than an unorthodox Neoplatonist view, probably preserved through the *Commentary on the Parmenides* of Porphyry. The physician Galen had been the only source of exegetical information prior to Porphyry. As far as we can tell Neoplatonists from Plutarch to Damascius knew early interpretation only as Galen and Porphyry had wished to portray it. The picture is clearly incomplete, and tells us nothing of Middle Platonist views. Little help is received from the remains of the interesting anonymous commentary (Cod. Taur. F VI 1) as its authorship is so much disputed,[20] its remains contain no introductory material, and the only significant historical element concerns Speusippus (1.20)!

Nevertheless, this material has great value for showing us the arguments for various positions and the reasons known to Plutarch for rejecting them. It shows us other significant features too, such as the extensive use of the *Sophist* by a succession of interpretations.[21] Certain passages, one of them dealing with Plutarch, give us important information about the more complex metaphysical interpretation. The Athenian School apparently understood the terms 'One' and 'Others' to be *Pythagorean* ways of referring to incorporeal entities and corporeal entities respectively.[22] That view had probably accompanied this interpretation from the beginning, for its weakest point is that it takes very little account of Parmenides' decision to base the exercise *on his own theory* (137b). However, if he is in fact a Pythagorean, as the Pythagorean Nicomachus of Gerasa had maintained,[23] then he too should have believed that a number of different things might be designated 'one' and 'other'. In such a case the hypotheses could plausibly be depicting a range of different metaphysical entities.

The hypotheses of the *Parmenides* were now being used neither as evidence for Platonism proper, nor as an examination of Parmenides' own theory, but as a pathway back to the earlier, more austere philosophy of Pythagoras. As such, they were being treated more as a source document than as a text to be interpreted. Perhaps such a view did not originate in

Platonic commentaries at all, but rather in treatises that purport to reveal the core of Pythagorism:[24] treatises which did not even have to acknowledge the *Parmenides* as a source, but which could reserve this detail for study with an élite. A number of Neopythagoreans wrote on the subject of Pythagoras' metaphysical principles, and many scholars read an intricate interpretation into the Neopythagorean Moderatus, while others resist. I have chosen to support an extreme view that finds such interpretation widely among the Neopythagoreans.[25] Evidence is thin, but the Neopythagoreans would not have represented their work as Platonic exegesis and would have made very little impact upon the commentary tradition. This reading becomes exegesis proper only when it comes to be read by those whose primary purpose is to clarify the meaning *of Plato*, in spite of strong leanings towards Pythagoras. And commentaries on this work would have arisen only when sufficient confidence in the importance of its message had caused it to be read in Platonist schools.

iii. *Cratylus*

In the *Cratylus* the character Hermogenes calls upon Socrates to help resolve an argument between himself and Cratylus over whether names are natural or conventional. After an involved discussion, it is not at all certain where Plato's sympathies lie. Consequently, the dialogue is best known for a long series of etymologies which it offers, and which supposedly reflect reality. This is particularly so in respect of the names of gods and other major immaterial and material forces of the universe, and of major ethical qualities. Time and again the ancient Platonists, and others, wanted to make use of the *Cratylus* as an authority for particular etymologies. One might thus suppose that the overall interpretation of the work would be of some importance, though extant writings seldom confirm this. That the dialogue was a study of 'the correctness of names' is implied in Thrasyllus' subtitle (DL 3.58), and also by its function in the late Neoplatonist curriculum.[26] Dillon (1993, 85) claims with good reason that 'by the ancients it was seen as a serious contribution to the theory of language'. We do not even hear of it being treated as a polemical work attacking Heraclitus, although some certainly recognised it as being concerned with Heraclitus' doctrines.[27]

Though debate was seldom attested, it is remarkable that the *Cratylus* is the one work for which Alcinous offers an *interpretation*. This takes the form of an appendix to his sixth chapter, which is largely on formal logic. It concentrates on showing how Plato had anticipated Aristotle in matters of syllogistic, analysis of sophisms, categories, and etymology, therefore constituting the complete logician – even before Aristotle. The works that perform the major role in demonstrating this thesis are *Parmenides*, *Euthydemus*, and *Cratylus*. This should remind one of how Galen had grouped the *Euthydemus* with other 'logical' works, and how he apparently took these dialogues to be offering an illustration of dialectical method rather than its discoveries.[28] A corresponding view of the *Cratylus* would involve an emphasis on the etymological theory, without commitment to any of the examples that Plato employed. Alcinous certainly makes little or nothing of individual etymologies from the *Cratylus*, just as he makes minimal use of doctrinal content from *Parmenides*, *Sophist*, *Politicus*, and *Euthydemus*.[29] He therefore seems to be assuming that none of these works is as important for the content that they bring to light as for the methods that they employ.[30]

Shortly after a statement that Plato treated the whole etymological question in the *Cratylus*, Alcinous commences his appendix as follows:

> The content of the *Cratylus* has this overall meaning. He is inquiring about whether names are by nature or by allocation. He believes that the correctness of names is a matter of allocation, but not without qualification and in chance fashion, but so that the allocation takes place in conformity with the nature of the thing. For the correctness of the name is nothing other than the allocation in tune with the nature of the thing. Arbitrary allocation is not adequate or sufficient for correctness, nor is nature and the first attempt to designate, but a combination of the two. And so the name of each thing is imposed to suit the thing's nature. (*Didasc.* 6.160.3-14).

It is clear that Plato is depicted as taking a moderate line between the excesses of the Peripatos (for which names were conventional) and the Stoa (for which they were natural).[31] Alcinous goes on to emphasise that the name is an instrument for teaching the thing, and stresses the role of the dialectician in the correct use of names as well as an advisor to the name-giver. The logical result of Alcinous' concerns with using names in accordance with the best name-allocator (the one who allocates names that naturally designate objects) would be a close concern with the terminology that Plato himself had preferred. Such a concern is certainly found in some parts of the work.[32] Either Alcinous or an influential source had been personally interested in the status of language. This material would not otherwise have been included. The question remains whether it is the *philosophic issue* or the *interpretative* one that was of primary concern. The former is probably more important, but the latter would have become so as pro-Aristotelian and pro-Stoic interpreters tried to utilise the work for their own ends.

Since we do have a condensed version of Proclus' *Commentary on the Cratylus*, it would be worth glancing briefly at what it tells us. One point of relevance is the lack of historical material that is provided, demonstrating *either* less controversy over the dialogue *or* an epitomator's lack of interest. Proclus' view of the aim of the dialogue, however, is worth comparing with that of Alcinous:

> The aim of the *Cratylus* is to demonstrate the generative activity of souls at

the lowest level (*en eschatois*) and their power of constructing similarities, which, being allocated it in their nature (*ousia*), they reveal through the correctness of names. But since the divided activity of souls often misses its proper goal, just as divided nature does, even those names that are undefined and go into circulation at random can reasonably have a place. Not all of them are the products of intellective knowledge or aim to achieve an affinity to things [signified]. (*In Crat.* 1)

Like Alcinous, Proclus seems to believe that names should be, but are not always, an accurate signifier of the thing designated. He continues to see nature as in itself inadequate to produce this accuracy. The correctness of names remains a key part of the explanation. The difference here is that the traditional elements are in danger of being swamped by the new metaphysical framework. Instead of attending to the human being who has allocated names, Proclus speaks of that part of the human soul which is of such a character as to generate names. Name-giving has become a creative, artistic activity as distinct from the technical one that Alcinous has made it.

In section 51 there is more explanation of why names may be better or worse. Plato is said to be setting up his name-legislator as *analogous* to the Demiurge of the Universe.[33] The Demiurge is seen as the primal name-giver, naming the Same and the Other, so the legislator, who invents names, is his human equivalent, and is accordingly called a demiurge at *Cratylus* 389a. A hierarchy of names arises, since they can be given by gods, clever men, or men in touch with intermediate demons. The dialogue has taken on a new *theological* significance, which is in agreement with the space that it allots to the discussion of divine names. This joint investigation of the nature and function of names together with the metaphysical lessons embedded within names now becomes important. It is seen by Proclus as a typical case of the metaphysical lessons advancing at the same time as discussion of dialectic:

> Just as in the *Parmenides* Plato hands down the entire dialectical art not as a bare outline but along with the investigation of reality, so too he now propounds the correctness of names along with the knowledge of reality. (*In Crat.* 7)

Interpretation of all the 'logical' dialogues is following similar rules. Plato's manner of giving instruction in logic is contrasted sharply with that of Aristotle, following the now familiar pattern of showing how Plato's approach to logic was actually more *advanced* than that of his successor:

> The *Cratylus* is both logical and dialectical, but not in the Peripatetic manner of dialectical pursuits – stripped of implications for the world. It is more in the style of the great Plato, who knew that dialectic was appropriate only to those whose reason is completely purified, educated through mathematics, and purged of juvenile traits through virtues. These, to put it simply,

are people who have done philosophy properly. For dialectic is the keystone of mathematical learning (*Rep.* 534e2). It leads us up to the one cause of all things, the Good, and is what is said by him (*Phlb.* 16c) to have come to humans from the gods via Prometheus along with the brightest of fire. (*In Crat.* 2)

Ultimately we see that the difference between Alcinous and Proclus in tackling 'logical' dialogues is that the latter has advanced to a far more exalted concept of what dialectic is. For Plato, he holds, logic can never be just logic.

iv. *Sophist*

The *Sophist* is yet another potentially perplexing dialogue. Has Plato here abandoned a metaphysical Theory of Ideas, or is he actually advancing it further? What is the relation of the dialectical frame, which hunts for a definition of the sophist by means of dichotomic division, and the central discussion that aims to show how an imprecise image can be part of reality? Are the Five Greatest Kinds, or *Megista Gene* (254b-255e), of this central discussion meant to indicate Plato's present idea of the structure of reality? Is the structure of language that is implied here meant to mirror the architecture of the World of Ideas? In short, even for us the supreme questions relate to whether this dialogue is an exercise in dialectic, metaphysics, the two separately, or both simultaneously.

The basic topic of the dialogue was much disputed in antiquity.[34] Thrasyllus labelled it 'On Being', suggesting an overriding metaphysical significance. The TS interpretation of the *Theaetetus* thought it concerned things which were knowable, seemingly having the Platonic Ideas in mind, and believing that the various examples of genus and species which abound within the work are indeed Ideas. The al-Farabi account of the evolution of the dialogues makes sophistry the concern of the work. This simple view is rejected by the anonymous *Prolegomena* on the ground that the sophist is a case of something that is not-F, not some particular thing. He believes that the dialogue may be united by seeing it as about what is not-X, where X may be any predicate at all. It seems that others before had also claimed that the dialogue was 'On Non-Being', seemingly the opposite of the Thrasyllan subtitle, but in practice not far removed. To these three different views could be added the Galenic one, that it is a dialogue about division.[35]

In the Middle Platonist period Plutarch detected serious metaphysical content in the work, particularly in the *Megista Gene* passage, which determines that reality should consist of at least five basic kinds: Being, Rest, Motion, Sameness, and Difference.[36] This passage, capable of strictly logical interpretation is introduced in a metaphysical and epistemological context. Plotinus again took the *Megista Gene* in a metaphysical sense when he found in them the categories of the intelligible world, after 255c had long been seen as having a bearing on Plato's theory of categories.[37] Iamblichus' rejection of this, not entirely approved by Proclus, does not imply the rejection of a metaphysical reading.[38]

It is Iamblichus who is responsible for what may seem at first sight the strangest account of the subject of the *Sophist*, but the one that does most to reconcile conflicting views. We quoted his view extensively in Chapter 7 iii. In making the work's ultimate target the demiurge of the sublunary world he sought to relate all the definitions of the sophist ultimately to this one divine figure, the many-headed sophist himself! This figure is a maker of images, closely related to non-being, but looks to the eternal, to true being itself. And the art of division is itself an art of imitation, imitating (as Iamblichus claims) the procession of entities from the One. Division imitates the course of Reality, sophists imitate all sorts of things, and the Sublunary Demiurge imitates the Heavenly Demiurge. Sophists, Being, Non-Being, Division, and Sublunary Demiurge: all are linked closely together in Iamblichus' account of the unified *skopos* of the *Sophist*. Logic, metaphysics, and theology are closely intertwined. Iamblichus' account has that same seductive quality as he attributes to the Sublunary Demiurge himself: bewitching the soul into remaining at the level of images.

Proclus may perhaps be following Firmus when he suggests that the subject is the many-headed sophist at *In Parmenidem* 637, but *In Rempublicam* 1.8.24-8 confirms that he inclines to this view in any case.[39] It does not have the complexity of Iamblichus' position, but it is broadly in agreement bearing in mind that the Sublunary Demiurge *was* the supreme and many-headed sophist. It is this kind of position that the *Prolegomena* attack.

What we have seen shows that this dialogue attracted considerable interest from interpreters, with interpretations ranging from quite simple to highly complex, from the non-metaphysical to the theological, mirroring closely the range of interpretations of the *Parmenides*.

v. *Politicus* and conclusion

We have spoken briefly of the *Politicus*, and, since others have recently spoken of its reception,[40] I do not wish to tackle it exhaustively. Clearly, however, it is important to divide possible interpretations into those which give precedence to its methodological lessons, such as advanced division and the use of examples, from those which consider its philosophic content more important. These in turn should be divided into those giving precedence to its ethics and politics, and those giving precedence to its physics, metaphysics, or theology as seen through the myth. The problem is our lack of knowledge concerning 'logical' and 'political' interpretations. Later Platonism tends to be shy of tackling political subjects, and a strictly 'logical' interpretation was surely a little less attractive in this case than in that of other such dialogues.

Persons known to Proclus at *On the Republic* 1.8.28-9.4 show us something about an orthodox view of the *Politicus*. They used the work's being named after the Statesman (rather than the cosmic revolutions of the myth) to show that all dialogues without a personal name-title were named after their principal topic. That this should be used as evidence points to a time when the work was an acknowledged investigation into the Statesman, *even though* much attention was being paid to the myth.

Thrasyllus' subtitle was 'On Kingship' (DL 3.58), and there is reason to suppose that the work had been thought to illustrate the practical art needed for guidance towards happiness in the arrangement known to al-Farabi.[41] If so, then the *Politicus* is seen as tackling a useful art, as opposed to the *Sophist* that tackles an unhelpful one. Such a purpose would in this case accord with Thrasyllus. There is a reasonable chance that *Sophist* and *Politicus* were again separated in the arrangement of Theon, with the *Politicus* being placed with works of positive ethical and political content.[42]

It is remarkable that the late Neoplatonic curriculum preserved the Thrasyllan sequence *Cratylus-Theaetetus-Sophist-Politicus*, and particularly regrettable that a lacuna prevents us from knowing exactly what roles were given to the *Sophist* and *Politicus*.[43] It seems clear to me that the *Cratylus* was seen as dealing with names (*onomata*) and the *Theaetetus* as dealing with notions (*noêmata*), as also that the *Politicus* was thought to deal with the physical world (*physika*). The key question is whether this last held for the *Sophist* as well. I suspect that it did not, and that the *Sophist* was thought to be about imitations (*mimêmata*). In this way we should have two contrasting pairs: concepts and the names that reflect them, the natural world and the image-making that mirrors it. This comes quite close to name, *logos*, image, and paradigm from the influential digression of the *Seventh Epistle* (344b). We have seen the importance of images or imitations for Iamblichus' understanding of the *Sophist*, and it is little less clear that he would have associated the *Politicus* with the Demiurge of the Heavens,[44] who was liable to be imitated. At any rate the *Politicus* is contrasted with the 'theological' works that follow: *Phaedrus*, *Symposium*, and *Philebus*. This perhaps indicates that the Demiurge of the Heavens, detected in the *Politicus* myth, was seen at the pinnacle of the physical world.

Among those who had made much of the myth of the *Politicus*, and had therefore seen it as including some serious reflections on physics and theology, were Plutarch, Severus, and Numenius.[45] Plutarch also found the work useful for demonology.[46] Of these Plutarch certainly and Numenius probably had made important metaphysical use of the *Sophist*.[47] Plutarch, speaking *in propria persona* at *Moralia* 746b, took the theology of the *Cratylus* to be serious Platonic theory: 'Plato himself thinks he is tracking down the attributes of the gods using names like footprints.'[48] Numenius too introduces the *Cratylus* into a metaphysical discussion at fr. 6.13-14. Either of these two prominent interpreters, it seems, would have agreed with Apuleius, that although Plato took physics, ethics, and logic from different predecessors, he made them inseparable (*On Plato* 1.3.187).

Accepting that important metaphysical doctrine resided in one 'logical' work opened the door wide to such doctrine in the others. There was in principle no argument by which either Plutarch or Numenius could rule out positive metaphysical teaching in the *Parmenides*. Though Plutarch shows little interest in the work, it seems to me difficult to deny that this dialogue's first three hypotheses lie beneath the discussion of the first and second/third gods, and their degrees of oneness, in Numenius fr. 11.11-20. By his time Platonists and their Pythagorean allies were likely to adopt a unified approach to all 'logical' dialogues. If Albinus, Galen, and (for the most part) Alcinous thought none contained any real philosophical doctrine, Numenius and orthodox Neoplatonists held that they all did. Proclus at *In Parmenidem* 634-8 provides useful confirmation of this when he reveals that the debate about the *Parmenides* had been linked with similar debate about the *Sophist*.

13

Extracting the doctrine

i. Levels of doctrine

As most readers will be aware, most of the dialogues that were uniformly important in antiquity are still to be tackled. Once the extreme proponents of the sceptic reading of Plato had failed to achieve any lasting credibility, a number of works were routinely taken to be expounding Platonic doctrine: by Middle Platonists, Neoplatonists, and others who wished to make use of Platonic texts. Among them was the single work on the physical world, the *Timaeus*, the two long political works, *Republic* and *Laws*, the two works on love, *Symposium* and *Phaedrus*, the *Phaedo*, and finally the *Philebus*. There are extant ancient commentaries on all except the *Symposium* and *Laws*, and consequently we know a considerable amount of detail about aspects of the debate.

Modern literature has tackled some of the material in detail. One thinks of the work of Matthias Baltes on details of the interpretation of the *Timaeus*;[1] of Anne Sheppard's work on Proclus' *Commentary on the Republic* (1980); of Westerink's work on the *Phaedo*-commentaries of Olympiodorus and Damascius (1976-7); of significant new research on the Nachleben of the *Philebus*;[2] and of important articles on the *Phaedrus* in the second century.[3] Now we have Julia Annas' perceptive study (1999) of the ethical aspects of many of these dialogues. It would be unwise to attempt to duplicate their efforts here, and not especially relevant to the main aim of this book, which has been to discuss issues of meta-interpretation, with emphasis on the period before Plotinus. Nevertheless it seems perverse to preserve a Pythagorean silence about the interpretation of these dialogues, and about ancient responses to some of the principal issues.

The most obvious question about dialogues that, according to accepted opinion, expound doctrine, is whether one should attach a similar status to everything which a principal speaker says, or whether some styles of address are to be afforded more weight. At one point there is argument from agreed premises to a conclusion, and assent by the interlocutor to this conclusion. At another, there is the use of elaborate analogies. At another, there is a puzzling mathematical passage. At another, a myth that 'Socrates' is said to believe, but not to be sure of. At another, Plato's speakers appeal to the authority of some figure from the revered past. At another simply an argument against the contrary view. Does all this reveal doctrine, and if so does it all have the same status?

Clearly, the responses to these questions would vary from interpreter to interpreter. The Alexandrian School of Ammonius regarded assertions without the backing of demonstrative arguments as being inferior, and the reliance on the authority of anybody but oneself as misguided.[4] Even so, they could pay a considerable amount of attention to non-demonstrative means of conveying Plato's message, such as the poetic and mythical parts of Socrates' arguments against Callicles at *Gorgias* 492-9.[5] The importance of philosophic myths and of appeals to religious beliefs is fundamental virtually throughout later Platonism, but for the Alexandrians they had simply ceased to be the revelations that they had become for the Athenian School.

Mathematical passages and analogies of all kinds were the source of considerable attention from Plutarch's exegetical works (and before), right through until late Neoplatonism. In general the assumption seems to have been made that such passages were far more than exercises to make us think things through, but the source of deeper doctrines that Plato was reluctant or unable to express more directly. One would have expected the Athenian Neoplatonists, with their insistence on seeing deep meaning even in introductory passages, to discover serious philosophy in whatever devices Plato chose to employ. However, there was an impressive level of debate in Middle Platonism too about the mathematics of the *Timaeus*, the colourful descriptions of matter in the same dialogue, the Sun, Divided Line, and Cave of the *Republic*, and the significance of the myths of the *Phaedo*, *Phaedrus*, and *Republic* 10. Indeed, it might almost be said that such passages were the 'bread and butter' of extant Middle Platonist exegesis.

One Middle Platonist approach to interpretation is perhaps well illustrated by the famous distinction attributed to both Gaius and Albinus (Test. 3 Göransson) between two grades of Platonic doctrine. There is a knowledge-producing doctrine, associated with true reality, and the likeness-producing type, associated with the physical world. 'Likeness-producing' doctrines (*eikatologikos*) sound like the type that would readily employ a variety of analogies and images to convey the intentions of the author, demonstration being presumably unavailable. However, it was certainly not generally accepted that the more oblique means of conveying doctrines were employed for discussions of inferior subject-matter. Plutarch, Numenius, and virtually the whole of Neoplatonism would expect such devices also in the communication of the more religious aspects of Platonism. To deprive Platonic texts of their mysteries was for them to remove the very thing that made Platonism most distinctive, and to make the mistake of assuming that the highest entities could be approached by conventional scientific and philosophic inquiry. It is not surprising that Albinus became associated with a rather literal, rather mechanical approach to Plato (Test. 16).

ii. *Phaedo*

The *Phaedo* at first sight looks to be a dialogue with a fairly straightforward didactic purpose. It is there to charm us, rather as Socrates has been charming Simmias and Cebes, so as to alleviate the fear of death. It is vital that Socrates himself is seen to face death with equanimity. It is perhaps the antecedent of Aristotle's lost *Gryllus* and the whole genre of consolation-literature thereafter. Its strategy is the opposite of that of Epicurus, trying to convince us that death will have a positive outcome for those who have lived with death in mind. Rather than total removal of all awareness (and hence the removal of ills), Plato argues for the removal of only those sensations that impede the progress of the mind, so that our immortal part returns to its rightful state. Plato must claim that which Epicurus must deny: the immortality of the soul.

Even so, there was room for disagreement about the work's dominant purpose. It had been known from an early date as *On the Soul* rather than by its current title.[6] This title would suggest that it was viewed as Plato's primary text on psychology, and that it was seen as being more treatise-like than those dialogues named after a key participant in the conversation. That title became Thrasyllus' subtitle, yet he saw the purpose of the first tetralogy in general as being the depiction of the philosophic life (DL 3.57). The two can easily be reconciled, for there is nothing to prevent the action of the dialogue (with help from the words) as illustrating proper philosophic conduct, while the subject of debate is the nature of the soul. Albinus also saw the work as offering a picture of the philosopher and his pursuit, but adds that it shows us how Platonism proceeds on the basis that the soul is immortal. So for him too it combines the study of psychology with the more general topic of the philosophic life. For al-Farabi it was about death being preferable to life (as was the *Apology* too),[7] and the picture of Socrates' last day was again an indispensible part of the dialogue. The author of the *Prolegomena* (21) actually knew of interpreters who gave the work a triple purpose, discussing (i) the immortality of the soul, (ii) how to die well, and (iii) the nature of the philosophic life. He rejects any such multiple aim (*skopos*), and it appears from 26 that the Iamblichan curriculum had made the purification of the soul from the influence of the body central to their conception of the work. The fundamental purpose of the *Phaedo* was thus something that could generate considerable debate, and few ancient interpreters would readily see it simply as an attempt to prove the immortality of the soul. A possible exception is Alcinous, whose love of collecting arguments causes him to treat the *Phaedo* in chapter 25 as little more than a catalogue of self-standing arguments for immortality.[8]

The *Phaedo* argues its way towards its conclusions with a persistence unusual in Plato, and it would be perverse to deny that he is committed to the theory of immortality which he propounds. Unable to accept that this was really Socrates, Panaetius denied either the authenticity of the dialogue or the authenticity of its Socrates.[9] The major quarrel, however, was exactly how much 'soul' Plato had in mind when he spoke of immortality. *Timaeus* 69c speaks of the lesser gods building another mortal kind of soul into the body, a kind responsible for the mortal passions of pleasure, pain, cheer, fear, temper, and hope. Is it only the reasoning part of the soul, then, which Plato wanted to make immortal? That solution too would have its difficulties, particularly for those who took seriously the theory of transmigration, whereby a human soul could find itself descending into some animal body. Do cattle have rational souls, or fish, or flies? Harpocration of Argos apparently did regard ants and flies as endowed with immortal souls,[10] but clearly most shunned such conclusions. It is interesting that Alcinous raises the issue about whether rational soul alone is immortal at *Didascalicus* 25.5, without making any final determination on the matter: a rare case of suspension of judgment in this work.

The debate over the extent of the soul's immortality is reported by Damascius,[11] who of course concentrates on the positions of the prominent Neoplatonists, most of whom made only the rational part immortal (Porphyry, Proclus), or the rational and irrational parts (Iamblichus, Plutarch of Athens). This last position is also claimed to have been that of Speusippus and Xenocrates. Somewhat more subtle positions are attributed to Plotinus and Numenius. Undoubtedly the problem here was in trying to reconcile the psychological doctrines of different dialogues, but the problems have their germ in the *Phaedo* itself, for the immortal soul after death is assumed to have faculties analogous to the very ones that it looks forward to being freed from. It also seems clear that commentaries on the *Phaedo*, which was from quite early a favourite work for commentators,[12] were the likeliest location for Platonist discussions of these general psychological issues. We have seen already that they seem to have been the ordinary place for discussion of the Theory of Recollection.[13]

iii. *Symposium* and *Phaedrus*

It seems logical to group these two works together, since they have the shared themes of love, beauty, and speech-making. They were extremely popular, having a wide appeal among the literate classes. Thus they are alluded to regularly not only in the esoteric philosophy of those such as Plotinus, not only in philosophic writers such as Philo of Alexandria, Plutarch, or Apuleius, but also in the comic and parodic works of entertainers such as Lucian. A proper appreciation of Lucian's *Symposium or*

Lapiths relies on a knowledge of Plato's *Symposium*, and references to the myth of the *Phaedrus* in particular abound in his works. Thanks to Aulus Gellius we have Taurus' disdainful comments about the youth of his day, who demand to begin their study of Plato with the *Symposium* (especially for Alcibiades' revelry) or *Phaedrus* (especially for Lysias' seduction-speech).[14] These works were popularly viewed as entertainment, and the philosopher clearly struggled to get his young clients to see a deeper meaning in them. We know that this applied to the well-known speech by Pausanias in the *Symposium*,[15] and his distinction between a higher and a lower Love, associated with a higher and a lower Aphrodite, was particularly popular.

Even so, Platonists such as Alcinous and Apuleius could claim that Plato really postulated *three* kinds of Love, apparently preferring the testimony of the Athenian Stranger at *Laws* 837 to that of Pausanias and Eryximachus in the *Symposium*.[16] They possibly thought that Plato's full authority in the *Symposium* resided only in the words attributed (via Apollodorus, Aristodemus, and Socrates) to Diotima. Diotima's account of the ascent to the Beautiful (210a-d) is interpreted by Alcinous as a means of discovering god, hence as a theological passage. He no doubt anticipates the late Neoplatonist equation of the divine with the good, the beautiful, and the wise.[17] The ascent passage must lie behind the Thrasyllan subtitle for the work, 'On Good', and it must be this passage that has assured it the penultimate place in Iamblichus initial canon of ten dialogues, after the *Phaedrus* and before only the *Philebus*.[18]

Also of importance in the words of Diotima was the description of Eros as an intermediate *daemon* rather than a god (202c-204c),[19] but it was important *for demonology* rather than for Eros. Unsurprisingly in view of the *Phaedrus'* very different approach, there is a reluctance among such authors as Plutarch (in the *Eroticus*) and Alcinous to follow the *Symposium* in denying the existence of a god Eros. Plutarch is particularly interesting, insofar as his own religious and sexual inclinations are very different from those that a literal reading of the *Symposium* would encourage, so that he not so much uses it as *creatively reinterprets* it. Here was a work that could scarcely be denied the status of inspired literature, but which encouraged an in depth understanding of love that would lead one to discard that very vehicle upon which the understanding was built.

The pervasive importance of the *Phaedrus*, and above all of its myth, did not prevent argument about its primary concern. Thrasyllus labelled it 'On Love' (DL 3.58); the author of the *Prolegomena* thinks of it as 'On the Beautiful' (21.13) or 'On all-pervasive Beauty' (22.6), and he criticises those who make it 'On Rhetoric' (22.4).[20] Even so, Neoplatonism took this work's contribution to the Platonic notion of rhetoric very seriously, and it is regularly studied alongside the *Gorgias* for this reason.[21] Prose writing did arise early in the work, and is the main topic under investigation towards the end, so that it may well have been treated like a work on rhetoric by the rhetorical schools. The rich and picturesque language of the myth could be seen by some as contributing as much to a rhetorical education as to a philosophic one, but not to the committed Platonist.

The *Phaedrus* shows us how even Plato's bluntest statements could generate heated debate. The famous statement 'All soul is immortal' (245c5) was central to the debate already considered about the extent to which this immortality went. Did Plato mean here only that soul as a whole was immortal, without any implication for individual immortality? Did he mean that all rational or at least all reasonable soul was immortal? Was it only human soul that he was interested in here? Or did immortality extend to the animating principle of ants and flies: of all things animate in fact, so that even the 'vegetative soul' becomes immortal.[22] Later Platonists certainly did their best to justify Plato's concerns about how the written word can be interpreted, but no more perhaps than we do today!

iv. *Republic*

It is no easy task to write briefly on ancient interpretation of so rich and varied a work as the *Republic*, particularly as we have essays by Proclus on several of its major themes. These essays are collectively known as the *Commentary on the Republic*, but a work concentrating so heavily on Plato's treatment of the poets is not a commentary in an orthodox sense.[23] In fact we do not know whether any ordinary commentary on the work was ever written in the ancient world. Commentaries are attributed by the Suda to Potamo and Onosander, both writing in the first hundred years of the Roman Empire, and Theon's (*Expos.* 146) cannot have been written long after. Other topics that received detailed treatment included the Myth of Er (Dercyllides, Proclus), the Divided Line (Plutarch), and the psychology of Book 4 (Posidonius, Plutarch, Galen).[24] While mathematical aspects of these passages were a particular attraction to ancient interpreters, the famous Nuptial Number of Book 8 had again attracted the attention of the mysterious Dercyllides.[25]

Alcinous, however, utilises a wide range of material from the *Republic*. He attaches a relatively low priority to mathematics in ch. 7 (which is based on *Republic* 7), and discusses the tripartite soul in relation to the virtues (ch. 29) rather than psychology. In general, one might suspect Alcinous of seeing the *Republic* as a work of predominantly moral and political significance, regarding its more 'theoretical' features as secondary. The brief summary of the *Republic* given by al-Farabi's Middle Platonic source likewise concentrates on moral and political issues and ignores metaphysics. It might be useful here to compare Albinus (*Prol.* 5) for whom the work is important for its contribution to educational theory and its illumination of the path to virtue.

For those interpreters who are not seduced into giving psychology, mathematics, and metaphysics pride of place, the key issue is whether the work was a contribution to personal ethics or to politics. The opening and close would suggest the former, but books 3-9 might suggest that the political agenda was more important. The character-classification had treated the *Republic* as one of a small group of dialogues with the *political* character, though we should not suppose that this means that its purpose or subject-matter was political. Rather it seems that 'character' was an indication of the *approach* that a work was taking,[26] and a political approach can be taken to solving problems more concerned with *individual* than community happiness. Programmes of education through the dialogues tended to place the *Republic* late, close to the *Laws* and other 'political' works,[27] but this did not guarantee that it was seen as political itself, for the 'physical' *Timaeus* routinely followed it. Rather it was held to be part of a group outlining good order within the individual, the state, and the cosmos, and giving emphasis to the analogies between them.

Proclus reports that some subtitled the work 'On Justice' and others 'On Constitution'.[28] The former made appeal to (i) the content of Book 1, (ii) the fact that justice in the state is examined to solve the problem of justice in the individual, (iii) Socrates' reminders to the company that they are trying to find justice, and (iv) the justice-theme of the final Myth of Er. The latter appealed to the antiquity of the title itself, which they believed had to illustrate the principal topic,[29] to the alleged treatment of it as a political work at *Laws* 739b-e, and to the fact that it is treated as a work about a constitution in the *Timaeus* (17b-19a). It might very well be that the first party had intended to question the seriousness of the political content of the dialogue, while the second party was trying to defend it. Nevertheless, there is no sign that such a sharp distinction was routinely maintained among Middle Platonists. Proclus certainly rejects it himself: 'The thing which is justice in an individual soul is exactly this kind of constitution in a well-governed state.'[30] For Proclus the macrocosm-microcosm analogy is so perfect that justice and constitution are alternative manifestations of the same thing. Already, surely, the term 'constitution', in Greek *politeia* with obvious connections to the community or *polis*, had become a standard term for the inner organisation of the parts of the soul,[31] and there was no longer any difficulty in making the *skopos* of the *Republic* 'On Constitution'.

A recurrent issue in modern debate is the extent to which Book 1 fully belongs with the rest of the *Republic*, bearing in mind that it resembles dialogues about the nature of a particular virtue, such as the *Charmides*. There is no doubt that the ancients were aware of a certain discontinuity here, but the issue is not one of the earliness or Socraticity of Book 1, but rather of its manner or 'character'. The ancients were well aware that Thrasymachus belonged to the same type of undesirable character as the orators of the *Gorgias* or the sophists of other dialogues.[32] In Diogenes this is the only case of a character who is introduced for the sake of refutation in an instructional dialogue, and there is no doubt that if the Book had been taken alone it would have been seen as *zetetic* or inquisitive. Proclus is not disturbed by such an anomaly, because he sees the mixture of instructional and inquisitive elements as being characteristic of the *Republic*, which, though perceptive, rather downplays the extent to which Book 1 stands out, and seems to misunderstand what 'zetetic' had meant.[33] Proclus does, however, make a distinction between the place of the first book and of the remainder, for he situates the latter in the city itself rather than the Piraeus.[34] This alleged change of scene is justified in terms of the turbulence of the Piraeus (and of debates concerning justice), as opposed to the more philosophical calm of the city. So the gap between Book 1 and the remainder of the work resurfaces in Proclus in a new way that many would find equally detrimental to the literary unity of the work – a unity which Proclus of course takes as given.

v. *Laws*

I include here a few words about the *Laws* as its length and political subject make it directly comparable with the *Republic*. I find, however, little to suggest that lively debate had taken place over it despite its supposed status as Plato's last work.[35] This is in part because interpreters simply took note of what they wanted to. Some passages were well known, including the classification of goods in Book 1 (631), parts of Book 5 (715-16, 731), and the theological content of Book 10. In this last Plutarch found clear reference to the status of an evil principle.[36] Overall, however, the *Laws* was not subject to much interpretative activity, but was rather used as a source for passages that might confirm one's interpretation of high-profile dialogues.

vi. *Timaeus*

It is ironic that the work in which Plato's assumed spokesperson speaks most directly was often the source of complaints of obscurity.[37] It was certainly the cause of fierce debates over all sorts of issues of detail. If one were to examine these issues it would take another volume (at least), and there is little point in offering an overview here. There was general consensus that it was a didactic work about the physical world and the divine machinery that governed it, and also that it stood in the Pythagorean tradition. Its connections with the *Republic* and the *Critias* were not doubted. The issues arose principally in connection with literal or non-literal interpretation, the relation of details to possible parallels in other dialogues, the way to understand some unusual notions (such as the disorderly motion in the receptacle), and the correct decoding of the mathematical passages.

Of these the most important for our purposes is the question of literal or non-literal interpretation, since it is one that has a bearing on other works too. This issue has been addressed in Chapter 4 ii, and it is one which persisted from Plato's immediate successors until the end of antiquity. Did Plato ever mean to postulate a temporal beginning for the universe? Did he mean us to take his creator-god seriously, or is that divinity merely the on-going organiser of the universe? Is he serious about all obscure details of physiology and psychology? Is there a strong moral purpose underlying the work, which has in fact determined much of the physical detail? Literal interpretation had the disadvantage that it made it far more difficult to reconcile the *Timaeus* with other works of Plato. Non-literal interpretation had the disadvantage that it was difficult to know where it should stop. There was also the problem that to disregard the *Timaeus'* account of Platonic physics often left one with nothing, for in this area there was very little comparable material. The *Timaeus* threw out the challenge to find the mean between the pulpit-style fundamentalism of an Atticus and the relative anarchy of many others. That this work had become a respected authority made it all the more important to work out just how this authority operated.

The more non-literal an interpretation became the more it was likely to depend on a message that was thought to take precedence over the teaching of physics. From the days of Stobaeus' source at *Eclogues* 2.49-50, often assumed to be Eudorus, the *Timaeus* was recognised as one of the principal sources for Plato's moral goal – assimilation to the divine. This is clear again in Albinus (*Prologus* 5). Particularly in the context of the eighth Thrasyllan tetralogy, or any other grouping which respected its explicit connections with the *Republic* and *Critias*, the *Timaeus* had to be recognised as having a message for human life. Any reading that began to doubt the seriousness of the physical message would naturally incline towards finding an ethical one, and that would have been a natural tactic for a stoic-minded writer around the second century AD. The *Timaeus* would be a source of obscure metaphysics for the Pythagorean sympathiser; for the practical philosopher it could be expected to have a very different significance.

vii. *Philebus*

For the greater part of the twentieth century the *Philebus* was a comparatively neglected dialogue. Its lack of immediate literary appeal, tortuous paths to an uncertain goal, and general obscurity ensured its unpopularity. It was as far as any Platonic dialogue from engaging with modern problems in an acceptable modern manner, and probably depended crucially on the reader's awareness of the debate on pleasure within the Old Academy. The *Philebus* is a tricky dialogue to interpret, and constantly presents us with problems in relating its material to that of other middle/late dialogues.

It would be a great mistake to believe that the ancients shared our view of this work. It seems to have had a key role in the Neoplatonic curriculum, perhaps as the final dialogue of the preliminary decad. It regularly attracted interest in the Middle Platonic period, in part because of the enormous interest in strategies for countering hedonism, but in part too because of the obscure metaphysical passages that the modern reader tends to find unattractive. Being more familiar than we are with Old Academic writers such as Speusippus and Xenocrates, and just as familiar with Aristotle's reports of unwritten metaphysical doctrine, the Middle Platonists rightly anticipated some modern writers in detecting esotericism in the *Philebus*.

Perhaps the earliest text that concerns me here was the account of Plato's various divisions of the good in Stobaeus *Eclogues* 2.54-5, which may be connected with Eudorus. The final obscure classification of 'goods' at 66a-d is interpreted as listing: (i) the Good itself, (ii) the combination of intelligence and pleasure, (iii) intelligence, (iv) the combination of knowledge and correct opinion, (v) pleasure. The tendency to 'translate' Plato into simpler terms is evident, and the pattern simple-mixture-simple-mixture-simple might be of some relevance.[38] Dillon has suggested with good reason that Eudorus' account of Pythagorean metaphysics[39] draws on the metaphysics of *Philebus* 23c-30e.[40]

When we come to Plutarch (*Mor.* 391c-d) we find a different approach to the passage. Rather than five 'goods' it is said to show five 'kinds' in which the Good manifests itself: (i) what's measured, (ii) what's symmetrical, (iii) intelligence, (iv) knowledge, crafts, and right opinions in the soul, (v) any pure pleasure. Taking these as areas where one may look for goodness agrees well with Plato's oblique approach to the Good at *Philebus* 64-5. Plutarch is depicting his own younger self as trying to discover some special significance in Plato of the number five, for which purpose he has also used the *Megista Gene* of the *Sophist* and the metaphysical classification of *Philebus* 23c. It can scarcely be doubted that Plutarch would dearly like to relate the 66a classification to the 23c one (which is explicitly related to the *Sophist*),[41] most probably along these lines:

(i) what's measured	separative cause	Different
(ii) what's symmetrical	mixed product	Being
(iii) intelligence	cause of combination	Same
(iv) knowledge etc. in soul	limiters	Rest
(v) any pure pleasure	unlimited	Motion

Academic caution prevents him from dogmatising about any of these connections, but it is interesting that Plutarch would be identifying the obscurely hinted cause of separation (23d9-11) with the most obscure element of the final classification. How could one find the highest human good in the cause that *separates* the mixed life? This is where the Middle Platonist insistence on the unity of the Platonic corpus is crucial. They would have recalled that according to *Phaedo* 81-4 the philosopher finds the highest good when he succeeds in separating his intellectual inner person from the pleasures and pains that come with life in the body. The highest good for humans is the one that allows us to leave the human state behind. The Middle Platonist goal of assimilation to a god, discovered by Alcinous (28) in *Theaetetus*, *Republic* 10, *Phaedo*, and *Phaedrus*, automatically implied transcending the human life, and there is a strong suggestion in the *Philebus* itself (33b) that a divine life would transcend all pleasure and pain, and consequently rise above the mixed life that alone is satisfactory for humans.

The *Philebus* did in fact include some encouragement for the observant reader to see death behind the first good at 66a. It is found in the region of measure and what's measured (*to metrion*), which clearly suggests an *absolute* measurement when contrasted with the symmetry (*to symmetron*) of the second good. And Plato adds *to kairion* to suggest that this absolute measure comes at an appropriate point of time. None of this would have been lost on the young Plutarch as he searched the more obscure passages of Plato for an underlying five-fold metaphysic: always in a Delphic context.[42]

The impulse to find some underlying meaning of significance behind *Philebus* 66 has also left its mark upon Alcinous. In chapter 10 (164.31-4) we meet two lists of five terms applied to his first god. He is eternal, inexpressible, self-complete, ever-complete, all-complete; and he is divineness, beingness, truth, symmetry, good. The traditional hunting for parallels to Alcinous' colourful vocabulary has not greatly advanced the understanding of this passage, and an alternative approach is needed, actually relating Alcinous' lists to a reading of Plato. Bearing in mind Alcinous' well-known tendency subtly to alter Plato's original expression,[43] we must look at the *meaning* rather than the word chosen.

The first list seems to be related to a reading of the first five hypotheses of the *Parmenides*, though the first and second items need ideally to be transposed.[44] The inexpressible character of the One emerges strongly at the close of the first hypothesis (142a). Its omnitemporal nature emerges almost at the close of hypothesis two (155c8-d6). Its being complete *in itself* is captured by the words 'the One, if it is, would undergo all these experiences' (157b). Every kind of change can be accomplished by the One itself. The fourth and fifth hypotheses are really examinations of the Others, so greater difficulty is expected in extracting a message about the One. Nevertheless, the fourth hypothesis makes it clear that what is viewed perpetually apart from the One is indeterminate, suggesting strongly that *all* determination *always* must be associated with the One (158c5-7). Finally the fifth hypothesis concludes by claiming that if the One is, then it is all things (160b). The series 'inexpressible, omnitemporal, self-complete, ever-complete, all-complete' would have constituted an excellent attempt to find some major message about the One in each of the first five hypotheses of the *Parmenides*.[45]

There are two vital things to be noticed here. First, there is no suggestion that there is any but a single god or One in view. Second, it would still not be possible to be examining this One from the same point of view, since the different hypotheses come to contradictory conclusions. The five different pictures of the One would have to have emerged in relation to different things, or at different levels. We are not dealing with a Neoplatonic-style interpretation, but rather with the type of interpretation that we have associated with Firmus. The One is throughout to be identified with Parmenides' One, and all the emphasis on total, everlasting, self-sufficient completion is in agreement with Parmenides B8. The ready talk of those things that are other than the One may be strange to us, but it is entirely in conformity with the Platonising view of Parmenides as found in Plutarch and others.[46]

It may seem rash to claim that these five epithets of the first god have been somehow applied in relation to different things or at different levels. However, when Alcinous tackled the Ideas in chapter nine he did indeed say what they were in relation to each of five metaphysical entities.

Idea in relation to:		
God	=	his thought
Us	=	primary intelligible
Matter	=	its measure
Sensible world	=	its paradigm
Itself	=	substance

One might also suspect that a list of five *Timaeus*-based names attributed to matter in chapter 8 (162.30-1) were intended to highlight its relation to different things,[47] though there are difficulties in finding what matter might be in relation to a transcendent god![48] However, the one parallel is sufficient to suggest that Alcinous' source is choosing five terms to describe god in relation to different metaphysical levels.

So now we come to the second of Alcinous' lists of five 'epithets' to describe god: divineness, beingness, truth, symmetry, good. There is no doubt that Dillon is correct in linking the last three terms with the *Philebus*, and he speaks of 65a in particular.[49] Rather he should be thinking of the final classification, which was clearly a popular passage and which again involves truth, symmetry, and good. That this passage is in view is confirmed by the fact that beauty, completion, and symmetry are linked immediately after, in a passage intended to offer some explanation of the terminology employed. Though missed by both Whittaker and Dillon, this clearly parallels *Philebus* 66b1-3. However, the relation of our five terms to this context is by no means simple, and must involve thinking of how the first divinity *is made manifest* at successive levels, much as in Plutarch. After all, what could it mean to call the first god 'divineness' (*theiotês*) or 'symmetry' or even 'truth' in his own right? Further, Alcinous himself suggests shortly afterwards that the first god should *not* be called good (165.8), because he does not participate in goodness. 'Good' at 164.34 must mean archetypal *goodness*.[50]

Alcinous goes on to provide us with most of the solution to the problem of these pseudo-epithets. He follows the list by asserting that he is not making any distinction between the terms, such as would compromise the unity of the first god.[51] What he maintains is that the prototypes of these qualities are present *in a primal undifferentiated way* in the first god:

> And (i) he is good, because be benefits all things to the best of his ability, being responsible for every good; and (ii) he is beautiful because he himself is in his own nature complete and symmetrical (*symmetron*); and (iii) he is truth because he constitutes the source of all truth, as the sun is source of all light. And (iv) he is father, by his being the cause of all things .... And (v) he is unspeakable (*arrhêtos*) ....

Though this has been much obscured by a struggle for brevity, we should have encountered in the original that Alcinous followed explanations (where necessary) of the terms in reverse order. The explanations began with the final term of the second list of five, then tackled the penultimate and the antepenultimate terms, and concluded with the second term of the first list.[52] Alcinous should have taken the term 'symmetrical' rather than 'beautiful' as the *explanandum*, but it is likely that his source had said 'symmetrical and beautiful', following *Philebus* 66b1 (*to symmetron kai kalon*). The relation of the first god to truth makes use of *Republic* 508d-e.

How the term 'father' has crept in as one requiring explanation is at first sight obscure, but it ought to be the case that the paternal activity of god had in fact been the explanation of another of the pseudo-epithets. The focus is on his creative role, which is mediated by the intellect of the cosmic soul. He imparts himself to all things (165.1), and is the cause of all things (164.40), not of their goodness or beauty or truth this time, but *simply* of their being. Originally, then, this had been the explanation of the *beingness* of god, that is cause of the being of all else. But that is not quite all. He is also the cause of the intellect of the cosmic soul, and is *specifically* this intellect's father. In this case it is not so much its being that god is causing as its divinity. The source had conflated the explanation of the divineness and beingness of god, by showing how he passes down a *divine order* to another power, so that this power can give *being* to the things of this world.[53]

Alcinous' treatment of his source is a complicated matter, and of great relevance for understanding his methods more generally. However, what concerns us now is his source's treatment of the final classification of the *Philebus*, like the hypotheses of the *Parmenides*, as a source for theology. How exactly does our fivefold list of pseudo-epithets relate to Plato's five 'goods'? The 66a classification concerns things good for humans. The five 'goods' are presumably supposed to be of five basic *types*, all of which are prefigured in the nature of the first god, the ultimate source of all goodness. It is easy to see that the symmetry, beauty and sufficiency of the life blended from knowledge and pleasure can relate to the symmetry, beauty and completion of god,[54] and that truth in our intellects can relate to the truth embodied in him. But what of knowledge, what of pure pleasure, and what of the good that concerns measure? Are we wrong to look for these behind Alcinous at all?

I propose that we solve the problem in the following way. Divineness relates only to the first good, the good involved with correct measure and timing. Beingness extends to the second good, symmetry etc., the qualities of the mixed life, which is the good that needs to be brought into being. Truth proper extends as far as wisdom and intelligence, which have this as their special concern (58d-59d). Beauty/symmetry, though associated with all that has preceded, extends to knowledge, craft, and true opinion. Goodness extends even to pure pleasure. That different goods should extend down to different levels, with the good extending even to matter, is a feature of late Neoplatonism too.[55]

Fortunately, the details are not crucial. What is important is that we find in Alcinous a *Philebus*-based theory of the gifts given by the first god, implicit in him, explicit in the lives in which they are manifested. Just as the first list employed the *Parmenides* as a theological text, so the second used the *Philebus* as little short of that. The author is not claiming that its sole significance is of this kind, as he uses it also for epistemology, psychology, and ethics, but this theological use will strike us as stranger. Proclus, however, unhesitatingly read it for its theological insights.[56] Furthermore, on the Neoplatonist reading of the dialogue, from Iamblichus on, it was a work 'On the Good'.[57] The Good of the *Republic* and the Beautiful of the *Symposium* and *Phaedrus* were both seen as relevant to understanding the *Philebus*. The position of the dialogue in the third Thrasyllan tetralogy, between the *Parmenides* and the *Symposium*, might have encouraged Alcinous' source to find theology in it. *Symposium* (210-11) is used shortly after as source of one of Alcinous' ways of knowing god (165.27-35).[58] The *Republic* and *Timaeus* were the only dialogues, other than those of tetralogy three, to exert a major influence on the theological chapter.

Plutarch and Alcinous have showed us ways in which the *Philebus* has been used for metaphysical and theological purposes, but it is much more difficult to say exactly how the dialogue fitted in with their metaphysics. The principles of limit and unlimited which dominate the early part of the work were themselves very flexible, capable of being employed in very different ways at 16c and 23c. Plutarch is in any case a very flexible thinker, guided by Academic caution, and unwilling to be dogmatic about what the *Philebus* means. In Alcinous we have come to expect a consistent underlying metaphysical system, but such an expectation always leads to disappointment. Alcinous, whether or not he plunders incompatible sources, shows considerable flexibility in the presentation of doctrine, and the *Timaeus*-dependent chapters on physics (12-22) are well known for being difficult to square with the metaphysics. Yet the author could feel comfort from the idea that Plato was many-voiced, and preserve something of these many voices in his account of Platonic doctrine *without implying that Plato was doctrinally inconsistent.*[59] Alcinous was flexible too. One should not underestimate the extent to which Platonic interpretation, and the plurality of dialogues interpreted, was affecting presentation of doctrine.

Hence if one wishes to see exactly how the *Philebus*-dependent theology fits into Alcinous' (or his source's) metaphysics, one should not expect everything to fit together perfectly. Metaphysical patterns are present in chapter 10, but they too are flexible. If we return to the five entities in relation to which the Ideas were examined, they were God, Ideas, Humans, Sensible World, and Matter (9.14-17). My contention is that the five 'goods', primally present in god, of the *Philebus* were relevant to:

(i)   something partaking in quasi-divine status, i.e. the heavenly intellect
(ii) something partaking in quasi-paradigmatic status, i.e. the real mixed life
(iii) something partaking in quasi-truth, i.e. our human quasi-intellect
(iv) something partaking of quasi-formal status, i.e. knowledge etc.
(v)   something partaking of quasi-material status, i.e. pleasure.

The beginning of the theological chapter had shown that Alcinous habitually finds us humans a particular place in the metaphysical scheme of things (164.13-18), and they surely have a place in the hierarchy that follows at 164.18 ff. Below the first god are:

(i)   An intellect ever thinking all objects of thought (= the heavenly intellect)
(ii) The objects of thought themselves (= the Ideas)
(iii) Something incompletely partaking in intellectual activity (= us humans)
(iv) Soul separated from intellect (nature)
(v)   [no lower grade mentioned]

Our author's representation of Plato's Ascent to the Beautiful as a way of knowing god channels *Symposium* 210a-11c into a basic fivefold pattern.[60] It involves the beauty of bodies, of soul, of laws/customs, of 'the vast ocean of beauty', and of the Good itself *together with* the first god. A persistent but flexible pattern emerges: the material, the natural, the human, the ideal, and finally the divine. The pattern belongs not to Alcinous but to his metaphysical source, some author in whom the young Plutarch too seems to have been interested. It presumably lies behind the five 'causes' (final, paradigmatic, motive, formal, material) of Seneca's *Epistle* 65.7-10, and perhaps with other passages in Middle Platonism.[61] The role that the *Philebus* played in promoting this metaphysical pattern is uncertain. From Plutarch one gathers that it was of some importance, with the tantalising theory of unlimited, limit, mixed product, and dual causes (23c-d) perhaps being crucial.[62]

viii. Conclusion

We are now stepping outside the realm of interpretation proper. The principal interpretative task of reconciling a variety of texts has produced a flexible pattern that is imposed upon texts. Interpreters acquire visions, visions fuelled by, but other than, the texts that they interpret. Visions may have difficulties that their originators do not fully see.[63] When the vision is imposed upon the text, instead of teased out of it, then interpretation proper gives way to doctrine. Plutarch's flexibility, and his caution about 'private conceptions' (*Mor.* 1000a), ensure that he remains an interpreter. In Alcinous, whose aim is to record *Platonic* doctrines, interpretation and doctrine become fused. With Neoplatonism we step, for some time at least, into a new world where visions cloud interpretation. Hence interpretation becomes the interpretation of an earlier vision rather than of a text. Plato becomes one of those whose texts preserve the vision until the Alexandrian school of Ammonius is forced by political circumstances to take a more objective view of Plato once again.

This is not to say that I consider the interpretative activity of Proclus to be in any way uninteresting. The very relation of the interpretation to the underlying vision, derived in part from Plotinus, in part from Iamblichus, and in part from Syrianus, can be well worth serious study, but that is a different book. Proclus is not a *fresh* interpreter, as many of the Middle Platonists were. So many of the alternative strategies that occur to the fresh interpreter could never have been considered by later Neoplatonists. Studying Proclus will not in the same way encourage *us* to become fresh interpreters, which is what this book aims to encourage. Fresh interpretation does not need to be raw interpretation. It does not need to fall into the same mistakes as have often been made before. We may learn the lessons of history, and still throw off the burden of tradition. Fresh interpretations need not be radical. They need not come to any conclusions that have not previously been entertained. However, the end will be all the more satisfying if we have been again to the beginning and chosen our route for ourselves.

In examining early interpretation we have been forced to concentrate largely on Middle Platonism. We have found intense debate both over the principles of interpretation and over the details. We have done so by adopting two strategies that will appear unorthodox. Firstly, we have studied interpretation largely as interpretation, not as doctrine. This strategy may have its flaws, but it will be a useful corrective to the opposite strategy, which hunts down little but doctrine. Secondly, we have declined to concentrate on the high profile dialogues, for the interpretative exercise involved a corpus as a whole, and the major issues appear in sharper focus in relation to less fashionable dialogues.

A long conclusion from our study is unwarranted. If there is anything of value in it, then most of it will lie in the detail rather than in any sweeping themes. However, a few points need to be made. Antiquity struggled with many of the issues that concern Platonic interpretation today. The level of debate was such as to encourage close reading of most of the corpus. It was alive to the need to give adequate attention to dramatic features of the dialogues without forgetting that they had a positive educational purpose. It often looked for meaning *beneath* the text, and often used intertextual strategies. It was alive to possibilities of esoteric meaning, but aware of the need to retain the written text as an arbiter. It approached texts without many of our modern philosophic tools, but it approached them though the Greek language and with all the tools known to the Old Academy. It approached them with a conviction that Plato had something worthwhile to say, though not necessarily that he was right. In fact *in what way* he was right was perhaps a more important issue than whether he was right.

Like us, antiquity found the need to postulate groups of texts that could profitably be studied together. While occasionally aware that chronology could have a bearing on this, they did not usually attempt any chronological arrangement. Groups were formed on the basis of common purpose or common communicative strategies, and seldom on the basis of common subject-matter or common doctrine. Didactic works were separated from exploratory and from polemical works, and for some reason the 'later' didactic works were often seen in relation to one another. This is perhaps because *Parmenides*, *Sophist*, *Politicus*, *Timaeus*, and *Philebus* were all seen as semi-Pythagorean. Seeing the *Laws* as rather different, and placing the *Theaetetus* in a very different group, had results from which we can profitably learn.

In that last remark, and in many that have preceded, my own reading of Plato will become evident. That reading, however, will remain flexible. I shall be ready to learn from ancients and moderns alike, and there is virtually nothing that I wish to insist upon. Dogmatic interpretation closes off options – options that may be invited by the text, and were never intended to be closed off by its author. The Platonic texts themselves encourage us to retain our options, to go on learning into old age like Socrates, and above all to be aware of how little of our knowledge about Plato is really known. Platonic interpretation is not in its infancy, but we may still approach it as if it were. Though the *Phaedo* rightly advises us to exorcise the trembling little child inside us, we should in no way try to expel the child from our approach to Plato. As Socrates well knew, to persist with naïve inquiries often has more useful results than to refuse to sink beneath a demanding level of sophistication.

Notes

1. What kind of text is this?

1. See in particular the expectations of the candidates for a chair of Peripatetic philosophy at Athens in Lucian, *Eunuchus* 4.

2. An early indication of this can be seen in Posidonius' attack on the psychology of Chrysippus (as reported by Galen in *Plac*. IV-V) who is assumed to deviate not only from Plato but also from Zeno, *Plac*. 4.416 = p. 280 De Lacy. Another would be the historical debate involving Philo of Larissa and Antiochus of Ascalon as seen through Cicero's *Academica*. An extreme case would be Lucian, *Piscator* and *Symposium*. See also the attack on the Cretan Platonist who claimed Plato's support for drunkenness, Gellius *NA* 15.2, on which see Tarrant 1996b, 177, and Numenius' attack on the New Academy for having deserted the heritage of Plato (frs 24-8 des Places).

3. Diogenes Laertius 3.61.

4. The papyrus may be consulted in Haslam 1972 and 1977. Material on Aristotle's mention of Alexamenos' dialogues overlaps with DL 3.48.

5. This still seems to be a discussion of the origin of the 'dramatic' dialogue, only the qualification has been dropped, thus to give an unbalanced view of Plato's predecessors, since other Socratics are likely to have anticipated Plato in the use of 'narrated' dialogue.

6. Tarrant 1993, 103-7.

7. Albinus, *Prologus* 1-2, who defends a definition virtually identical with that of DL 3.48: 'A dialogue is a *logos* composed of question and answer, on some philosophic or political topic, with the appropriate characterisation of the *dramatis personae* employed and use of diction.'

8. *De Plat*. 1.2.185.

9. See Sandy 1997, 191-2.

10. On Lucian's writings, see particularly Branham 1989.

11. Glucker, 1997, 80; but cf. pp. 66-7 which show that they were also aware of similarities.

12. DL 3.51: 'to give an exemplar of what the philosophic life would be like', Albinus *Prologus* 5 speaks of the dialogue as showing us who the philosopher is, what the philosophic life is, and upon what hypothesis it is based.

13. See Panaetius frs 127-9 = Ascl. *In Met*. 90, *Anth. Pal*. 9.358, Syrianus in Elias; Panaetius is said to regard the work as *nothos* (spurious), but it is hardly likely that this means Panaetius rejects *Plato's authorship*; Panaetius is extremely interested in the validity of the portrait of Socrates in various Socratic authors (frs 126, 132-4), and it is the inaccurate picture of Socrates he objects to. What it shows is that Panaetius is requiring that a dialogue depicting Socrates, in whom the Stoics were independently interested, should depict his views accurately, i.e.

Panaetius perhaps holds the modified transcript theory in relation to other 'Socratic' dialogues, and is disappointed to find that it cannot be held here.

14. See DL 3.58-60: *Apology* has none; *Critias, Clitophon, Menexenus,* and *Euthydemus* have as second titles adjectives in *-ikos* and *logos* must be supplied; *Protagoras* and *Epinomis* have other types.

2. Are there doctrines here?

1. I do not exclude the possibility that this was Plato himself, though I lean towards the other view. On this see the study of Roochnik 1984.

2. On this phenomenon see in particular Sandy 1997, pp. 73-7, 214-23. The phrase 'short cut to glory' appears in Lucian, *Sale of Lives* 11 in relation to Diogenes. Sandy 1997, 73 speaks of 'Lucian the declared enemy of short cuts to specious learning'; even so, it is a practice which he seems not to have scorned himself, for see Anderson 1976, where 'some short cuts to wisdom' appears in the very title of an article designed to show that much of Lucian's 'erudition' is owed to his familiarity with stock examples from rhetorical handbooks etc.

3. Much useful work is being done on the doxographe.s by Jaap Mansfeld and David T. Runia; see their 1996.

4. Vander Waerdt 1994.

5. Socrates affirmed only that he knew that he knew nothing; Arcesilaus was not prepared to do so (*Acad.* 1.45).

6. This is how I interpret *nihil certi dicitur*, which must surely differ in substance from claim (1), *nihil adfirmatur*. Annas (1994, 326) takes *adfirmatur* as 'is assented to', but this seems to me to be turning a claim about what is written in books into a psychological claim [*nihil adfirmatur* may also mean 'nothing is confirmed', 'nothing is proven', but this scarcely fits here]; she then takes claim (4) as meaning 'nothing firm is said', which could be misconstrued as a statement about how Cicero views the status of Plato's utterances, rather than how Plato views it.

7. Anon. *Proleg.* 10.

8. This reversal in direction is noted by the anonymous *Theaetetus*-commentator in fr. B, using the key verbs *kataskeuazein* and *anaskeuazein*, which do indeed imply argument for and against.

9. See particularly *Soph.* 223-33.

10. The change of direction takes place at *Plt.* 267c-268a, and is picked up again, after the myth that illustrates the problem, at 274e.

11. I relate it to the Academic Sceptic Favorinus, Tarrant 1996b.

12. See DL 9.69-70.

13. See Tarrant 1985, 27, 69-71, Annas 1994, 313-14; the difference may be that Tarrant relates Cicero's verbs of inquiry to the Greek *zētētikos*, and Annas to *skeptikos*.

14. On these arguments see Annas 1994, 327-30.

15. Sometimes the increasing hesitancy of an interlocutor might be explained by Plato's desire to achieve a realistic picture of him being dragged into assent as at *Euthyphro* 7d-8a: (i) 'Necessarily.' (ii) 'You are correct.' (iii) 'Of course.' (iv) 'Quite.' (v) 'That's likely.' (vi) 'Possibly.' This is not the case in the *Philebus* passage.

16. See below, Chapter 11.

17. Albinus, *Prologue* 3, DL 3.49-50; the *Epistles* jointly make a thirty-sixth work.

18. That Plato *dogmatises* in specifically mentioned in chapter 52 of Diogenes Laertius, which I should certainly take to be following the same source as for the character-classification. On the nature of this source Tarrant 1993, 1995, and Mansfeld 1994, differ.

19. i.e. *zêtêseis* do not permit one to *apophainesthai* on the topic under investigation. See columns 54-9.

20. *Meno* 100b; the importance of the work is clear from the fact that it is supposed to contain the answer to the very question that the *Theaetetus* is investigating (cols. 3 and 15), besides being one of two principal texts for the theory of recollection (81-6), which is likewise of great importance for the commentator.

21. Trapp 1990. Most famous of all, perhaps, was the picture of the plane-tree at 229-30, which inspired the opening of Cicero's *De Legibus*, and is clearly one of the highlights of Platonic literature for Lucian: *Vit. auct.* 16, *Dom.* 4, *Amores* 31, *Philopatris* 3.

22. See Tarrant 1983b, Runia 1986b.

23. See Tarrant 1993, ch. 5; depending on where the Thrasyllan material in Porphyry's *Commentary on Ptolemy's Harmonics* (=T23, p. 12 Düring) actually ends, one might also claim that he also used esoteric material from *Epistle* VII (p. 14 Düring).

24. For the *agrapha dogmata* see particularly the appendix of Gaiser 1963. Much useful work relating to them continues to be done, particularly in Germany, e.g. Szlezak 1985.

25. See particularly Sayre.

26. See Stobaeus *Ecl.* 1.36.6-37.3 and 1.123.7-8 Wachsmuth ('Aetius' = frs 101, 213 Isnardi-Parente) on Xenocrates' account of divinities and of the first principles. In the former passage note the term *metapephraken* at 1.37.3, implying that his views are an adaptation of Plato.

27. See Damasc. *in Phd.* 1.177 = Xenocr. fr. 211 I-P.

28. Speusippus F48 Tarán = Proclus *In Prm.* pp. 38-40 Klibansky.

29. Plut. *Mor.* 1012d-1013a, 1013d-e; Xenocrates fr. 188 I-P.

30. See Chapter 4 ii.

31. See Chapter 5 i.

32. Hermodorus frs 7 and 8 I-P = Simpl. *Phys.* pp. 247-8.

33. Kahn 1996 etc.

34. DL 3.63-4, Tarrant 1993, 180-1, Sedley 1997b.

35. The language of initiation is occasionally applied to philosophy by Plato himself, but the theme was more elaborately developed in the first century BC, where it is most evident in the *Introduction to Platonic Mathematics* by Theon of Smyrna. See Tarrant 1993, 98-107.

36. There is a persistent gulf here between those who have and have not philosophised; cf. Sandy 1997, 132: 'Approximately the first twenty-seven chapters are devoted to developing and maintaining the implication that only the ignorant misconstrue the actions of philosophers.'

37. Fr. 24.47-64 des Places.

38. Even if there were some truth in the rumours of esoteric doctrine in the Academy of Arcesilaus, SE *PH* 1.234, they scarcely imply anything akin to Plato's alleged esotericism.

39. *Symp.* 177d, *Lys.* 204c, *Tht.* 149-51 etc.

40. *Symp.* 216e, cf. 218d; see Vlastos 1991, 33-42, cf. 1987.

41. e.g. 'Meno' at *Meno* 71bc.

42. e.g. 'Callicles' at *Grg.* 481b-c.

43. *In Grg.* 34.3

44. Socratic irony at *In Alc.* 52-3, *In Grg.* 28.5, 32.13; it is not characteristic of Plato himself, *In Alc.* 2.150, and where it is found in Plato there is always truth in the words, *In Alc*. 88. It is more usually Polus who is thought of as ironic, *In Grg*. 18.3, 6, 10-15; 19.11, 13; 20.1.

45. Plutarch *Mor*. 999c-d, anon. *Tht*. 58.42-59.2.

46. See *Brutus* 299.

47. See *De Or*. 2.270, *Brutus* 292, 299, *Acad*. 2.15. The topic is fully covered by Glucker 1997.

48. *Brutus* 292, *De Or*. 2.270.

49. *Acad*. 2.74; on *Brutus* 299, Glucker, who views Cicero as having converted from stoicising Antiochian views to New Academic ones, asks 'Can one conclude that, even by the time of the *Brutus*, Cicero already refused to take Lucullus' confessions of ignorance as mere irony?' ,1997, 67.

50. See Lévy 1992, 187-94, Glucker 1997, 72-5 for attempts to explain this phenomenon. There may be a significant difference between Varro and Lucullus, representing Antiochian and Stoic views respectively (Glucker 74).

3. Where do I look for Plato's doctrines?

1. Tarrant 1999c.

2. Material on Aristotle's mention of Alexamenos' dialogues overlaps with DL 3.48.

3. Possibly 'he conceals Plato'. What follows is likewise conjectural.

4. Tarrant 1993, 103-7.

5. 'Socrates' from *Republic, Cratylus, Minos, Theaetetus, Euthyphro, Apology, Crito, Phaedo*; Timaeus from *Timaeus*; the Eleatic Stranger from *Sophist* and *Politicus*; and the Athenian Stranger from *Laws* and *Epinomis*. No spokesman is needed for the *Epistles* and the remaining work is the *Critias*: which (i) does not purport to offer doctrine, and (ii) has the appearance of an unfinished work, so that another character might have had the final say.

6. O. Gigon 1986, 136-7; Tarrant 1993, 17-21; 1995, 152-4; Mansfeld 1994, 58-107.

7. Schröder 1934, pp. 10.26, 11.19, 21, 25, 32, 12.15, 17.12, 21.31, 23.10, 24.24; excerpts from book IV found in Rhazis do assume that 'Tymeos' (variously spelled) speaks (ibid. 28.4, 15, 32.2, 34.10, 14), but this is unlikely to reflect Galen's practice.

8. *Plac*. 2.7.19.9, 8.7.2.3, *Trem*. 631.10, 632.1 K; Schröder vii-viii.

9. Kraus and Walzer 1951 IX 28, X 1, XI 27, XIV 16, XV 17, XXII 1. An exception is XXI 33.

10. nos. 2, 4, 5, 7, and sometimes 8. Plutarch does not always mention Plato by name, though it is usually clear that he means Plato. He actually says 'Plato himself demonstrates' in 5 at 1004a, again names Plato in 7 at 1004d and 1006a, and in 8 at 1007c-d; but 8 begins with a reference to what 'Timaeus' says at 42d (1006b).

11. And seemingly *Republic* 4 (1007e).

12. *Phd*. 1013d, *Rep*. 1029c, *Phdr*. 1013c, 1016a, 1026d, *Sph*. 1013d, *Plt*. 1015c-d, *Phlb*. 1014d, *Laws* 1013e-f, 1015e, *Tim*. passim.

13. The tactic of Plutarch is argued against by his successor Taurus (text 23B.44-8 Lakmann = Philop. *Aet*. 6.21), who denies that other dialogues such as the *Critias* and *Politicus* can tell us anything about the meaning of 'generated' within the *Timaeus* and reaffirming that in these works too the universe could be 'generated' in one sense and not in another.

14. *Compendium* 1.26-31, 2.9-11; pp. 36-9 Kraus and Walzer.

15. That Socrates was subject to various influences of the divine in prison is strongly suggested by the prophetic dream at *Crito* 44a-b, the Corybantic effect of the voices of the arguments at *Crito* 54d, and the dreams at *Phaedo* 60e which though not recent assumed a new importance apparently linked with the will of Apollo. Finally, it is surely no accident that the *Phaedo* itself refers at 84e-85b to the phenomenon of the swan-song, the song of the swan just before death which is supposed to be particularly beautiful; this is interpreted by Socrates as being linked with their being sacred to Apollo, and able to see into the future that death brings them. Socrates here seems less than flattered that the company should think his own prophetic abilities to be inferior to those of the swan, so that clearly we are supposed to be listening to his voice as if to the voice of a prophet. Whether or not this involves assuming that Apollo is speaking through him is not clear, though the theory of divine inspiration outlined in the *Ion* would allow for this.

16. Winkler 1985.

17. 613d, 634a; the allusions were noted by Jones 1980, p. 116.

18. e.g. Plut. *Erot.* 752b, 764b. Another example from a second-century Platonist is Apul. *Apologia* 12: 'mitto enim dicere alta illa et divina Platonica, rarissimo cuique piorum ignara, ceterum omnibus profanis incognita: geminam esse Venerem deam, proprio quamque amore et diversis amatoribus pollentis; earum alteram vulgariam ... alteram vero caelitem ....' The bipartition, however, is probably not Apuleius' preferred division of Eros, as can be seen from the tripartition in *De Plat.* 2.14, and this again suggests that the need was felt to look deeper than Pausanias for guidance. Compare here Alcinous, *Didasc.* 33.

19. See Chapter 5 ii.

20. Manuscripts preserve ancient doubts about the authenticity of xii.

21. See DL 3.37, anon. *Proleg.* 24.13-19.

22. On this question see Tarrant 1993, 24; 1995, 150-1.

23. See Chapter 8 vi.

24. See anon. *Proleg.* 26.7-9, 45-7, Festugière 1969, and for *Rep.* Tarrant 1997a.

25. *Strom.* 2.19.100.3; see Runia (1995).

26. DL 9.72; Plutarch too frequently underlines the provisional nature of its conclusions.

27. See Chapter 5 ii on Panaetius and 5 v on Posidonius; Panaetius fr. 59 = 76 derives from Proclus' *In Tim.* and relates to *Timaeus* 24c; Posidonius F 85, 290-1 Kidd. Material comes from Plutarch, Sextus Empiricus, and Theon of Smyrna.

28. See *Strom.* 1.10.48.2.

29. The 'logical' works (*Crat., Sph, Plt., Prm.*) have become *zetetic* in Albinus (*Prol.* 6).

30. Philop. *De Aet. Mundi* 6.21, 27 = Taurus TT23B, 24 Lakmann.

31. See Chapter 11.

32. For Vlastos it is the last, 1991, 46; 1994, 135.

33. Boulanger, 1968, 212: 'Sa méthode consiste essentiellement à vouloir mettre l'adversaire en contradiction avec lui-même.'

34. *Phdr.* at 2.34, 459, *Laws* at 2.50, 304, 4.17, *Menex.* at 2.341, *Plt.* at 2.348, *Ap.* at 2.349, *Euthd.* at 2.457.

35. See Plut. *Mor.* 370e-f, anon. *Proleg.* 24.13-19.

36. See DL 3.35, anon. *Proleg.* 3.28-31; Riginos 1976, 55.

37. See Dover 1980, viii.

38. *Mor.* 1028a-b, on which see Cherniss in the Loeb vol. xiii a.

39. See Lycos 1994; Jackson et al. 1998, 25 on the significance of myth within the Iamblichan curriculum. Iamblichus or somebody similar founded their interpretation of the *Gorgias* on the myth, ibid. 23-8, 57. Good examples of 'commentary' dominated by the discussion of myth are to be found in Proclus: *In Rep.* and *In Crat.*

40. Pythagoras' association with the doctrine of the transmigration of souls led to his association with Platonic accounts of the soul's afterlife and also with the theory of recollection. Olympiodorus seems to associate philosophic use of myth closely with the Pythagoreans, certainly the Water-Carriers myth (*In Grg.* 29.3-4), though the discussion of the final myth is also introduced with a reference to the Pythagoreans (46.1), the purpose of which is unclear. Above all myth needed to be symbolically interpreted, and the Pythagoreans are associated at 29.4 with symbolic interpretation. In relation to mathematics note that Plutarch, following the passage quoted, goes on to talk of those who import obvious Pythagorean material into their understanding of Plato's mathematics.

41. See DH 25.209, DL 3.37, Quint. *Inst.* 8.6.64 = Anecdote 137, Riginos 1976, 185.

42. In this work the summary of the theory of the ideal state and the initial rendering of the story of Atlantis both seem largely irrelevant to the basic principles of the cosmology that will follow and which we know to have been the main object of exegetical activity (see Ferrari 1998). Proclus does indeed regard the whole of what precedes Timaeus' account of the cosmos, up to 27b, as introductory, *In Tim.* 1.204.16. Severus had not thought any of this worth interpreting, Longinus had been interested in the Egyptian story of Atlantis, and Porphyry and Iamblichus had felt obliged to relate the whole to the aim of the dialogue as they conceived it. Something of the attitude of these interpreters is discernible at 1.19, 27, and 87.

43. SE *Math.* 7.112-14.

44. See Chapter 5 i.

45. *In Tim.* 1.97.30ff.

46. *In Tim.* 1.77.2-9; 83.25-8; 86.25-30; 93.7-15; also Panaetius (!) and other Platonists at 1.162.11-15.

47. Anon. *Proleg.* 15-16, Proc. *In Alc.* 10. On this whole question see Coulter 1976.

48. See particularly *In Alc.* 18-19.

49. *In Alc.* 12, alluding to *Rep.* 597e, 602c.

4. Defending and attacking Plato's work

1. The earliest extant report is Aristoxenus, *Harm. Elem.* 2.30-1; Simplicius, *In Phys.* p. 151, tells us that Speusippus, Xenocrates, and Aristotle all reported the event, and gave similar accounts of its central theme: that the basic principles of the universe were the One and the Indefinite Dyad.

2. *Euthd.* 290bc (dialecticians and mathematicians), 291c (the royal art), 301a-b (predication and self-predication); again, I think here particularly of Kahn's 'proleptic' or 'ingressive reading' of some early works now consolidated in Kahn 1996.

3. For a collection of the unwritten doctrines, see Gaiser 1963.

4. See frs 1-6 Isnardi-Parente.

5. The theory of matter seems clearly related to the concept of the indefinite at *Phlb.* 23c ff., and the theory of categories seems to owe something to *Sph.* 255c. Other texts might also be cited.

6. I think particularly of fr. 62 I-P = F48T = Proc. *In Prm.* pp. 38-40 K/L, where Speusippus is said to be giving an account of the doctrines of the ancients (*narrans tamquam placentia antiquis*). He explains how they thought the One higher and better than Being, and how, when they envisaged it in isolation, they realised the need for another principle, since the One alone could not account for generation. This principle they now called the Indefinite Dyad. Since the One and the Indefinite Dyad are the principles of the so-called unwritten doctrines, it seems that explaining Plato must be a part of the exercise, but Plato himself cannot easily be described as 'the ancients'; hence he was being described in terms of earlier theory, perhaps with both Pythagorean and Eleatic elements. For a full and cautious discussion of the impossibility of using this fragment as proper evidence for Speusippus' own doctrine, for Plato, and for ancient Pythagoreanism see Tarán 1985, 350-6.

7. In fr. 83 I-P the three Fates, Atropos, Clotho, and Lachesis are related to three epistemological levels; in fr. 213 I-P Hades, Posidon, Demeter, and Zen are introduced into the doxographic account of his theology. Story-telling is likewise associated with Heraclides Ponticus, particularly in his work *On the Breathless Woman* frs 76-89 Wehrli; see Gottschalk 1980, who speaks of 'his love for the events of a shadowy, mythical past'.

8. *De Caelo* 1.12, 2.2.

9. Xenocrates is the best-known figure in this regard, frs 153-8 I-P, but the scholiast on Arist. *De Caelo* 1.10 279b32ff. includes the name of Speusippus also (fr. 95 I-P = 61bT), and Tarán 1985, 383-5, accepts this as good evidence, suspecting that Heraclides also understood the *Timaeus* in that way.

10. Aristotle (*De Caelo* 1.10 279b32) already speaks of his opponents as 'trying to bring a defence', and the scholiast repeats what may still have been a military metaphor.

11. *In De Caelo* 303-4 = Xenocrates fr. 154 I-P.

12. This work certainly invites reflection upon the distinction between *mythos* and *logos*, particularly at 26e, where 'Socrates' appears to accept that Critias' story of Atlantis will be the latter rather than the former. The account of the physical world, however, is not consistently referred to as a *mythos*.

13. This would be true not only of early myth-like cosmologies, but of Parmenides' *Doxa* (B9 and following), Anaxagoras (for whom all things were originally together, B1, before the cosmos evolves through a generation-process), Archelaus (who generates his universe from a primeval slime), and Democritus (for whom the vortex generates our world).

14. On the traditional unclarity (*asapheia*) of the *Timaeus* in Middle Platonist times see Ferrari 1998, 16-22.

15. See Sayre 1983, Gaiser 1963, Krämer 1959, etc.

16. As Mayhew 1997, 69.

17. See Ross 1924, I xxxix-xli; Kahn 1996, 87.

18. *Pol.* 2.2.1; this feature is treated extensively, and at times technically, by Mayhew 1997.

19. Apollo may easily be given the false etymology not-many (*a-pollon*), and though this does not occur in the *Cratylus*, one etymology there (405b-406a) is simple ([*h*]*a-plous*). For full discussion of the theme of unity in the *Republic* see Krämer 1959.

20. It is often supposed that the story of Aristotle and Xenocrates leaving Athens on the succession of Speusippus implies that they were candidates for the Headship, but his age would suggest otherwise. Even so Xenocrates became Head on the death of Speusippus after only eight years, and he is said to have done so because he had more voter appeal than Menedemus or Heraclides and Aristotle was away in Macedon (Philod. *Academica* col. VI). If Aristotle could have been a serious candidate for the Headship at that time, then he would surely have had to have commanded Plato's respect for some time.

21. Following the theories of Jaeger 1923/46.

22. Kahn 1996, 82: 'We know nothing of the personal relations between Plato and Aristotle (who was his junior by nearly forty-five years).'

23. 'This fact [the high fictional content] is to a large extent obscured *for us* by the extraordinary realism or verisimilitude of Plato's dialogues' (p. 34: my emphasis). One may compare p. 33, where Kahn would extend to the *Memorabilia* and *Symposium* Momigliano's unobjectionable observation (1971, 55) that the fictitious nature of the *Cyropaedia* would have been understood in the light of previous Socratic writings.

24. Compare *EN* 1145b23-4 with *Prot.* 352c1-2; see also *EE* 1246b32-5.

25. See *EE* 1229a15 and 1230a7, and compare *Prot.* 360a-d; also *La.* 194e ff., where, however, the view is not being sponsored by Socrates as would seem to be the case in the *Protagoras*.

26. See *EE* 1246b32-5, and compare *Prot.* 352b-d.

27. See *EE* 1247b15, and compare *Euthd.* 279d.

28. See *EE* 1235a37, and compare *Mem.* 1.2.54 (cf. Kahn 1996, 82n).

29. *Meno* 71d might seem to be behind *Pol.* 1260a20-4; *Menexenus* 235d relates to *Rhet.* 1367b7-9 and 1415b30-2; and *Rhet.* 1419a8-12 refers to *Ap.* 27c-e. On all these texts see Deman 1942, texts XVIII-XX and XXII.

30. The *Protagoras* was the Platonic work which Isocrates was thinking of at the beginning of the *Helen*, where he speaks of those who make the virtues a single thing, and says that there a is a single science of them all; the *Euthydemus* was clearly intended to come to Isocrates' attention too, to judge from the presence of the Isocrates-like figure at 304d ff., so that there is little doubt that both were intended from the beginning to circulate publicly as written documents. Of works usually supposed to have antedated the main body of the *Republic* I believe that only those presented in narrative form were intended for wide circulation; see Tarrant 1996a.

31. Speusippus frs. 96-7 I-P = F54a/bT; Xenocrates frs. 165-201 I-P.

32. Tarán 1985 369-71, appeals to 'the very wording of Speusippus' definition' which he thinks links it with *Timaeus* 35a7 ('idea') and 36e2. Isnardi-Parente (1980, 337) writes 'Speusippo probabilmente inteso difendere Platone dall' accusa mossagli da Aristotele, *De An.* 407a2-3, di aver confuso l'anima con una grandezza spaziale, puntualizzando il fatto che per Platone l'anima non è grandezza, ma *idea* della grandezza.'

33. *De Communi Mathematica Scientia* 9 = fr. 97 I-P; Moderatus can be plausibly identified on the basis of Stob. *Ecl.* 1.49.32, p. 364.10 & 20-3 Wachsmuth.

34. *Mor.* 1007c = Xenocr. fr. 171 I-P. Xenocrates is not 'ancient' in relation to Plato.

35. Fr. 169 I-P = Aet. 4.2.1 and fr. 170 = Theodoretus *GrAC* 5.17; Nemesius (*Nat. Hom.* 44 = fr. 190) is more expansive.

36. Them. *In De An.* 32.19 = fr. 262 I-P.

37. Aristotle speaks of 'Plato in the *Timaeus*'.

38. Damasc. (formerly known as Olympiodorus) *In Phd.* 1.177 = Speusippus fr. 99 I-P = F55T = Xenocrates fr. 211 I-P. Tarán (1985, 373-4) compares *Phdr.* 245c.

5. The struggle for Socrates and Plato

1. See Scofield 1991.

2. See Long 1988, Striker 1994.

3. *Plac.* 8.5.14-15.

4. This is usually taken to mean that he took the charge very seriously; but surely there was irony involved, and Plato is actually shown to have treated the charge with total contempt, not defending himself but making the most extreme counter-claims, which claimed *Solon's* authority for an *Egyptian* admission that Athens had all along been the true home of the ideal state.

5. He is champion of the view that it is *historia psilê*, which signifies a bare narrative rather than unadulterated history in our sense.

6. Evidence is delicate. In Strabo 2.3.6 (= Posid. fr. 13T, 49 EK) the view that Atlantis was fiction seems to have been taken by somebody who used the words 'he who invented it destroyed it', and at 13.1.36 we learn that Aristotle used these words *for something*, though the context is there Homeric. Consequently, it is often asserted that Aristotle made the remark about Atlantis.

7. One is reminded here of the dubious help and advice that Herodotus received from Egyptians in Book 2.

8. For such a view, and indeed for useful discussion on this passage of Proclus in general, see Dörrie 1987, 328-31.

9. Proc. *In Tim.* 1.277.8.

10. Plut. *Mor.* 1013a.

11. ibid, 1013d-e.

12. See Long 1988.

13. Fragments in van Straaten 1962, fr. 127 (from Asclepius), fr. 129 (Elias).

14. Note that there is an anecdote which represents Phaedo of Elis as denying any knowledge of the conversations that Plato had represented him as narrating, Athen. 11.505e, Riginos 1976, 108.

15. Clem. *Strom.* 5.14 = SFV 3 Antipater 56.

16. I have benefited from unpublished work by Christopher Gill and from Julia Annas' (1999, 31-51) comments on these issues prior to publication. Cf. also Striker 1994.

17. See again Annas 1999, 42-4.

18. The famous phrase 'Plato before, Pyrrho behind, Diodorus in the middle', which was adapted from Homer and applied to Arcesilaus by Aristo (SE *Math.* 7.234), clearly implies that Arcesilaus had a Platonic face.

19. Precisely what it was that he acquired, and whether he did so on his own behalf or that of the school, is open to dispute. DL 4.32.

20. Proclus *In Prm.* 631-3 (*Menex.* and *Phdr.*); Olymp. *In Grg.* proem 4 and anon. *Proleg.* 22.

21. We are aware of this attitude towards *Prm.* and *Tht.*, Proc. *In Prm.* 631-2, 657; the latter passage shows how the *Theaetetus* as a whole was treated at times as an attack on Protagoras, see Sedley 1996a.

22. Even Sextus doubts the reports of Arcesilaus' esoteric teaching at *PH* 1.234, and other evidence is equally unsatisfactory.

23. See below, Chapter 9.

24. The terminology is that employed by Sextus Empiricus *PH* 1.235.

25. On these see Glucker 1978, 13-81, Tarrant 1985, and now Mansfeld 1997.

26. His name is coupled tantalisingly with those of his fellow-Solians Crantor and Clearchus in Plut. *Mor.* 1022c-d, but only to note a difference in his manner of representing the 1/2/3/4/8/9/27 schema from *Tim.* 35b ff. (cf. 1027d). For the regular solids see *Mor.* 427a-428a.

27. See T13-T16 Tarrant.

28. Of the *Quaestiones Platonicae* nos. 3, 5, and 9 have important mathematical aspects, and a good deal of the treatise *On the Generation of the Soul in the*

Timaeus is heavily mathematical. Mathematical explanations are also sought for the Delphic E, *Mor.* 387e-391e.

29. See Anecdote 31, Riginos 1976, 84, first attested in Plutarch *Mor.* 52d, *Dio* 13.4, and Anecdotes 98-101, Riginos 138-47, of which 98 is not found before the fourth century AD, 99 is from Eratosthenes, 100 appears first in Plutarch again (*Mor.* 718e-f, *Marcellus* 14.9-11), and 101 comes from Cicero *De Rep.* 1.17.29, and reworks a story usually applied to Aristippus.

30. *Expos.* p. 103 Hiller = F291 EK; one might compare the material on the cosmological significance of the number seven in Philo, *Opif.* 89-128, cf. 13-14, 47-52.

31. *Math.* 7.93 = F85 EK.

32. *Mor.* 1023b-d = F141a EK.

33. Compare SE *Math.* 7.93 = F85 EK with Crantor at *Mor.* 1012f-3a.

34. F142-6, 150-3 EK from books 4 to 6 of Galen *PHP*. On this material see now Cooper 1998 and Gill 1998.

35. See here Gill 1997, 267-8.

36. Seneca *Ep.* 94.38 = F178 EK. I take Seneca to mean that Posidonius attacked the prefaces to the individual laws encountered within the book as a whole, but the matter is not critical for our discussion.

37. Hermeias *In Phdr.* p. 102 Couvreur = F290 EK. This position is contrasted with that of Harpocration, who apparently made the passage apply even to the souls of totally insignificant creatures like ants.

38. On Antiochus see Tarrant 1985, Barnes 1989.

39. *Acad.* 2.113, 131-2, 136, 139, 143.

40. See SE *Math.* 7.145-9 = Speusippus F75 Tarán and Xenocrates 83 I-P.

41. Cic. *Or.* 8-10, *Acad.* 1.30; *Leg.* 1.25, *TD* 1.57-8.

42. In Varro they are supposed to emerge from the mind of the supreme god in the same way that Minerva emerged from the head of Jupiter.

43. Note that 1.113 expresses the worry that the Peripatetic tradition, including Cratippus, may be trying to include normal scientific predictions among 'prophecies'.

44. 'id percipi posse ... si impressum esset e vero.' There is no suggestion that it has to be an impression of such a kind that an identical one could not be false.

45. Cicero's provocative insistence in the *De Officiis* that Cratippus' Peripatetic philosophy did not differ much from his own Academic one is the statement of one who was less an adherent of Antiochus than of Philo of Larissa, for whom the Academics neither accepted the Stoic criterion nor made any deliberate attempt to deny that things are cognitively grasped

46. See Chapter 10.

47. See Chapter 5 vi.

48. Philo *Opif.* 102, *Her.* 156, Seneca *Ep.* 65.7, Nic. *Intr.* 1.2.4, Alcinous *Didasc.* 9.163.14, 31-4. It is significant that Alcinous combines the notion of Ideas as thoughts of god with the doctrine of three principles, in which the Ideas apparently have the same independence from god that matter has.

6. The re-establishment of Platonic philosophy

1. One should perhaps mention here the sensible view of Hershbell 1987, 239, that Eudorus is Plutarch's doxographic source in the *De Animae Procreatione*.

2. Physics: a One that is above the One opposed to the Dyad, Simpl. *Phys.* 181; ethics: the injunction 'follow God', and, as the goal, an early version of Plato's 'assimilation to the divine in accordance with what's possible', Stob. *Ecl.* 2.49.8, 16, which *probably* preserves Eudorus' view.

3. 1016f, 1017e-f, 1018e-f, 1020e-f, 1029f; it is pointless to speculate about possible Eudoran sources. It was probably a commonplace to see the *Timaeus* as a text requiring Pythagorean interpretation, since there is a precedent in Posidonius (F85 EK) while Cicero dedicated his Latin version of part of the work to the Pythagorean Nigidius Figulus; the work is still seen in a Pythagorean light by Proclus, *In Tim.* 1.1.25-7. The Pythagorean work of 'Timaeus Locrus' is of course both a product and a perpetuator of this trend, attempting to recreate Pythagorean cosmology from the *Timaeus* and then being seen as Plato's Pythagorean source.

4. Stob. *Ecl.* 2.49.25-50.5, 2.55.5-21.

5. Göranssion 1995, 188; the passage in question is 2.45.11-57.12.

6. Göranssion 1995, 219-26; he was anticipated by Kenny 1978, 21-2.

7. Stob. *Ecl.* 2.49.24, 2.53.8-11, 2.54.10-55.4, 2.55.20-1, 2.57.10. There are six references to the *Timaeus*.

8. See Runia 1986a for an exhaustive treatment of the *Timaeus* in Philo. For use of the Theory of Recollection see his 1986c. My problem in using Philo is that his ultimate goal is the interpretation of non-Platonic texts.

9. Mansfeld and Runia 1997. Both authors have also published other relevant articles.

10. Ps.Plut. 1.3 cf. 1.9-10, Stob. *Ecl.* 1.10.16, cf. Alcinous 8-10.

11. Such five-fold lists are encountered also in Alcinous 10.2, Maximus Tyrius 29.7; they may also be applied to matter: Ps.Plut. 1.9, Stob. *Ecl.* 1.11, Alcinous 9.1. See Chapter 13 vii.

12. Stobaeus *Ecl.* 1.1, less fully in Ps.-Plut. 1.7.

13. Only at Stob. *Ecl.* 1.12.

14. Only at Stob. *Ecl.* 1.20.

15. Ps.Plut. 2.6, Stob. *Ecl.* 1.22.

16. Ps.Plut. 4.2, Stob. *Ecl.* 1.49.

17. See Göransson 1995, 203-18.

18. See above, Chapter 6 i.

19. Counting the ten books of the *Republic*, the twelve of the *Laws*, and the thirteen *Epistles* as one work each.

20. On Thrasyllus see Tarrant 1993, 1995; Mansfeld 1994.

21. See Tarrant 1993, ch. 5 and T23.

22. At 3.52 Plato is said to prescribe doctrine about truths he has comprehended, to refute falsehoods, and to suspend judgment on whatever is unclear, using sophistic characters to espouse positions needing refutation and Socrates, Timaeus, and the Strangers for expounding doctrine. At 3.65 interpretation involves determining whether something is a *Platonic message* or just an illustration, distinguishing what is offered as doctrine from things said to undermine an interlocutor's position, and finally whether it has been rightly said.

23. It is true that Albinus, writing in the middle of the second century AD, does link 'character' with a *rough* reading-order (*Prol.* 6), but then he is not the author of the classification, but is already revising it. Furthermore the whole of his doctrinal class of dialogues, including those of ethical, political, and physical character, is bunched at the third step of the education-programme, and both 'anatreptic' and 'endeictic' characters come at the final stage. Had the classification had a close link with a reading order then one should have expected different stages for each of the eight 'characters'. Diogenes, perhaps trying to be too schematic, does add the 'characters' when recording the members of the tetralogies, but this is probably a late addition as the *Critias* is wrongly labelled. See

Tarrant 1993, 25. Another argument that is of some significance here is the argument from silence: the anonymous *Prolegomena* (24-5) speak of unsatisfactory reading orders that had preceded Iamblichus, and mention the tetralogies and an attempt at chronological ordering. But dialogue-character is not mentioned here, even though the author actually employs a reduced version of the classification for his own purposes at 17.19-27; the initial division between instructional and inquisitive dialogues is essentially the same, while the secondary divisions are (i) into theoretical and political (a slip for 'practical'?) and (ii) into gymnastic and agonistic as in DL and Albinus.

24. Stob. *Ecl*. 2.49.18-23.

25. Quint. *Inst. Orat.* 2.15.24 (below, Chapter 9 iii), Sextus *PH* 1.221, Albinus *Prologus* 3, Galen *PHP* 2.3.9-10 de Lacy = 2.179 Müller, Proc. *In Prm*. 631, possibly following Middle Platonic material on the *Parmenides*. In this last case we are dealing with a division between *parts* of the one dialogue, not between whole dialogues. The basic division seems also known to anon. *In Tht*. (Tarrant 1985, 69-71), where *zetetis* is a large part of what Plato is doing in the *Theaetetus*, though other parts do allow him to reveal doctrine.

26. Tarrant 1993, 48.

27. cf. Tarrant 1993, 51-7.

28. cf. Galen *Plac*. 2.3.9-10 de Lacy = 2.179 Müller: the testing of a young person's suitability for maieutic precedes their being led on to make a discovery. Perhaps read *apokuêsai* for *aporêsai*.

29. T19a-b = Porph. *V. Plot*. 20-1.

30. Into (i) a generic sense of the term, and, in diminishing order of distinction, (ii) God, (iii) Ideas, (iv) immanent forms, (v) things that exist in conjunction with forms (men, animals, things), and (vi) abstracts like time and void – but not in the strict sense of the word. Qua objects of sensation ordinary things and animals are in a state of flux, and do not 'be' in the strict sense of the term.

31. i.e. Aetius' *pros ho* (see above, Chapter 5 ii) is the Greek origin of Seneca's *ad quod*.

32. Ps.-Plut. 1.9, 1.19, Stob. *Ecl*. 2.11, 2.18.

33. Ps.-Plut. 1.10, Stob. *Ecl*. 1.12.

34. Ps.Plut. 1.3 cf. 1.10, Stob. *Ecl*. 1.10.16.

35. Bastianini-Sedley 1995, 254-6. The text was originally edited by Diels and Schubart 1905.

36. Opsomer 1998, 35-6, doubts the early dating but is again duly cautious, and unlike some scholars respects the caution which I had also exercised. He appears to consider the date quite close to that of Plutarch.

37. Tarrant 1993, 98-103.

38. See Tarrant 1993, 58-68.

39. Albinus *Prol*. 4.

40. Tarrant 1993, ch. 6 ii.

41. See Porph. *V. Pyth*. 53.

42. Porph. *V. Plot*. 20.71-6, 21.1-9 = Thrasyllus T19 Tarrant.

43. Fr. 17; but Being-Itself would not be one of those things which *participates* in Being, so that he would transcend being to exactly the same extent as the Idea of the Good would transcend participated goodness.

44. He does refer to Nicomachus in the *Parmenides*-commentary (619), and finds some use for Numenius and Cronius in his discursive *Republic*-commentary (2.20, 2.96, 2.109; Numenius fr. 35). On references in the *Timaeus*-commentary see below.

45. Porphyry tells us that Plotinus read them (*V Plot*. 14), and himself preserves important information of Moderatus (*V Pyth*. pp. 44-8) and Numenius (*De Antro Nymph*. 21-3, 28, 34).

46. See Chapters 12 ii, 13 vii. On Clement, Choufrine 1998.

47. *In Tim*. 1.381.26-382.12, cf. 384.4

48. 1.76.30-77. 6 (fr. 37) leads into a discussion of Porphyry's debt (1.77.21-4); 2.274.10-14 (fr. 40 dP) is about Theodorus' debt to Numenius on the nature of soul; 1.303.27 ff. (fr. 21 dP) leads up to 1.304.22-305.6 where Harpocration is introduced, and said to follow Numenius; then 3.103.28-32 (fr. 22 dP) leads forward to a discussion of Amelius' evident debt; similarly Numenius is linked with Amelius at 3.33.33-4.3 (fr. 46c dP). The fleeting mention at 2.9.4-5 (fr. 51 dP) has an almost doxographic quality, and suggests no close acquaintance, while 3.196.12-19 (fr. 50 dP) is a reference to 'those about Numenius' and could easily have been taken from one of these others who follows Numenius on this issue.

49. Numenius fr. 35, *In Tim*. 2.128; see Dillon 1977, 364.

50. Proc. *In Tim*. 1.204.17. But Severus is by no means an overall source, since they differ over the figure needed to explain the harmonic numbers of the World Soul at 35b (Calc. 32, Proc. *In Tim*. 2.171.9).

51. A number of texts (= F22a-26b Lakmann) are to be found in Philoponus.

52. See Tarrant 1996b.

53. So Proc. *In Tim*. 1.284.13-14, 3.247.12 (= fr. 24 dP).

54. Proc. *In Tim*. 1.276.31-277.7 = fr. 19 dP.

55. *In Tim*. 3.247.15.

56. *In Tim*. 1.305.6 = fr. 12 dP.

57. *In Tim*. 1.20.21-6 = fr. 16 dP.

58. Proc. *In Tim*. 1.305.6.

59. Dillon 1977, 337-8.

60. Certainly this seems to have been the case with doxographic handbooks, see Mansfeld and Runia 1996, particularly on the nature of Pseudo-Plutarch.

7. The principal Neoplatonist interpreters

1. In particular see Proc. *In Tim*. 1.204.24-7.

2. On his life and works see Dillon 1973, 3-25.

3. See Festugière1969, Westerink et al. 1990, lxvii-lxxiii, Jackson et al. 1998.

4. Here Iamblichus is of course drawing on the famous 'Cave' passage of *Republic* 7, particularly 516e, and while it seems somewhat eccentric to involve other dialogues in one's interpretation of such a lemma, he has of course chosen that dialogue which has been partly 'served up' by Socrates the day before, and which will be alluded to in what follows.

5. Or at least the reciprocity argument, the recollection argument, and the argument from similarity, *In Phd*. frs 1, 3, 4 = Olymp. *In Phd*. 10.1, 11.2, 13.4.

6. I read here *empodiôn* for *enantiôn*, cf. *Sph*. 230c6, d2.

7. Dillon's translation, 'able to produce change', neglects the original text in which the slippery, changeable nature of the hard-to-catch sophist is often in evidence, 216cd, 218d, 226a, 231c, 235a-c, 236c-d, 240c, 241b. The sophist is in fact a kind of Proteus.

8. This role of Epimetheus is quite atypical of Neoplatonism, see Dillon's discussion, 1973, 258-9, and also Olymp. *In Grg*. 48.6 where Prometheus is again associated with a descent, that of rational souls, but where Epimetheus is associated with irrational soul – certainly not with reversion to a higher world.

9. At one point (fr. 23 = *In Tim*. 1.174.28-175.2) Proclus claims that Iamblichus understands the reference to Athens' crushing the Atlantean invasion of Europe and Asia entirely literally, apparently reacting against certain predecessors whose symbolic interpretation contributed nothing to a unified reading of the dialogue. At least one such opponent and predecessor, Porphyry, can surely be identified (see Dillon 1973, 293)

10. According to Olympiodorus (*In Grg.* 46.4-7) the big difference between philosophic and poetic myth is that the former may harmlessly be understood at the literal level, while poetic myths are both absurd and harmful when taken literally. He does not assert that the surface meaning of philosophic myths is actually true, for he denies any temporal progression in the divine order, but he does take much that is stated in the myths of the afterlife (or *nekuiai*) as literally true.

11. The latter part even of this is extant only in Latin translation. The evidence of Damascius strongly suggests that Proclus had covered the whole work. Evidently the tastes of those who have preserved Proclus' commentaries did not stretch to less theologically exciting passages at the end.

8. The so-called early dialogues

1. I am more concerned with ancient doubts about authenticity, which involved most of tetralogy IV: *Alcibiades II*, *Hipparchus*, and *Erastae*. See Tarrant 1993 24; 1995 150-1.

2. See *Prologue* 5 and Chapter 13 ii.

3. This is so even before the activity of Thrasyllus in systematically supplying dialogues with second titles. For references see Chapter 13 ii.

4. See DL 3.56.

5. Saffrey and Westerink 1997. The Plato section of the index locorum runs from 204 to 217!

6. Segonds 1985-6.

7. Whittaker 1990; in Dillon's index (1993) we find no reference to either work.

8. Dillon 1977, 150 (cf. 12c-13c) and 332 (12e).

9. *Mor.* 459b (12b); 480d; *Or.* 3.2b (2b-3a).

10. *Didascalicus* 28.3 (*Hippias Major* 296e), 30.1 (*Laches* 193a-d), 30.2 (*Lysis* 216d), 33.4 (*Lysis* 205b-206b); references in Dillon 1993, who draws attention to signs of neglecting the *Lysis* (p. 199).

11. Anon. *Proleg.* 10; see Chapter 2 i.

12. Cic. *TD* 1.57, *Div.* 1.115, Plut. frs 215-17, anon. *Tht.* 46-7, Albinus *Prol.* 6, Alc. *Didasc.* 4.155.24-8.

13. The indirect tradition is complex, and anon. *Tht.* (3, 15) seems to preserve a different reading: see Tarrant 1989, but cf. Carlini 1995.

14. See in general Tarrant 1989, more specifically Bastianini-Sedley 1995, 485-6.

15. On the levels of virtue in Plotinus and others see Dillon 1983; for Olympiodorus see Tarrant 1997, Jackson et al. 1998.

16. See anon. *Tht.* cols. 4 and 11, Alcinous *Didasc.* 30, and Dillon 1993, 183-9.

17. *LA* 3.249-50, Stob. *Ecl.* 2.131.14 ff. Ierodiakonou (1999) has collected the evidence for 'middle' virtues across various schools, with particular reference to the Peripatetic Aspasius.

18. 47.37-48.7, cf. 46.43-47.7.

19. See above, Chapter 5 viii. The ecstatic divination normally associated with the seer was actually explained rather differently in Cicero, but still with reference to a shared body of knowledge that can be accessed in certain circumstances. It is significant that the politician's decisions are closely linked with predicting what will arise in certain cases.

20. *aneu nou* becomes *ouk aneu nou*. I shall speak throughout as if the received text of Plato is correct at 99e6, and Clement's text wrong; our text ought to be right, as it agrees with *noun mê echontes* used of seers at 99c8.

21. Dillon's translation (p. 7).

22. On the formulaic phrase 'not without' at 156.5-14 see Chapter 11 vi.

23. Two further uses involve sensation and opinion. Commentators agree on the relevance of *Timaeus* 28a here, particularly the phrase *noêsei meta logôi perilêpton*; it has most obviously inspired 156.11-14. Alcinous' *perilêpsis* (156.6) recalls *perilêpton* there (twice). For the wider context see Whittaker 1975.

24. The statement in the *Symposium* that all become pregnant both in soul and in body is said to refer to the fact that all have intellectual visions when disembodied.

25. Jackson et al. 1998, 42-3, 164 etc.

26. Cic. *Acad*. 2.74.

27. See Chapter 2 v.

28. See *De Orat*. 2.270, *Brutus* 292.

29. The opponents here are not named, but, since belief that Socrates offers a theory of knowledge and belief that he is not serious about his ignorance go hand in hand, they are probably to be identified with some at least of those who make the *Theaetetus* a dialogue about the criterion of truth (see col. 2, fr. D), who actually do believe that a positive epistemological doctrine underlies (i) the work and (ii) the way in which Socrates handles the conversation. Hence Socrates, revealing parts of a genuine theory of knowledge, can scarcely be ignorant himself.

30. Compare with such ancient attitudes the challenging remarks of Jonathan Lear in his review of Alexander Nehemas, *The Art of Living*, *New York Times* 25.10.98: 'Let me simply state, without argument, that irony is one of Socrates' least important features. What is important is that others take Socrates to be ironic – both figures inside the dialogues ... and figures outside ....'

31. I owe this reference to David Sedley.

32. *In Grg*. 28.5, 32.13.

33. Galen speaks of arguments which the dialectician will not use for the establishment of truths, but rather for gymnastic purposes or refuting sophistry (*Plac*. 2.3.10), and this is in agreement with observations in Alcinous *Didascalicus* 6 of how Plato uses eristic arguments against persons like Euthydemus and Hippias, while he used *endoxa* against both sophists and young men.

34. *In Alc*. 2.150.

35. *In Alc*. 52-3, *In Grg*. 28.5, 32.13.

36. *In Grg*. 28.5, trans. Jackson et al. 1998, 201.

37. The strength of the feeling against Epicurean hedonism is well illustrated by Taurus' attitude in Gellius *NA* 9.5.8.

38. See for instance Olymp. *In Grg*. 3.13, 9.7, 25.1, 26.15, *In Alc*. 7, 42, 55, 146; Proc. *In Alc*. 152.

39. Cic. *Fin*. 5.67, Philo *VMos*. 2.7, *Sacr*. 82, anon. *Tht*. 9-11, Alcinous, *Didasc*. 29.3-4, Apul. *Plat*. 2.6, Plot. *Enn*. 1.2.7, Olymp. *In Grg*. 35.2; see Dillon 1993, 181.

40. Alcinous, *Didasc*. 29.4, Apul. *Plat*. 2.6.

41. So Apuleius, *Plat*. 2.9, but their perfection will of course entail their complete subservience to the rational soul.

42. *Theol*. 1.4.19.1-2, 1.5.24.20, 1.6.28.23-24, 5.24.87-91, 5.34.124.3-4.

43. *Mor*. 98d (note the phrase *kata ton Platôna*, though this need mean no more than 'in the words of Plato'), cf. *Prt*. 321c. Plutarch also alludes to the myth (321c) at 593a and fr. 11, (326b) at 8c. Porphyry makes some use of it (322b) at *De Abstinentia* 1.10.3-11.1. Other authors from the second century who appear to make use of it regularly include Clement of Alexandria, Maximus Tyrius, and Lucian.

44. See Jackson et al. 1998, 318.

45. 316b-c, 318a, and especially c7-d1

46. Tarrant 1993, 52-4. The chief alternative is to suppose that the word means the same as *epideictic*, which would mark the dialogue as a work of sophistic display, probably linking it with use of the verb at *Prt.* 317c7 to describe the sophist's enthusiasm to show off in front of his rivals. This term would certainly capture one feature of a sophist's activity, and one which Socrates himself slips into in the *Protagoras*, but there would be no marked contrasted with the over-turning type of dialogue. Furthermore it would be a little difficult to see how a work of display could belong to the 'inquisitive' class to which exercise, inquiry, and refutation of falsehoods were apparently fundamental.

47. 322d5-323a4, 324c5-d1, 326e2-5, 327b4-c4, 327e1-328a8.

48. 331b8-c3; d1-e3, e6-332a1.

49. 333e1-2.

50. Even in the literary digression (338e-347a) the actual nature of virtue and vice remains in the forefront of the discussion at the expense of sensible interpretation of the poets' words.

51. See Kraus and Walzer 1951, intro.

52. 27.4-5; see Dillon 1993, 170-1.

53. *In Grg.* 3.9, 19.2.

54. *Strom.* 1.25.168.3, 2.4.18.2.

55. *In Grg.* 42.1, 6.11.

56. See Chapter 9.

57. See Jackson et al. on 8.1 and *Euthd.* 305a, as well as *Tht.* 167e-168c.

58. Albinus, *Prologus* 3.

59. See Rosenthal and Walzer 1948; Tarrant 1993, 32-8.

60. Cic. *Fin.* 5, especially 5.28.

61. The term *epimeleia* recalls the standard Socratic concern with *psychês epimeleia*, or care for the soul. The term is prominent at *Alc.* 124a7: Alcibiades is about to learn what he must take care of, and this will be soul rather than body or possessions, 132c.

62. See Reis 1997; I have previously had something relatively modest to say: Tarrant 1993, 38-41.

63. Anon. *In Tht.* commented on both works, and material deriving from the *Phaedo* elsewhere often suggests an origin in a commentary, e.g. Plut. frs 215-17, and some Harpocration fragments.

64. See Reis 1997; I do not simply mean that 32 different orders would have been *practically* impossible, but that many of the dialogues would have to be regarded as quite perverse initial texts for *any* pupil to be encountering, among them the *Politicus*, *Epinomis*, and *Critias* which are clearly the sequels to *Sophist*, *Timaeus*, and *Laws*. He arrives at his conclusions as a result of an excessively detailed application of Albinus' comparison between the corpus and a circle, on which there is no fixed starting-point.

65. *prosêkousan taxin ... têi kata Platôna didaskaliai.* I strongly suspect that the words which follow this in the text *tôi ta Platônos hairoumenôi* are the result of either a misguided gloss, or a well-aimed gloss from which the negative has been omitted. The second dative phrase is clearly grammatically superfluous.

66. Proclus *In Alc.* 12-14, Olymp. *In Alc.* 1.

67. On this arrangement see Tarrant 1993, 32-8.

68. The *Minos* at least is missing, but perhaps this is due to transmission-problems, which have also made it difficult to identify the positions of *Symposium*, *Lysis*, and *Philebus*.

69. The one passage which is regularly mentioned as of relevance is 116, which has influenced the syllogistic of *Didasc.* 6.

70. See 3.572; 4.29-36.

9. From false art to true

1. See on this Tarrant 1999b.

2. See Jackson, Lycos & Tarrant 1998, intro. 23-8.

3. Cic. *De Or*. 1.47, 87-92. In Cicero's philosophical works *Grg.* is used most obviously in the *Tusculan Disputations:* 470de (5.12.34), 484c (2.1.1).

4. See Sedley 1996a, 81, 89.

5. See the discussion of the history of Parmenides-interpretation at In *Prm*. pp. 631 ff.

6. It is clear from *De Oratore* 3.119-20 that Cicero's 'Crassus' does not regard the present Academy as teaching what *he* would term 'rhetoric', since their treatment of the broader themes of rhetoric still did not go beyond a general introduction, and even under Philo's leadership (the most innovatory of the New Academy), the treatment of specific cases was in its infancy. Yet this shows how far Philo did promote the teaching of rhetoric, and the rhetorical skills of the Academy had been evident to the Romans since Carneades' day, many of whom sought to improve their skills through contact with philosophers who not only argued regularly both for and against a thesis, but also traced their heritage back to Plato, who was widely believed to demonstrate consummate oratorical skills when attacking oratory (see particularly 'Crassus' at *De Oratore* 1.47).

7. See also SE *Math*. 2.43, where the observation that there are two types of rhetoric, one used among the wise and the other among the mediocre, is recorded as the *objection* of unnamed persons *against* the Academic arguments of Charmadas and Clitomachus.

8. cf. Olymp. *In Grg.* 2.2, 12.1; also Sextus in *Math*. 2. On this trend see of Karadimas 1996, 163-9, 237.

9. Moreschini 1994 observes connexions between Aristides and Apuleius on the two-rhetoric theme, but might have considered more authors in this connexion; this was not simply a second-century theme.

10. In Sextus we again have a distinction between two rhetorics, one operating among the wise and one among mobs; this is spelt out more fully at 2.43 by *opponents* of the New Academy.

11. New Academics also at 2.61, Critolaus at 2.12, 2.20, 2.61; also Xenocrates and the Old Academy at 2.6, 2.12, 2.61, Zeno, Aristo, and the Stoics at 2.6-7, 2.10, 2.61, an Aristotle at 2.8-9 and 61.

12. On Aenesidemus see now Decleva Caizzi 1992.

13. 'Plato in the *Gorgias* using some such method of division seems to be giving a definition of rhetoric cumulatively (*ex episyntheseôs*).' The pieces come from 450bc, 452e-53a, 454e-55a.

14. Albinus, *Prologus* 3.

15. Tarrant 1993, 58-72. This group, which might be described as 'apotreptic' follows a seemingly protreptic group comprising most of the other zetetic dialogues.

16. Tarrant 1993, 31-8, suspecting that it may be Galen's arrangement. The failings of Parmenides are of a lesser order.

17. *velut coactus a Socrate*, 2.15.10.

18. *pauca ex Gorgia Platonis a prioribus imperite excerpta*; the reference would seem to imply the existence at this stage of a genre involving the précis of selected materials from a single work.

19. For Sextus see *PH* 1.221 and cf. unnamed persons at Proc. *In Prm.* 631; Albinus, *Prologus* 3; see above, Chapter 6 ii.

20. Jones 1980 lists 9 parallels + 4 possible parallels on pp. 144-6 and 20 parallels + 4 possible parallels on p. 116. This seems to place the work behind *Tim.*, *Rep.*, *Leg.*, *Phdr.*, *Symp.*, *Phlb.*, and *Phd.*, as well as behind the *Epistles*, in its rate of use by Plutarch. Similar impressions are received from Helmbold and O'Neill 1959 who find some 33 references to *Grg*. Whittaker's edition of Alcinoos cites 13 passages of *Grg*. in its index. In Middle Platonic times there was no disproportionate use of any one passage of *Grg.*, as there is of highlights from *Tht*. This applies to Maximus Tyrius; Philo; Apuleius; Clement of Alexandria; and Alexander of Aphrodisias. See too the collection of information on ancient *Grg.*-exegesis in Dörrie-Baltes 1993, p. 195.

21. Aulus Gellius, *NA* 7.14, on which now see Lakmann 1995, 82-94: (mostly at 10.22, where subtle use is made of Callicles' attack on mature-age philosophising. See Tarrant 1996b).

22. As at DL 3.52.

23. In Gellius, *Noctes Atticae* 17.20.4 ff.

24. On the connexions between oratory and philosophy in the second century see Michel 1993.

25. Notably in the speech *For the Four*. Olympiodorus' first-hand knowledge of this work is questioned by Behr 1968, who assumes that he follows Ammonius, who follows Porphyry's attack on Aristides in the lost *Against Aristides*. But it is clear that Aristides' criticisms have remained an important issue, and the vagueness of references to Aristides reflects Olympiodorus' usual practice of not looking up references in the classroom when he recalled the overall thrust of what had been said.

26. See Behr 1994, 1140-1233, and 1968, 41-60, particularly p. 54: 'Perhaps influenced by discussions with the more superficial members of this group ...'. The group was the 'School of Gaius', who was presumed have functioned there, though this is not clear (Göransson 1995, 35 n.3, 39 n.7). Certainly, however, this school dominated in the practice of Platonism on the Asia Minor coast, and Galen goes to Ephesus to seek out Albinus (*De Libris Propriis* p. 97.6 ff.) who is closely associated with Gaius and certainly promoted his kind of Platonism. The likelihood that Platonists were the first to provoke even the work *Against Plato on behalf of Rhetoric* may be judged from reference to people who particularly admire the scathing treatment of rhetoric at *Gorgias* 463a-465c, section 20. There are certainly other, seemingly Cynic, opponents of rhetoric in these works, particularly in *Against Plato, in Defence of the Four* (3.663-85 Behr), but one might heed the following words of Karadimas 1996, p. 31 n. 142: 'Furthermore, there are phrases in *DRhet*. itself which seem to point to the Platonists of Aristides' own day; see *DRhet*. 12, 60, 272, 440. All of them cannot be explained as general rhetorical apostrophae ....'

27. See Karadimas 1996, 31 n. 143, who points out that section 366 is clearly directed against partisans of Plato.

28. *In Tim*. 3.234.15-18.

29. Certainly Albinus continued to see the *Gorgias* as an *anatreptic* work, designed to overturn the work of Plato's opponents, but by placing this whole group of works at the fifth and final stage of his education process in *Prologus* 6 he seems to imply that they have an advanced part to play. For him (3) the whole 'zetetic' class of dialogues, to which the polemical or 'agonistic' group belongs, does have as one of its purposes – perhaps the primary purpose: see Göransson 1995 103 – the refutation of what is false, not simply mental exercise and the challenging of what may or may not be false. 'Proving that not' can be just as useful a step towards knowledge than 'proving that', and in some ways differs mainly in respect of the author of the thesis. To prove that virtue is not (not teachable) scarcely differs from proving that it is teachable, except insofar as the former would naturally have an opponent's ideas in view, and the latter would have one's own or one's ally's in view. Hence to prove that injustice is *not* more beneficial than justice or that rhetoric does *not* yield 'power' may be as important in our moral education as proving that justice is no less beneficial and philosophy no less powerful. A stronger purpose is thus detected in 'zetetic' dialogues, which is precisely what enables the 'logical' works (*Crat.*, *Sph.*, *Plt.*, *Prm.*) to be reclassified as 'zetetic' by Albinus (6); their contribution to knowledge is not in doubt.

30. See Boulanger 1968, 232-3.

31. See particularly 3.351. It is characteristic of the over-literal interpreter to speak of what 'Plato says'; and Proclus also tells us that the school of Gaius saw *Plato* expounding *doctrine* both demonstratively and *eikotologikôs* – i.e. doctrine of a kind is being expressed even in passages of a more myth-like character.

32. Boulanger 1968, 212: 'Sa méthode consiste essentiellement à vouloir mettre l'adversaire en contradiction avec lui-même.'

33. In Plutarch's *De Animae Procreatione* the *Timaeus* is interpreted with a view to *Rep.*, *Phdr.*, *Sph.*, *Plt.*, and *Laws* etc. (see p. 36), and Taurus is seen in Philoponus (*De Aet. Mundi* 6.21) to have taken works such as *Plt.* and *Critias* into account when defending his view of *Tim*. One may of course compare Plutarch's tactics when attacking the Stoics in *De St. Repugn.*, of showing how often one passage *disagreed* with another.

34. *Phdr.* at 2.34, 459, *Laws* at 2.50, 304, 4.17, *Menex.* at 2.341, *Plt.* at 2.348, *Ap.* at 2.349, *Euthd.* at 2.457.

35. 2.446f, 3.537-8. See also Moreschini, 1994, 1246-7.

36. On the two rhetorics in Apuleius and Aristides see Moreschini 1994, particularly 1246-7, where, observing connexions between Aristides and Apuleius, 'potrebbe darsi, però, che i due passi che abbiamo citato, quello di Aristide e quello di Apuleio, si sorregnano a vicenda, e qua la scuola platonica del secondo secolo averse tracciata una differenza tra la forma peggiore della retorica.' On rhetoric in Apuleius see also O'Brien 1991, 39-50, and on Apuleius' learning Sandy 1997.

37. This material, though not the material on rhetoric, has its parallel in that other Middle Platonist Platonic handbook, Alcinous' *Didascalicus*. Alcinous has no separate section dedicated to rhetoric.

38. 463a-65c: the passage to which Aristides had so objected in *In Defence of Oratory*.

39. On this whole question see Tarrant 1999b.

40. *Proleg.* 22. See above, Chapter 9 i.

41. On the self-seeing intellect see Jackson et al. 1998, 27-8. The myth involves sight in two ways: judges and judged are now naked, making the quality of their souls visible (523d-e), and Zeus already realises the problems that Pluto reveals to him (523e6-7). Neither feature suggests self-sight.

42. Westerink 1970, 3, refers to passages in Proclus which concern Amelius: *In Tim.* 1.306.1-14 and *Theol.* 5.5.23.2-18 SW. It seems that Amelius, in discussing the scope of Plato's demiurge from the *Timaeus*, postulated a triple demiurge, three intellects or three kings, he who is, he who holds, and he who sees. The second *holds* the first, and the third *holds* the second but merely *sees* the first (8-9). We do not find the required reflexivity here.

43. Jackson et al. 1998, 23-8; Iamblichus, *In Sophistam* fr. 1 Dillon; cf. Proclus, *Theol.* 1.5.25.16-18. Contrast Westerink 1962, xxxviii.

44. 1.6.28.25-29.3: note 'He composes his myths for the sake of his preferred targets'.

45. e.g. Olymp. *In Grg.* proem 6, *Prolegomena* 22; on the meaning of *politikos* in this context see Jackson et al. 1998, 28-31.

46. See Tarrant 1997; Jackson et al. 1998, 28-32.

47. For the unifying role of wisdom see *Phd.* 68c-69c; also Dillon 1983.

48. This contrasts with the natural virtues or *euphuiae* which may be found in isolation from each other, as at *Meno* 88b.

49. Note that, though present in Olympiodorus (46.7), the view that the myth shows the paradigm of constitutional well-being is absent from the schematic discussion of proem 6 and other relevant passages.

50. See Jackson et al. 1998, 58 n. 19, though Porphyry should be added to the list of authors employing this scheme.

10. Recollecting Plato's Middle Period

1. See Kahn 1996, 42-8.

2. It was adequately refuted by Thesleff 1982, 154-5; and the fact that a second preface circulated in antiquity (anon. *Tht.* column 4) must call into question whether the *dedicatory* preface was part of the original work.

3. Compare *Sph.* 216a1 with *Tht.* 210d3.

4. That the *Timaeus* uses refers to the ideal state depicted principally in book 5 of the *Republic*, or that the *Critias* employs a chief speaker who has appeared in the *Charmides*, is very seldom thought to indicate proximity of date.

5. Criteria which seem to me to be relevant are positive and negative responses, the rate of *ontôs* as opposed to *tôi onti* for 'in truth', and the handling of vocatives. On average both works seem to be closer to Book 5 of the *Republic* than to later or earlier books, but they include more characteristically 'late' forms as well as more characteristically 'early' ones, suggesting a long gestation.

6. See Tarrant 1984.

7. DL 7.165 = SVF 1.411: the term *anhypoptôtos* replaces *ametaptôtos* here. The interesting thing about the Herillus fragment is that it appears in itself to postulate two kinds of *epistêmê*, one which is the telos, and is to be identified with living by referring all things to life with *epistêmê*; the other which is the *epistêmê* referred to within this definition of the higher *epistêmê*, and which must be some less grand notion of knowledge to avoid circularity. It would be plausible for an ancient commentator to have interpreted the latter as some kind of partial knowledge, which the sage's overall knowledge must consult in the course of life's decisions.

8. See Stob. Ecl. 2.74.16 ff. = SVF 3.112: the wording in this case is *hexin phantasiôn dektikên ametaptôton hypo logou*, and one contrast is with *sustêma ex epistêmôn technikôn ex hautou echon to bebaion*; the virtues are considered to be an example of this. For more on this passage see n. 66.

9. See Mansfeld 1983.

10. 74b-76a, 82b-86a, 86e-87b

11. cf. Tarrant 1984, 97.

12. The work, originally edited by Diels and Schubart 1905, should now be consulted in the edition of Bastianini and Sedley 1995. On the author and date see particularly 246-56. See also Sedley's further recent papers relating to anon. *Tht.*

13. The lemma is critical for a proper appreciation of what TC has to say, even though it remains, for us, a slightly strange response to that lemma, and dependent upon the fact that TC views the distinction between simple and complex knowledge as fundamental for the understanding of the *Theaetetus* and *Meno*. That the subject of the *Theaetetus* is regarded as simple knowledge may be seen at 2.18-21; that this is also what is described at *Meno* 98a, where reasoning sets right opinions on the path to becoming knowledge, is claimed at 2.39-3.7.

14. See Mansfeld, p. 61; Tarrant, 1984, 99 n. 9.

15. *to hypo tais geômetriais ... legeis.*

16. The singular is used 25 times in Plato, 10 in *Rep.* 7, the plural five times only, four from *Rep.* 6-7 (refs. above), and again for geometrical problems at *Meno* 76a (contrast *peri pasês geômetrias* (gen. sing.), 85e2). See Brandwood 1976.

17. cf. 536d5.

18. One key text is perhaps DL 7.47 (SVF 1.68, 2.130) where knowledge is defined as either 'secure apprehension' (which is clearly a case of simple knowledge as viewed by TC) or 'a hexis in the reception of presentations which is impervious to reason' (which is how TC described Zeno's simple knowledge). Another is Stob. Ecl. 2.74.16 ff. (SVF 3.112) where definitions along the same lines as those given by DL are separated by two further definitions which refer to some kind of *systema* (either a compound of the type of apprehensions referred to above or a compound of 'skilled knowledges' which has its own guarantee, such as the virtues are). In both cases the knowledge must clearly be both complex and systematic, the only apparent difference being in whether the guarantee is to be encountered in each of the elements of the complex or alternatively within the complex itself. The notion of a system of knowledge is actually better established in the definition of craft (*technê*), SVF 2.93-7. For two kinds of knowledge in Herillus, see above, n. 7.

19. Surely an important qualification: note the *nun*, 529a6, and cf. 523a, 527a, 531a.

20. Certainly that much is suggested at 533b6-c6, where the use of sensation within the mathematical disciplines is not raised; this is an important passage for our purposes as it raises the theme of the unknowability of complexes so long as the beginnings (elements?) are unknown. As at 510d2 it is noted that the results are agreed upon, yet this agreement is said not to constitute knowledge.

21. It is evident from Plutarch, notably the *De Animae Procreatione*, and from Theon Smyrnaeus, himself a mathematical interpreter, that much early interpretation of Plato had been mathematically focussed. The names of Eratosthenes, Clearchus, Theodorus of Soli, Adrastus, and Dercyllides readily come to mind as interpreters who concentrated on mathematical aspects. Certainly Dercyllides and Clearchus seem to have written on specifically mathematical aspects of the *Republic*, see Dörrie-Baltes 1993, 80.1, 80.3.

22. 201d-206b: the theory demands that, in physical theory and in linguistic theory, there should be knowable complexes, which can be fully explained in terms of their elements, while the elements themselves remained unknowable and inexplicable: approachable only by sensation. While nowadays we might hesitate to relate this theory directly to the *Republic*, there is no doubt that it would have attracted comparison with the mathematical sciences as described in *Republic* 6 in our period, when authors were searching for ways of explaining one dialogue in terms of another, as if looking for handles by which interpretative problems could be grasped. There is the additional point that much the same theory appears to be rejected within the *Republic*, at 7 533c3-5, albeit without ever raising it as a serious possibility.

23. SVF 3.548-56.

24. See above, n. 14

25. Similarly in the *De Animae Procreatione* the Posidonian view of the World Soul (1023b-c) rigidly separates mathematicals off from 'first intelligibles'.

26. Theon, *Expos.* pp. 2-5 Hiller; Alcinous, *Didasc.* 7, p. 162.10-23, seems to show that Plato was thought of as postulating a separate kind of cognition for mathematical objects. Alcinous also has a seemingly unrelated use of the key term 'simple knowledge' at *Didasc.* 4, on which however see below.

27. See fr. 23 des Places, where the second god belongs to the level of intellect, while the third belongs at the level of that which thinks discursively.

28. But on Plotinus see Blumenthal 1996, 91-3.

29. 533c5, 511d1, d4.

30. Lies are *not to be approved* (*Tht.* 151c-d) *in general*, but they are *necessary* (*Rep.* 389b) *on certain occasions*, 59.2-34; *all human beings* (*Smp.* 206c) conceive in soul *in some existence*, but *some* are psychically sterile (*Tht.* 151b) *in this life*, 57.15-41.

31. See 98a4-5, which appears to link the binding-process with recollection on the part of he who opines.

32. It may be worth noting that, when Cicero speaks of the Recollection-Theory as found in the *Meno* at *TD* 1.57, he actually uses the unusual neuter plural term *geometrica*, which may suggest familiarity with the distinction between simple and complex knowledge as applied to such passages.

33. One can surely know the road to Larissa and still be ignorant of how one should reach any of the other major towns of Thessaly. It would be possible to compare such a person with somebody who, using diagrams rather than general geometrical theory, has arrived at knowledge of a single geometrical calculation.

34. I shall argue below that a determined interpreter could have detected systematic knowledge at certain points of the *Meno*, but that does not invalidate the basic point being made here.

35. It is here relevant that TC finds in Theaetetus' words which introduce the knowledge = sensation theory evidence that this is the theory that Theaetetus is himself employing: see 61.1-9, *hôs ge nuni phainetai*.

36. I do not assert that the hypothetical method in *Meno* is identical with mathematical method in the *Republic*, only that it would have been tempting for Ur-C to affirm such an identification, particularly in view of the absence of accepted ideas about Plato's chronology during the period.

37. A second hypothesis, clearly of a different sort and lacking any 'if', is that excellence is good, 87d3. Such a 'hypothesis' might well be the kind which Ur-C would have expected to operate at the *noêsis*-stage of the Divided Line, 511b5.

38. It is always difficult to translate the term *aitia* into English: here 'reason' is in many ways a better translation than 'cause', but it has the effect of stripping any metaphysical associations which it would have had for the Platonist. I therefore utilise transliteration.

39. Greg Horsley has kindly pointed out to me that the quality of the script indicates that we are dealing not with a lecturer's notes, but with a text in circulation.

40. My thanks to the participants at a seminar at King's College London where the notion of stylistic variation was discussed, and in particular to Verity Harte.

41. This is assumed by Tarrant 1983 and Sedley-Bastianini 1995 (252, 255, 500), but the origin of Pseudo-Hero (see Mansfeld 1983) suggests that the reading could possibly have been corrected since Taurus.

42. Hence TC's text of 98a3-4 is well suited to the idea that acquisition of knowledge requires an *aitia* for a *logismos* already in place, as opposed to a *logismos* in support of a hitherto unargued *aitia*. I previously argued that there was no special reason why TC should have *needed* his reading of 98a, and indeed that he interpreted it much as if he had the MS reading (Tarrant 1989, cf. Sedley-Bastianini p. 485). In that case TC has not arrived at his reading through deliberate emendation. It now seems possible, though not likely, that Ur-C had done so.

43. The *Meno* too seems harsh on those who try to explain what one doesn't know in terms of what one doesn't know (75c-d), and seems to take an agreed matter of common knowledge as the starting-point for any genuine explanation (d5-6). Certainly it rejects an attempt to give an account of a definiendum which would employ the definiendum or a part thereof in the definiens (79a-c).

44. Long accepted by the Stoics, such notions now become critical to inter-school debate in such works as Plutarch's *De Communibus Notitiis* and Alexander's *De Fato*.

45. Following the likely restoration of *haplê* by Wilamowitz at 17.37.

46. It may be important that an argument cast in syllogistic form is described as 'unpacked' (*diêrthrômenos*) at 16.33 according to Sedley's admittedly uncertain restoration.

47. There may be a significant contrast here with interpreters such as Albinus (*Prol.* 6) who emphasise the cathartic nature of many 'Socratic' works, particularly of the 'peirastic' type (which includes the *Theaetetus* so far as we know), and sees the 'maieutic' works (those involving midwifery) as intended to awaken the natural notions as a *preliminary* to the direct handing down of doctrine.

48. It would surely have been noticed that Plato's tactic in the *Meno* had been to illustrate dramatically various cognitive conditions.

49. TC realises that the *Symposium* makes all persons conceive in soul as well as body, and endeavours to reconcile the two with reference to this 'in a way', and by restricting this qualified non-pregnancy to this life (57.26-8, 33-9). 'In a way not pregnant' will mean not having the natural notions 'at hand' (*procheira*), an adjective that recalls the condition of unaccessed knowledge like birds flying loose in Plato's 'aviary' (*Tht.* 198d7, cf. b10). This is presumably a clue to how TC interpreted the aviary section

50. This will include Anytus, the seer-politician, 92b-c, who has some correct intuitions about sophists.

51. See Glucker 1999.

52. It is possible that this was the normal place for ancient commentators to discuss the Theory of Recollection, since the *Meno* apparently did not attract commentaries; this might explain the inclusion of the set of material relating to *Meno*-style epistemology, ascribed to Plutarch of Chaeronea (frs 215-17) though not uncontroversially so, in a manuscript devoted to the Olympiodorus and Damascius *Phaedo*-commentaries. Cf. also Alcinous, *Didascalicus*, ch. 25, 177.45-178.10 (the author seems not to take account of the *Meno*'s recollection passage, except possibly at 6, p.185.4), Atticus, fr. 7.17-28 des Places. Cicero, *TD* 1.57 describes the slave-boy experiment in the *Meno*, but follows this (57-8) with a more extended appeal to the discussion of recollection in the *Phaedo*, where he believes that Plato explains his theory in greater detail, and where he shows full awareness of the important role now played by the Ideas.

53. See 23.7, 46.43-47.45, 53.46, 56.34.

54. Note *ennoia*, 73c9, *ennoein*, 73c8, 74a6, b6, c8, d1, d9, e2, 75a1, a5, a6, a11,

76a3; Cicero *TD* 1.57: *tot rerum atque tantarum insitas et quasi consignatas in animis notiones quas* ennoias *vocant*.

55. Tarrant 1993, 128-30.

56. Note that, following an interpretation of *Symposium* 206c, a trace of recollectable knowledge is presumed to be present in everybody, but that many are unable to access it in this life (57.15-39). On 'queste tracce predialettiche' see Bastianini-Sedley 1995, 535-6, who relate it also to our ability to know what a given craft is even before we understand what knowledge is (23.15-25).

57. Perhaps one should include as an alternative here the notion that Intelligence governs the world which is put forward as an explanatory principle in the *Phaedo* 97c-98b, though the chances are that a unitarian would interpret this passage in relation to *Republic* 6 anyway.

58. Plato quotes only so much of *Od.* 10.492-5 as to employ the verb *pepnusthai*, but the Homeric context demonstrates that this is to be understood in terms of the possession of *phrenes* and *noos*.

59. Also 66e3, 68a7, 69a-c, and, from the end of the work, 111b4, 114c7.

60. 65c3, e2-3, e6-66a3.

61. The terminology of *dianoia* is found four times at 65e-66a, and of *logismos* three times from 65c2 to 66a. There is clearly a link between the two in Plato's mind.

62. 74c4, c8, d3, 74b2, b4, c8, 75b5, c1, c8, d4 (plural), d9, d10, e4 (plural), e5, 76a4, a5, a9, b1, b5 x 2, c1, c6, c15 (plural); also the verb *oida* at 74a9 (compound), 75d8, d9, which 75d8-10 shows to be very closely related, and *gnôsis* terminology at 73c7 and d7.

63. I hesitate to say the language of 'concepts', since this is not a broad enough translation here. For refs. see above, n. 54.

64. We are not, however, talking of these acts of knowledge-recovery as if the knowledge could not form part of a wider whole, as thought association is usually the trigger for recollection (73c-74a).

65. The single use of *dianoia* (*en têi dianoiâi*, 73d7) seems to mean no more than 'mind', and there is no occurrence of *logismos*.

66. Also by the singular at 76c6 and verb at 76c1; the plural recurs at 75e4, 76c15.

67. The use of *logismos* at 84a7 may be incidental, and linked with the verb's occurrence at a2. There is no talk now of *epistêmê*, but some of *noêsis* and *noêta*, which as in the *Republic* might have suggested a higher type of knowledge, where one's understanding of the object of contemplation is linked in with one's understanding of all else (80b1, 81d7, 83b1, b4).

68. The 'grasp' (*epilambanein* at 79a3) or acquisition was of course conceived as being pre-natal, as can be seen from the use of *lambanein* at 75b5, c2, c4, c7, d5, d7, d9, e2, 76a2, c14, d3. The recollection can be described by the use of the verb *analambanein*. This-worldly contemplation can also be described the verb *ephaptomai* (79d6), which seems entirely compatible with the notion of making contact with what is within our memories.

69. 525c, 529d-530b, 531b-d.

70. An obvious objection is that, on such an interpretation, the simple/complex distinction is irrevocably linked in the *Republic* with the Platonic Ideas as objects of knowledge, that it is not *exclusively* linked with them in the *Phaedo*, and that it is not linked at all in the *Meno* or *Theaetetus*. Equally obviously, such an objection cannot be accepted by any interpreters working with a unitarian approach either to the corpus as a whole or at least to these four dialogues. The epistemologies of the *Phaedo* and *Republic*, particularly of *Republic* 5 477a ff., make it necessary that knowledge in the other two dialogues should somehow be linked with knowledge of Ideas, in the mathematical sciences as elsewhere. Any uses of the term *epistêmê* to refer to anything that in no way involved Ideas, common notions, etc. would be seen as using that term in a figurative sense only.

71. See Sedley-Bastianini 1995, p. 499; Mansfeld 1983, pp. 63-5.

72. *Met.* A, 981a5-6; this passage comes only a little before that in which Aristotle characterises knowledge by our awareness of 'why P' in addition to 'that P', equated with knowledge of an *aitia*, a passage clearly influencing TC at 3.1-7: where the concept of simple knowledge is being first explained.

73. See *EN* 6.3, 1139b19-24, where *epistêmê* is a *hexis apodeiktikê*, and concerns things unable to be otherwise, unlike *technê* (*EN* 6.4, 1140a10-16).

74. To the latter is appended the observation that some say that this is grounded in *tonos* and *dynamis*. For the text see Long and Sedley 1987, 42H, pp. 258-9, where the key point is that the definitions are represented in the manuscript tradition as definitions applying to four different types or conceptions of knowledge, not four definitions of one thing. The second definition actually speaks of a system of 'such knowledges', using the plural, to refer back to the single cognitive acts referred to in the first. Long and Sedley assert that 'Stobaeus reports four different senses of *epistêmê*, starting with the most particular ... and concluding with the most general.' Ur-C may have disagreed about the last.

75. Tarrant 1985 p. 116 with p. 168 n. 36.

76. This theory is most notably expounded in Cicero, *Academica* 1.37 and *De Legibus* 1.38. The only Stoic to whom Cicero appeals in these contexts, where the compatibility of orthodox Stoic doctrine with Plato and Aristotle is stressed, is Zeno himself.

77. See Cic. *Acad.* 2.30-1.

78. Even these, or the greatest of them, are embryonically present among nature's original gifts in the Antiochian account of 'Peripatetic' ethics in the fifth book of Cicero's *De Finibus*. See Tarrant 1985, 121-4.

79. Important discussions of the assimilation doctrine, which both contribute towards its rehabilitation in our understanding of Plato, are to be found in Sedley 1997c and Annas 1999.

80. Tarrant 1993, 120-47.

81. Dörrie-Baltes 1993, 80.1, 3, 5, with commentary.

82. Dörrie-Baltes 1993, 80.2, 4. The former, a contemporary of Augustus, did not regard himself as a Platonist but as an 'eclectic' (DL 1.21), but without knowing his reasons we cannot totally rule out the possibility that he is Ur-C. The latter is identified by the Suda with the writer of *Tactica* of the first century AD.

83. Simple knowledge at 155.33, common notions at 155.27-32, *perilêpsis* (regarded as unusual by Whittaker 1990, p. 86, the noun does not occur in TC, who, however, uses the verb *perilambano* regularly in relation to the *embracing* of an Idea within a definition, 26.11, 37.10-46, 45.48) at 156.6.

84. So Bastianini-Sedley 1995, p. 499.

85. It is interesting that in the *Didascalicus* only chapters 3 (possibly) and 4 use the verb *kalein* in the context of what *Plato* calls something. Chapter 4 does so up to 5 times, at 154.40, 155.4, 17, 26, and 32. In general a study of *kalein*, *onomazein*, *prosagoreuein*, along with relevant uses of *legein* (+ *eipein* + *eirêsthai*) and *phêmi*, will show that there is considerable concern about what things are called in chapters two to four of the work, which is nowhere matched and approached only in chapters 25-30. My figures for each page of Hermann's Teubner (pp. 152-89) are as follows: p. 155 (=4): 11; pp. 153 (=2-3) and 154 (=3-4): 6 each; pp. 158 (=6), 162 (=7-8), and 179 (=26-7): 4 each; pp. 178 (=25) and 187 (=33): 3

each; pp. 152, 166, 169, 175, 181-3: 2 each; pp. 156, 159, 160, 171, 173, 177, 180, 185, 188: 1 only; pp. 157, 161, 163-5, 167-8, 170, 172, 174, 176, 184, 186, 189: no relevant occurrence.

86. 155.13, 17, and 32; elsewhere it is more often general philosophic or platonist vocabulary that he explains, though Plato is specified in chapter 1 (152.28), 7 (162.10), and 27 (180.15).

87. Obviously, we cannot speculate as to what the source of *Didasc.* 4 commented on.

88. See Dillon 1993, 71-2.

89. For Stoicism see Dillon 1993, 64-6.

90. 154.29-30: 'knowledge-producing reason has reliability ... because it concerns sure and stable foundations', 32-4: 'the foundations of *epistêmê* ... and opinion are intellection and sensation', 155.28-32: 'intellection is the foundation of knowledge-producing reason'. These passages make it entirely possible that a genuinely recollected awareness of the Idea should have been thought of as that which anchors the reasoning that produces knowledge, just as the original vision of the Idea(s) had been the source of that reasoning.

91. Twice Alcinous speaks of cognition which was *then* called intellection, but is *now* called a natural notion (155.26-8, 31-2). Translators have no option but to take this in the natural sense, as claiming that one and the same experience used to be correctly termed *noêsis* while the soul was disembodied, but came to be correctly called natural notion on embodiment. But this fudges the careful distinction between *noêsis* proper and *physikê ennoia*, making them the same thing after all but giving them different names at different times. An alternative at 26-8 would be to understand Alcinous in both passages as referring only to embodied cognition of the Ideas, but saying that this process *used to be called noêsis* (as of course it was in Plato) and *has since been termed noêsis* (as in early imperial philosophy). 29-32 shows that Alcinous himself did not mean it in this way, but his source might indeed have intended to distinguish between past and present ways of referring to embodied intellection.

92. Whittaker 1990, p. 7.

93. Whittaker 1990, xix-xxvi.

94. I am in sympathy with Göransson 1995, pp. 24-5 etc., who argues that the *Didascalicus* should be regarded as a compilation from a number of sources, and hence that one should specify the source of a given section, be it larger or smaller. With regard to chapter 4 one may note (i) that he adduces the fact that the different use of *dialektikê* in chapter 7, which would puzzle one who had just read 4, goes without comment (p. 114), and (ii) that, because of the absence of criteriology from the division of logic in 3, this cannot be from the same source as 4 which assumes that it is such a division (p. 115). This enables Göransson to claim (p. 130) that 'Of the chapters on dialectics, chapter 4 obviously has no connection with the others'.

95. *Meno* 85d9 is, on the basis of the received text, perhaps the only clear example of this, but in general Plato's talk of recovering knowledge tends to suggest that in one sense we have had knowledge all along.

96. Particularly the phrase *noêsei meta logôi perilêpton*; it has most obviously inspired 156.11-14. Alcinous' *perilêpsis* (156.6) recalls *perilêpton* there (twice). For the wider context see Whittaker 1975.

97. The phrase 'not without' has become formulaic at 156.5-14; strangely the preposition *aneu* is very rare elsewhere in the *Didascalicus*, being found only at 5.157.3 and 14.170.3 (where it is prompted by the *chôris* of *Tim*. 30b3). A negative is present in both of these cases. There are similarities with the usage of the preposition in TC, where there is a negative present in every case; here it first occurs in the phrase *ou mentoi aneu logou* (5.41-2), then at 23.8 in a discussion of the relevance of definition to the unravelling of the common notions: 'this does not arise in one grasping each genus and the differentiae'. This context is very like that at *Didasc.* 5.157.3: one must use the division of the genus firstly into species for discerning each things real substantive being; this couldn't arise without a definition. Definition by genus and differentia(e) is necessary in each case for such cognition of the Ideas as we are permitted in this existence. Next we have the phrase 'without knowing *epistêmê*' at 23.16-17, and finally the phrase 'not without motion at least' at 73.10. Three uses of the 'not without' phrase in Alexandrian authors should be mentioned: Clement, *Strom.* 5.83.4 (in whom the phrase is found 13 times) preserves an apparently deliberate emendation of *Meno* 99e6 by which *aneu nou* becomes *ouk aneu nou*. This is an emendation to a dialogue important for our present purpose, and one which is once again of epistemological relevance. Potamo, again from Alexandria and author of early exegesis of the *Republic*, utilised the phrase in his description of the moral goal, DL 1.21. Philo of Alexandria also uses *ouk aneu* frequently (26 times), usually in non-technical ways, but one epistemological passage should be mentioned: 'Everything which sensation experiences does not abide without *nous*', *LA* 2.41. This compares with low figures in Plutarch (all genuine: 6), Plotinus (4), Porphyry (5), Sextus (4), and a rather higher use in Alexander of Aphrodisias (14) and the vast Galen (41), in both of whom the Stoic quasi-causes *hôn ouk aneu* are much discussed. One further use seems particularly relevant to this paper: DL 7.47 (= SVF 2.130, but is it 'old'?) follows his two Stoic definitions of knowledge, including that used by Ur-C, with 'but [they say that] not without the study of dialectic will the sage remain unerring in reason'.

98. I have here interpreted the tantalising verb *anhaploô* rather colourlessly as 'explicate', and hence as similar to *diarthroô*, literally 'divide at the joints'. But in view of the very real importance of the concept of *haplê epistêmê*, one might interpret both as a process of reducing the common notions to their simplest elements. In this context *anhaploô* has probably been prompted by the discussion at 19.4-20 of things simple and complex, where 'knowledge' is simple and 'geometry' complex, because the latter embraces the idea of the former. To *anhaplôsai* geometry, one would presumably have to give its genus 'knowledge' and its differentia.

99. It is not really a problem that the term *noêsis* does not occur in extant pages of TC, for the verb *noein* is used regularly, 10.28, 10.31, 23.24, 27.41, 41.32-3, 62.46; while TC's use seems a little wider, at 23.24 it is used in the required sense of grasping a concept (there of a given 'knowledge' in the absence of a concept of knowledge as a whole).

100. See above, n. 97.

101. On the questions of whether Arius Didymus is a major source of Alcinous, and who Arius was, see now the sceptical voices of Göransson 1995, particularly 182-218, and Bremmer 1998.

102. See Texts 1 (Eusebius/Hieronymus), 2 (Delphic Inscription III 4.91), and 18 (Suda) Lakmann for Beirut, but Text 3 (Philostratus *VS* 2.1) for Tyre!

11. The debate over the *Theaetetus*

1. Sedley 1996.
2. On Socratic Irony see Chapter 8 iii.
3. See above, Chapter 2.

4. That is as a result of Diels and Schubart reading *all' e[nioi] phasin* at 32-3 where Sedley-Bastianini have *all' hout[oi] phasin*, which may fit the traces better. In view of the little that remains I suggest that our minds should be open to the possibility of *alloi [de] phasin*: 'But others say ...'. Since *delta* occupies double the space of many letters this should be possible.

5. With the popular *men ... de ...* construction.

6. *prothemenon* (proposing) is directly related to *prothesis* (proposed topic), as is *prokeitai* (it is proposed) at 2.18.

7. Cornford 1935; cf. Bastianini-Sedley 484.

8. For the limited equivalence of 'through which' and 'by which' (*di' hou*; *hôi*) see *Tht.* 184bc, Bastianini-Sedley 483.

9. The simple distinction between the criterion 'through which' and the criterion 'by which' is clearly made by Alcinous (4.1-2), but he appears to see reason both as a criterion 'by which' and as a criterion 'through which'. Ptolemy, *On the Criterion* 2, distinguishes agent, instrument, and means (mind, sensation, reason).

10. It is possible that Thrasyllus had benefited from the debate that we are witnessing, but one only has to bear in mind his comparable lack of influence on Plutarch to realise that the implications for TC's date are not strong.

11. Insofar as TC has provided the strongest justification for taking the topic of knowledge at face value, his work might have been known to Thrasyllus.

12. But he gave the *Sophist* the subtitle *On Being* (DL 3.58), which agrees well with TS.

13. Though see Mansfeld 1994, 58-107, for an alternative view.

14. Purification and elenchus were considered by Albinus to be features of the *peirastic* dialogue; see *Prol.* 6; Bastianini-Sedley 481.

15. Bastianini-Sedley (481) refer to the genuine parallel at anon. *Proleg.* 10.31-3; however, their reference to Proc. *In Prm.* 631 is evidence of an interpretation which made *Tht.* an attack on Protagoras in the same way as they made *Prm.* an attack on Zeno of Elea. Polemical works could not be regarded as *peirastic*, for this 'character' is concerned with the testing of the young.

16. Sedley 1997a.

17. Sedley relates this to the more immediate context, but I suspect that anon. is not limiting himself to this.

18. This fragment (on the mis-perceptions of 157e) sees Plato as having outlined Protagoras' theory in 152-7 *only to undermine it in 158 ff.*

19. *orthôs hypemnêsas; isôs gar ouk apo kairou ....*

20. cf. Tarrant 1999a. Another echo of the same passage occurs at Ph. *Ebr.* 154 at the beginning of what is probably the most important epistemological passage of Philo that we possess, most likely to stem from a Pyrrhonist source *filtered through* an Academic-Platonist channel whose ultimate purpose was to distinguish our usual vain conceits of knowledge founded on sensation or reasoning from a higher vision which is revealed when the eye of the soul is purified. This contrast is fully present in Philo, in his comments on Abraham's return to 'sobriety' at *Sobr.* 3-5; the terminology here is suggestive of Platonism.

21. I do in fact believe that space suggests the reading *kai ta eirêmena de hypomimnêiskei hêmas* where Sedley and Bastianini do not think to include *de*.

22. cf. Tarrant 1999. Sedley has 'and are reminding us that his preceding words were a summary account of the criterion "by which" judgement is made ...'.

23. A word beginning 'X ...' strongly suggests the presence of the name of Xenophanes, who is easily regarded as saying something almost Platonic about the extent to which man may be a measure, SE *Math.* 7.50, 110. Just before we seem to read 'like the ...-ists', possibly Pyrrhonists.

24. Sedley 1997, 141-3.

25. This possibility has been explored with perhaps too much relish by T. Göransson, *Albinus, Alcinous, Arius Didymus*, Göteborg, 1995, pp. 24-5 etc. With regard to chapter 4 he notes (i) that Alcinous employs without comment a different use of *dialektikê* in chapter 7, which would puzzle one who had just read 4 (p. 114), and (ii) that, because of the absence of criteriology from the division of logic in 3, this cannot be from the same source as 4 which assumes that it is such a division (p. 115). This enables Göransson to claim (p. 130) that 'Of the chapters on dialectics, chapter 4 obviously has no connection with the others'. I tend to agree, chiefly because I believe that much more of Alcinous has gone into this chapter than into some others. However, this does not mean that he has based the chapter directly on Plato rather than on his interpreters.

26. Notable exclusions from my list of demonstrable sources are *Meno* and *Republic* 6-7, whose influence, if any, is confined to doctrines discussed in other works.

27. Note, however, that the term *organon* is used at 184d4.

28. Sedley 1996b.

29. In fact his acceptance that the wax tablet from 191c is Plato's *seat of sensation* (155.12-13) is scarcely compatible with such a view, which allows no seat of sensation to be fixed.

30. This much is compatible with TC's own view that Socrates tries to awaken an interlocutor's natural notions with samples of theory from elsewhere (47.35-48.7), though column 2 already makes it clear that TC sees the Protagorean samples as *false*.

31. Nevertheless, he shows no sign of seeing the work as being about knowledge either, and some features of his epistemology are foreign to TC's approach – e.g. a heavy emphasis on linking types of cognition with types of objects, avoided by TC at 2.39-52.

32. For Plutarch and the *Theaetetus* see Opsomer 1998, 78-82.

33. In the *De Animae Procreatione* which is of course based on the *Timaeus* Plutarch openly supplements his understanding of that work with reference to *Rep.*, *Phdr.*, *Critias*, *Plt.*, *Phlb.*, *Laws*, as well as *Sph.* For this last see 1013d. The list is surprising insofar as Plutarch has no conception of a 'late' group of dialogues.

34. See *E at Delphi* 391b, *De Defectu* 428c.

35. We find in this passage the verb *krinein* four times, and the noun *kritês* once.

36. It is significant that there is an allusion to *Sph.* 230b-e when discussing midwifery at *Mor.* 999e.

37. The problem of reconciling the sterility of some individuals (151b) with the creativity of all humans at *Symp.* 206c is tackled differently (and less convincingly) by TC at 57.15-42, and was surely pondered by Plutarch whose discussion of midwifery involves Socrates' erotic art, 1000d. But Plutarch holds that Platonic recollection is not 'generation' because what is recollected is not constructed by the individual, which TC actually admits elsewhere (55.30-3) in spite of making the contrary assumption at 57.20-2. 'Generation' is for Plutarch the production *of one's own ideas*, something foreign to the critical faculty.

38. *noêsis, noêta*; e.g. 1001c ff., 1024f ff.

39. Similarly Alcinous in *Didascalicus* 4 speaks of human reason as being considerably less secure than the kind of reason that god is capable of, and reduces human intellection (*noêsis*) to a hazy recollection in this world of a vision from another.

40. In the very next sentence we read: 'otherness, in its difference from being, strays into the generation of non-being'.

41. *Mor.* 746b, on his affection for B35.

42. *Mor.* 385c, cf. also *Quaestiones Conviviales* 680c-d where *Tht.* 155d is again an issue.

43. The *dia ti* and the *didaskalia tês aitias*.

44. Ammonius uses terms such as *eikotôs* and *eoiken* at 385c, where he also seems to think it providential that many of the world's more important truths are hidden from us.

45. It is surely worth noting, however, that on the key question of a *positively* sceptical account of our cognition of the sensible world *even when backed by reason*, and a Platonising contrast with things which are open to some higher under-standing *though they do not seem to be readily understandable by reasoning processes*, Ammonius must be seen to be very close to Philo at *Ebr.* 154-205 and *Sobr.* 3-5; the latter would thus appear to come from early in this Academic-Platonist tradition, and one may add that *Sobr.* 5 probably alludes to the Theory of Recollection as assimilated in both Plutarch and anon. to the awakening of natural common notions.

46. 1001c, 1002a, 1002d x 2.

47. 1109e, 1114d, 1123f; the remaining case is *Mor.* 448b.

48. Philo of Alexandria, though using the term 22 times, is comparable in this respect, and tends to identify as criteria only the individual sensations, sensation as a whole, and intellect.

49. Fr. 83 I-P = SE *Math.* 7.147-9.

50. cf. Sedley 1996b, 312: 'Alcinous is confident that *doxa* at [*Tim.*] 28a is simply a shorthand for "doxastic *logos*".'

51. *Adiapseustos* as translated by Dillon 1993, p. 5: but note that he interprets the passage as meaning '*only* free from error when it is engaged in the cognition of reality'. This 'only' is present by way of interpretation, and suggests that error is possible in other activities; Dillon identifies these with the cognition of non-reali-ties, apparently taking *tôn pragmatôn* as a reference to Ideas (62-3), though use of the term at 154.19 makes it doubtful whether that could be meant. Whittaker 1990, p. 5 translates 'l'autre et à l'abris de l'erreur dans la connaissance des réalités'.

52. I believe that the reason why opinion has been introduced here as an alternative to opinion-giving reason is simply that the theory of the opining faculty is closely connected with *Timaeus* 28a, which uses the simple 'opinion' at this stage. Cf. Sedley 1996b, 311-12.

53. See Porphyry *Harm.* pp. 12-13 Düring, Tarrant 1993, ch. 5. The key point is that the demiurgic god employs this *logos* in the creation-process as a result of which it is closely bound up with matter, and it then becomes a crucial element in logic and cognition.

54. 157b3-4: *ho tôn sophôn logos*, b7: *ean tis ti stêsêi tôi logôi*. The meaning for us is now an 'account' of the world and now 'speech', but it could have suggested more to others.

55. For an extensive study see Decleva Caizzi, 1988. She considers that this unusual passage in Sextus is in some way connected to Asclepiades of Bithynia and his new materialism, possibly to Asclepiades' use of Plato (p. 465) and perhaps to another strange testimony concerning Protagoras' sensation-theory at DL 9.51 which is also probably linked with Asclepiades (p. 469): on how he used to say that soul is nothing but the senses *as Plato says in the Theaetetus*!

56. Asclepiades is no doubt an important interest for Sextus because he was important for Aenesidemus too.

57. Göransson 1995, 203-18; see also Bremmer 1998.

58. The 26 occurrences compare with low figures in Plutarch (all genuine: 6), Plotinus (4), Porphyry (5), Sextus (4), and a rather higher use in Alexander of Aphrodisias (14) and the vast Galen (41), in both of whom the Stoic quasi-causes (*hôn ouk aneu*) are much discussed.

59. So his proposed criterion of the most accurate presentation would imply. One should note that TC sees Plato as attacking a Protagorean theory that gave pride of place to the senses, using language that is reminiscent of the Stoic criterion (*plektikon*: see Opsomer 1998, 41) and Potamo's (*akribeia*), 3.7-15.

60. As seen from the reference to intervening space at 156d6 and to sense organs and sense objects being filled with sensation and quality respectively.

61. Since 62.8 anon. had been showing how Plato was very much aware that Theaetetus and Protagoras differed in their view of knowledge.

62. *Ebr.* 171-205.

63. See *Quis Heres* 246.

64. Sedley 1996a, 81, 88-9.

65. Proc. *In Prm.* 631, 657; Dam. *Princ.* 3.169.32.

66. 201e-202a, cf. 152d.

67. In *Menex.* Plato is supposed to try to outdo his rival, in *Prm.* to overthrow him, and in *Phdr.* to combine these strategies.

68. Curiously, even *Prm.*, which is treated as competing *by opposition*, is seen as *going beyond* Zeno in its use of opposing arguments.

69. Favorinus, the 'Academic' immediately springs to mind, but there would have been many others with an interest in Plato.

70. SE *PH* 1.222: the alternative view has to assume that the term *stasis* could be used for an official school of philosophy (or, with Decleva Caizzi 1994, for a mere 'view' that Sextus is about to express) rather than for a controversial opinion or philosophical stance which is opposed to one or more other positions. I can only believe that Menodotus and Aenesidemus are being seen as principal exponents of the aporetic interpretation of Plato. However, the coupling of the two Pyrrhonist leaders together may be akin to many other such couplings in Sextus, and indicate that our author is following the second's view of the first, rather than giving an independent view of the earlier as well. See also my 1985, 75 and 161 n. 33, Annas & Barnes 1994, 58.

71. The translation follows Morrow and Dillon, 1987, 29-30.

72. See Winter 1997.

73. If I am right about this kind of interpretation, then it is most likely to have reached Proclus from Favorinus, probably via Galen, who evidently subscribed to the 'logical' interpretation of the *Parmenides* that follows, and improves upon, the polemical interpretation. For Galen on *Prm.* see Tarrant 1990, 25; 1993, 35; for the logical interpretation see Steel 1997.

12. The 'logical' dialogues

1. DL 3.49-50 = Thrasyllus T20.

2. On this work see Dillon 1992, Schicker 1992.

3. The myth is mentioned at 46.8.

4. This latter name is a mistake for Hermogenes, see Westerink et al. 1990, 51.

5. Had anon. accurately recorded the name Hermogenes, this would have had the effect of cancelling the influence of Cratylus, since they stand for opposite theses in the *Cratylus*, but the error allows a pro-Heraclitan reading.

6. See Chapter 3 i.

7. See Chapter 11 vii.

8. Denied by Mansfeld 1994, but see Tarrant 1995.

9. See Dillon 1993, 108; Whittaker 1990, 106 (with helpful references).

10. Plotinus tends to use the *Parmenides (Enn.* 5.1.8-10) as if he did not expect any challenge on the grounds that such use is wrong *in principle*. This may be explained either by such uses being already normal, or by the esoteric nature of his writings.

11. See Tarrant 1990, p. 25 n. 6, on *Prologus* 6.

12. See Steel 1997, 79; *Theol.* 1.9.35.5-7; note that the *Platonic Theology* is even less concerned with doxographic accuracy than *In Prm*.

13. This is the natural inference of Proclus' account of their view of the hypotheses, that it is *nothing but* an example of how to reason, taking *what could have been any thesis at all* as suitable for examination, like the *Sophist*'s angler-paradigm.

14. See Kraus and Walzer 1951 for the remains of all these compendia, and Dam. *VIsid.* 244 for Marinus' reversion to the Galenic interpretation of the *Parmenides*.

15. See *PHP* 9.7.15, pp. 630-1 de Lacy.

16. I have associated this work with a later stage, which might be correct (1993, 34). The anomaly is explained on 36.

17. There seems also to be more than historical concern when Proclus tackles this interpretation at length at *Theol.* 1.9.

18. In *Theol.* 1.9.37.15-39.6 Proclus supplements this passage of the *Theaetetus* with *Sophist* 217c which again refers reverently to this same encounter with the elderly Parmenides.

19. The 'Firmus' interpretation does not accept that Parmenides was ever normally thought of as positing a One in this stricter sense, and appeals to *Sph.* 244e-5b.

20. On this work see now the work of Linguiti 1995. A connection with Porphyry is generally supposed.

21. *In Prm.* 634, 637, 638; *Theol.* 1.9.37.3, 38.13.

22. *In Prm.* 1048, 1059; *Theol.* 5.39.143.15-17.

23. See Proc. *In Prm.* 619.

24. Compare the style of Numenius, who constantly has passages of Plato in mind, but is in fact giving an exposition of an alleged Pythagorean system.

25. Tarrant 1993, 148-77.

26. Anon. *Proleg.* 26.40-1: *ton Cratylon hôs peri onomatôn didaskonta.*

27. Anon. *Proleg.* 4.7-9.

28. The example given by the Galenic interpretation at *In Prm.* 634 is how Plato does not try to define the angler in the *Sophist* in order to discover the nature of the angler, but as an illustration of the dichotomic method of division.

29. The relevance of the *Parmenides* for negative theology in ch. 10 is disputed; apart from definitions concerning dialectic (4, 155.17-20), *Sophist* and *Politicus* become important only for the discussion of the statesman and sophist (34-5, 198.5-27), which are added more or less as an afterthought to the political section; *Euthydemus* briefly becomes important for ethics at 181.2-10 because of the digressions in which Socrates teaches Cleinias; *Cratylus* is mentioned in Whittaker's index only in relation to chapter 6, though Dillon refers to it also in relation to linguistic details of chapters 10 (165.4) and 27 (181.5-6).

30. This had probably been what Albinus too had had in mind when he consciously assigned the 'logical' dialogues to the *zetetic* rather than the *hyphegetic* type (*Prol*. 6), linking their role with the consolidation of doctrine through argument, rather with its teaching.

31. On this background see Whittaker 1990, 91-2.

32. Chapters 3-4 and 25-30. See above, Chapter 10 x.

33. Appealing to *Tim*. 41e, 42d, and *Laws* 716.

34. Proclus, *In Rep*. 1.8.23-8, seems to know the subtitles 'On Being', 'On Non-Being', and 'On the Sophist'.

35. *PHP* 9.5 (566.10-11 de Lacy): 'the diairetic method, in which Plato has given us a training in the *Sophist*', cf. Proc. *In Prm*. 634.

36. *Mor*. 1013d, cf. 391b, 393b, 1115d-e (with Dillon's discussion, 1977, 227). There is an excellent chance that Numenius too read the *Sophist* as a central metaphysical text, cf. Dillon 1977, 368-9.

37. Plot. *Enn*. 6.2, and for the rejection of Aristotelian categories, 6.1. On earlier use see Dillon 1977, 8, 133; though Atticus (fr. 2 des Places) of course rejects the relevance of quasi-Aristotelian categories for Platonism.

38. Proc. *Theol*. 1.11.52.2-10.

39. Contrast *Theol*. 1.4.18.13-20, where the dialogue is treated like a discussion of Being.

40. Dillon 1992, Schicker 1992.

41. Tarrant 1993, 33-7.

42. Tarrant 1993, 61-8.

43. Anon. *Proleg*. 26.40. I am closer to agreeing with Trouillard and Segonds than with Westerink concerning the restitution of the text.

44. See Proc. *Theol*. 1.4.19.13: *ho men politikos ... tên en ouranôi demiurgian [apeikonizetai]*. The Demiurge of the Heavens is present in the discussion of the *skopos* of the *Sophist*, Iambl. *In Sph*. fr. 1 translated in Chapter 7 iii.

45. Plut. *Mor*. 1015c, 1017c, 1026e-f (and possibly 429b, 720b: Jones 1915, 149); Severus in Proc. *In Tim*. 1.289.7-13, Numenius fr. 11.14-19 and 12.17-22 des Places (note *epithymêtikon êthos, aperioptos, eis tên heautou periôpên*, and cf. *Plt*. 272e4-6). Confirmation for Numenius may also be sought from fr. 16.10-12, where I read *dêmiourgos nûn, epeita theôrêtikos holôs*: 'a demiurge at one moment, contemplative the next.' Note that *eis tên heautou periôpên* means 'to self-contemplation' in later Platonism.

46. See Dillon 1977, 217, on *Mor*. 416f.

47. For Plut. see above, for Numenius see Dillon 1977, 369, on fr. 6.6-12, which relates not only to 248e but also to the subsequent *Megista Gene* passage.

48. Reference to *Crat*. 397d, 401c, and 415c-d in the important *De Iside* (375d) will confirm this stance.

13. Extracting the doctrine

1. 1976-8; also Ferrari 1998, on Galen's interpretation.

2. Mr. G. van Riel is working on this topic at Leuven, and see Laurenti 1996 on Plutarch.

3. Notably Trapp 1990.

4. Olymp. *In Grg*. 41.9. Galen in general adopts similar attitudes.

5. See Lycos 1994.

6. See [Plato] *Epistle* XIII 363a, Callimachus *Epigr*. 25.

7. Rosenthal and Walzer 1943, 13.

8. That the arguments were self-standing is also the view of Iamblichus,

Olymp. *In Phd.* 10.1.11-14, 11.2.1-5, 13.4.6-18 = Iamb. *In Phd.* frs 1, 3-4, cf. Dam. *In Phd.* 1.207.1-6. Olympiodorus resists his position strenuously.

9. See above, Chapter 5 ii.

10. Hermeias *In Phdr.* 102.

11. Often cited as Olymp. *In Phd.* (= p. 124 Norvin), but in fact Dam. *In Phd.* (1.177). Olymp. does in fact discuss the issue at *In Phd.* 10.7 in relation to Iamblichus = *In Phd.* fr. 2.

12. See TC 48.7-11, Albinus in Tertullian (see Göransson 1995, 68-71), Plut. frs 215-17. *Phaedo*-related material was prominent in Harpocration's giant *Commentary on Plato*.

13. See above, Chapter 10 v.

14. *NA* 1.19.9 = Text 4 Lakmann.

15. *NA* 17.20 = Text 14 Lakmann.

16. *Didascalicus* 33.3, *De Platone* 2.14.239-40; Dillon 1993, 200-2.

17. Anon. *Proleg.* 11.5-9, Proc. *Theol.* 1.25.112.25-113.6.

18. Unfortunately the text of anon. *Proleg.* 26 has obscured this.

19. The passage has left its mark on the *Didascalicus* in chapters 15 (171.25-6) and 33 (187.34-7) and often in Plutarch.

20. The commentary of Hermias confirms the importance of these last two attempts to characterise it. See Westerink et al. 1990, 71 n. 186.

21. See above, Chapter 9; Jackson et al. 1998, 8, 18 etc.

22. For Posidonius' view that the statement was about universal soul see above, Chapter 6 v. For Harpocration's view that immortality extended to the lowest creatures, see Chapter 13 ii. The 'vegetative soul' is explicitly mentioned by Olymp. *In Phd.* 10.7.4-5.

23. The imbalance of the commentary may partly but not wholly be attributed to the nature of its transmission.

24. Dercyllides in Theon *Expos.* 201, Proclus *In Remp.* 96-359, Plut. *Mor.* 1001c-2e, 1007e-9b, Galen *Plac.* 5 often (including Posidonius frs 142-5, 150a).

25. Proclus *In Remp.* 2.24-5.

26. Compare anon. *Proleg.* 17.19-29, where what had once been termed the 'character' of a dialogue is now called the 'mode of engagement'. Here the *Republic* is affirmed to be an instructional dialogue of the political mode.

27. The big exception is the earliest known arrangement: Aristophanes of Byzantium placed it at the opening of the *first* trilogy (DL 3.62).

28. *In Remp.* 1.7-14

29. The *Sophist* and *Politicus* are regarded as analogous cases of titles that illustrate the primary purpose of the work, so that this view was evidently held by persons who thought that these two works were about the sophist and the statesman respectively. This suggests something of a 'fundamentalist' approach to the dialogues.

30. *In Remp.* 1.11.12-13.

31. Jackson et al. 1998, 29-31; Tarrant 1997a.

32. Olymp. *In Grg.* proem 1, 1.1, 18.1; DL 3.52.

33. *In Remp.* 1.15.19-27; anything involving real two-sided dialogue seems to be regarded as 'zetetic'.

34. *In Remp.* 1.17.1-18.5, cf. 1.16.2-8. The distinction is related to Proclus' assumption that the beginning of the *Timaeus* relates directly to books 2-10 of the *Republic*, thus situating them at the Panathenaia rather than the Bendidia.

35. *Proleg.* 24.13-19, DL 3.37, Plut. *Mor.* 370f.

36. *Mor.* 370f, cf. 1013e-f, 1015d-e, 1016e.

37. See Ferrari 1998, on Galen and Calcidius in particular.

38. cf. Plut. *Mor.* 943a-b, where we meet the pattern intelligence (single), *logos* (compound), soul (single), [sensation or emotions?] (compound), body (single).

39. Dillon 1977, 127; Simpl. *Phys.* 181.

40. Though not presented as Pythagorean, this account is clearly related to Philolaus.

41. Note that the notion of the Good appearing in five 'kinds' (*genê*) picks up Plato's term for the *Megista Gene* and Plutarch's own *en pente genesi* (in five kinds) that applied to the 23c classification as well as the *Sophist*. Plutarch again tries to make the *Megista Gene* the basis for some underlying metaphysic in the late dialogues at *Mor.* 428c.

42. The treatise *De Defectu Oraculorum* is the only other one to show strong inclination towards seeing a five-fold metaphysic in Plato, 426e-431a, where again Plutarch is a junior figure, who meets with rather sceptical reactions from his master Ammonius.

43. Whittaker 1990, xix-xxv.

44. Alcinous would surely have allowed himself the privilege of altering the order of five epithets in his souce.

45. It might also solve the problem about 'inexpressible' appearing in a list of otherwise positive attributes (Dillon, 1993, 103), for 'inexpressible' applies only to the One of the first hypothesis, and explicitly not to that of the second (155d-e).

46. See Parmenides A34 = Plut. *Mor.* 1114d.

47. 163.14-17: *ekmageion, pandeches, tithênê, mêtêr, chôra.* I should punctuate strongly after 'he names' (*onomazei*), as the next term to follow (substrate: *hypokeimenon*) has nothing to do with Plato, and the following epistemological phrases have been *adapted* from *Tim.* 52b, and are not 'names'.

48. The term 'mother' does in fact serve to capture the relationship with god, insofar as it is contrasted with the 'father' at *Tim.* 50d2-3. The receptacle is the 'nurse' of coming-to-be (49a), as if to humans. It is the mould of all physical nature (50c), but all-receiving in relation to the Ideas (51a-b). It is space, perhaps, in its own right (52a8). All this could have been brought out by a source keen to show the force of the various appellations of the receptacle.

49. Dillon 1993, 105. To appeal to 65a, as he rightly sees, makes it odd that Alcinous leaves out beauty, but we should not emend the text.

50. Clearly it should be taken as a substantive here, since the other members of the list are all nouns.

51. Whittaker aptly compares Clement, *Strom.* 5.12.82.2, on which see now Choufrine 1998.

52. Note that I have claimed that this term *should* have been the first; it would have been the first if the source had been faithfully followed.

53. Above all, the first god's beingness should be the source of the Ideas, which are being (*ousia*) in their own right (9.1), while his divineness should be the source of the divinity of the heavenly god who contemplates them.

54. Symmetry and completion are better understood as divine attributes if one bears in mind that the author sees Plato's god as identical with Parmenides' one-being from B8.

55. See Jackson et al. 1998, 92 etc.

56. *Theol.* 1.5.24.12-17: in this it has the same status as *Phd.*, *Phdr.*, *Symp.*, *Sph.*, *Plt.*, *Crat.*, and *Tim.*, though a lesser status than *Prm.* The work was supposed to teach us about the One-Good, much as in Alcinous' source, and about the two primary principles, i.e. limit and unlimited, which were also popular with Middle Platonists.

57. Iamblichus fr. 1 = Dam. *In Phlb.* 5, which also mentions Syrianus and

Proclus. Damascius qualifies this (6). The Thrasyllan subtitle was 'On Pleasure', for the *Symposium*'s was 'On the Good'. The *Prolegomena* criticise the notion that pleasure is the *skopos* (23.3-7), claiming that it is actually the rank of the six goods. We have no hard evidence that any Middle Platonist saw the work as simply a discussion of pleasure, though it included that, as Alcinous (32) acknowledged.

58. Tetralogy 3.4, *Phaedrus*, is perhaps alluded to in this theological chapter. Whittaker cites in the apparatus 246e5, 247c6, and c7-8.

59. See above, Chapter 6 i.

60. 165.27-34. Plato organises the ascent according to an educational pattern, including the appreciation of successive bodies and of universal physical beauty (210ab, 211c), and for him the beauty of soul is not mentioned separately at 211b.

61. Of significance may be five terms applied to matter in Numenius fr. 4a.2-6: limitless (in itself), formless (compared with nature), irrational (compared with us), unknown (in comparison with Ideas), unordered (in relation to god). Also Aetius' list: the One, the Single-Natured, the Monadic, the Really Real, and the Good (all describing God), of which the final two seem related to items 1 and 2 of Alcinous' list 2, while the first three might have some relation to the *Parmenides*.

62. The correspondence here is unlimited (material), limit (natural), mixed (ideal), cause of combination (human intelligence), cause of separation at right moment (the Good).

63. In this case, I believe, particular difficulties over the ideal level, insofar as the ancients (just like us) had difficulties in detecting the Ideas within the *Philebus*.

Bibliography

Anderson G. 1976, 'Lucian's Classics: Some Short Cuts to Wisdom', *BICS* 23, 59-68.

Annas J. 1994, 'Plato the Skeptic' in Vander Waerdt (1994), 309-40.

Annas J. & Barnes J. (tr.) 1994, Sextus Empiricus: *Outlines of Pyrrhonism*, Cambridge, CUP.

Annas J. 1999, *Platonic Ethics, Old and New*, Ithaca, Cornell UP.

Baltes M. 1976-8, *Die Weltentstehung des platonischen Timaios nach den antiken Interpreten I & II*, Leiden, Brill.

Baltes M. 1996, 'Muß die "Landkarte des Mittelplatonismus" neu gezeichnet werden?', review of Göransson, *Göttingische Gelehrte Anzeigen* 248, 91-111.

Baltes M. 1997, 'Is the Idea of the Good in Plato's *Republic* beyond Being?', in Joyal 1997, 3-25.

Barnes J. 1989, 'Antiochus of Ascalon' in Barnes & Griffin 1989, 51-96.

Barnes J. & Griffin M. (eds.) 1989, *Philosophia Togata*, Oxford University Press.

Barnes J. & Griffin M. (eds.) 1997, *Philosophia Togata II, Plato and Aristotle at Rome*, Oxford, OUP.

Bastianini G. & Sedley D.N. (eds.) 1995, Anonymous *In Theaetetum*, Corpus dei papiri filosofici greci e latini, *iii*: Commentari, Firenze, 1995, 227-562.

Behr C.A. 1968, *Aelius Aristides and the Sacred Tales*, Amsterdam, Hakkert.

Behr C.A. 1994, 'Studies on the Biography of Aelius Aristides', *ANRW* 34.2, 1140-233.

Blumenthal H.J. & Clark E.G. (eds.) 1993, *The Divine Iamblichus*, London, Duckworth.

Blumenthal H.J. 1996, 'On soul and intellect' in Gerson (ed.), *The Cambridge Companion to Plotinus*, Cambridge, 82-104.

Boulanger A. 1968, *Aelius Aristide et la sophistique dans la province d'Asie au IIe siècle de notre ère*, Paris, Boccard.

Boys-Stones G. 1997, 'Plutarch: Thyrsus-bearer of the Academy or Enthusiast for Plato' in J. Mossman (ed.), *Plutarch and his Intellectual Background*, London, Duckworth.

Brandwood L. 1976, *A Word Index to Plato*, Leeds, Maney.

Branham J.B. 1989, *Unruly Eloquence*, Cambridge Mass, Harvard.

Bremmer J. 1998, 'Aetius, Arius Didymus and the Transmission of Doxography', *Mnemosyne* 51, 154-60.

Brenk F.E. 1992, 'Darkly beyond the Glass: Middle Platonism and the Vision of the Soul' in Gersh & Kannengiesser 1992.

Carlini A. 1995, 'Plato, *Meno* 98a3' in L. Belloni et al. (eds.) *Studia Classica Iohanni Tarditi oblata*, Milan.

Charrue J.-M. 1978, *Plotin Lecteur de Platon*, Paris, Les Belles Lettres.

Choufrine A. 1997, 'The Aspects of Infinity in Clement of Alexandria', *Journal of Neoplatonic Studies* 6, 3-44.

Cleary J. 1997, *The Perennial Tradition of Neoplatonism*, Leuven, Leuven UP.

Cooper J. 1998, 'Poseidonius on the Emotions', in J. Sihvola & T. Engberg-Pedersen (eds.), *The Emotions in Hellenistic Philosophy*, Dordrecht/Boston, Kluwer Academic Publishers, 71-111.

Cornford F.M. 1935, *Plato's Theory of Knowledge*, Cambridge, CUP.

Coulter J.A. 1976, *The Literary Microcosm: Theories of Interpretation of the Later Neoplatonists*, Leiden, Brill.

Decleva Caizzi F. 1988, 'La "matteria scorrevole": sulle tracce di un dibattio perduto' in J. Barnes & M. Mignucci (eds.), *Matter and Metaphysics*, Naples, Bibliopolis, 427-70.

Decleva Caizzi F. 1994, 'Aenesidemus and the Academy', *CQ* 42, 176-89.

Diels H. and Schubart W. 1905, *Anonymer Kommentar zum Theätet, Berliner Klassikertexte ii*, Berlin.

Dillon J.M. 1973, *Iamblichi Chalcidensis in Platonis dialogos commentariorum, Philosophia antiqua* 23, Leiden, Brill.

Dillon J.M. 1977, *The Middle Platonists: A Study of Platonism, 80 BC to AD 220*, London, Duckworth.

Dillon J.M. 1983, 'Plotinus, Philo and Origen on the Grades of Virtue' in H.-D. Blume & F. Mann (eds.), *Platonismus und Christentum*, Festschrift für H. Dörrie, *Jahrbuch für Antike und Christentum, Ergänzungsband* 10, Münster, 92-105.

Dillon J.M. 1987, intro. in Morrow & Dillon.

Dillon J.M. 1992, 'The Neoplatonic Exegesis of the *Statesman* Myth' in Rowe 1992, 364-74.

Dillon J.M. 1993, *Alcinous: The Handbook of Platonism*, Oxford, OUP.

Dillon J.M. 1996, 'An Ethic for the Late Antique Sage', in Lloyd P. Gerson (ed.), *A Cambridge Companion to Plotinus*, Cambridge, CUP, 314-35.

Dillon J.M. 1997, 'The Riddle of the *Timaeus*: Is Plato sowing Clues?', in Joyal 1997, 25-42.

Dodds E.R. 1928, 'The *Parmenides* of Plato and the Origins of the Neoplatonic One', *CQ* 22, 129-42.

Donini P. 1992, 'Il *De Facie* di Plutarco e la teologia medioplatonica' in Gersh & Kannengiesser 1992.

Donini P. 1994, 'Testi e commenti, manuali e insegnamento: La forma sistematica e i metodi della filosofia in età postellenistica', *ANRW* II.36.7, 5027-5100.

Dörrie H. 1987, *Der Platonismus in der Antike*, Band I, *Die geschichtlichen Wurzeln des Platonismus*, Stuttgart-Bad Cannstatt, frommann-holzboog.

Dörrie H. & Baltes M. 1993, *Der Platonismus in der Antike*, Band III, *Der Platonismus im 2. und 3. Jahrhundert nach Christus*, Stuttgart-Bad Cannstatt 1993, frommann-holzboog.

Dover K.J. 1980 (ed.), *Plato: Symposium*, Cambridge U.P.

Ferrari F. 1998, 'Galeno interprete del Timeo', *MH* 55, 14-34.

Festugière, A.J. 1969, 'L'ordre de lecture des dialogues de Platon aux Ve/VIe siècles', *MH* 26, 281-96.

Gaiser K. 1963, *Platons Ungeschriebene Lehre*, Stuttgart, Klett.

Gersh S. 1986, *Middle Platonism and Neoplatonism: The Latin Tradition*, 2 vols., Notre Dame, University of Notre Dame Press.

Gersh S. & Kannengiesser C. (eds.) 1992, *Platonism in Late Antiquity*, Notre Dame, University of Notre Dame Press.

Gigon O. 1986, 'Das Dritte Buch des Diogenes Laertios', *Elenchos* 7, 136-7.

Gill C. & McCabe M.M. (eds.) 1996, *Form and Argument in Later Plato*, Oxford, OUP.

Gill C. 1997, 'Galen versus Chrysippus on the Tripartite Psyche in *Timaeus* 69-72' in T. Calvo & L. Brisson (eds.), *Interpreting the* Timaeus-Critias, Sankt Augustin, Academia.

Gill C. 1998, 'Did Galen understand Platonic and Stoic thinking on Emotions?', in J. Sihvola & T. Engberg-Pedersen (eds.), *The Emotions in Hellenistic Philosophy*, Dordrecht/Boston, Kluwer Academic Publishers, 113-48.

Glucker J. 1978, *Antiochus and the Late Academy*, Göttingen, Hypomnemata.

Glucker J. 1999, 'A Platonic Cento in Cicero', *Phronesis* 44, 30-44.

Glucker J. 1997, 'Socrates in the Academic Books and Other Ciceronian Works', in Inwood & Mansfeld, 58-88.

Göransson T. 1995, *Albinus, Alcinous, Arius Didymus*, Göteborg, Acta Universitatis Gothoburgensis.

Gottschalk H.B. 1980, *Heraclides of Pontus*, Oxford, OUP.

Hadot P. 1968, *Porphyry et Victorine*, Paris, Etudes Augustiniennes.

Haslam M. 1972, 'Plato, Sophron, and the Dramatic Dialogue', *BICS* 19, 17-38.

Haslam M. 1977, 'Treatise on Plato', *POxy*. 45, 29-39.

Hershbell J.P. 1987, 'Plutarch's *De Animae Procreatione in Timaeo*: an Analysis of Structure and Content', *ANRW* II 36.1.

Ierodiakonou K. 1999, 'Aspasius on Perfect and Imperfect Virtues' in L. Alberti & R. Sharples,

Aspasius: the earliest extant Commentary on Aristotle's Ethics, Berlin, De Gruyter, 142-61.

Inwood B. & Mansfeld J. (eds.) 1997, *Assent and Argument: Studies in Cicero's Academic Books*, Leiden, Brill, Philosophia Antiqua.

Isnardi-Parente M. 1980, *Speusippo: Frammenti*, Napoli, Bibliopolis.

Jackson R., Lycos K., Tarrant H. (tr.), Olympiodorus: *Commentary on Plato's Gorgias*, Leiden, Brill, 1998.

Jaeger W. 1923/46, *Aristotle: Fundamentals of the History of his Development*, tr. R. Robinson, Oxford, OUP.

Jones R.M. 1980, *The Platonism of Plutarch*, Garland reprint, London & New York.

Joyal M., 1997, *Studies in Plato and the Platonic Tradition. Essays presented to John Whittaker*, Aldershot, Ashgate.

Kahn, C.H. 1996, *Plato and the Socratic Dialogue*, Cambridge, CUP.

Karadimas D. 1996, *Sextus Empiricus against Aelius Aristides: The Conflict between Philosophy and Rhetoric in the Second Century AD*, Lund, Lund UP.

Kenny A. 1978, *The Aristotelian Ethics*, Oxford, OUP.

Krämer H.-J. 1959, *Arete bei Platon und Aristoteles*, Heidelberg, Abhandlungender Heidelberger Akademie der Wissenschaften, phil.-hist. klasse.

Kraus P. & Walzer R. 1951, *Galeni Compendium Timaei Platonis aliorumque Dialogorum Synopsis quae extant Fragmenta*, London, Warburg Institute.

Laurenti R. 1996, 'Il Filebo in Plutarco' in P. Cosenza (ed.) *Il Filebo di Platone e la sua fortuna*, Napoli, D'Auria.

Lévy, C. 1992, *Cicero Academicus: Recherches sur les Académiques et sur la Philosophie Cicéronienne*, Collection de l'école française de Rome 162, particularly 567-88 on *ND* III and the *Timaeus*, and 602-17 on *De Fato* and *Phaedrus*.

Lilla S. 1997, 'The Neoplatonic Hypostases and the Christian Trinity', in Joyal 1997, 127-90.

Linguiti A. (ed.) 1995, *Commentarium in Platonis Parmenidem*, Corpus dei papiri filosofici greci e latini, *iii*: Commentari, Firenze, 1995, 63-202.

Long A.A. 1988, 'Socrates and Hellenistic Philosophy', *CQ* 38, 150-71.

Long A.A. & Sedley D.N. 1987, *The Hellenistic Philosophers*, vol. 2, Cambridge, CUP.

Lycos, K., 1994, 'Olympiodorus on Pleasure and the Good in Plato's *Gorgias*', *OSAP* 12, 183-205.

Mansfeld J. 1983, 'Intuitionism and Formalism: Zeno's Definition of Geometry in a Fragment of L. Calvenus Taurus', *Phronêsis* 28, 59-74.

Mansfeld J. 1994, *Prolegomena: Questions to be Settled before the Study of an Author, or a Text*, Leiden, Brill.

Mansfeld J. & Runia D.T. 1996, *Aetiana* I, Leiden, Brill.

Mansfeld J. 1997, 'Philo and Antiochus in the lost *Catulus*', *Mnemosyne* 50, 45-74.

Mayhew R. 1997, *Aristotle's Criticism of Plato's Republic*, Lanham, Boulder, New York: Rowman & Littlefield.

McAvoy M. 1999, *The Profession of Ignorance: with Constant Reference to Socrates*, Lanham, University Press of America.

Merlan P. 1960, *From Platonism to Neoplatonism*, 2nd ed., The Hague, Nijhoff.

Michel A. 1993, 'Rhétorique et philosophie au second siècle après J.C.', *ANRW* II 34.1, 3-78.

Momigliano A. 1971, *The Development of Greek Biography*, Cambridge Mass, Harvard UP.

Moreschini C. 1994, 'Elio Aristide tra retorica e filosofia', *ANRW* II 34.2, 1234-47.

O'Brien M. 1991, 'Apuleius and the Concept of a Philosophical Rhetoric', *Hermathena* 151, 39-50.

O'Meara D.J. 1993, 'Aspects of Political Philosophy in Iamblichus' in Blumenthal & Clark 1993, 65-73.

Opsomer J. 1998, *In Search of Truth: Academic Tendencies in Middle Platonism*, Brussels, Verhandelingen van Koninklijke Academie voor Wetenschappen, Letteren en Schone Kunsten van Belgie.

Pépin J. & Saffrey H.D. (eds.) 1987, *Proclus: Lecteur et interprète des Anciens*, Paris, Centre National de la recherche scientifique.

Press G. 1996, 'The State of the Question in the Study of Plato', *Southern Journal of Philosophy* 34, 507-32.

Reis B. 1997, 'The Circle Simile in the Platonic Curriculum of Albinus', in Cleary 1997.
Riginos A.S. 1976, *Platonica: the Anecdotes concerning the Life and Writings of Plato*, Leiden, Brill.
Roodchnik D. 1984, 'The Riddle of the Cleitophon', *Ancient Philosophy*, 4, 132-45.
Rosenthal F. & Walzer R. (eds.) 1943, *Alfarabius: De Platonis Philosophia*, London, Warburg Institute.
Rowe C.J. (ed.) 1992, *Reading the Statesman*, Proc. III Symp. Plat., Sankt Augustin.
Runia D.T. 1986a, *Philo of Alexandria and the Timaeus of Plato*, Leiden, Brill.
Runia D.T. 1986b, 'Redrawing the Map of Early Middle Platonism: Some Comments on the Philonic Evidence' in A. Caquot et al. (eds.), *Hellenica et Judaica: Hommage à Valentin Nikiprowetzky*, Louvain & Paris.
Runia D.T. 1986c, 'Mosaic and Platonist Exegesis', *Vig. Chr.* 40, 209-17.
Runia D.T. 1995, 'Why does Clement of Alexandria call Philo "The Pythagorean" ', *Vig. Chr.* 49, 1-22.
Russell D.A. (ed.) 1990, *Antonine Literature*, Oxford, Clarendon.
Saffrey H.D. & Westerink L.G. (eds.) 1968-97, *Théologie platonicienne*, Paris, Les Belles Lettres.
Sandy G. 1997, *The Greek World of Apuleius: Apuleius and the Second Sophistic*, Leiden, Brill.
Sayre K. 1983, *Plato's Late Ontology: a Riddle Solved*, Princeton, Princeton UP.
Schicker R. 1992, 'Aspekte der Rezeption des Politikos im Mittel- und Neuplatonismus' in Rowe 1992, 381-8.
Schleiermacher F.E.D. 1973, *Introductions to the Dialogues of Plato* tr. W. Dobson, New York, Arno.
Schofield M. 1991, *The Stoic Idea of the City*, Cambridge, CUP.
Schröder H.O. 1934, *Galeni in Platonis Timaeum Commentarii Fragmenta*, Leipzig and Berlin, Teubner.
Sedley D.N. 1989, 'Philosophical Allegiance in the Greco-Roman World' in Barnes & Griffin, 97-119.
Sedley D.N. 1993, 'A Platonist Reading of *Theaetetus* 145-7', *PAS* suppl. vol. 67 125-49.
Sedley D.N. 1996a, 'Three Platonist Readings of the *Theaetetus*' in Gill & McCabe.
Sedley D.N. 1996b, 'Alcinous' Epistemology' in K.A. Algra et al. (eds.), *Polyhistor: Studies in the History and Historiography of Ancient Philosophy Presented to Jaap Mansfeld on his Sixtieth Birthday*, Leiden, Brill.
Sedley D.N. 1997a, 'A New Reading in the Anonymus "Theaetetus" Commentary (PBerol. 9782 Fragment D)' in *Papiri Filosofici: Miscellanea di Studi* I, Firenze, Olschki, 139-44.
Sedley D.N. 1997b, 'Plato's *Auctoritas* and the Rebirth of the Commentary Tradition' in Barnes & Griffin, 110-29.
Sedley D.N. 1998, *Lucretius and the Transformation of Greek Wisdom*, Cambridge, CUP.
Segonds, A.Ph., 1985-86, Proclus: *Sur le premier Alcibiade de Platon*, Paris, Les Belles Lettres, I-II.
Sheppard A.D.R. 1980, *Studies on the 5th and 6th Essays of Proclus' Commentary on the Republic*, Göttingen, Vandenhoeck & Ruprecht.
Sheppard A.D.R. 1987, 'Proclus' Philosophical Method of Exegesis: The Use of Aristotle and the Stoics in the Commentary on the *Cratylus*', in Pépin & Saffrey.
Shields C.J. 1994, 'Socrates among the Sceptics' in Vander Waerdt (ed.), 341-66.
Sluiter I. 1998, 'The Dialectics of Genre: Some Aspects of Secondary Literature and Genre in Antiquity' in Depeu M. & Obbink D (eds.), *Matrices of Genre*, Cambridge, Mass, Harvard UP.
Steel C. 1997, 'Proclus et l'interprétation "logique" du Parménide', in L.G. Benakis (ed.), *Néoplatonisme et philosophie médiévale*, Brepols.
Steel C. 1999, ' "Negatio Negationis": Proclus on the First Lemma of the First Hypothesis of the *Parmenides*', in J. Cleary (ed.), *Traditions of Platonism*, Aldershot, Ashgate.
Striker G. 1994, 'Plato's Socrates and the Stoics' in Vander Waerdt P.A. (ed.), 241-51.
Szlezak T. 1985, *Platon und die Schriftlichkeit der Philosophie*, Berlin & NY, De Gruyter.
Tarán L., 1985, *Speusippus of Athens*, Leiden, Brill.
Tarrant H. 1983a, 'The Date of Anonymous *In Theaetetum*', *CQ* 33, 161-87.

Tarrant H. 1983b, 'Middle Platonism and the *Seventh Epistle*', *Phronesis* 28, 75-103.

Tarrant H. 1984, 'Zeno on Knowledge or on Geometry: the Evidence of Anon. *In Theaetetum'*, *Phronesis* 29, 96-9.

Tarrant H. 1985, *Scepticism or Platonism? A Study of the Fourth Academy*, Cambridge, CUP.

Tarrant H. 1989, 'By Calculation of the Reason?', in P. Huby & G. Neal (eds.), *The Criterion of Truth*, Liverpool, Liverpool UP, 57-82, also *LCM* 14.8, 1989, 121-2.

Tarrant H. 1990, 'More on Zeno's *Forty Logoi'*, *ICS* 15, 23-38.

Tarrant H. 1993, *Thrasyllan Platonism*, Ithaca, Cornell UP.

Tarrant H. 1995, 'Introducing Philosophers and Philosophies', *Apeiron* 28, 141-58.

Tarrant H. 1996a, 'Orality and Plato's Narrative Dialogues', in I. Worthington (ed.), *Voice into Text*, Leiden, Brill, 129-47.

Tarrant H. 1996b, 'Platonic Interpretation in Aulus Gellius', *GRBS* 37, 173-93.

Tarrant H. 1997a, *'Politikê Eudaimonia*: Olympiodorus on Plato's *Republic'*, in K. Boudouris (ed.), *Plato's Political Theory and Contemporary Political Thought*, International Association for Greek Philosophy and Culture, Athens, vol. II, 200-7.

Tarrant, H. 1997b, 'Olympiodorus and the Surrender of Paganism' in L. Garland (ed.), *Conformity and Non-conformity in Byzantium*, *Byzantinische Forschungen* 24, 1997, 181-92.

Tarrant H. 1999a, Review of F. Adorno (ed.), *Papiri Filosofici: Miscellanea di Studi* I, *CR* 49, 264-5.

Tarrant H. 1999b, 'The *Gorgias* and the Demiurge' in J. Cleary (ed.), *Traditions of Platonism*, Aldershot, Ashgate.

Thesleff H. 1982, *Studies in Platonic Chronology*, *Commentationes Humanarum Litterarum* 70, Societas Scientiarum Fennica, Helsinki.

Thesleff H. 1994, 'Notes on Eros in Middle Platonism', *Arctos* 28, 115-28.

Thesleff H. 1997, 'The Early Version of Plato's *Republic'*, *Arctos* 31, 149-74.

Trapp M.B. 1990, 'Plato's *Phaedrus* in Second-Century Greek Literature', in Russell 1990.

Vander Waerdt P.A. (ed.) 1994, *The Socratic Movement*, Ithaca, Cornell UP.

Vlastos, G. 1983, 'The Socratic Elenchus', *OSAP* 1, 27-58.

Vlastos, G. 1987, 'Socratic Irony', *CQ* 37, 79-96.

Vlastos, G. 1991, *Socrates: Ironist and Moral Philosopher*, Cambridge, CUP.

Vlastos, G. 1994, *Socratic Studies*, Cambridge, CUP.

Volkmann-Schluck K.-H. 1966, *Plotin als Interpret der Ontologie Platos*, Frankfurt, Klostermann.

Westerink, L.G. (ed.) 1962, *Anonymous Prolegomena to Plato's Philosophy*, Amsterdam, North Holland.

Westerink, L.G. 1970, Olympiodorus, *In Platonis Gorgiam*, Leipzig, Teubner.

Westerink, L.G. 1971, 'Damascius, commentateur de Platon', in *Le Néoplatonisme*, Paris, 253-60.

Westerink L.G., Trouillard J., Segonds A.Ph. (eds.) 1990, *Prolégomènes à la Philosophie de Platon*, Paris, Les Belles Lettres.

Whittaker J. 1975, 'Seneca *Ep*. 58.17', *Symb. Os.* 50, 143-8.

Whittaker J. 1987, 'Platonic Philosophy in the Early Centuries of the Empire', *ANRW* II, 36.1, 81-123.

Whittaker J. (ed.) 1990, Alcinoos, *Enseignement des Doctrines de Platon*, Paris, Les Belles Lettres.

Winkler J.J. 1985, *Auctor and Actor: A Narratological Reading of the Golden Ass*, Berkeley etc., University of California Press.

Winter B.W. 1997, *Philo and Paul Among the Sophists*, Cambridge, CUP.

Indexes

The indexes are correlated with the main text. They include references, but not mere examples, from the text, and references in the notes that apply directly to discussion in the text.

Index locorum

References to the pages of this book are in **bold** type.

Index to Platonic works and passages

References to the pages of this book are in **bold** type.

Index of names